Biography Today

Profiles of People of Interest to Young Readers

Volume 13 — 2004
Annual Cumulation

Cherie D. Abbey
Managing Editor

Kevin Hillstrom
Editor

615 Griswold Street
Detroit, Michigan 48226

Omnigraphics, Inc.

Cherie D. Abbey, *Managing Editor*
Kevin Hillstrom, *Editor*

Peggy Daniels, Sheila Fitzgerald, Leif Gruenberg, Laurie Lanzen Harris,
Kevin Hile, Jeff Hill, Laurie Hillstrom, Sara Pendergast, Tom Pendergast, Diane Telgen,
Sue Ellen Thompson, Matt Totsky, and Rhoda Wilburn, *Sketch Writers*

Allison A. Beckett, Mary Butler, and Linda Strand, *Research Staff*

* * *

Peter E. Ruffner, *Publisher*
Frederick G. Ruffner, Jr., *Chairman*
Matthew P. Barbour, *Senior Vice President*
Kay Gill, *Vice President — Directories*

* * *

Liz Barbour, *Permissions Associate*
Dave Bianco, *Marketing Director*
Leif A. Gruenberg, *Development Manager*
Kevin Hayes, *Operations Manager*
Barry Puckett, *Librarian*
Cherry Stockdale, *Permissions Assistant*

Shirley Amore, Don Brown, Margaret M. Geist, Kevin Glover,
Martha Johns, and Kirk Kauffman, *Contributing Staff*

This book is printed on acid-free paper meeting the ANSI Z39.48 Standard. The infinity symbol
that appears above indicates that the paper in this book meets that standard.

Printed in the United States

INDEXED IN
Children's Magazine Guide

Contents

3

Preface

Biography Today is a magazine designed and written for the young reader—ages 9 and above—and covers individuals that librarians and teachers tell us that young people want to know about most: entertainers, athletes, writers, illustrators, cartoonists, and political leaders.

The Plan of the Work

The publication was especially created to appeal to young readers in a format they can enjoy reading and readily understand. Each issue contains approximately 10 sketches arranged alphabetically. Each entry provides at least one picture of the individual profiled, and bold-faced rubrics lead the reader to information on birth, youth, early memories, education, first jobs, marriage and family, career highlights, memorable experiences, hobbies, and honors and awards. Each of the entries ends with a list of easily accessible sources designed to lead the student to further reading on the individual and a current address. Obituary entries are also included, written to provide a perspective on the individual's entire career. Obituaries are clearly marked in both the table of contents and at the beginning of the entry.

Biographies are prepared by Omnigraphics editors after extensive research, utilizing the most current materials available. Those sources that are generally available to students appear in the list of further reading at the end of the sketch.

Indexes

A new index now appears in all *Biography Today* publications. In an effort to make the index easier to use, we have combined the **Name** and **General Index** into one, called the **Cumulative Index**. This new index contains the names of all individuals who have appeared in *Biography Today* since the series began. The names appear in bold faced type, followed by the issue in which they appeared. The General Index also contains the occupations, nationalities, and ethnic and minority origins of individuals profiled. The General Index is cumulative, including references to all individuals who have appeared in the *Biography Today* General Series and the *Biography Today* Special Subject volumes since the series began in 1992.

In a further effort to consolidate and save space, the Birthday and Places of Birth Indexes will be appearing only in the September issue and in the Annual Cumulation.

Our Advisors

This series was reviewed by an Advisory Board comprised of librarians, children's literature specialists, and reading instructors to ensure that the concept of this publication—to provide a readable and accessible biographical magazine for young readers—was on target. They evaluated the title as it developed, and their suggestions have proved invaluable. Any errors, however, are ours alone. We'd like to list the Advisory Board members, and to thank them for their efforts.

Gail Beaver
Adjunct Lecturer
University of Michigan
Ann Arbor, MI

Cindy Cares
Youth Services Librarian
Southfield Public Library
Southfield, MI

Carol A. Doll
School of Information Science and Policy
University of Albany, SUNY
Albany, NY

Kathleen Hayes-Parvin
Language Arts Teacher
Birney Middle School
Southfield, MI

Karen Imarisio
Assistant Head of Adult Services
Bloomfield Twp. Public Library
Bloomfield Hills, MI

Rosemary Orlando
Assistant Director
St. Clair Shores Public Library
St. Clair Shores, MI

Our Advisory Board stressed to us that we should not shy away from controversial or unconventional people in our profiles, and we have tried to follow their advice. The Advisory Board also mentioned that the sketches might be useful in reluctant reader and adult literacy programs, and we would value any comments librarians might have about the suitability of our magazine for those purposes.

Your Comments Are Welcome

Our goal is to be accurate and up-to-date, to give young readers information they can learn from and enjoy. Now we want to know what you think. Take a look at this issue of *Biography Today*, on approval. Write or call me with your comments. We want to provide an excellent source of biographical information for young people. Let us know how you think we're doing.

Cherie Abbey
Managing Editor, *Biography Today*
Omnigraphics, Inc.
615 Griswold Street
Detroit, MI 48226

editor@biographytoday.com
www.biographytoday.com

Congratulations!

Congratulations to the following individuals and libraries, who received a free copy of *Biography Today* for suggesting people who appeared in 2004:

Kay Altland, York, PA
Miranda Becker, Danville, IL
Amanda Bents, Bonifay, FL
Kylie Blackburn, Parsons, KS
Dolly Bloomquist, Roosevelt Elementary
   Media Center, Mankato, MN
Tonya Carpenter, Vernon, FL
Mary Dotts, DeWitt, MI
Blythe Enke, Salt Lake City, UT
Priscilla Fernandez, Orlando, FL
Dawn Foster, Elmwood Park, NJ
Beverly Harrington, Chicago, IL
Helen Ideno, Chicago IL
Nichole Jones, Edgewater, CO
Leigh Jordon, Lancaster, SC
Lucille Koors, Indianapolis, IN
Erin Lounsbury, Farmingville, NY
Abigail Nicoloff, Waco, TX
Marissa Rayford, Riverdale, MD
Rose M. Rivas, San Antonio, TX
Sheron Rundall, Dallas, GA
Miranda Trimm, Allegan, MI

Natalie Babbitt 1932-

American Children's Author and Illustrator
Creator of the Children's Classic *Tuck Everlasting*

BIRTH

Natalie Babbitt was born Natalie Zane Moore on July 28, 1932, in Dayton, Ohio. Her father, Ralph Zane Moore, changed jobs frequently but at one point worked as a labor relations specialist for General Motors. Her mother, Genevieve (Converse) Moore, was a college graduate and a talented artist who did not pursue a career after her children were born. Natalie has one sister, Diane, who is two years older.

One of Natalie's ancestors was Zebulon Pike, the explorer who discovered Pike's Peak in Colorado. Others were among the earliest American settlers of Ohio and West Virginia. The town of Zanesville, Ohio is named after a member of her father's family.

YOUTH

Babbitt was born during the Great Depression, a time of economic hardship for many American families following the stock market crash of 1929. Despite the family's economic troubles, however, Genevieve Moore wanted her daughters to have every possible advantage. She took them to the opera, to symphony concerts, and to the theater, and she made sure they received lessons in art, piano, and horseback riding. Her social and economic ambitions for the family were one of the reasons why Ralph Moore changed jobs so frequently, moving his family every few years before finally settling down in Cleveland.

> *Babbitt describes herself as a "loner who spent a lot of time drawing and reading, but who liked birthday parties and going to a friend's house after school. A good child who did plenty of bad things. I never got away with anything, though. No matter how clandestine I tried to be, my mother always found me out."*

"There was something indomitable about my parents," Babbitt told an interviewer many years later. "We always managed to have a good time, and my mother saw most of her careful plans for my sister and me come remarkably close to full realization." Genevieve Moore, who had never had a chance to pursue an artistic career herself, decided that Diane would grow up to be a writer and Natalie would be an artist, and she went out of her way to encourage their talents in these directions. She read them all the classic children's books, such as Lewis Carroll's *Alice in Wonderland*, Charles Kingsley's *The Water Babies*, and Booth Tarkington's *Penrod*. Natalie spent much of her time trying to imitate the drawings of glamorous women she'd seen by the Spanish artist Louis de Vargas, who was very popular during the 1940s. By the time she was nine, she decided she wanted to be an illustrator.

Babbitt describes herself as a "fairly average child" who was "by turns confident and scared to death. A loner who spent a lot of time drawing and reading, but who liked birthday parties and going to a friend's house after school. A good child who did plenty of bad things. I never got away with anything, though," she adds. "No matter how clandestine I tried to be, my mother always found me out."

EARLY MEMORIES

When Natalie was less than a year old, her father lost his job and the family had to give up their house. They moved to Indian Lake in northwestern Ohio, where her grandmother owned a cottage. The period during which they lived at the lake had a strong influence on Natalie's later development as a writer and illustrator. Both her grandmother's cottage and the lake itself would reappear in many different forms in her novels. And the heroes and heroines of her books would often be lonely children who had been separated from their homes. Natalie says that as a result of this experience in early childhood, she developed "a deep anxiety about being alone in strange places" that has been with all her life.

EDUCATION

Because her family moved so often, Babbitt attended a number of different elementary schools. As a high school student, she attended the Laurel School for Girls in Shaker Heights, graduating in 1950. She describes herself at Laurel as an underachiever who had little in common with her older sister, a reader of serious literature with a large vocabulary. "She was a straight-A student—a hard and conscientious worker—while I avoided everything that didn't come easily," Natalie admits.

The summer after she graduated from Laurel, Babbitt took a course in fashion illustration at the Cleveland School of Art and decided that she was more interested in creative drawing than in sketching shoes, handbags, and dresses. That fall she began her studies at Smith College, where she majored in art and found herself competing with other students who were just as talented as she was, if not more so. "I had always done what came easily, and what came easily had always been good enough," she recalls. "It was not good enough at Smith, and would never be good enough again."

Although art was her major, Natalie also studied writing at Smith. By that point, she was dating Samuel Babbitt, a student from Yale who wanted to be a novelist. She envisioned a life in which he would write books and she would do illustrations. They were married shortly after her graduation from Smith in 1954.

BECOMING A WRITER AND ILLUSTRATOR

After graduation and marriage, Natalie took a job in the freshman dean's office at Yale University while her husband stayed home and worked on a novel. When he discovered how lonely it was to be a writer and decided to accept a job at Yale as an administrator, she quit her job there and started raising a family.

For the next 10 years Babbitt was busy as a stay-at-home mother and the wife of a college administrator, first at Yale and later at Vanderbilt University in Nashville, Tennessee. Then, in the mid-1960s, when her husband was back at Yale studying for his Ph.D., Natalie had an idea for a children's picture book. She persuaded her husband to write the story while she concentrated on a series of pen-and-ink drawings with contrasting areas of black and white. The result was *The Forty-Ninth Magician,* a story about a young king who promises to look after the sons and grandsons of a court magician who is getting old. Soon after its publication in 1966, Natalie's husband accepted a job as president of Kirkland College in upstate New York, and once he again he put aside the idea of becoming a writer.

After moving to Clinton, New York, where they would live for the next 12 years, Natalie read Betty Friedan's nonfiction work, *The Feminine Mystique.* During the early days of the feminist movement, this influential book inspired many women to develop their talents and pursue their own careers. Although she had been very successful as a homemaker and an academic administrator's wife, she realized that she was not completely happy. "Then Betty Friedan's book came out and I understood why I was so frustrated," she says. She realized that if she wanted to pursue a career as a book illustrator, she would have to write the books herself.

CAREER HIGHLIGHTS

Early Picture Books and *The Search for Delicious*

Babbitt decided to try writing children's books herself. She was encouraged to give it a try by Michael di Capua, the editor at Farrar, Straus, & Giroux who had worked with her husband on his book. Over the next two years, she wrote and illustrated two picture books with stories in rhyming verse. *Dick Foote and the Shark* (1967) tells the tale of a Cape Cod poet in the 19th century who tries to convince his father, a fisherman, that writing poetry is a worthwhile venture. Their difference of opinion is finally resolved when Dick saves himself and his father from a shark attack by reciting a poem. Critics praised the book for its "bouncing rhythms and ingenious rhymes" as well as for its black ink drawings with a sea-green wash.

Babbitt's second picture book was *Phoebe's Revolt* (1968), about a turn-of-the-century tomboy named Phoebe who hates the frilly dresses that are the accepted style for girls her age. Her father decides to teach her a lesson by forcing her to wear his clothes for a week. She eventually compromises by agreeing to wear the sailor dresses that her mother has made for her. Babbitt's illustrations for this book showed a more extensive use of shading and a sepia (brownish) wash, which gave the entire book an antique look.

After the success of these picture books for young readers, di Capua urged Babbitt to try writing something longer. The result was *The Search for Delicious* (1969), a novel about a 12-year-old boy named Gaylen and his search for the perfect definition of the word "delicious." Gaylen is the adopted son of the Prime Minister, who is writing a dictionary and can't quite decide on the best definition for this word. So he sends Gaylen on a journey through the kingdom to conduct a national poll on its meaning. During his travels he meets a minstrel named Canto, who gives him the key to an underwater house belonging to a mermaid named Ardis. When Gaylen emerges from his visit to Ardis's underwater world, he does so with a new maturity and sense of his mission in life. It is only then that he can successfully confront Hemlock, the villain of the story, who is trying to hoard the kingdom's water supply. With Ardis's help, Gaylen is able to thwart Hemlock's plan and bring about widespread agreement on the true meaning of the word "delicious."

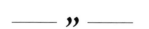

> *Writing for young people isn't all that different from writing for adults, according to Babbitt. "I believe that children are far more perceptive and wise than American books give them credit for being."*

The Search for Delicious was Babbitt's first work of fantasy. According to *Horn Book,* it showed her willingness to "explore complex themes and ethical dilemmas." The book was also praised by critics for its intricate plot as well as its humor and "haunting language." The *New York Times* selected it as the year's best novel for 9 to 12 year olds.

Myths, Monsters, and Mansions

In the early 1970s Babbitt published four more books for children. *Kneeknock Rise* (1970) tells the story of a young boy, Egan, who visits relatives in the small town of Instep, located at the foot of a small mountain called Kneeknock Rise that is home to a mythical monster called the Megrimum.

One of Egan's uncles has disappeared and may have been captured by the Megrimum. When Egan and his dog climb Knee-knock Rise to search for his Uncle Ott, they discover that there is a perfectly logical explanation for the moaning sound that people have heard coming from the mountain. But the inhabitants of Instep would rather hold on to their illusions than give up their village's only claim to fame. *Knee-knock Rise* was a John Newbery Honor Book and was cited as a Notable Book by the American Library Association.

The Something (1970) is a picture book for young readers that was inspired by Babbitt's own fear of the dark when she was a child. Its hero is Mylo, a troll-like child with buck teeth, skinny arms and legs, and a fur-covered body who is terrified of the "something" that lurks in the dark. He finally comes to terms with his fear by making a statue of "The Something" from the clay that his mother has bought him. Babbitt's illustrations for this book are more cartoon-like and have more shading than those created for her earlier picture books. The overall effect is darker, making Mylo's fears easy to imagine.

The mystery *Goody Hall* (1971) was inspired largely by Babbitt's memories of her own mother, who died when Babbitt was only 24 and who had dedicated her life to the pursuit of wealth and social acceptability. Goody Hall is a Victorian mansion where Mrs. Goody lives with her son, Willet. Her husband, a wealthy miser named Midas Goody, has disappeared, prompting Hercules Feltwright, her son's tutor, to investigate. The story has many parallels to the myth of Hercules, who performed 12 difficult "labors" or tasks and became a god after his death, as well as references to the story of the mythical King Midas, who had the power of turning everything he touched into gold. Although some critics found the book's happy ending too contrived, others praised its "high-spirited, hugely complicated plot."

Babbitt followed that up with *The Devil's Storybook* in 1974. This collection of ten short stores is about a devil who tries to lure more people to Hell but usually ends up being tricked. It revealed Babbitt's skill in writing traditional tales and led to the 1987 sequel, *The Devil's Other Storybook,* 13 years later.

Babbitt's Masterpiece: *Tuck Everlasting*

With three picture books, three novels, and a volume of short stories behind her, Babbitt was ready to combine her interest in fantasy, folk tale, and mythology in *Tuck Everlasting* (1975), the book for which she would become famous. It takes place in the late 19th century in a place that recalls both Babbitt's grandmother's lakefront cottage in Ohio and the Adirondack Mountains, where Babbitt was living when she wrote the book. Winnie Foster, the heroine of the story, is a 10-year-old girl who lives a very protected, orderly life until the day she decides to explore the woods surrounding her fenced-in yard. There she discovers a spring that bubbles up from the trunk of an old oak tree. She is about to drink from it when she is stopped by Jessie Tuck, a 17-year-old boy who explains that whoever drinks the water will become immortal. He and his family—his parents Angus and Mae Tuck and his brother, Miles—took a drink from the spring 87 years ago and are now trapped in the bodies they will inhabit forever.

> *Babbitt remains bothered by the fact that so many students are being forced to read her book.* "Tuck is not a crowd-pleaser," *she said.* "But it has apparently come to seem useful, particularly for classroom discussions about death — though that is not, to my mind, its central theme." *She often says that she would rather have children* "examine their own reactions to it as a piece of fiction, and not simply talk about whether they would like to live forever or not."

The Tucks kidnap Winnie to ensure that she keeps their secret. The villain of the story, referred to only as "the man in the yellow suit," witnesses her kidnaping and offers her parents a trade: he will rescue their daughter if they will turn over ownership of the woods. He has heard rumors about the Tucks and their magical spring, and he is obsessed with finding them so that he can bottle the water and sell it. He tries to force Winnie to drink from the spring, but Mae Tuck steps in. Winnie's efforts to help Mae show that she is mature enough to make decisions for her own future.

Alexis Bledel as Winnie Foster in the movie Tuck Everlasting, *with Amy Irving as her controlling mother and Ben Kingsley as "The Man in the Yellow Suit."*

Because it dealt with such important issues as death, immortality, and change, *Tuck Everlasting* appealed to adult as well as young readers and quickly became a children's classic. It reminded many readers of their favorite fairy tales, and teachers welcomed the book for the lively discussions it provoked about whether or not living forever was really a good thing. Critics compared *Tuck* to other notable children's classics, including E. B. White's *Charlotte's Web*. The International Board on Books for Young People placed Babbitt's book on their honor list, and novelist Anne Tyler, who reviewed the book for the *New York Times,* called *Tuck Everlasting* "one of the best books ever written — for any age."

Tuck Everlasting was later made into a movie starring Alexis Bledel from television's "The Gilmore Girls," as well as Jonathan Jackson, Ben Kingsley, William Hurt, and Sissy Spacek. (For more information on Bledel, see *Biography Today*, Jan. 2003.) The 2002 movie earned mixed reviews. Some critics praised its sensitive handling of deep issues and claimed that it would appeal to a wide audience. "*Tuck Everlasting,* a sweeping romantic fable about love and mortality, targets an audience of girls in their early teens, but has been made with such skill and sensitivity that its appeal spans generations," Kevin Thomas wrote in the *Los Angeles Times.* But other reviewers felt that the movie did a poor job of capturing the magic of the novel. "*Tuck Everlasting* is the softest, sorriest excuse for so-called 'inspirational cinema' that Hollywood has produced this year," wrote Craig Outhier in the *Orange County Register.* "It's overnarrated and underwritten, unimaginatively filmed and inflated with gaseous platitudes that rise, helium-like, into a vast and featureless sky of strained morality."

Despite the success of the novel over the past 25 years, Babbitt remains bothered by the fact that so many students are being forced to read her book. "*Tuck* is not a crowd-pleaser," she said. "But it has apparently come to seem useful, particularly for classroom discussions about death — though that is not, to my mind, its central theme." She often says that she would rather have children "examine their own reactions to it as a piece of fiction, and not simply talk about whether they would like to live forever or not."

The Eyes of the Amaryllis and *Herbert Rowbarge*

In her subsequent works, Babbitt continued to explore what became one of her favorite themes: people who, like the Tucks, are "frozen in time." Her next book, *The Eyes of the Amaryllis* (1979), tells the story of an old woman on Cape Cod named Geneva Reade, who loses her sea captain husband when his ship, the *Amaryllis,* sinks before her eyes. She spends the next 30 years combing the beach after every high tide, waiting for her husband to send her a sign of his enduring love. Her own son, George, marries and moves inland to escape his mother's obsession, but when Geneva breaks her ankle it is Jenny, George's daughter, who comes to take care of her.

Jenny and Geneva are the only two people who have seen Seward, a ghostly character they meet while beach-combing one evening, who turns out to be the artist who carved the original figurehead for the *Amaryllis.* Seward has struck a bargain with the sea: he will guard the sea's treasures in return for his immortality. When the figurehead washes ashore one day, Geneva quickly seizes it as the sign she has been waiting for, but Seward tries to persuade her to return it because the sea cannot guard the wreck without the figurehead's eyes. A terrible storm erupts, and Geneva almost loses her house and her life as she struggles to hold onto the figurehead that the sea is trying to reclaim. Like *Tuck Everlasting, The Eyes of the Amaryllis* was made into a movie, although it received only lukewarm reviews.

Just as Geneva Reade spends her whole life waiting for a sign from the husband she lost as a young woman, the main character in *Herbert Rowbarge* (1982), Babbitt's next novel, spends his entire life thinking about a twin brother from whom he was separated as a very young child. Herbert and Otto are abandoned as babies and end up in an orphanage. Otto is

adopted soon afterward, while Herbert grows up in the orphanage and never quite recovers from the loss of his twin. He becomes a rich and powerful man who owns a huge amusement park, but even his marriage to a banker's daughter and the birth of his twin girls fail to bring him happiness. The story is told partly from the perspective of the twins, Babe and Louisa, as middle-aged women who must come to terms both with their own long separation from each other and with their father's inability to love them.

Herbert Rowbarge didn't enjoy the same widespread success that *Tuck Everlasting* did. Perhaps this was because the main character is an adult for most of the story and because its style, according to the *New York Times Book Review,* was "so fine and subtle" that only adults could fully appreciate it. Still, it was Babbitt's favorite book up to this point in her career. One reason that she was so attached to the book was that its setting closely resembled the lakefront cottage and town where she and her sister used to spend their summer vacations. "It's about Ohio, where I grew up, and it's about Midwestern things and people," she explained in an interview. "I tried to make it a book for kids, but it did not want to go that way. It's for women over 40."

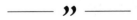

Babbitt's books begin, she says, "with a word or phrase that strikes some kind of sympathetic chord. . . . From this, a group of characters evolves. The characters assume more and more positive personalities, and the events that follow stem from the actions and reactions they might logically be expected to have."

The Valerie Worth Books and More Recent Titles

Early in her career, after her husband abandoned his plans to become a writer, Babbitt had decided that she wouldn't illustrate books that had been written by other people. But she soon dropped that idea and began working with the well-known poet Valerie Worth. In 1972 Worth published a very popular collection called *Small Poems.* Babbitt did a small ink drawing for each poem that captured the subject matter of the poem with great delicacy and accuracy. The result was so successful that she and Worth collaborated on eight more volumes of poems for young readers, which *Booklist* praised for the "small ink drawings [that] embody the realistic and make us imagine much more." Their final joint effort, *Peacock and Other Poems* (2002), was published after Worth's death in 1994. Again the quiet detail of the illustrations earned praise, as Carolyn Phelan wrote in *Booklist*: "Babbitt's precise pencil drawings accompany the

poems, reflecting the words in a quiet and unassuming way."

In addition to illustrating the Valerie Worth poetry books, Babbitt has focused on children's picture books in recent years. *Nellie: A Cat on Her Own* (1989) is about a marionette cat whose creator dies and who must be persuaded that she can still dance without her mistress there to pull the strings. The *Los Angeles Times Book Review* praised Babbitt's watercolor illustrations and called it a book about "the risks and the joys in growing up to be strong and independent." *Bub, or the Very Best Thing* (1994) is a picture book fantasy about a young king and queen who want to find "the very best thing" for their young son, the prince. They look for ideas in books and consult everyone they meet as they walk through the castle grounds. But when they ask the prince himself, he replies "Bub" — a response that the cook's daughter interprets for them as "love." *Elsie Times Eight* (2001) is Babbitt's most recent picture book for children about a fairy godmother who is hard of hearing and has a tendency to misinterpret people's wishes. When Elsie makes a wish, the fairy godmother misunderstands the word "before" and thinks she means there should "be four" Elsies. When Elsie's father shouts, "No! Wait!" she thinks he is saying, "No! Eight" and makes four more Elsies.

Dedicated to Writing for Children

Babbitt says that she is often asked why she doesn't write books for adults. "This question invariably comes from people who do not understand that only in a child's book can a writer take advantage of the widest range of symbolism, express a basic optimism, and have at his disposal the whole vast richness that only fantasy can offer," she explains. She has published numerous essays about literature for children in which she points out that writing for young people isn't all that different from writing for adults. "I believe that children are far more perceptive and wise than American books give them credit for being," she says.

As a result, Babbitt's books never "talk down" to their audiences. In addition to their constant references to folklore, mythology, and classic literature, they treat such complex themes as love, death, immortality, and loyalty. The plots and settings may be fantasy, but the issues they raise are familiar and realistic. At the same time, her books are not filled with as much heroism and violence as most pure fantasy books. They're more likely to focus on a single tragic or violent act and its effect on the rest of the characters.

When she sits down to write, Babbitt always reminds herself, "Don't preach, don't be dishonest, and don't be earnest." Perhaps one of the reasons her books have been so popular with young readers over the years is that they're more interested in telling an entertaining story than in trying to teach a lesson.

Writing Process

Babbitt's books begin, she says, "with a word or phrase that strikes some kind of sympathetic chord. . . . From this, a group of characters evolves. The characters assume more and more positive personalities, and the events that follow stem from the actions and reactions they might logically be expected to have." *Goody Hall*, for example, began with the single word "smuggler."

"I think my writing style and my pictures come out of the same place," Babbitt says. "They're mutually informed by what I see in my head. When you're writing a story, it's like watching a movie—you describe what you're seeing in your head. And illustrating is the same thing—you draw what you see in your head."

MARRIAGE AND FAMILY

Babbitt and her husband, Samuel Fisher Babbitt, have been married since 1954. They have three grown children—Christopher, who is a psychologist; Thomas, who is a composer and rock musician; and Lucy, who is a children's novelist—and three grandchildren. After leaving his posi-

> **"**
>
> *"I think my writing style and my pictures come out of the same place," Babbitt says. "They're mutually informed by what I see in my head. When you're writing a story, it's like watching a movie—you describe what you're seeing in your head. And illustrating is the same thing—you draw what you see in your head."*
>
> **"**

tion as president of Kirkland College, Samuel Babbitt became vice president at Brown University. For many years the Babbitts have lived in Providence, Rhode Island, and spent their vacations on Cape Cod.

FAVORITE BOOKS

Babbitt's favorite books are *Alice in Wonderland* and *Through the Looking-Glass* by Lewis Carroll. "These books are full of transformations," she says. "I loved the pig baby and the Cheshire cat and the caterpillar." But she also liked the fact that "Alice wasn't changed at all by her Wonderland experiences. . . . Lewis Carroll didn't want Alice to change. He only wanted to point out, I think, the endless absurdities of the adult world."

SELECTED WRITINGS

As Author and Illustrator

Dick Foote and the Shark, 1967
Phoebe's Revolt, 1968
The Search for Delicious, 1969
Kneeknock Rise, 1970
The Something, 1970
Goody Hall, 1971
The Devil's Storybook, 1974
Tuck Everlasting, 1975
The Eyes of the Amaryllis, 1977
Herbert Rowbarge, 1982
The Devil's Other Storybook, 1987
Nellie: A Cat on Her Own, 1989
Bub, or The Very Best Thing, 1994
Elsie Times Eight, 2001

As Illustrator

The 49th Magician, 1966
Small Poems, 1972
More Small Poems, 1976
Still More Small Poems, 1978
Curlicues: The Fortunes of Two Pug Dogs, 1980
Small Poems Again, 1985
Other Small Poems Again, 1986
All the Small Poems, 1987

All the Small Poems and Fourteen More, 1994
Peacock and Other Poems, 2002

SELECTED HONORS AND AWARDS

Best Books of the Year (*The New York Times*): 1969, for *The Search for Delicious;* 1982, for *Herbert Rowbarge*
Notable Children's Books (American Library Association): 1970, for *Kneeknock Rise;* 1974, for *The Devil's Storybook;* 1976, for *Tuck Everlasting;* 1977, for *The Eyes of the Amaryllis;* 1999, for *Ouch! A Tale from Grimm*
Best Book of the Year (*School Library Journal*): 1974, for *The Devil's Storybook*
Christopher Award for Juvenile Fiction: 1976, for *Tuck Everlasting*
Recognition of Merit Award (George C. Stone Center for Children's Books): 1979
Children's Literature Festival Award (Keene State College): 1993
Blue Ribbon Book (*Bulletin of the Center for Children's Books*): 1998, for *Ouch! A Tale from Grimm*

FURTHER READING

Books

Authors and Artists for Young Adults, Vol. 51, 2003
Beacham's Guide to Literature for Young Adults, Vol. 5, 1992
Contemporary Authors New Revision Series, Vol. 38, 1993
Levy, Michael. *Natalie Babbitt,* 1991
Something about the Author, Vol. 106, 1999
Something about the Author Autobiography Series, Vol. 5, 1988
St. James Guide to Children's Writers, 1999

Periodicals

Horn Book, Mar. 2000, p.153
New York Times, Oct. 6, 2000, p.15
New York Times Book Review, Nov. 14, 1982, p.44
Publishers Weekly, Feb. 21, 1994, p.229

Online Databases

Biography Resource Center, 2003, articles from *Authors and Artists for Young Adults,* 2003; *Contemporary Authors Online,* 2001; and *St. James Guide to Children's Writers,* 1999

ADDRESS

Natalie Babbitt
Children's Marketing Department
Farrar, Straus and Giroux
19 Union Square West
New York, NY 10003

WORLD WIDE WEB SITES

http://www.fsgkidsbooks.com
http://www2.scholastic.com
http://www.kidsreads.com/authors/au-babbitt-natalie.asp

David Beckham 1975-

English Soccer Player
Captain of England's National Team, Former Player for
Manchester United, Currently Playing for Real Madrid

BIRTH

David Robert Joseph Beckham was born on May 2, 1975, in
Leytonstone, England. He is the son of Sandra, a hairdresser,
and Ted, a former heating engineer and kitchen renovator who
once played for the local Kingfisher soccer club; Sandra and Ted
Beckham recently divorced. Beckham has two sisters: Lynne,
who is three years older, and Joanne, who is five years younger.

YOUTH

Soccer has dominated Beckham's life since he was a young boy. "All I ever wanted to do was kick a football about," he said, using the European term for soccer. "It didn't enter my head to do anything else. I think I was programmed by my dad to some extent. . . . It wasn't imposed on me, though, and I'm grateful for that." He first started kicking the ball around in his backyard, "but I was murdering the flowerbeds." So he and his friends would go to a nearby park "and just practice and practice for hours on end." By the time he was seven years old, he had started following his father to Wadham Lodge, a small soccer field near their home where he would watch the Kingfishers practice. "It had a little wall all around it and two dugouts. It seemed like a massive stadium to me at the time," Beckham recalled. "I dreamed about playing on that field one day."

> "All I ever wanted to do was kick a football about. It didn't enter my head to do anything else. I think I was programmed by my dad to some extent. . . . It wasn't imposed on me, though, and I'm grateful for that."

But Beckham had an even bigger dream than that: he wanted to play for Manchester United, a team that is as famous in England as the New York Yankees are in the United States. In fact, United is considered the most popular sports team in the world, with 53 millions fans. There are fan clubs all over the world, including Africa, New Zealand, Japan, Iceland, and the United States. His father was a huge fan of United, and Beckham has said that this influence was the main factor in his wanting to play there. "I don't know about United born; I was definitely United bred. And what kept me going was the idea that, eventually, I'd get the call I'd been waiting for ever since I'd first kicked a ball."

The Rovers

While he was growing up, Beckham played soccer on multiple teams — on his school teams, on his church team, and also on a youth team called the Ridgeway Rovers beginning at age seven. The Rovers didn't just play in local games, though. The team traveled as far as Germany and Holland, "so we gained the same sort of experience as a professional playing in an international tournament," said Beckham. His father helped with the coaching, and he and other parents became very involved with the Rovers.

This made it a great family experience for the kids during the six years of the team's existence.

When he was ten, Beckham began attending the Bobby Charlton Soccer School each summer. The school ran a well-known skills competition, which Beckham won his second year there. The prize for winning the competition was a training camp trip to Barcelona, Spain. Although he was the youngest player to train at the Barcelona camp and the other players didn't speak English, he found that "if we were playing, we could make ourselves understood. It was the first time I'd been in a professional set-up, training with professional players. It opened my eyes."

EDUCATION

As a student, Beckham wasn't very strong academically, but he loved playing rugby and soccer. He first attended Chase Lane Primary, whose coach made a big impression on him. "I can still remember Mr. McGhee, the teacher who used to coach us: a Scotsman and passionate with it, a bit like [Manchester United coach] Alex Ferguson in fact." In addition to playing for his primary school, Beckham also played for his church's team, the Cubs, "which you could only do if you went to church on Sunday. So all the family . . . made sure we were there every time, without fail."

When he started going to Chingford High, Beckham was disappointed because the school had a rugby team rather than a soccer team. It was coached by a man he admired greatly: John Bullock, whom he described as "tough and disciplined but a lovely man. He was great with all of us and always seemed to have a lot of time for me." Bullock was not interested in soccer, but Beckham and his friends pestered him until the coach agreed to form a school team. "As soon as we had a school soccer team, we started winning leagues and cups, which was great for us. It was great for the school, as well. Maybe the soccer helped me to be happy there. I wasn't that interested in [academic] lessons."

Beckham dropped out of high school in 1991, at age 16, which officially ended his formal education. It was time for him to concentrate on becoming a professional soccer player.

CAREER HIGHLIGHTS

United Trainee

While he was still in school, Beckham had attended a soccer academy run by the Tottenham Hotspurs (known as the Spurs). Tottenham was interested in his potential, but Beckham's favorite team had also taken notice of

*Beckham played for Manchester United Youth in 1993,
his last year before turning pro.*

the boy. The Spurs soon offered him a six-year contract, which would start
with four years in training, followed by two years as a professional. The
offer was tempting. But when United laid the same cards on the table,
Beckham decided that he would rather play with his favorite team. He

signed as a United trainee on July 8, 1991 — the same year that he decided to leave high school.

In European professional soccer, which they call football, many clubs have a farm system, with multiple teams at varying levels of play. When young players like Beckham are signed to a club, they often start their careers by playing on teams at lower levels and then try and work their way up to the top team. In England alone there are 92 teams in four different divisions; the top is Premier, then First, Second, and Third. Manchester United fields a team in the Premier League, the top level. Teams play against other teams in their home country as well as against other teams in Europe and around the world. There are many different tournaments and awards each year. In England, the Premiership is awarded to the champion in the Premier League. The FA Cup, the world's oldest national cup competition, is awarded to the winner of the English Football Association tournament. The champion teams of the various European countries play against each other in an annual tournament whose winner receives the European Cup. Perhaps the most popular and prestigious event is the World Cup, which occurs every four years. It's an elimination-type competition where the number of contenders is reduced through a series of qualifying rounds. Eventually, only two teams are left to play the finals, and then only one team emerges as the winner, the World Cup champion.

When Beckham first started with United, he participated in what is called the Youth Training Scheme (YTS). He remained in this training program for young players while he was getting ready to turn pro. He and his team-mates soon proved their skills when they won the Milk Cup, a tournament in Northern Ireland; in 1992 they won the Football Association's Youth Cup, the first time a United team had done so since 1964. Although they lost the next year, Beckham had convinced United that he was a solid player. He was signed to a professional contract on January 22, 1993, though he continued to play on the youth team throughout 1993. His team didn't win the Youth Cup that year, coming in as the runner-up instead. The following year, Beckham played primarily on the United reserve team.

Dreams Come True

For Beckham, playing for Manchester United at their Old Trafford stadium was a dream come true. He began playing for United in 1994, making his debut that September as a substitute in a match against Brighton. Beckham could barely realize that he was wearing the jersey for the team of his dreams. "I'd wake up every morning hardly able to believe what was going on around me," he said. "I'd drive into training, thinking to myself: 'I'm a first-team player. I'm doing my work on the main field. . . . I've got my own spot in the car park, with my initials there in white paint.' When I went to the training ground for the first time as a boy, those white lines marked out with the initials of the United players I idolized seemed to represent everything I dreamed of achieving for myself. Now, I belonged and it might have been easy to get swept away with it all. People at the club, though, and the manager in particular, didn't let that happen."

———— " ————

"[Beckham] is a genius with an innate sense of physics," **Sports Illustrated** *writer Frank Deford once reported. "He has, says one software company, figured out how to balance the kick angle, kick speed, spin, and direction in order to get the optimal turbulent laminar transition trajectory. What trajectory Beckham's brain calculates in seconds from instinct would, engineers say, take computers hours to figure out."*

———— " ————

In the 1994-95 season, the United coach eased Beckham into his role on the team at right midfield. He was even loaned out to another team, Preston North End, to gain experience. He played five matches and scored two goals there. He finally made his Premier League debut at home near the end of the season, in April 1995. But things really started to improve for Beckham in the 1995-96 season, when he established himself on the first team. That was also when he first started to show his talent for scoring. United won the Double that year, winning two major tournaments: the FA Cup and the Premiership, the league title.

Beckham started the next season, 1996-97, by scoring his most famous goal. In a game against Wimbledon, the young player proved his remarkable skills by kicking in a goal from 57 yards away—halfway down the soccer field. The stunning play gained him instant fame. His performance that year helped United win the Premiership. In addition, he was named the Professsional Footballers' Association Young Player of the Year.

Beckham was gaining fans, too, who were impressed by his ability to make a soccer ball curve into the net when he kicked it. He is especially good at this when performing a free kick after a penalty. Puzzled by the soccer player's ability, engineers in Japan and Europe have even made it a subject of scientific study. "The conclusion," *Sports Illustrated* writer Frank Deford once reported, "is simply that he is a genius with an innate sense of physics. He has, says one software company, figured out how to balance the kick angle, kick speed, spin, and direction in order to get the optimal turbulent laminar transition trajectory. What trajectory Beckham's brain calculates in seconds from instinct would, engineers say, take computers hours to figure out." His famous kick would later lend itself to the title of a 2002 movie, *Bend It Like Beckham,* about a girl who wants to play soccer as well as her hero.

Recognized Talent Leads to the National Team

The next season, 1997-98, was disappointing for United. They finished second in their league, lost in the FA Cup, and were knocked out of the Champions League quarterfinals. But for Beckham, there was some consolation when he was called up by England's national team. This did

Beckham helped Manchester United win the Premiership in 1997. Here, he celebrates after scoring a goal.

not mean he had to leave his home team, Manchester United. Instead, soccer players who represent their national teams also play for the local teams from which they are selected, like an American professional basketball player would continue to play for their NBA team even when named to the American national team for the Olympics. "It's an honor for any player to represent his country," noted Beckham. "But you can't make it happen for yourself. All you can do is concentrate on playing for your club and hope that you catch the eye of the right person. . . . That first Double-winning season [winning the FA Cup and Premiership], though, brought all of us into the limelight — and into the reckoning as far as England was concerned. When it happened for me, it all came quicker than I could have imagined, and was a bigger thrill than I'd ever let myself dream it might be. Almost overnight, it seemed I went from being a promising player at my club to being a regular part of the England team challenging for a place in the 1998 World Cup in France."

At first, things seemed to be going fine for the England team in 1998. They played well enough to enter the World Cup playoffs. Expectations for Beckham, the team's new rising star, were high. He played as a substitute in a match against Romania; then, in the next game against Colombia, he scored his first goal as an England player. This meant England would make it to the second round, in which they would have to face their archrival, Argentina.

———— " ————

"It's an honor for any player to represent his country," noted Beckham. "But you can't make it happen for yourself. All you can do is concentrate on playing for your club and hope that you catch the eye of the right person. . . . Almost overnight, it seemed I went from being a promising player at my club to being a regular part of the England team challenging for a place in the 1998 World Cup in France."

———— " ————

The Infamous Red Card

England and Argentina had a long history of bitter rivalry, both on the field and off. This dates back to the Falkland Islands War in 1982, when the two nations had clashed over the islands in the south Atlantic off the coast of Argentina. They had even fought a war over it, with Britain coming out the victor. Their hostile feelings were often expressed on the soccer field in intense, aggressive play.

The England players were holding their own against Argentina that June day when a goal set up by Beckham to teammate Michael Owen tied the game at 2-2 at half-time. Early in the second half, though, something happened that would haunt Beckham for years. One of the Argentina players, Diego Simeone, fouled Beckham, and the English player fell to the ground. Beckham described what happened next: "While I was down on the ground, he made as if to ruffle my hair. And gave it a tug. I flicked my leg up backwards towards him. It was instinctive, but the wrong thing to do. You just can't allow yourself to retaliate. I was provoked but, almost at the same moment I reacted, I knew I shouldn't have done. Of course, Simeone went down as if he'd been shot. 'I've made a big mistake here. I'm going to be off.'"

It would prove to be the biggest mistake of Beckham's career. Simeone drew a yellow card (a minor foul), but Beckham was given a red card (a

In this 1998 game between the national teams for England and Argentina, Beckham earned a red card and was ejected from the game. Here, he is sent off by the referee after striking out at Simeone.

major foul) and ejected from the game. England had to play short-handed for 73 minutes and eventually lost in penalty kicks. The match ended in a tie, but England had needed a win to go to the World Cup. Without it, England was out of the competition, and Beckham's major penalty made him the scapegoat. Some of his most loyal fans in Manchester still supported him. But most soccer fans throughout England were outraged and vilified him. The once-adored soccer star was lambasted in the newspapers (one headline read, "What an Idiot!"), was heckled wherever he went, and was even burned in effigy outside one London pub.

The public's scorn even escalated to death threats. Beckham recalled one particularly disturbing occasion: "I received a letter at my house in Worsley that contained two bullets in it and a scrawled note saying there's be one for each of us [him and his wife]. I can still remember standing by my pool table and the sound of the cartridges dropping out of the envelope and onto the table in front of me." Though nothing happened to him, threats such as this are taken very seriously by soccer players like Beckham, who no doubt recall how Colombian player Andres Escobar was murdered after he accidentally lost a World Cup game by kicking the ball into his own team's goal.

Redemption and the 2002 World Cup

Beckham was greatly troubled by the public's reaction to his foul, but he responded by playing some of his best soccer ever. The 1998-99 season proved to be a terrific year, both for Beckham and for Manchester United. Executing fantastic passes and goals, he helped lead United to what is known as the Treble, or Triple Crown. That means the team won three championships: the FA Cup, the English Premiership, and the European Champions Cup, which is considered the ultimate club prize in European soccer. United also won the Inter-Continental Cup in 1999. Also known as the World Club or Toyota Cup, the Inter-Continental Cup is awarded to the winner of a match between the champions of two continents, Europe and South America. The season was the most successful year in the history of the Manchester United club.

The following season, 1999-2000, the team won another English Premiership. Beckham was voted second in two competitions, best player in Europe and best player in the world; he lost to Rivaldo of Barcelona and Brazil in both contests. In the 2000-01 season, United again won the English Premiership and Beckham was named Britain's Sportsman of the Year. But his main achievements were in international play. He first captained the England national team in a friendly in Italy (a friendly is an exhibition game). He then kept the captain's armband after that, in World Cup qualifying play. In 2001, he led England to a 5-1 win against Germany in a World Cup qualifier. He later shot a last-minute goal on a free kick to win a game against Greece in the final qualifying round. That goal secured England's place in the World Cup finals.

In the World Cup finals, England was slated to play their archrivals, Argentina. Beckham was excited but nervous about playing against Argentina, because the humiliation of the 1998 red card incident was still fresh in his memory — and in that of his fans. "I have waited for this game for four years," he said. "I was nervous, but what I had to do was go forward." This game was made even more difficult because he was recovering at that time from an injury to a metatarsal bone in one of his toes — although luckily the injury was to his left foot, not his right or kicking foot.

Beckham knew this was his chance to make things right. The score was tied at 0-0 when he was fouled by an Argentina player. The referee didn't

Beckham scores a goal during the 2002 World Cup match against Argentina.

call it, but that didn't matter because another England player, Michael Owen, was quickly fouled, too. It was time for a penalty kick, and Beckham took the ball. "I remember forcing in two big gulps of air to try and steady myself and take control," he said. "For the last two penalties I'd taken for

United, I'd hit the ball straight down the middle of the goal and the keepers [a line of opponent players protecting the goal], diving to one side, had been nowhere near them. 'Same again now, David.' I was far too nervous to try to be clever. Not nervous for myself any longer. This was all about the team I was captain of. I've never felt such pressure before. I ran forward. And I kicked the ball goalwards as hard as I could. *In.* The roar. *IN!"*

After the kick, Beckham ran directly to the stands filled with Argentine fans, tilted his head back, and roared. England had won it, 1-0. "It's been a long four years. It's been up and down, but this has topped it all off," he later said. "It doesn't get any sweeter than that. As a footballing nation, we have waited a long time for this." In the next round, the quarter-finals, England played against Brazil. Unfortunately, England lost to Brazil, the eventual World Cup winner. But Beckham's redemption was complete.

Popularity

Over the years, Beckham has won a huge fan following. Yet some sports analysts feel that his fan following is not commensurate with his skill and that he is not the most talented player on the field. As British sportswriter Kevin McCarra once put it, "Beckham's talent . . . is deep rather than broad. He is one-paced, cannot trick his way past a fullback, tackles erratically, and has occasionally been faulted for his defensive positioning. All of that has been overshadowed by the precision with which he hits long, diagonal crosses and passes."

Over the past few years, Beckham has become overwhelmingly popular in Britain. Certainly part of his appeal is his physical attractiveness, which cemented his allure to women. Another part is his flashy lifestyle with his wife, Victoria Adams (also known as Posh Spice), a former singer with the Spice Girls. Together, they're the most famous celebrity couple in England. Beckham also has a large following among gay fans, a fact that he embraces: "Being a gay icon is a great honor for me. . . . I'm quite sure of my feminine side, and I've not got a problem with that at all." On the other hand, he sometimes wears gold chains and styles his hair in cornrows, which lends him a certain appeal to black fans. And although he is rich now, his roots are grounded in his blue-collar family background, so he appeals to working-class fans. In this way, Beckham has managed to appeal to all types of people. This has made him a huge asset to his commercial sponsors, which include Adidas, Pepsi, mobile-phone company Vodafone, and Police brand sunglasses. He sometimes models for these companies, and he also has his own clothing design business.

Final Years with Manchester Grow Tense

The first years of the new millennium were good ones for Beckham, or so it seemed. Manchester United had won the English Premiership in 2000 and 2001, though the team had fallen short of the FA Cup and Champions League titles and had won no titles in 2002. The team won the Premiership again to close the 2002-03 season.

But despite such successes, the relationship between Beckham and Alex Ferguson, the coach of Manchester United, was growing increasingly tense. By 2003, Beckham's stardom had become a liability for him professionally. His image as a cultural icon greatly disturbed Coach Ferguson. Especially after Beckham's marriage to Posh Spice, Ferguson felt that his player's mind was not on the game as much as it should be and that he was distracted by such things as photo shoots and family events. Two incidents particularly set Ferguson off: when Beckham missed a practice to be with his son Brooklyn, who was sick, and when he went to Buckingham Palace to meet the queen rather than following orders to take a vacation in order to recuperate from a broken rib.

"What happened then doesn't seem real now, thinking back to that afternoon," recalled Beckham. "The boss [Coach Ferguson] took a step or two towards me from the other side of the room. There was a boot on the floor. He swung his leg and kicked it. At me? At the wall? . . . I felt a sting just over my left eye, where the boot had hit me. I put one hand up to it and found myself wiping blood off my eyebrow. I went for the manager. I don't know if I've ever lost control like that in my life before."

Beckham's relationship with Ferguson became more and more tense, until it all blew up one day after United lost a game to Arsenal. Ferguson blamed Beckham for the loss, but Beckham felt that the whole team had played

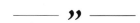

poorly and resented taking all the responsibility. "What happened then doesn't seem real now, thinking back to that afternoon," recalled Beckham. "The boss took a step or two towards me from the other side of the room. There was a boot on the floor. He swung his leg and kicked it. At me? At the wall? . . . I felt a sting just over my left eye, where the boot had hit me. I put one hand up to it and found myself wiping blood off my eyebrow. I went for the manager. I don't know if I've ever lost control like that in my

*Playing for Real Madrid in 2003, Beckham fights off
Santiago Ezquerro Marin of Athletic Bilbao.*

life before." At the end of the 2002-03 season, Beckham was traded and had to leave Manchester United.

Several reasons for the trade have been given, including a desire to change playing tactics and a need to bring in fresh players. This is an issue because Beckham's salary is enough to pay for several less-experienced players. But many observers believe the breakdown in the coach-player relationship was the deciding factor. Knowing that he would be traded, Beckham insisted the only other team he would play for would be Real Madrid, a powerhouse club that had a lot of stars of its own. United agreed, and the Madrid team happily signed him to a six-million-euro-per-year contract, plus bonuses. Having to leave his beloved Manchester United team was a blow for Beckham, but he is still on the England national team as its captain.

Beckham started with Real Madrid in the 2003-04 season. After playing a few games, he finds that he enjoys his new teammates. "This team not only can play great football," he said enthusiastically, "but they can play hard attacking football and they've got a lot of character." Financially, the deal works well for Beckham, too. Not only does he receive an excellent salary from his new team, but some of his major sponsors—Pepsi, Adidas, and Vodafone—are also associated with Real Madrid, so he can continue his sponsorship deals.

In his ten years of playing professional soccer, Beckham has accomplished a great deal. With the England national team, he earned 60 "caps," meaning 60 appearances in international competition, and scored 11 goals. With Manchester United, he made a total of 394 appearances with the club, scoring 85 goals. As part of United, he helped the team win two FA Cups and six Premierships, plus the European Champions Cup and the Inter-Continental Cup. It's an unprecedented winning streak, comparable to the New York Yankees or the Chicago Bulls.

Fame has naturally been one consequence of Beckham's success. But while he appreciates the media, he feels they exaggerate his spending habits and desire to be in the spotlight. "None of it is true," he once protested, "and I can't sue or I would end up doing it every day." For Beckham, it really all comes down to one passion: "I have always wanted to be a well-known footballer and all the things that come with it are an amazing bonus. But the important thing for me is to play football."

———— **"** ————

Beckham started with Real Madrid in the 2003-04 season. After playing a few games, he finds that he enjoys his new teammates. "This team not only can play great football," he said enthusiastically, "but they can play hard attacking football and they've got a lot of character."

———— **"** ————

MARRIAGE AND FAMILY

Beckham was married on July 4, 1999, to pop singer Victoria Adams. His fairy-tale wedding at a romantic Dublin castle was compared with the royal wedding of Charles and Diana. And when Becks and Posh, as they are known in Great Britain, bought a mansion in Hertfordshire, it promptly became known to the English public as "Beckingham Palace" (a play on

Victoria Adams, known as Posh, shows off her diamond solitaire engagement ring in 1998, after she and Beckham announced their plans to marry.

Buckingham Palace, the name of the royal family's home). The Beckhams have two sons: Brooklyn, who was born in 1999 in the New York City borough he was named after, and Romeo, who was born in 2002 and is named after the singer from So Solid Crew.

Beckham is known to be devoted to his family. He even got into trouble with his Manchester United coach because he put his family before soccer. Although Beckham has said that "without my football I'm a lost soul," he has also that "the most important thing to me is my family."

The Beckhams would seem to have it all: money, good looks, and fame. They are certainly idolized for their glamorous lifestyle and commitment to each other and their children. But there is another side to their celebrity lifestyle: the family has received death threats and has been the target of several kidnaping threats. Fortunately, these have all been avoided with the help of the police and increased security measures.

MAJOR INFLUENCES

Other than the early influence of his father, Beckham has found inspiration in his hero Bobby Moore, who is the only captain of an English team to win the World Cup, as well as former England coach Glen Hoddle.

HONORS AND AWARDS

Young Player of the Year (Professional Footballers' Association): 1997
Sir Matt Busby Award: 1997
Player of the Year (Nationwide Football Awards): 2000
Most Valuable Player (Western Union): 2001
Britain's Sportsman of the Year: 2001
BBC Sports Personality of the Year: 2001
Sports Personality of the Year (British Broadcasting Corp.): 2001
Order of the British Empire (Government of Great Britain): 2003

"I have always wanted to be a well-known footballer and all the things that come with it are an amazing bonus. But the important thing for me is to play football."

FURTHER READING

Books

Beckham, David. *My World,* 2000
Beckham, David. *Both Feet on the Ground: An Autobiography,* 2003
Newsmakers, Issue 1, 2003
Who's Who in the World, 2001

Periodicals

Economist, July 5, 2003, p.57
Los Angeles Times, Aug. 5, 2001, p.D10
Newsweek, Oct. 16, 2000, p.64
New Statesman, Feb. 10, 2003, p.57
New York Times, July 2, 1998, p.A21
People, May 4, 1998, p.71; June 19, 1999, p.58; June 9, 2003, p.63
Soccer Digest, Aug.-Sep. 2003, p.38
Sporting News, July 7, 2003, p.56
Sports Illustrated, Sep. 7, 1998, p.28; June 23, 2003, p.60
Time, June 30, 2003, p.49
Time International, Apr. 28, 2003, p.65

Times (London), Mar. 21, 1998, Magazine sec., p.18; Apr. 15, 2000, p.31; Mar. 27, 2001, Sports sec., p.9; June 21, 2001, p.Times2:2; June 2, 2002, Sports sec., p.2; Mar. 27, 2003, p.11; June 19, 2003, p.43; Sep. 17, 2003, Sports sec., p.42; Sep. 14, 2003, Sports sec., p.6
USA Today, June 10, 2002, p.C12
Vanity Fair, Sep. 1999, p.298

Online Databases

Biography Resource Center Online, 2003, article from *Newsmakers,* 2003

ADDRESS

David Beckham
CM Publicity — 19 Management
Unit 32 — Ransomes Dock
35-37 Park Gate Road
London SW11 4NP
UK

WORLD WIDE WEB SITES

http://www.manutd.com
http://www.realmadrid.com

Francie Berger 1960-

American Lego Builder and Marketing Manager
First Professional Lego Builder and Designer in the
United States

BIRTH

Francie Berger was born on April 3, 1960, in Queens, a borough of New York City. Her father, Harvey Berger, was a traffic manager, while her mother, Rhoda, was a medical tran-
scriptionist. Berger was three years old when her only sibling,
Adam, was born. He is now an attorney.

YOUTH

Berger was raised in the New York City borough of Queens. She began playing with Lego bricks at age three, after her parents gave her a set of the plastic interlocking building blocks. "I got my first Lego set when my brother was born," she said. "I guess my parents just wanted to keep me busy." She quickly became captivated by the toy; in fact, she would rather build a house than play house. One favorite project was when "my dad and I created this little fire truck, and I always wanted to rebuild it." She recalls this fire truck with affection because they designed it themselves; this was before Lego even sold a fire truck kit. Berger's Lego collection grew as she received more blocks for her birthday and at Hanukkah. She also picked out Lego sets to give her brother, and remembers how excited she was by a Swiss villa set she chose for her brother's birthday. Not only was it was a house set, it featured a brand new arch-shaped piece. She gave the set to him for his birthday, but now jokes that "if you ask him, he'll say he never got to play with it."

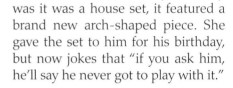

"I got my first Lego set when my brother was born," Berger said. "I guess my parents just wanted to keep me busy."

Back in the 1960s, playing with Lego blocks could sometimes be frustrating. The Danish company first began making building blocks in 1949, but they didn't appear in the United States until 1961. When Berger was a child, there were just 200 different shapes — today there are over 2,000 — and the bricks were only available in red and white. As a result, she remembers, "I always built striped houses." As her projects grew bigger, she began writing to Lego Systems, the American maker of the blocks, to ask if she could order customized sets. The stores offered small sets of assorted bricks, but "I wanted to buy red bricks so I didn't have to build striped houses." The company said they couldn't help her, but she would occasionally write them to make other requests or suggestions.

As Berger grew older, her friends grew out of playing with Lego toys. She never did, even though her junior high friends didn't think it was very cool. "It was one of many things that set me apart," she recalled. "I was an athlete, and 'girl things' didn't interest me that much. I was the one who got a baseball mitt for my 16th birthday." She also had a newspaper route to earn extra pocket money, and played organized baseball and softball. Although there weren't many sports teams for girls in the 1970s, her high school did have a softball team and she competed as a pitcher. She still spent her free time with Lego, however, and remembers getting a Lego set to pass the time when she was hospitalized briefly at age 16.

EDUCATION

In 1978 Berger graduated from Benjamin Cardoza High School in Bayside, Queens, New York. Her mother wanted her to go to business school, "because everyone knew I would own a toy store one day." She decided to study architecture instead, since designing buildings seemed the field of study closest to her passion for Lego: "Architecture is just building bigger houses with bigger bricks." She chose Virginia Polytechnic Institute (Virginia Tech) because it offered a five-year architecture program that included an entire year's internship in a real-life setting. Another bonus was the guest lecturer program, in which architects and designers visited the university to speak about their work. During her freshman year, Berger heard a lecture by a toy designer that opened her eyes to the possibility of finding a job in the toy industry. "That was when a light bulb went off in my head, and I said to myself, 'This is where I belong.'"

At Virginia Tech, students had the option to spend their fourth year in an off-campus internship. When it was time for her fourth year, Berger managed to get a position in New York City with that lecturer's toy company, Environmental Programs. During her internship, Berger helped work on the company's design for Johnson & Johnson's toy-of-the-month program. It was the encouragement of her mentor at Environmental Programs that led her to pursue her dream of becoming a Lego builder. She wrote letters to Lego Systems, asking about a job. She kept calling and writing until she finally got in touch with the right person and convinced him to see her. She went to their Connecticut headquarters to give them a presentation of her work. She was ready to quit school and begin working right way, but they asked her to finish school instead, then send them her résumé.

Berger returned to Virginia Tech for the final year of study for her architecture degree. She was still thinking of Lego blocks, however; for her senior project she designed a scale model of a farm using Lego bricks, with the

> *Berger decided to study architecture, since designing buildings seemed the field of study closest to her passion for Lego: "Architecture is just building bigger houses with bigger bricks."*

Berger (seated at right) and other designers critique a model built by Lego master builder Kurt Zimmerle (seated at left).

largest buildings standing about 12 inches tall. She worked from photos of actual farm buildings, then drew up blueprints for reproducing them in Lego blocks. Her design had 14 buildings, including a farmhouse, cow and horse barns, a chicken coop, a pigsty, a shed, a small tractor, and even a little outhouse. She did not construct most of the buildings, as she would have needed thousands of bricks to complete them all, but her detailed plans fulfilled the requirements for her project. In 1983 she graduated from Virginia Tech with her degree in architecture.

CAREER HIGHLIGHTS

Getting Her Dream Job

After college, Berger continued writing to Lego Systems, figuring they still might need a skilled Lego builder. "I knew they had guys in Denmark who designed huge models that were shipped all over the world. I wrote and told them they had the bricks here, why not let me design them here?"

She sent them an updated résumé (including photos and schematics of her senior project) and then left on a cross-country tour for three months in a 1977 Volkswagen Beetle. She came back on a Wednesday, and two days later got the phone call from Lego Systems: her efforts had paid off with a job offer. "I think they had finally gotten tired of listening to me on the phone," she said. "Figured if they saw me in person, maybe they could make me go away. [They] agreed to see me in person, and they never got rid of me." Actually, landing her dream job was a matter of timing, perseverance, and tenacity, Berger added; Lego happened to be ready to start their model department in 1983, and her persistence meant she was the first person they thought to hire.

Before Berger joined the company, the American division of Lego had no builders on their staff. If they needed a Lego model for a special display, they had one made by an artist in the main office in Denmark. Then the model would have to be shipped across the Atlantic to the United States. Berger began working in Lego America's new model shop in February 1984. She began with a tour of the Lego offices in Enfield, Connecticut; when she visited the department responsible for handling public relations, everyone in the letters department knew who she was. The best part, however, was her new work area, filled with an endless supply of Lego blocks in all the colors and shapes she could want.

"I think they had finally gotten tired of listening to me on the phone," Berger said about her many calls to Lego. "Figured if they saw me in person, maybe they could make me go away. [They] agreed to see me in person, and they never got rid of me."

Berger's job started out with relatively small projects: she repaired older models that had been traveling around the country and made a few small models for display in mall stores. These models might be displayed in a store like Sears or JC Penney, which were major retailers of Lego in the 1980s. Bigger models, perhaps of animals, people, or cars, were needed for Lego displays at malls and toy trade shows (where toy makers introduce new products to prospective retailers). Later, when Lego established their own specialty stores at Minnesota's Mall of America and Florida's Disney World, Berger helped create models for permanent display in the stores.

How Professionals Build a Model

When Berger first began designing her own models for Lego, it involved lots of trial and error to make sure she produced just the right shapes, even curves. "When we build a model, we don't use any bricks that you can't buy in stores, and we don't alter them or cut them or do anything weird to them," Berger explained. It is possible to create the illusion of something round (like a head) with cube-shaped Lego blocks, but it takes careful design and practice. Eventually Berger's department adopted the technique used by the Danish modeling department, using the company's specially designed graph paper to plan their models. Like an architect's drawings, these would include a plan view, looking down from the top, and an elevation view, shown from the side.

> **“**
>
> *When Berger first began designing her own models for Lego, it involved lots of trial and error to make sure she produced just the right shapes, even curves. "When we build a model, we don't use any bricks that you can't buy in stores, and we don't alter them or cut them or do anything weird to them," Berger explained.*
>
> **”**

With the new graph paper, Berger could sketch out her designs and then use them as a guide for building her projects. The "best part of the job," she said, was that with over 2,000 shapes and 20 colors, "you have all the bricks you want, in any color and any size." After constructing an unglued model, she would turn it over to one of the department's model builders. The builders would then make an exact copy of Berger's design from the ground up, gluing it as they put it together. (The modelers actually use a strong chemical solvent that fuses the plastic together, forming a stronger bond than glue.) They make it as hollow as possible, to keep it light, and once the model is completed and bonded it can be transported for display.

While this method allowed for some changes during the building, it could lead to disaster. Berger recalled one time when she was building an unglued model of a life-sized human figure some six feet high. One day a woman in Lego's public relations department was showing the design lab to a reporter; with the wave of an arm she ruined six weeks' work. (Luckily, since the model broke apart in big chunks, it only took a few days for Berger to piece it back together.) Her co-worker apologized with flowers; when

This golfer made from Lego blocks demonstrates the challenge of creating round objects with square blocks.

another gentleman in the office did the same thing, the culprit appeased her with a "gorilla-gram."

Over the next few years, Lego began hiring other designers and builders, and Berger became a supervisor in her department. First she oversaw the work of the model builders, who built projects from other people's designs. Around 1992 she was named model design supervisor, overseeing the work of other designers. The special events department grew larger, including not only model designers and builders but display designers and carpenters, who created the settings in which these marvelous Lego sculptures were presented.

Sharing Enthusiasm for Lego Worldwide

Berger's creations during her years in Lego's model design department included some amazing projects. She created a six-foot-tall pirate, complete with red beard, for a display in the famous New York City toy store F.A.O. Schwartz. The flagship Toys "R" Us store in New York's Herald

Berger with her model of the U.S. Capitol building, made with one-half million Lego blocks.

Square once featured an animal amusement park with a six-foot Lego roller coaster that Berger created. Minnesota's Mall of America displayed her department's tallest work, a 24-foot-high clock tower that took four months to create. One of her most intricate models was a copy of the U.S. Capitol building, complete with steps and lampposts, that measured 27 feet wide and traveled the country in a special Lego exhibit of national landmarks. It was made from half a million Lego bricks. Berger and her fellow designers might consult photos or plans when copying a real building, or look at storybooks when designing an elf or a pirate. One of her favorite projects, however, came straight from imagination: a six-foot-tall surfing hippopotamus.

While she was part of Lego's design department, Berger often traveled around the country, building models on site. The models were used to promote Lego products at stores, toy fairs, and in the company's traveling museum. She left her position as head of the model design department in 1998 to spend two years in Mexico City. There she helped Lego Mexico start their own special events department. While in Mexico, she not only planned special Lego events, she also helped create several Lego models, including some six-foot tall models of parrots, which are native to the country. Her favorite building project during her time in Mexico, however, was a version of the Aztec sun calendar that would be featured in Lego Mexico's offices. Also known as the sun stone or calendar stone, the Aztec sun calendar is one of Mexico's national symbols, with the original discovered in the main temple of the Aztec capital Tenochtitlan (now Mexico City). Filled with detailed carvings, the stone uses pictures to represent the Aztec calendar, which has 18 months of 20 days each, plus five festival days. Berger's model was 54 inches in diameter and featured many different colors.

While Berger was working for Lego Mexico, the American office underwent a corporate restructuring. In 1999 the model design department was cut from more than 50 people to 10, and later down to just four. Computers had made designing models much simpler by using a special "Legolizer" computer program. Using this program, which company staffers created themselves, a designer could create a three-dimensional (3-D) model on screen and the computer would translate it into a building plan. The plans could be sent to builders anywhere in the world, perhaps to those at the new Legoland California theme park, which opened in 1999 and has a model-building staff on hand to repair the park's numerous models and build new exhibits. So when Berger returned to the United States in 2000 she switched jobs, moving into Lego's promotional events department as an in-store project manager. "I felt I had taken it as far as I could," she said of her job as a model designer.

Moving into Marketing

Currently, Berger's new job as an in-store project manager is to develop "retail-tainment" events: hands-on events for specific retailers. For example, she might take one of Lego's newest products and develop a two-hour event for a local Toys "R" Us or Wal-Mart store to host for its customers. She also works on designing a specific look for Lego's store displays so that customers can instantly recognize the space as the "Lego section." Sometimes she travels to supervise interactive Lego events, such as the time she went to the Kennedy Space Center in Florida, where she helped visitors build the world's largest Lego space shuttle. On these trips

Berger's favorite model is this replica of Cinderella's castle at Disney World in Orlando, Florida.

she helps her audience work together to build a project, and she says "the best thing [is] coming out here and working with the kids."

Besides traveling all over the United States and Mexico, Berger has visited cities in Canada and Costa Rica, as well as a children's museum in Guatemala. Her favorite model that she made during her travels was a replica of

Cinderella's castle built at Disney World in Orlando, Florida. She built the model, which grew to be 15 feet tall, with the assistance of the park's guests, and calls it "the absolute highlight of my career here." Her current position doesn't require as much travel, but that's no sacrifice for Berger—it gives her more time to spend at home with her daughter, Seneca. Occasionally the two of them will play with Lego blocks at home, but not very often: her daughter prefers other toys. Besides, Berger says, "it's odd to have to build with a limited amount of bricks again."

Berger's unusual occupation has brought her a curious kind of notoriety. She has been profiled in newspapers, magazines, a book called *Odd Jobs,* and even on a television TV show about "Our Favorite Toys." Her job sometimes makes casual chat challenging. Answering the simple question "what do you do?" turns into a conversation stopper as everyone in the room gathers around to hear more about her work. The envy of other adults is understandable: Berger has seen her childhood dreams come true. In working for Lego, she says, "what it always comes back to is that this is fun."

> *Berger's job sometimes makes casual chat challenging. Answering the simple question "what do you do?" turns into a conversation stopper as everyone gathers around to hear more. The envy of other adults is understandable: Berger has seen her childhood dreams come true. In working for Lego, she says, "what it always comes back to is that this is fun."*

HOME AND FAMILY

Berger was married in 1988; her wedding invitation featured a photo of two hippos dressed as a bride and groom—made entirely of red Lego bricks and standing three feet tall. She separated from her husband in 2001, however. She has a daughter, Seneca Rasey, born in 1995, and the two of them live in Ellington, Connecticut, in an old Victorian house Berger is restoring.

HOBBIES AND OTHER INTERESTS

Berger devotes much of her free time to restoring the 1891 Victorian house where she lives. In her spare time she also enjoys creative arts like scrapbooking and photography, as well as building dollhouses and model trains. She loves to travel when she gets the chance. In the past, Berger has volunteered for literacy programs, teaching English as a second language.

FURTHER READING

Books

Schiff, Nancy Rica. *Odd Jobs: Portraits of Unusual Occupations,* 2002

Periodicals

Baltimore Sun, Apr. 9, 1995, p.J1
Chicago Tribune, May 23, 1995, p.C4
Christian Science Monitor, Dec. 2, 1997, p.16
Hartford Courant, Feb. 8, 2003, p.B3
Los Angeles Daily News, Dec. 8, 1997, p.SV3
New York Times, June 2, 1996, sec. 13CN, p.1
New Yorker, Jan. 14, 1991, p.24

Online Articles

http://www.cbsnews.com/stories/2003/02/18/earlyshow/living
/main541087.shtml
(*CBS News*, The Early Show, "Help Wanted: Lego Builders,"
Feb. 19, 2003)

Other

Phone interview with Francie Berger by Diane Telgen, conducted May 20, 2004.

ADDRESS

Francie Berger
Lego Systems, Inc.
555 Taylor Road
P.O. Box 1600
Enfield, CT 06083-1600

WORLD WIDE WEB SITE

http://www.lego.com

Tony Blair   1953-

British Political Leader
Prime Minister of the United Kingdom

BIRTH

Anthony Charles Lynton Blair was born on May 6, 1953, in
Edinburgh, Scotland. He was the second child born to Leo
Blair, a lawyer and university professor, and Hazel (Corscaden)
Blair, a homemaker. He has an older brother, William, and a
younger sister, Sarah.

YOUTH

Shortly after Tony was born, the Blairs moved with their two sons to Glasgow, Scotland, where Leo Blair worked as a tax inspector while studying for a law degree. In 1954 they moved again, this time all the way to southern Australia, where Leo had been hired to teach law at the University of Adelaide. Still wearing diapers, Tony entertained the other passengers on the long boat trip to Australia with his dancing. His younger sister Sarah was born in Adelaide, while Tony attended pre-school and continued to show a flair for performing in public.

The Blairs returned to England after three years, settling in the northern city of Durham. There, Leo Blair taught law at the University of Durham and got involved in local politics. In 1963 he ran for Parliament (see box on pages 15 and 16) as a member of the Conservative party, but during the campaign he suffered a serious stroke. Tony was only 11 at the time, but he remembers this event as "the day my childhood ended." "My father was a very ambitious man," he later told his biographer, John Rentoul. "He was successful. He was a go-getter. One morning I woke to be told that he had had a stroke in the middle of the night and might not live through the day and my whole world then fell apart." But, he goes on to explain, "It taught me something. It taught me the value of the family, because my mother worked for three years to help him talk and walk again. But it taught me something else, too. When that happened, the fairweather friends—they went. That's not unusual. But the real friends, the true friends, they stayed with us. They helped us, and they stuck with us for no other reason than that it was the right thing to do." Years later, when Blair was running for public office and was accused of having led a privileged life as a child, he would often refer back to this experience and how it taught him to value loyalty and a clear sense of right and wrong. He would also mention how his father's sudden change from a young, healthy man to a bedridden one made him more

> *Blair remembers the day his father had a stroke as "the day my childhood ended." "My father was a very ambitious man," he later said. "He was successful. He was a go-getter. One morning I woke to be told that he had had a stroke in the middle of the night and might not live through the day and my whole world then fell apart."*

aware of "the changes that can happen overnight and the fact that you can go down as well as up in the world."

Leo Blair was only 40 at the time of his stroke, and he was eventually able to resume work as a lawyer. But his political career was over. The family was just beginning to adjust to his new situation when Tony's younger sister, Sarah, developed a form of rheumatoid arthritis. "My sister was in the hospital for two years, as they treated the illness quite differently then," Blair said. "It was a terrible thing because she had to have all sorts of drugs. My mum was coping with that and my dad at the same time and she was an absolute rock. I didn't see her break down, never once." Sarah's illness, combined with Leo Blair's slow recovery, caused severe emotional and financial stress for the family. But once again, this difficult period instilled in young Tony some of the qualities that would later account for his success. He learned the value of hard work and responsibility, he came to admire his mother's ability to bear up under an enormous amount of strain, and he would eventually prove that he had inherited his father's political ambition.

> "It taught me the value of the family," Blair said about his father's stroke, "because my mother worked for three years to help him talk and walk again. But it taught me something else, too. When that happened, the fairweather friends — they went. That's not unusual. But the real friends, the true friends, they stayed with us. They helped us, and they stuck with us for no other reason than that it was the right thing to do."

EDUCATION

After spending his early years at a "pre-prep" school called Western Hill, Tony enrolled in the Durham Choristers School as a day student at age eight. This was a private school—which in England is referred to as "public." In addition to his studies, he played cricket and rugby and performed in school plays. He was often referred to as "Blair Two" because his older brother, William, also attended the school. Although he was considered smart enough to skip a grade, Tony was primarily interested in sports.

It is common for children from middle- and upper-class British families to be sent off to boarding school in their early teens. At age13, Tony went to

Blair with his parents and brother in 1956.

Fettes College in Edinburgh, the city in Scotland where he had been born. Fettes was the most prestigious private secondary school in Scotland, and it was often described as the Scottish version of Eton, the well-known English boarding school where upper-class and even royal families send their sons. Although he claims he "did not shine at anything" during his years at Fettes, he played basketball and rugby and was captain of the cricket team (a game that combines elements of baseball and croquet). He also displayed a rebellious streak, particularly when it came to rules that he thought were unfair. Fettes encouraged the tradition known in England as "fagging," where younger boys are forced to run errands and perform menial chores for older boys, who beat them with a cane if they don't do their jobs right. Tony hated this custom, and at the beginning of his second year at Fettes he tried to run away. He was forced to return to school, but these were not the happiest years of his life.

After graduating from Fettes in 1971, Tony took what is commonly referred to as a "gap year," which is a year off between high school and college. He spent it in London, hauling musical equipment around the city for rock bands in an old van. He and a friend thought they could set up a business promoting and managing rock bands, and Tony spent much of his time handing out leaflets and trying to book performances for a band called Jaded. But he was unable to support himself on his earnings, so he had to take on a number of odd jobs as well. After sleeping on sofas in his friends' apartments for a year, he decided he was ready to go back to school and complete his education.

In 1972, Blair entered St. John's College at Oxford University, where he studied law. At that time, in the early 1970s, student protests against the Vietnam War were disrupting many college campuses. But Blair didn't get involved in campus politics or anti-war protests at Oxford. He grew his hair long, wore bell-bottom jeans and colorful shirts, and sang in a rock band called the Ugly Rumors, but he avoided the drug culture that was so prevalent on college campuses at the time. Instead, he became very interested in religion, especially after making friends with Peter Thomson, an Oxford classmate who was studying theology. Thomson introduced Blair to the teachings of Scottish philosopher John Macmurray, who believed that people should work for the benefit of the community rather than to meet their own individual needs. Blair was deeply affected by Macmurray's ideas. "My Christianity and my politics came together at the same time," he recalls. He was confirmed in the Church of England at the end of his second year at Oxford, and he began thinking of ways that he could put his religious beliefs to work for the good of a larger community. Blair graduated from Oxford in 1975.

"She knew she was dying but she was very, very lucid," Blair said about his mother. "She saw each one of us in turn and went through things with us. . . . She was very keen as to what type of future life we should lead. . . . I was always the wildest of the three [and] Mum was worried I might go off the rails."

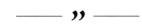

Two weeks after Blair graduated from Oxford, his mother died of throat cancer at the age of 52. Her death—much like his father's stroke 12 years earlier—had a profound effect on Blair. "She knew she was dying but she was very, very lucid," he recalled. "She saw each one of us in turn and went through things with us. . . . She was very keen as to what type of future life we should lead. . . . I was always the wildest of the three [and] Mum was worried I might go off the rails." Before she died, Hazel Blair made both her sons promise "that we'd get ourselves sorted out and not do stupid things."

Tony Blair suddenly realized that if there were things he wanted to accomplish in his life, he'd better not waste any more time. "My life took on an urgency that has probably never left it," he said. Planning to practice law, he immediately completed a one-year law course in preparation for the bar exam. He passed the bar in 1976.

CAREER HIGHLIGHTS

After completing his law studies, Blair began an unpaid apprenticeship — known as a "pupilage" — at a law firm run by Derry Irvine. Irvine had also taken on another pupil, Cherie Booth, who had graduated first in her class at the London School of Economics and would later become Blair's wife. Irvine could only choose one of his pupils for a "tenancy" or permanent job with the firm at the end of their year-long pupilage. Blair had performed only marginally on the bar exam while Booth had achieved one of the top scores, but it was Blair who was asked to join Irvine's firm. "One of his principal skills was absorbing enormously complicated material," Irvine recalls. "He had a very keen sense of what was relevant. He was very good at getting to the point . . . [and he possessed] an excellent facility with the English language."

Becoming a Member of Parliament

It was around this time that Blair began to get involved in the Labour party, one of Great Britain's two dominant political parties (see box on pages 15 and 16). The Labour party had traditionally been dominated by trade unions. But a series of strikes in the late 1970s seriously disrupted British life and commerce, and many people became disenchanted with the Labour party. Many Labour voters switched their support to Conservative party candidates in the election of 1979, when Margaret Thatcher became Prime Minister. In 1982, Blair decided to run for Parliament as a Labour candidate from Beaconsfield, a district west of London that had almost always voted Conservative. He won only 10 percent of the votes, but he made a very good impression on party leaders during his campaign. The following year he ran again, this time in Sedgefield, an industrial area near Durham, and won.

Once he became a Member of Parliament (MP), Blair proved himself to be a quick learner. While Margaret Thatcher and the Conservatives continued to run the government, Blair rose rapidly through the ranks of the Labour

*The Houses of Parliament at the Palace of Westminster,
with Big Ben shown at the right.*

Government in the United Kingdom

The United Kingdom consists of England, Scotland, Wales, and Northern Ireland. The U.K. has a parliamentary form of government, which means that the lawmaking body known as Parliament is the supreme authority. The Parliament consists of the *monarch* (currently Queen Elizabeth II), the *House of Commons*, and the *House of Lords*. The role of the monarch is largely ceremonial with no real power, and the term "Parliament" is often used to refer just to the two law-making bodies, the House of Commons and House of Lords. There is no written constitution that gives Parliament its authority. Its power has evolved over many centuries and is based not only on law, but also on custom and tradition. The two houses of Parliament meet in the Palace of Westminster, which is located in London next to the River Thames. The building has three sections, one for the House of Commons, one for the House of Lords, and a royal apartment for the monarch. Although still considered a Royal Palace, the last monarch to live here was Henry VIII, who moved out in 1512. The clock tower Big Ben is also part of the building.

The **House of Commons** has 659 members (known as *Members of Parliament* or MPs) who are elected by the voters, much the way

Americans elect their senators and congressional representatives. There are currently two main political parties, the Conservative party (also known as Tories) and the Labour party. Whichever party wins the most seats in the House of Commons during a general election (see below) gets to choose its leader as the *Prime Minister*. For example, the Labour party won the most seats in the 2001 general election, so its leader, Tony Blair, became the Prime Minister. The main function of the House of Commons is to pass laws and to oversee "the Government."

In the U.K., "the Government" consists of the Prime Minister and about 100 members of the political party that is currently in power. These 100 members can be from either the House of Commons or the House of Lords. They work in government departments to manage public services.

The **House of Lords** has approximately 700 members, known as peers, who are not elected. There are 500 *life peers*, who are appointed by the Queen on the recommendation of the Prime Minister and who have typically served the country in other capacities in the past. They hold their positions for life. This group includes about 12 *law lords*—high-ranking judges who act as a final court of appeal. There are 26 bishops or *lords spiritual* representing the Church of England, which is the official church of the British government. Finally, there are 92 *hereditary peers,* who have inherited their seats in Parliament from the families. These peers have traditionally been members of British nobility. The hereditary peers at one time dominated the House of Lords, but today their influence has been reduced, and most hold their position for life rather than passing it on to their children. The main function of the House of Lords is to review legislation passed by the House of Commons.

General elections must be held at least every five years. During that period of time, it is the Prime Minister's responsibility to call for a general election. A general election is also held when Parliament votes that it has "no confidence" in the Prime Minister and his cabinet, or when Parliament defeats a measure that the Prime Minister considers absolutely essential. When a general election is called for, the Prime Minister and all elected Members of Parliament lose their positions and must go home to campaign for them all over again.

Blair (right) is shown working with fellow members of the Labour party in 1993.

party. In late 1984 he was promoted to the position known as "front bench," or spokesperson for treasury and economic affairs. Less than three years later he became his party's spokesperson on trade and industry. Just as the Conservatives had their cabinet ministers, the Labour party had what is known as a "shadow" cabinet, and in 1989 Blair was appointed to the position of "shadow" secretary of state for employment. The idea was that if the Conservatives should lose their hold on the government in the next general election, the Labour party would already have its experts in place and be ready to step in.

Labour Party Leader

By 1992, the Labour party had been defeated in four consecutive elections and John Major had succeeded Margaret Thatcher as Prime Minister. Neil Kinnock, the Labour party's leader, resigned in response to this dismal record and his deputy, John Smith, took his place. But then, in May 1994, Smith died unexpectedly of a heart attack. Blair decided he would try for the party leadership position, even though it meant competing against Gordon Brown, an old friend and colleague. Members of the Labour party voted and Blair won, largely because he was regarded as the party's best hope of winning the next general election.

Blair had been working for several years to "modernize" the Labour party, and now he was in a position to really push for change. In the past, the party had strongly supported trade unions, government-controlled industries, and social welfare programs that were paid for by the government. Blair proposed returning industry to private ownership and promoted free enterprise and competitiveness. He took some of the power away from Britain's trade unions, which had traditionally played a major role in choosing candidates and determining the party's policies. He also turned his attention to fighting crime, particularly after the case of Jamie Bulger — a two-year-old who had been murdered by two 10-year-old boys in 1993. This terrible crime had horrified the country and made many people start to worry about Great Britain's rising crime rate. And, finally, he concentrated on raising educational standards and fighting inflation.

> "
>
> *In the 1990s, young people who could not remember a time when the Conservatives had not been in power were drawn to Labour by Blair's energy and youthful appearance. In his speeches he described Labour as no longer a "tax and spend party, but rather a responsible party, a law and order party, a pro-business party."*
>
> "

By the end of Blair's first year as leader, membership in the "New Labour" party had increased by a third. Middle-class voters, who had traditionally seen themselves as Conservatives, began to take notice of the Labour party's new agenda. Young people who could not remember a time when the Conservatives had not been in power were drawn to Labour by Blair's energy and youthful appearance. In his speeches he described Labour as no longer a "tax and spend party, but rather a responsible party, a law and order party, a pro-business party." The British public responded to his message. In the 1997 general election, the Labour party won by a landslide, and Tony Blair replaced John Major as the new Prime Minister.

Prime Minister Blair

In 1997, at the age of only 43, Tony Blair became Britain's youngest Prime Minister since 1812. He moved into 10 Downing Street, the Prime Minister's official London residence, and wasted no time continuing his effort to move the Labour party toward the political center. "The individual thrives best in a well-functioning community of people," he reminded Britons. With that goal in mind, he set out to free the country from its traditional class-consciousness and to minimize racial and economic distinctions.

Blair greeting voters in 1994.

Less than four months after taking office, however, Blair was faced with an unexpected crisis: Diana, Princess of Wales, was tragically killed in a car accident in Paris. He managed to handle the situation with tact and eloquence, referring to Diana as "the people's princess." Diana's death came at a time when she was divorced from her husband, Prince Charles, the future king of England. In the wake of their separation, the royal family had distanced themselves from her. After her death, Blair persuaded the notoriously private royal family that she must be given a public funeral broadcast over loudspeakers so that the British people had an opportunity to participate in the mourning. He also advised the royal family to appear in public at the gates to Buckingham Palace, where flowers and other tributes to Diana were piling up daily. Without putting himself in the spotlight, Blair was responsible for avoiding what could have been a public relations disaster for the royal family and for providing ordinary people with an outlet for their grief over Diana's death.

As Prime Minister, Blair continued the reforms he had begun as head of the Labour party, emphasizing crime prevention and law enforcement, closer relations with the European Union, and improvements in the education and health care systems. He gave Scotland and Wales limited self-government by allowing them to establish regional parliaments of their own. He tackled the issue of British rule in Northern Ireland, which has long been a source of controversy, by opening up communications with

Blair with President Bill Clinton in the Oval Office of the White House, 1996.

Sinn Fein, the political division of the Irish Republican Army. He came out in favor of NATO (the North Atlantic Treaty Organization) taking military action to stop the ethnic strife and bloodshed in Kosovo in 1999; he described the situation there as a "battle of good against evil, between civilization and barbarity, democracy and tyranny." He even went to Moscow to meet with President Vladimir Putin — the first Western leader to do so.

At home, Blair showed that he was serious about changing the face of Great Britain. One of his more controversial moves was an unsuccessful attempt to ban hunting foxes with hounds, a traditional British upper-class sport that also provided jobs for many working-class people. There was a tremendous public outcry, particularly from the upper-class Britons who enjoyed fox hunting and the workers in rural areas who made their living as blacksmiths, gamekeepers, grooms, and other hunting-related occupations. This public outcry caught Blair off guard, and the bill never made it through the House of Lords. An even more radical move was to change the organization of the House of Lords. He abolished the 650 seats for hereditary peers (see box on pages 15 and 16) and replaced them with 500 life peer positions, along with 92 hereditary peers who were allowed to remain until further reforms were passed. His goal was to make the House of Lords less elitist and more "compatible with a democratic society."

Comparisons with President Clinton

At the end of his first year in office, Blair's popularity had actually grown. He had a 72 percent approval rating from the British public — higher than that received by any British Prime Minister at the end of his first year in office since World War II. But after 2000 he began to lose his appeal to voters. Some attributed this to what they called his morally superior attitude and the frequently unpopular stands from which he refused to back down, even when it became obvious that the majority of the British people didn't agree with him. People began to see him less as a fresh-faced idealist and more as a politician. Although he won reelection in the 2001 general election, voter turnout was the lowest it had been in 50 years.

Blair was often compared to Bill Clinton, the American president who was in office throughout most of the 1990s. Blair's youthful good looks and campaigning skills, like Clinton's, had earned him as many votes as his policies; and like Clinton, he was married to a successful attorney with a thriving career. They were also frequently compared due to their political policies. The American press referred to Clinton as a "New Democrat" for his ability to shift the Democratic party's agenda toward the political center. In a similar vein, many said the policies put forth by Blair and his "New Labour" party were moving toward the center and, in fact, were not really all that different from what the Conservative party had supported for years. The British press actually referred to him as "Tony Blinton," or sometimes "Tony Blur," because he had a talent for stating his objectives in broad, non-threatening terms that would appeal equally to middle-class suburban voters and poor and working-class people.

As Prime Minister, Blair wasted no time continuing his effort to move the Labour party toward the political center. "The individual thrives best in a well-functioning community of people," he reminded Britons. With that goal in mind, he set out to free the country from its traditional class-consciousness and to minimize racial and economic distinctions.

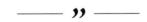

Blair meets with President George W. Bush at the White House, shortly after the terrorist attacks on September 11, 2001.

One thing that set Blair apart from Clinton was his squeaky-clean personal life. Although both he and Clinton had studied at Oxford, Blair had never been caught smoking marijuana or doing anything that might embarrass him in later life. And unlike Clinton, who had a history of extramarital affairs, Blair was obviously devoted to his family and spent as much time with them as he could. Still, his manner, which was often described as "righteous" or "preachy," began to rub voters the wrong way.

Siding with the U.S. in the Iraq War

The United States and Great Britain have had a long history of friendship, which had been cemented by the close personal relationships between Margaret Thatcher and President Ronald Reagan in the 1980s and between Blair and Clinton in the 1990s. Then in September 2001, terrorists attacked the United States, hikjacking airplanes that struck the World Trade Center, the Pentagon, and a field in Pennsylvania. At the World Trade Center, a number of British citizens were also killed. These attacks provoked an outpouring of sympathy and support for America, and the majority of Britons supported the U.S. decision to attack terrorist strongholds in Afghanistan later that year. But then President George W. Bush began to talk about invading Iraq and getting rid of the Iraqi dictator Saddam Hussein. The majority of the British people thought Bush was going too far. Tony Blair, however, steadfastly supported Bush in his plans for war, even when it became clear that the U.S. would go ahead with the invasion without the support of the United Nations. Blair sent British troops to support the U.S. in the Persian Gulf, and his popularity took a sudden nosedive. One of his cabinet ministers even quit in protest.

As the war proceeded and British soldiers began dying, Blair lost much of the support he had gained in the preceding six years. Since most European countries were opposed to the war, Britain's involvement in Iraq undermined attempts to build closer ties between Great Britain and the European Union, an economic and political association of European countries. Then a report by the British Broadcasting Corporation (BBC) said that Blair had "overstated" the facts regarding Iraq's weapons of mass destruction—a primary reason for the invasion. The BBC report said that Blair had done this in order to justify his decision to send British troops to war. The subsequent failure of U.S. troops and weapons experts to uncover any evidence that Iraq was still manufacturing weapons of mass destruction made it look as though Blair had been lying.

Blair steadfastly supported Bush in his plans for war with Iraq, even when it became clear that the U.S. would go ahead with the invasion without the support of the United Nations. Blair sent British troops to the Persian Gulf, and his popularity took a sudden nosedive. One of his cabinet ministers even quit in protest.

Blair's reputation was soon damaged even further by revelations regarding David Kelly, a weapons expert for the British Defense Ministry who had been named as the source of the BBC report. Kelly committed suicide after being questioned by a parliamentary committee and being overwhelmed by media attention. There was speculation that the government had deliberately subjected Kelly to humiliation, thus contributing to his decision to kill himself. Blair and his government were eventually absolved of blame. A report was issued by a senior judge, Lord Hutton, on how the government had handled the intelligence information it had received prior to the Iraq war. The report declared that, in fact, it was the BBC that was responsible for overstating the case on weapons

Blair addresses British troops on a surprise visit to Iraq. "It's a great honor for me to be here today," he told the troops. "The first thing I want to say is a huge thank you for the work you're doing here."

of mass destruction. Although the head of the BBC stepped down in response to the report, a broad spectrum of the British public still believed that their Prime Minister had involved the country in a war under false pretenses.

British and American casualties in Iraq began to mount, and civil unrest there threatened to undo whatever good the invasion might have achieved. Soon, the strain on Blair began to take its toll. In October 2003 he was hospitalized for several hours with an irregular heartbeat. He returned to his office soon afterward and appeared to be in fine health. But it was clear that his determination to "stay the course" in Iraq—no matter how much it damaged him politically—was making life difficult. Even the capture of Saddam Hussein in December 2003, which Blair hailed as the beginning of "unity, reconciliation, and peace," gave him only a temporary boost in public support.

A Close Call

In January 2004, Tony Blair survived a crisis that could easily have spelled the end of his career as prime minister. Blair is a strong believer in privatization — private funding for industry and public services. He wanted to increase the amount of tuition that British college students paid from about $2,000 a year to $5,400. He insisted that without this additional income, British universities would not be able to compete with those in other countries.

Many Americans are accustomed to paying a high price for their education, so that increase might not sound excessive. But it was an extremely risky position for Blair to take in England, where poor and middle-class families are accustomed to paying very little for their children's education. The issue struck at the heart of what has divided the Labour party ever since Blair took office: "Old Labour" would like to keep the traditional system, under which the government pays for things like higher education and health care, while "New Labour," represented by Blair, wants to require individuals and families to pay more for such services.

When Parliament voted on January 27, 2004, New Labour won, but only by five votes. About 70 members of his own party voted against Blair and the tuition hike — the highest number to do so since the vote supporting Britain's participation in the Iraq war in March 2003. So even though Blair was victorious, the narrow margin of victory was seen as yet another indication of the struggle going on inside the Labour party. Several Members of Parliament claimed that they had been pressured about their votes, which didn't help. As one outspoken MP complained to *The Times*, "All the reasons for voting were to do with dear old Tony — 'Preserve Tony for the nation,' 'Don't vote with the Tories' — nothing to do with the [tuition] bill."

What Lies Ahead for Blair?

It seems likely that Blair will call for a general election in the fall of 2005. Many critics have charged that he has been spending too much time and energy supporting Bush in Iraq and not enough working on domestic issues like health care, education, and his country's transportation system, and he has recently begun to turn his attention to solving problems at home. But even on controversial domestic issues, like raising university tuition fees, Blair has shown a determination that some people regard as inflexible and unyielding. Once he makes up his mind, he is unlikely to change it — a characteristic that has made some Britons wonder whether he will still be their Prime Minister a year from now. But for the time being, his position appears to be secure.

Blair and his family pose for photographers at their vacation villa in Italy, 2000. Blair, who is holding his new baby, Leo, is accompanied by Kathryn, Euan, Cherie, and Nicky.

MARRIAGE AND FAMILY

In 1980, Blair married Cherie Booth, the young lawyer he had met in Derry Irvine's office when he was just out of law school. Booth uses two forms of her name: she uses her maiden name professionally and her married name when she is acting as the Prime Minister's wife. As one of Britain's most prestigious lawyers, she specializes in employment law. Booth has been named a "Queen's Counsel," which means that she argues legal cases on behalf of her country's government. It's an honor granted to only a small percentage of Britain's lawyers. Although she briefly considered a career in politics herself and actually ran for Parliament as a Labour party candidate in 1983, she has since abandoned politics to work in a human rights law firm and to earn money to support her family. Her work as a lawyer has frequently required her to take stands that oppose those of her husband and his party, but she has managed to keep her career separate from her role as the wife of the Prime Minister. Unlike American First Lady Hillary Clinton, who became a lightening rod for criticism during her husband's presidency, Cherie Booth has avoided negative publicity when she has gotten involved in government policy.

The Blairs live in London and spend their weekends at Chequers, the Prime Minister's country house. They have four children: Euan, born in

1984; Nicholas, born in 1985; Kathryn, born in 1988; and Leo, born in 2000. Cherie Booth made headlines during her husband's first term in office when she announced that she was pregnant at age 45. When Leo, named after Blair's father, was born in May 2000, he became the first child born to a Prime Minister in office in 152 years. Booth insisted that her husband make changes in his work schedule so that he could spend more time caring for Leo, and she has been a role model in many other ways for working mothers.

The Blairs have made a real effort to give their four children as normal an upbringing as possible. Cherie Booth is particularly aware of the dangers involved in having a famous father, since her own father was a well-known television actor; he starred in an English comedy series that was the model for the popular American TV series, "All in the Family." Tony Blair always has breakfast with his children and spends an hour with them at the end of the day, while his wife is often still working. They spend most of their weekends at Chequers and vacation in Europe in the summer.

HOBBIES AND OTHER INTERESTS

On the weekends he spends at Chequers, Tony Blair likes to swim in the pool there. Tennis is his favorite sport, and he can often be seen on the tennis courts at Chequers as well. When his schedule allows, he likes to play football with his children.

HONORS AND AWARDS

Charlemagne Prize (City of Aachen, Germany): 1999

FURTHER READING

Books

Hinman, Bonnie. *Tony Blair,* 2003
Rentoul, John. *Tony Blair: Prime Minister,* 2001
Wilson, Wayne and Jim Whiting. *Tony Blair: A Real-Life Reader Biography,* 2003

Periodicals

Atlantic Monthly, June 1996, p.22; July-Aug. 2003, p.27
Current Biography Yearbook, 1996
New York Times, May 14, 2000, Section 6, p.56
Newsweek International, Sep. 29, 2003, p.24

People, May 19, 1997, p.201
Reader's Digest, Mar. 2003, p.71
Time, Mar. 31, 2003, p.64; June 11, 2001, p.34; Feb. 2, 2004, p.24
Time International, Dec. 10, 2001, p.36
The Times (London), Jan. 28, 2004, p.A3

Online Articles

http://www.theatlantic.com/issues/96jun/blair/blair.htm
   (*Atlantic Monthly,* "The Paradoxical Case of Tony Blair," June 1996)

ADDRESS

Tony Blair
10 Downing Street
London SW1A 2AA
United Kingdom

WORLD WIDE WEB SITES

http://www.number-10.gov.uk/output/page2.asp
http://www.explore.parliament.uk/Parliament.aspx?id=3

Orlando Bloom 1977-

English Actor
Star of the Hit Movies *Lord of the Rings*, *Pirates of the Caribbean*, and *Troy*

BIRTH

Orlando Bloom was born on January 13, 1977, in Canterbury, England, a small, historic city about 60 miles southeast of London. His mother, Sonia Copeland-Bloom, runs a language school for foreign students. Her husband, Harry Bloom, was a South African human-rights activist and writer. He died when Orlando was four. During his childhood, Orlando believed that Bloom was his father. But when he was 13, he learned that his biological father actually was Colin Stone, a writer and family friend. Bloom has one older sister, Samantha, an actress.

Bloom's unusual name was chosen by his mother, who named him after the 17th-century composer Orlando Gibbons. Bloom often has to assure people that Orlando Bloom is his real name. It's "a hard one to live up to," he said. His nickname is "Orli."

― **"** ―

"When I realized the heroes on 'The A-Team,' 'The Fall Guy,' and 'Knight Rider' weren't real, I decided I wanted to act, because I thought I'd love to be any number of those guys," Bloom said. "I realized those larger-than-life actors that I saw on TV, in the movies, in the theater, even street performers, could be multiple characters, and I thought that was just great. You can be an action hero, you can be Jimmy Dean, you can be those characters."

― **"** ―

YOUTH

Bloom was shaped by his arts-loving family. His mother encouraged him and his sister to enter competitions to recite poetry and Bible passages. "That's where I got a real taste for performing," he said. "I'd love to stand up and perform, and I'd do quite well." He was an imaginative boy who played pirates and other make-believe games by the hour. Watching movies like *Superman* and his favorite TV shows made him see that acting was a way to transform himself again and again. "When I realized the heroes on 'The A-Team,' 'The Fall Guy,' and 'Knight Rider' weren't real, I decided I wanted to act, because I thought I'd love to be any number of those guys," he said. "I realized those larger-than-life actors that I saw on TV, in the movies, in the theater, even street performers, could be multiple characters, and I thought that was just great. You can be an action hero, you can be Jimmy Dean, you can be those characters." He especially admired the late American actor James Dean "because he put so much passion in his work," Bloom said.

Although Bloom was eager for an acting career, his first experience on stage was far from positive. At age four, he played a monkey in a monkey suit. "It was really hot onstage," he recalled. "I itched my [bottom] and the entire audience laughed at me." It was the "worst ever," he reported. In spite of this embarrassing start, Bloom continued to perform through his childhood and teens.

Off-stage, young Bloom was "full of action and full of ideas," his mother remembered. He was physically energetic and daring and had the scars to prove it. Over the years he has broken his nose, both legs, an arm, a wrist, a finger, a toe, and his back. He has also cracked his skull three times. "I was a little bit crazy," Bloom said. "Not crazy-crazy, but I was always the first one to jump off the wall or dive into the lake, without really thinking about the consequences."

When he was nine, Bloom broke his leg skiing and had to wear a cast for a year. It caused him to go through a chubby phase. "I sat at home really depressed because I couldn't play. I was eating biscuits [cookies] and chocolate bars." Bloom said. "I was a porker." He didn't get back on track with sports until he was 16. He admitted that he "wasn't very cool" and relied on his sister to buy him clothes — often funky items from second-hand shops. Bloom had more serious challenges, too. He has dyslexia, a condition that causes him to jumble the letters in words. It makes reading difficult. "I was teased about that because I couldn't spell properly," he said.

As he reached adolescence, Bloom had to come to grips with some surprising news: he learned that Harry Bloom was not his father; instead, his father was another man. In an interview in *GQ* (*Gentleman's Quarterly*), Bloom explained. "My mom was married to one man, but I was fathered by a second. I think she was waiting for me to be old enough to understand it. But when would you tell a kid about that stuff? It's very difficult." Harry Bloom, the man he had believed was his father, was a heroic figure. He fought for equal rights for black and white people in South Africa at a time when the country's white rulers denied equal treatment for black citizens. Harry Bloom wrote important books on the subject and even went to prison for his beliefs. He died when Bloom was four. "Harry was always a role model for me," Bloom said. "My mother spoke of him so fondly." Suddenly, at age 13, Bloom was asked to accept that his biological father was a family friend, Colin Stone. A writer, Stone had served as a guardian to Bloom from the time of Harry Bloom's death. "I don't know any family that doesn't have a little story somewhere," Bloom told *GQ*. "Besides, if you didn't have those things in your life, you'd be so bland."

EDUCATION AND FIRST JOBS

Because of his dyslexia, "education was always a bit tricky," Bloom said. "But I got all my exams and degrees. I just had to work harder to get them." He attended St. Edmund's, a private, co-ed school in Canterbury for students from age three to age 18. The school has a strong tradition in music and performance, and Bloom acted in school plays. His former drama teacher recalled: "Even at 14 or 15 he was getting lead roles against people who were 17 or 18. It's . . . easy to think he's a good-looking chap and that's why he's getting roles in Hollywood, but he was a very good character actor."

At 16, Bloom had completed the second stage of British schooling. Rather than remain at St. Edmund's for the last two years of pre-university education, he moved to London to join Britain's National Youth Theater. After two seasons, he won a scholarship for further training at the British American Drama Academy. While there, he won a couple of small television roles. Also, his performance in a play at a small North London theater won him an agent, a professional who helps an actor find roles. When Bloom had completed his scholarship, he played the lead role in the play *A Walk in the Vienna Woods*. He also made his movie debut in *Wilde*, a film biography of Oscar Wilde, the 19th-century Irish writer. The film was critically acclaimed, and Bloom was striking in his small part as a teenaged prostitute.

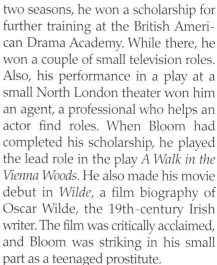

—————— " ——————

Bloom's former drama teacher recalled, "Even at 14 or 15 he was getting lead roles against people who were 17 or 18. It's . . . easy to think he's a good-looking chap and that's why he's getting roles in Hollywood, but he was a very good character actor."

—————— " ——————

Bloom was getting noticed as a promising young actor and, with the benefit of an agent, could have entered the professional world. Instead, he chose to continue his education. He was accepted into a degree program at London's Guildhall School of Music and Drama. Such acclaimed actors as Ewan McGregor and Joseph Fiennes have attended this prestigious school. "I always planned to go to drama school," Bloom said. "I suppose I could have trained in the industry more. But, instead, I chose an environment that would be more conducive to experimenting." During his three years at the Guildhall School, he acted in classics like *Twelfth Night* by William Shakespeare and *Uncle Vanya* by 19th-century Russian playwright Anton Chekov.

In 1998, Bloom had an accident that nearly ended his career and his life. While visiting some friends, he volunteered to force open the warped door to their roof terrace. The door needed to be kicked in from the outside. Bloom climbed from a window out onto a gutter—but the gutter couldn't bear his weight. It gave way, and he fell three stories to a terrace below. "I crushed one vertebra and fractured three others. The doctors thought I wouldn't walk again," Bloom said. He was offered an operation to bolt metal plates to his spine but it carried the risk of damage to his bones and nerves. Bloom decided to take the chance and hobbled out of the hospital on crutches 12 days later. For a year, he wore a brace, and with intensive rehabilitation, he taught himself to walk again.

"I was really depressed. I was in a lot of pain," Bloom recalled of his time in the hospital. "But I had this one great teacher who came to visit and said to me, 'This is going to be the making of you.' And it was." The incident helped him to refocus and to appreciate life, Bloom said: "It made me feel that every day I'm alive is an opportunity. It had a huge effect on my life, both as an actor and as a young guy just trying to get through."

Despite this difficulty, Bloom was able to finish his education. He graduated from the Guildhall School of Music and Drama in 1999, earning an honors degree.

CAREER HIGHLIGHTS

The *Lord of the Rings* Trilogy

Just days before he graduated, Bloom was handed the role of a lifetime. New Zealander film director Peter Jackson offered him the role of elf-warrior Legolas Greenleaf in his film version of the *Lord of the Rings* trilogy, which includes *The Fellowship of the Ring, The Two Towers,* and *The Return of the King.* The movies were based on the well-loved books written by the English author J.R.R. Tolkien, who had been a professor of medieval languages and literature at Oxford University in England. Tolkien set the stage for the trilogy and first introduced some of the characters in *The Hobbit,* published in 1937. The three books in the *Lord of the Rings* trilogy, which were originally published in the 1950s, have often been called the finest fantasy novels ever written. Together, they have sold more than 100 million copies worldwide. (For more information, see the entries on Peter Jackson in *Biography Today Performing Artists,* Vol. 2; J.R.R. Tolkien in *Biography Today,* Jan. 2002; and Elijah Wood in *Biography Today,* Apr. 2002.)

In the *Lord of the Rings,* Tolkien created a vivid ancient world complete down to its own languages. His world is populated with fantastic creatures including hobbits, dwarves, elves, orcs, and ringwraiths. Set in the mythical world of Middle-Earth, the story centers on an evil Ring of Power, which must be destroyed before it falls into the hands of the dark

Bloom as Legolas Greenleaf in the Lord of the Rings *trilogy.*

wizard Sauron. The only way to destroy the ring, however, is to throw it back into the fire where it was forged: the lava of Mount Doom in the dark lands of Mordor.

To destroy the ring, a group of nine is selected, called the "Fellowship of the Ring": the wizard Gandalf; the men Aragorn and Boromir; the elf Legolas; the dwarf Gimli; and the hobbits Frodo, Sam, Merry, and Pippin. They pledge to travel to Mordor and cast the ring into the flames of Mount Doom in order to save Middle-Earth from eternal darkness. Together, the Fellowship must overcome great obstacles and resist the power of the ring. They set out on a terrific journey of action, adventure, and heroism, as the members of the Fellowship are tested to determine their loyalty to their oath and their ability to overcome adversity in all forms.

Creating the Movies

Filming the *Lord of the Rings* trilogy represented a "first" in the industry: it was the first time three separate films would be made as one continuous production. The three films would then be released at one-year intervals, in 2001, 2002, and 2003. It was considered a very risky strategy, but it ultimately paid off. Jackson and Bloom didn't know it yet, but the films would be acclaimed by critics and wildly popular. "I remember meeting Peter Jackson when he came to see me at school and thinking this would be really amazing," Bloom said. "I could feel the mad energy and I was so excited."

Although he had planned to continue his acting training on the London stage, Bloom didn't hesitate to commit to the *Lord of the Rings*. "It wasn't like I was going to turn that down 'Oh, no, I think I'll go and do some theater,'" he said. "I was like, *'Yeah!'*" Instead of staying in London, 22-year-old Bloom found himself on the way to New Zealand in 1999 for an 18-month, three-film shoot. It was "like winning the lottery," Bloom said. "I mean, imagine being flown to this amazing country and being taught how to shoot a bow and arrow, learn to ride horses, and study swordplay — it was sick! I was pinching myself."

For the part of Legolas, dark-haired, brown-eyed Bloom had to be transformed into a blue-eyed blond with waist-length hair. He even had a specially designed wig. But in order to make it fit, Bloom had to shave part of his own hairline. Because bow and arrow are Legolas's chief weapons, he also had to get his archery skills up to speed quickly. "I found that I had a bit of a knack for it, to where I was shooting paper plates out of the sky, which is quite cool."

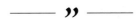

"[It was] like winning the lottery," Bloom said about spending 18 months in New Zealand. "I mean, imagine being flown to this amazing country and being taught how to shoot a bow and arrow, learn to ride horses, and study swordplay — it was sick! I was pinching myself."

For some scenes, though, he only had to fire an empty bow — the arrow was later added using computer graphics. He also learned to ride horseback. Luckily, the only "war wound" from the film for accident-prone Bloom was three cracked ribs when he fell from a horse.

Along with the thrills and excitement of filming, Bloom found his new role as Legolas, the regal elf warrior, somewhat intimidating. "Tolkien created the elves to be these perfect beings, to bring the world forward. It's quite a responsibility to take that to the screen." Like all of the elves in the *Lord of the Rings*, Legolas is immortal. At the time of the story he is 2,931 years old. Bloom saw Legolas as something of a superhero. "Elves have this superhuman strength, yet they're so graceful. I wanted him to have a balletic movement to him. A real grace, but he's . . . a red-blooded, full-on warrior elf. The movement was more sophisticated than your average human. . . . [It] was more like a samurai," Bloom said, referring to the aristocratic Japanese warriors from around the 17th century who followed a strict code of honor.

———— **"** ————

"Tolkien created the elves to be these perfect beings, to bring the world forward. It's quite a responsibility to take that to the screen," Bloom said about Legolas, whom he considered something of a superhero. "Elves have this superhuman strength, yet they're so graceful. I wanted him to have a balletic movement to him. A real grace, but he's . . . a red-blooded, full-on warrior elf. The movement was more sophisticated than your average human. . . . [It] was more like a samurai."

———— **"** ————

Along with the challenge of bringing a superhuman being to life, Bloom found himself performing with superstars of the acting profession. He said: "[Can] you imagine what it was like for me, coming right out of drama school, being thrown into a group of actors like Ian McKellen, Ian Holm, and Christopher Lee. . . . Yes, it was incredibly daunting." On the other hand, Bloom said, the cast members were the ultimate teachers: "I just watched how the other actors were going about what they were doing. In a way it was perfect. It was like a continuation of school."

During the year and a half of filming, New Zealand became something of a spiritual home for Bloom, and the cast was like a family. "We all got on so well and grew close, going fishing or on road trips together during free time," he said. Bloom lived in a house next to the sea. "You could almost spit in it," he said. "The Hobbits and I went surfing all the time." The filming itself was cloaked in secrecy. "I would have to wear a hooded jacket in the car on the way to the set and home every day, too, if I still had the elf ears on," he said. According to Bloom, the only negative side to making the *Lord of the Rings* was that it had to end. He recalled the celebration the cast and crew had after the last re-shoot had been completed: "The stunt guys did a hucker, which is a Maori kind of pole dance [Maori are the native people of New Zealand]. Peter said some amazing things. It was really sad and hugely emotional."

Scenes from the Lord of the Rings *trilogy.*

Today, Bloom wears an indelible souvenir of his experience on *Lord of the Rings*. He has a tattoo on his forearm of the "elvish" symbol for nine in honor of the nine members of Tolkien's fellowship. Each of the actors who portrayed a member of the fellowship got one. Not as visible, but just as permanent, is Bloom's feeling for his character. "I hope I carry a part of [Legolas] with me forever," he said. "He's a special, special character and of course, my first. I'm never going to let go of him." Bloom also said he will never stop being grateful to Peter Jackson for the experience he gave him. "Not just as an actor but as a guy getting to live in New Zealand and experience that culture," Bloom said.

After working on *Lord of the Rings*, Bloom next went to work on *Black Hawk Down* (2001), by the established director Ridley Scott. In this film about U.S. military personnel stationed in Somalia, a country on the coast of eastern Africa, Bloom has a small role as Pfc. Todd Blackburn, a young, inexperienced U.S. Army ranger. In a case of art imitating life, his character falls 70 feet from a helicopter. He breaks his back and many other body parts. He then is taken to safety in a convoy. Bloom recalled, "After I had my fall, I was in hospital lying right next to a young soldier with a paralyzing injury. It's surreal how life has these patterns."

Pirates of the Caribbean

In 2003, Bloom appeared in another huge hit film, *Pirates of the Caribbean: the Curse of the Black Pearl*. If the *Lord of the Rings* won Bloom won female fans' attention, his appearance in *Pirates of the Caribbean* sealed their affection. Funny, rollicking, romantic, and scary all at once, the film was a huge success with audiences. Johnny Depp steals the show with his mincing, comical portrayal of scalawag pirate Capt. Jack Sparrow. But Bloom is firmly the romantic heart of the film, as earnest blacksmith Will Turner, a good-hearted lad in love with the local beauty, Elizabeth (played by Keira Knightley). He teams up with swaggering Sparrow to rescue his fair damsel.

"It's all that fun, swashbuckling stuff, which is a good laugh," Bloom said. "I loved the boat-to-boat battles and all the swinging on ropes." Co-star Geoffrey Rush, with whom he also worked in *Ned Kelly*, recommended him for the role in *Pirates*. And when Bloom heard who else was in the cast, he signed right on. "Knowing that Johnny Depp was involved in this movie made it a no-brainer for me," he said. "Johnny is such a hero of mine. As a kid, I'd run to his movies." Knightley became the envy of females everywhere when she shared Bloom's first on-screen kiss. "He has an amazing future ahead of him," she said. "He's a very good-looking boy

LEFT AND ABOVE:
Scenes from Pirates of the
Caribbean.

BELOW: A scene from
Black Hawk Down *with*
Bloom (center) as Blackburn
and Josh Hartnett (right) as
Eversmann.

and a lovely person. . . . I have nothing but good things to say about the kiss." The chemistry of the actors, and the liveliness of the story, won *Pirates* a huge following. The film was critically acclaimed, as well as financially successful. A hotly anticipated sequel is already in the works, in which Bloom, Depp, and Knightley return to their original roles. Filming is to begin in winter 2005.

Recent Films

Bloom appeared in several 2004 releases, both smaller films and a big blockbuster. He returned to period drama in *Ned Kelly*, set in the 19th century in the outback of Australia. The film tells the story of the real-life Australian outlaw and gang-leader Kelly, played by Heath Ledger. Bloom plays the supporting role of Irishman Joe Byrne, Kelly's best friend. Kelly and his gang create havoc in their bush community as a reaction to the abuse dished out by the local authorities. The gang "feels they are hard done by and persecuted unjustly," Bloom explained. "I have to admit, I didn't know a lot about the real-life Ned Kelly or the members of his gang. In the end, it was so rewarding playing a character who was a hero in real life to so many Australians."

> **" In Troy, Bloom was happy to play a bad boy for a change. "Will in Pirates and Legolas — they're obvious hero types," he said. "Paris is an anti-hero, and this is the story of stories." "**

Bloom's next release, *The Calcium Kid*, marked his first chance to take a lead role in a film. In this lower-budget British comedy, Bloom portrays a young milkman, Jimmy, who accidentally discovers he has a gift for boxing. Before he knows it, to his surprise, he is pegged to face an undefeated American champion. "Jimmy is an everyday geezer," Bloom said of his character. "He's not trying to be anything. In fact, he's just like me." The film was released in Britain in 2004 to mostly negative reviews. It reportedly will go straight to video release in the United States.

Also in 2004, Bloom appeared in the big-budget historical epic, *Troy*. The film is based on the tales related by the ancient Greek poet Homer in his epic poem *The Odyssey*. As in the *Lord of the Rings* trilogy, Bloom was part of a large, ensemble cast, including such major actors as Brad Pitt and Peter O'Toole. The director, Wolfgang Petersen, is noted for his international hit *A Perfect Storm* and earlier success, *Das Boot* (*The Boat*), a German-language film. In *Troy*, Bloom plays the pivotal role of Prince Paris.

Bloom as Paris and Diane Kruger as Helen in scenes from Troy.

Paris is a lover more than a warrior, but when he steals the famous beauty Helen from the King of Sparta he ignites war. Bloom was happy to play a bad boy for a change. "Will in *Pirates* and Legolas — they're obvious hero types," Bloom said. "Paris is an anti-hero, and this is the story of stories." The film has received mostly positive reviews, though more for the scope and technical success of the movie than for the individual performances.

Upcoming Projects

Bloom has several new movies on the way. He has finished *Haven*, a small, independent film set in the Cayman Islands in the West Indies. Bloom portrays a happy-go-lucky British guy who gets involved with two criminals, played by Bill Paxton and Gabriel Byrne. In addition to starring in *Haven*, Bloom is the film's co-producer. "It's the first time I've done that," he said. "In terms of the role that I've been playing as a producer, it's been really just a sounding board; it's very much a collaborative effort."

> ———— " ————
>
> *"I never really wanted to be famous,"Bloom said. "I trained for three years at drama school to be an actor—not a celebrity."*
> *Indeed, director Peter Jackson praises Bloom for not letting fame go to his head."He [is] the same guy, fun-loving, enthusiastic, and supportive. He doesn't buy into the nonsense."*
>
> ———— " ————

Currently in production is *Kingdom of Heaven*, directed by Ridley Scott, with whom Bloom previously worked on *Black Hawk Down*. The story takes place during the Crusades, a series of military campaigns that were undertaken by European Christians against Muslim powers between the 11th and 14th centuries. The invaders were trying to seize the city of Jerusalem and other Holy Lands from the Muslims. As in *Pirates of the Caribbean*, Bloom plays a blacksmith with a noble cause. His character, Balian of Ibelin, becomes a knight in order to defend Jerusalem against the Crusaders. Along the way, he saves a kingdom and falls in love with Sibylla, Princess of Jerusalem (played by Eva Green). "I swore to myself I wasn't going to do another movie with a horse and a sword, but here I am," Bloom said. "It's cool." According to Scott, the film will be produced on a scale slightly larger than *Gladiator*, his Oscar-winning epic. The much-awaited film is expected in May 2005.

Once that wraps, Bloom is set to transform himself into someone completely different: a present-day American. As the lead in *Elizabethtown*, he will portray a depressed young man returning to Kentucky for his father's funeral. Kirsten Dunst co-stars as a possible love interest. The movie has been described as a romantic comedy with strong dramatic elements. The director is Cameron Crowe, known for *Jerry Maguire* and *Almost Famous*. And of course, Bloom's many fans are also anxiously awaiting the sequel to *Pirates of the Caribbean*.

*Bloom doesn't want his
status as a teen idol to
keep him from building a
varied and challenging
career. "You know the
heart-throb thing — I hope
that it won't stop me from
making more interesting
choices, because that's what
I intend to try and do."*

”

Bloom's Appeal

Since his first appearance in the *Lord of the Rings* trilogy, Bloom has won the hearts of fans. Judging from his stacks of mail, many of them are females. According to *Ned Kelly* director Gregor Jordan, "There's a reason why girls go crazy for him. He's in the long tradition of guys like James Dean and Russell Crowe. There's just something about him that makes people want to sit in the dark and watch him on a movie screen." Jerry Bruckheimer, the producer of *Pirates*, would concur. "He is so natural. He's got that look, as if he could have come from another time." Writing in *GQ*, Allison Glock also commented on Bloom's old-fashioned appeal. She wrote, "He is courtly and sweetly naive. His lithe body seems built for tights and ruffs. Even his face has the delicate features of a more civilized era."

Indeed, interviewers note that Bloom's behavior, as well as appearance, could come from another era. He has been described as soft-spoken, polite, and an attentive listener. One journalist said that he had an almost spiritual presence. Another reported that during the course of one interview, Bloom graciously gave autographs to fans and helped an elderly man whose wheelchair had broken down.

As for Bloom, he is uncomfortable with adoration and shrinks from his heart-throb status. "I never really wanted to be famous," he said. "I trained for three years at drama school to be an actor — not a celebrity." Indeed, director Peter Jackson praises him for not letting fame go to his head. "He [is] the same guy, fun-loving, enthusiastic, and supportive. He doesn't buy into the nonsense."

When it comes to making choices for his film roles, Bloom embraces Johnny Depp's advice: "Don't go for the money. Keep it real and follow your heart. Take your time." Bloom also plans not to let his status as a teen idol keep him from building a varied and challenging career. "You know the heart-throb thing — I hope that it won't stop me from making more interesting choices, because that's what I intend to try and do," he said.

As his career gets busier, he enjoys "down" time more. "When I'm not working I prefer to sit and do nothing," Bloom said. "Go to a beach. Go for a walk. The simple things have suddenly become more enjoyable."

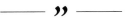

HOME AND FAMILY

Bloom is often on the road filming — in Mexico, Malta, Morocco, or the Caribbean, to name only a few of his recent movie locations. When he isn't working, he divides his time between Los Angeles and London. He remains close to his mother, sister, and old friends, whom he likes to see as often as he can. He is unmarried. Currently, he is reported to be dating actress Kate Bosworth, the star of *Blue Crush*. But Bloom is adamant about keeping his private life private. "I've got a lot of love in my life and I'm happy," he said.

HOBBIES AND OTHER INTERESTS

Bloom enjoys extreme sports, including skydiving, snow boarding, surfing, and bungee jumping. "When you're in front of a 150-foot drop with a piece of cord tied to your ankles, it's scary," he said. "But you confront that fear and get over it and it empowers you." His back injury in 1998 hasn't deterred him from what he loves to do. But it has made him more cautious. "Now I approach everything in a much less flighty manner," he said. "If I'm gonna get on a snowboard, I'm aware that I could do serious damage to myself." As his career gets busier, he enjoys "down" time more. "When I'm not working I prefer to sit and do nothing," Bloom said. "Go to a beach. Go for a walk. The simple things have suddenly become more enjoyable."

Bloom is a vegetarian. He reportedly likes shopping and antiques. He has studied photography and art; if he weren't an actor, he says he'd like to be a sculptor. A music fan, he enjoys Jeff Buckley, Coldplay, Radiohead, Jack Johnson, and Kings of Leon.

FILMS

Wilde, 1997
The Lord of the Rings: The Fellowship of the Ring, 2001
Black Hawk Down, 2001
The Lord of the Rings: The Two Towers, 2002
The Lord of the Rings: The Return of the King, 2003
Pirates of the Caribbean: The Curse of the Black Pearl, 2003
Ned Kelly, 2004
The Calcium Kid, 2004 (United Kingdom release)
Troy, 2004

HONORS AND AWARDS

Best Breakthrough Star Award (MTV Movie Awards): 2002, for *Lord of the Rings: The Fellowship of the Ring*

FURTHER READING

Books

Contemporary Theatre, Film, and Television, Vol. 43, 2002

Periodicals

Houston Chronicle, July 13, 2003, p.8
Interview, Nov. 2001, p.50
Newsday, Feb. 10, 2002, p.D3
The Record (Bergen County, NJ), July 6, 2003, p.E1
Teen People, Dec. 1, 2002, p.80; Feb. 1, 2004, p.78
USA Today, July 7, 2003, p.D1
YM, June 2004, p.80

Online Databases

Biography Resource Center Online, 2004, articles from *Contemporary Theatre, Film, and Television*, 2002

ADDRESS

Orlando Bloom
International Creative Management
8942 Wilshire Blvd.
Beverly Hills, CA 90211

WORLD WIDE WEB SITES

http://www.lordoftherings.net
http://disney.go.com/disneyvideos/liveaction/pirates/main_site/main.html
http://troymovie.warnerbros.com

Kim Clijsters 1983-

Belgian Professional Tennis Player

BIRTH

Kim Clijsters (pronounced KLEYE-sters) was born on June 8, 1983, in Bilzen, Belgium, a town in the Flemish-speaking region of the country. Her father, Lei Clijsters, was a renowned soccer star, while her mother, Els Vandecaetsbeek, was a champion gymnast. The Clijsters family later resided in the city of Bree, and in 1985 they welcomed another girl, Elke, into the family.

YOUTH

Clijsters grew up surrounded by sports. Her parents were both exceptional athletes, but they never pressured her into a career in sports. Instead, they supported her in all of her pursuits. Clijsters later commented about the physical gifts she received from her parents. "I got my build from my dad. I've never really touched weights or anything. I get my flexibility from my mum. She used to do gymnastics. For a strong girl like me, I think I'm very flexible as well. So I think it's a very good mix to have."

> "
>
> *"I got my build from my dad. I've never really touched weights or anything. I get my flexibility from my mum. She used to do gymnastics. For a strong girl like me, I think I'm very flexible as well. So I think it's a very good mix to have."*
>
> "

Clijsters gravitated towards tennis at the age of five after seeing other children playing the game in a local park. By the age of six, she was already participating in various competitions. A few years later, at the age of eight, she started taking private lessons. Still, her parents were reluctant to push her in that direction. "Tennis is still a hobby to Kim," her father once said. "If one day she doesn't like tennis, she should look for something else to do." Clijsters felt fortunate that her parents had that attitude. "My mum and dad, they've always told me from day one if you don't like it and you don't enjoy anything like traveling, hotel rooms, whatever, that's fine. You don't have to play tennis for us. I'm very lucky," she said.

But Clijsters was determined to succeed in the sport. By 1992, her family asked Bart Van Kerckhove to be her first coach. The move proved to be an important one, and a few years later, Clijsters won the Belgian Junior Championship at the age of 11. Before long, Van Kerckhove and others became convinced that she had the talent to be a world-class tennis player. Clijsters and Van Kerckhove eventually parted ways in 1996.

From there, the rising star went to tennis school in Antwerp. This was another positive experience for Clijsters, as she got a chance to showcase her talents and compete against many top international players her own age. At the training school, Clijsters met tennis coach Carl Maes. The pair hit it off, and Maes agreed to work with her. He once compared her style on the tennis court to her father's style on the soccer field. "Kim is really a very good copy of her father," Maes said. "Physically, she's very strong. Also, mentally, he was a very tough competitor. He wasn't the most elegant, technical player, but he was fun to watch. They are both very intuitive players — they just feel the game."

Soon thereafter, Maes began to accompany her to practices and tournaments all over the world. Her success was immediate, as Clijsters later recalled. "There are so many junior trophies in the attic that I won through the years I don't know what they all are." Her talent soon began to attract attention. By the time she was 15, she received a major break. The Belgian Tennis Federation gave her wild cards into three $10,000 events, giving her the chance to enter the events without actually qualifying. Clijsters did exceptionally well, winning one and making the finals in another. Her performance proved that she had what it took to turn professional.

But things weren't always rosy during this time. "Late in 1998, my mother Els got a very rare liver cancer and was told she only had two months to live," Clijsters once recalled. "I was just starting my career, playing $10,000 tournaments in Belgium, and it was very hard because at home there was always crying in the family. But tennis was good for me because it helped me take my mind off things." Eventually Els Clijsters had a successful liver transplant and made a remarkable recovery.

CAREER HIGHLIGHTS

Going Pro

In 1999, Clijsters entered the professional ranks with a bang. A month before she turned 16, she found herself in the Belgian Open. To the surprise of everyone but Clijsters and her entourage, she advanced all the way to the quarterfinals in the tournament. Later that year, she entered the legendary Wimbledon tournament. Wimbledon is one of many tournaments on the professional circuit of the Women's Tennis Association (WTA). But there are just four tournaments that make up the Grand Slam of tennis: the French Open, the Australian Open, Wimbledon (in England), and the U.S. Open. These are considered the most important tournaments in professional tennis.

Initially, Clijsters was a bit overwhelmed by the idea of playing at Wimbledon. "I have no idea what to expect. All I can do is try to enjoy it," she said at the time. But once again she made a name for herself, upsetting the 12th ranked Amanda Coetzer 6-2 and 6-4 in the third round. (In women's tennis, a player wins a match by defeating her opponent in 2 out of 3 sets, while men must win 3 of 5 sets. The first player to win 6 games usually wins the set, but if their margin of victory is less than 2 games, the set is decided by a tie-breaker. Shorthand notation is often used to show the score of a tennis match. For example, 6-2, 4-6, 7-6 means that the player in question won the first set by a score of 6 games to 2, lost the next set 4 games to 6, and came back to win the match in a third-set tie-breaker.)

Clijsters next had to go up against Steffi Graf, a player whose posters used to adorn her bedroom wall as a youngster. Before the match, Clijsters remarked, "Just going out to play her will be fantastic for me, and I will have to forget all my feelings for what she is and what she has achieved. It's so exciting." Ultimately, the experience proved to be a bit more humbling as her idol and seven-time Wimbledon champ defeated her twice by the score of 2-6. Clijsters was still a bit star-struck months after the match, especially when Graf later announced her retirement from the game. "The honor of being one of the last players to play Steffi is my best memory of 1999. After the match Steffi said to me I played tennis for the future. That meant so much to me."

> ———— " ————
>
> *"Just going out to play [Steffi Graf] will be fantastic for me, and I will have to forget all my feelings for what she is and what she has achieved. It's so exciting."*
>
> ———— " ————

Next up for Clijsters was a spot in the 1999 U.S. Open. In the third round, she faced the hottest star in women's tennis, Serena Williams. Clijsters started strong and almost derailed Williams's eventual championship run. In the third set, Clijsters had a 5-3 lead, but things fell apart when she dropped the last four games. Still, Clijsters viewed the experience as a positive one. "The match against Serena proved that I could play with her and maybe beat her," she remarked. "After that, I felt I wasn't just lucky. I could actually play with the top players."

Clijsters finally won her first WTA title that September at the Seat Open in Luxembourg. Her opponent in the final match was Dominique Van Roost, the No. 1 Belgian player at the time. Clijsters registered identical scores of 6-2 and became the fifth-youngest woman to win a tour event in the 1990s. She finished the year ranked No. 44, a fairly high position for a rookie. Later that year, she also received another honor. A panel of sports writers named her Belgium's Sportswoman of the Year. Soon after, Belgian tennis fans started referring to her as "Our Kim."

During her rookie season, Clijsters was thrilled to play at Wimbledon against her idol, Steffi Graf, 1999.

Developing Her Game

The year 2000 proved to be another successful one for Clijsters. A tough competitor, she disposed of top players like Anna Kournikova and Arantxa Sanchez-Vicario in various matches. At the U.S. Open she nearly upset Lindsay Davenport. One of her biggest wins came when she beat Elena Likhovtseva to capture the WTA Sparkassen Cup. In all, she played in 17 tournaments in 2000 and finished the year strong, winning 10 of her last 12 matches. She also vaulted 11 places in the player rankings to No. 20 while still maintaining the distinction of being the youngest player in the top 100. This exceptional performance prompted the Belgian sportswriters to name her Sportswoman of the Year for the second consecutive time.

Clijsters continued her upward climb in 2001. In March, she stunned the tennis world by upsetting Martina Hingis at the Tennis Masters Series. The match was a dramatic one, with scores of 6-2, 2-6, and 6-1. Clijsters's performance and dramatic style won over the crowd. In June 2001, she celebrated her 18th birthday by defeating fellow Belgian Justine Henin-Hardenne at the French Open. "I couldn't wish myself a better birthday than this one," Clijsters said at the time. Unfortunately, she later lost in the finals to experienced veteran Jennifer Capriati, but she remained poised and appreciative of all the support she received after the match. "I enjoyed it actually. I felt that I had to give something back to all the Belgian people who came to watch me today." Clijsters also noted the emergence of the other young tennis pros from her home country. "A lot of the new young players try to hit winners on every ball. We try to stay aggressive," she remarked. "If you see all the new upcoming players—Jelena Dokic, Justine Henin, Elena Dementieva—they all hit the ball very hard. I think this is probably the future of tennis." After her performance in Paris, Clijsters rose to No. 7 in the player rankings.

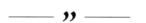

> *"People see me differently now, but I feel like the same player I've always been,"* Clijsters said in 2001. *"I am really happy with the way my career is going right now. I can't complain. When I was a top-50 player, I used to want to always beat a top-10 player, and now all the top-50 players want to beat me."*

The next stop for Clijsters was Wimbledon, and she was ready to put the French Open behind her. "I think Wimbledon is a place where I feel comfortable and I like the grass," she said. "I think I showed at the French Open that I can play at a very high level against the best players in the world. I think I can do well on any surface. Losing in Paris was disappointing, of course, but I take a lot of positives out of it."

This time, Clijsters achieved success at Wimbledon in the women's doubles final. She teamed up with Ai Sugiyama, the top-ranked female doubles player in the world, to defeat Virginia Ruano-Pascual and Paola Suarez by scores of 6-4 in each match. At the time, Ruano-Pascual and Suarez were the reigning French Open doubles champions. Clijsters and Sugiyama then faced the top-ranked Lisa Raymond and Rennae Stubbs in the finals and lost by scores of 6-4 and 6-3. Still, Clijsters enjoyed the experience of pairing up with Sugiyama. "It's my best result ever in women's doubles," she said at the time. "It's nice. We laugh on the court, we make jokes. It's relaxing a little bit." Clijsters didn't fare quite as well in the singles competition, bowing out to Lindsay Davenport by scores of 6-1 and 6-2 in the quarterfinals.

Clijsters rebounded in late July when she competed in the Bank of the West Classic. Suddenly, she wasn't an unknown quantity anymore and people were beginning to take notice of her game. "People see me differ-

Clijsters serves against Justine Henin-Hardenne in the semi-final match of the French Open, 2001.

ently now, but I feel like the same player I've always been," Clijsters remarked. "I am really happy with the way my career is going right now. I can't complain. When I was a top-50 player, I used to want to always beat a top-10 player, and now all the top-50 players want to beat me." Once again, Clijsters electrified the crowd with her style and flair. In the final match, when she defeated Lindsay Davenport, Clijsters literally burned a hole in her shoe and sock by running up and down the court and skidding her feet against the ground. "I actually bruised my toe. But it's OK, I'm still alive," she said after the match was finished.

But more impressive was Clijsters's game, which netted her $90,000 in winnings and vaulted her to No. 5 in the WTA rankings. "I am really happy to have a title this year," she said. "I've been in the finals, but I never took the extra step to beat the best players. This really means a lot to me." Still, she acknowledged that she still had to improve her game to meet her ultimate goals. "I have to keep working. I can still be fitter and serve better.

There are a lot of things I need to work on. I feel like I am getting closer. And I know against the best players, the star players, you just can't make mistakes." Even Davenport admitted that Clijsters had stepped up her game since they met at Wimbledon early in the month. "She is a better player than she was three weeks ago. She didn't play well at Wimbledon. She played will here." Clijsters had continued success through 2001, including a trip to the U.S. Open quarterfinals in September. Ultimately, she lost to Venus Williams 6-3, 6-1 in that tournament.

—— " ——

"This is definitely my biggest win and it feels incredible," Clijsters remarked after the 2002 WTA Tour Championships. Later, she said that "It's still pretty amazing for me to realize all of this and what I've achieved. I'm only 19. It's incredible."

—— " ——

Continued Success

It wasn't until May 2002 that Clijsters was able to get her revenge against Venus Williams. The stage was the Betty Barclay Cup, and Williams was the top seed and defending champion. Clijsters started the match off horribly, losing 1-6 in the opening set, but she came back strong and finished off Williams 6-3, 6-4.

Clijsters continued her 2002 assault on the Williams family by upsetting top-ranked Serena Williams 7-5, 6-3 at the WTA Tour Championship in November. Clijsters took home the top prize of $765,000 for her effort. "This is definitely my biggest win and it feels incredible," she remarked after the tournament. Later, she reflected further: "It's still pretty amazing for me to realize all of this and what I've achieved. I'm only 19. It's incredible." Williams also had high praise for the Belgian: "She's always done really well and had a lot of talent," she said. "We've always had some pretty competitive matches. She obviously has a very good future. We will see what next year will bring. I think she'll do very well."

At the Australian Open in January 2003, Clijsters once again found herself up against Serena Williams. This time it was Williams's turn to shine. Clijsters won the first set 6-4, but dropped the second 3-6. She was up 5-1 in the third and final set before falling apart and losing to Williams 5-7. Despite the collapse, Clijsters remained upbeat after the match: "I can't blame myself for anything," she said. "I just kept trying to hang in there. It just wasn't good enough at the end. Serena just started playing much more aggressively and hardly made any errors any more. If she plays her best

*Clijsters hugs
Serena Williams
after beating her
7-5, 6-3 at the
WTA Tour
Championships in
November 2002.*

tennis, it's very hard to beat her. That's what she did towards the end. Even though I lost, I enjoyed every moment. Big match, center court, and a Grand Slam. I still had a great time out there." Once again, Williams had kind words for her opponent. "Kim's not only a good tennis player, she's a great person, and I think she'll make a great champion because she's always so positive. Even if she's dying, she always looks positive."

Clijsters faced other difficulties in 2003. In a match against Silvia Farina Elia at Wimbledon in July, Clijsters was stung by a bee on her stomach. She still won the match, but the incident did cause some confusion for her on the court. "I didn't know if I should call the trainer or what. And I was very happy I didn't blow up out there, to know that I didn't have any allergies to it. It has never happened to me before and it hurt." Clijsters then advanced to the semi-finals, where she eventually lost to Venus Williams 4-6, 6-3, 6-1.

> ——— **"** ———
>
> *"I can't blame myself for anything,"Clijsters said after losing to Serena Williams in the 2003 Australian Open. "I just kept trying to hang in there. It just wasn't good enough at the end. Serena just started playing much more aggressively and hardly made any errors any more. If she plays her best tennis, it's very hard to beat her. That's what she did towards the end. Even though I lost, I enjoyed every moment. Big match, center court, and a Grand Slam. I still had a great time out there."*
>
> ——— **"** ———

Life at the Top

In August 2003, Serena Williams announced that she would be off the tennis courts for six to eight weeks while recovering from knee surgery. Venus Williams was also banged up and unable to compete. Because of this situation, and because she had a tour-leading six 2003 titles at the time, Clijsters found herself the No. 1 ranked female tennis player in the world. She was the 12th woman to receive the honor since the inception of the rankings in 1975.

While acknowledging her obvious talent and skill, many questioned if Clijsters was worthy of the ranking. They pointed out that she had yet to win a major tournament and stated that the whole situation wouldn't have happened if Serena Williams had stayed healthy. "Kim would probably rather win a Grand Slam than be No. 1," Lindsay Davenport said at the time. "People equate who wins Grand Slams with who is the best player."

Despite such comments, Clijsters took pride in her accomplishment. "This is a very special day I'll never forget. No matter what will happen the rest of my career, no one will ever take that away from me. It's something that I will always have on my resume," she said. "I'm only 20. I don't see the point of starting to worry about Grand Slams," she added.

An Intense Rivalry

In the absence of the Williams sisters, the biggest threat to Clijsters's No. 1 ranking turned out to be fellow Belgian Justine Henin-Hardenne. The pair had known each other since childhood, and Clijsters had fond memories of their relationship. "We grew up together. We've always kept in contact, and it's pretty amazing how we started at the same thing and ended up around the same ranking," she said. Henin-Hardenne also remarked on their closeness: "Kim and me, we are close friends. We speak about everything. But not of tennis. I think it's so good for a little country like Belgium to have two people like us."

> "This is a very special day I'll never forget. No matter what will happen the rest of my career, no one will ever take that away from me," Clijsters said after becoming the No. 1 ranked female tennis player in the world. "It's something that I will always have on my resume. I'm only 20. I don't see the point of starting to worry about Grand Slams."

But somewhere along the line, things went sour between Clijsters and Henin-Hardenne. In November 2002, Clijsters decided to skip Henin-Hardenne's wedding to spend time with her boyfriend. In early August 2003, at the Acura Classic in San Diego, Clijsters lost to Henin-Hardenne in the finals. At the end of the first set Henin-Hardenne took an extended time out to get treatment for some blisters on her feet. Clijsters complained that the move was a delay tactic designed to break her rhythm and concentration, something that she said Henin-Hardenne had pulled before with her. "I'm sort of getting used to it, she's done it in every match I've played against her. It didn't look like it was hurting because she was still running." Later she added: "It's a sign that she is not at her best and so she has to resort to other means to get out of scrapes. It is to her credit that she is able to turn matches around by acting this way." Henin-Hardenne, who had previously weathered similar accusations from Serena Williams, disputed Clijsters's comments. "She's disappointed she lost—that's the

Clijsters returns a shot to Henin-Hardenne during the 2003 Acura Classic.

only reason she's saying this," Henin-Hardenne said. "I don't know why all the players are talking about the incidents in my matches because I think I'm a fair player. She said it because she lost the match."

At the time of Clijsters's ascension to No. 1 in 2003, Henin-Hardenne was ranked No. 3. As it would happen, the pair met in the U.S. Open Finals in early September, with Henin-Hardenne once again emerging victorious. She beat Clijsters 7-5, 6-1. The situation turned ugly, this time with Clijsters's father Lei making comments to the press that Henin-Hardenne's gains in muscle and strength over the past year were unnatural and suggesting that the cause was performance-enhancing drugs. "You want me to tell you why Justine is beating Kim regularly?" he asked. "Because her muscle mass has doubled, and she now has an arm like Serena's." These comments enraged Henin-Hardenne and her camp. "I have never been tempted by doping," Henin-Hardenne claimed. "My only doping is my work. I am ready to undergo whatever test, wherever to prove that my body is clean." Carlos Rodriguez, Henin-Hardenne's coach, defended the tennis star and accused Lei Clijsters of jealousy. "In Belgium, what we are trying to do is to start a fight between these two girls. I swear on the heads of my two sons that she has never taken doping products. Justine is better than Kim and will win more often." Later, Clijsters tried to blame the press for the rift between her and Henin-Hardenne. "Everything is the fault of the media," she said. "The Belgian media don't know enough about tennis. They see the gossip that sells papers elsewhere and because we're stars now, they want to create something a little bit like that between us."

Clijsters finished the 2003 season strong, beating Amelie Mauresmo 6-2, 6-0 to win the final tournament of the WTA season, the WTA Tour Championships, with a prize worth over $1 million. "It's a dream come true," she said after the tournament. But when the computer votes were eventually tallied for the whole season, she found herself ranked No. 2, just behind Justine Henin-Hardenne. Still, Clijsters found a silver lining in the rankings. "Of course it's a little disappointing, but at least I got be No. 1. And I end the year No. 2 — that not too bad. I made the finals of two Grand Slams," she said.

A Controversial Decision

In December 2003, Clijsters drew heavy criticism from her home country when she announced that she would be skipping the 2004 Olympics in Athens, Greece, because of a conflict with Fila, one of her commercial endorsements. Adidas had the contract to supply the Belgian Olympic athletes with outfits for the games. Clijsters protested because of her existing contract with Fila. The Belgian Olympic committee made a concession and said that Clijsters could wear Fila clothes during tennis matches, but refused to let her wear them in a ceremony if she were to win a medal. International Olympic Committee President Jacques Rogge also criticized the move. "The wearing of the Adidas shirt will show solidarity," he said. "The problem is that 80 percent of athletes don't have enough financial support when they go to the Olympics." Despite such comments, Clijsters remained steadfast in her decision. "As long as my clothing remains an issue, it is impossible for me to go to the Olympics, even though I would like to go and even though I would be able to fit it into my schedule," she explained.

In late January 2004, Clijsters found herself in the finals of the Australian Open. This time her opponent was her nemesis Justine Henin-Hardenne. Although she was nursing a sprained ankle, Clijsters played tough, but eventually lost by scores of 6-3, 4-6, 6-3. As soon as the match ended, Clijsters offered her congratulations by kissing Henin-Hardenne at the net, but later expressed disappointment over the way the match was umpired. Television replays showed that French umpire Sandra de Jenken had

Clijsters stretches for a return during the 2004 Australian Open.

blundered a call that should have had Clijsters making a save on game point. "I'm not the type of player that's gonna start complaining after matches," Clijsters later said. "At the moment it's very disappointing. And a few people have told me that it was in. So that's even more disappointing then. But, you know, I'm not going to blame the umpire or anything because everyone makes mistakes. But of course it's disappointing."

MARRIAGE AND FAMILY

In March 2000, Clijsters was paired with Australian tennis star Lleyton Hewitt in a mixed doubles tournament in Miami, Florida. Later that year, the pair began showing up together at other tennis events, including the French Open and Wimbledon. It was soon confirmed that they were dating and spending as much time together as possible. Clijsters even opted out of a few tournaments so that she could be with Hewitt on the road.

As things heated up between Clijsters and Hewitt, their relationship became a hot topic for the press. "I love being with Kim because she is a great girl," Hewitt declared. "We measure up well. We understand each other and what we have to deal with to be in the top 10 in the world. A different girlfriend probably wouldn't connect." Clijsters also felt that the couple was on the verge of something special. "I know we're both very young, but I feel so comfortable with him," she remarked. "We can't be together every week but that is what makes it special." She continued: "What he does with his career definitely helps me on the court but we hardly talk about tennis. He comes to watch my matches, I watch his, but once we're together, it is different."

On December 23, 2003, Hewitt officially proposed to his girlfriend of four years during a cruise around Sydney Harbor. Clijsters accepted. Later, she commented on how the situation would affect her career: "I don't really plan to have a very long career because one day I wouldn't mind having a family as well. It's hard to put a number on it. It also depends how I'm feeling, the way my body is coping with the tough schedule. See how, you know, if I'm still enjoying it."

Clijsters continues to remain close to her parents and sister, so much so that she decided to build a house in her hometown of Bree on the same street where her parents and grandparents live. Clijsters is thankful for her close relationships with family, and also for the feelings of calm she experiences when she's home with her family in Bree. "It's probably the only place where I can go shopping and go to dinner. Everywhere else, it's different," she said.

"I know we're both very young, but I feel so comfortable with him," Clijsters said about her fiancé, Lleyton Hewitt. *"We can't be together every week but that is what makes it special."* She continued: *"What he does with his career definitely helps me on the court but we hardly talk about tennis. He comes to watch my matches, I watch his, but once we're together, it is different."*

HOBBIES AND OTHER INTERESTS

When she's not playing tennis, Clijsters enjoys spending time with her fiancé and their English bulldog Beauty. She also watches movies like *Gladiator* and *Dumb and Dumber* and cites Madonna, Live, and Savage Garden as her favorite musical acts.

HONORS AND AWARDS

Belgian Sportswoman of the Year (Belgian Sports Journalists Association): 1999, 2000, 2001, 2002
Most Impressive Newcomer (WTA Tour): 1999
Karen Krantzke Sportsmanship Award (WTA Tour): 2000, 2003
WTA Tour Player of the Month (International Tennis Writers Association): November 2002, May 2003, August 2003
Trophy for National Sporting Excellence (Belgian Government): 2002

FURTHER READING

Periodicals

Detroit Free Press, Nov. 22, 2003, p.B2
New York Times, Sep. 4, 2001, p.5
San Francisco Chronicle, July 27, 2001, p.E9
St. Petersburg (Fla.) Times, Aug. 12, 2003, p.C2
Tennis, Mar. 2000, p.16; Mar. 2002, p.44; Feb. 2003, p.79; Apr. 2003, p.12;
    May 2003, p.103
Washington Times, Aug. 18, 2002, p.C11

Online Articles

http://www.dispatch.co.za
    (*DailyDispatch.com*, "Clijsters Has No Complaints," Feb 2, 2004)
http://www.dailytimes.com.pk
    (*DailyTimes.com*, "Beaten Clijsters Opts for Short Career," Feb. 1, 2004)
http://www.theaustralian.news.com.au
    (*TheWeekendAustralian.com*, "Mind Game is Clijsters' Major Hurdle,"
    Jan. 31, 2004)

Online Databases

Biography Resource Center Online, 2004

ADDRESS

Kim Clijsters
WTA Tour
One Progress Plaza
Suite 1500
St. Petersburg, FL 33701

WORLD WIDE WEB SITES

http://www.kimclijsters.be
http://www.wtatour.com/players

Celia Cruz 1924?-2003

Cuban-Born American Singer
Known as "The Queen of Salsa"

BIRTH

Celia Cruz was born in Havana, Cuba, on October 21, some-
time between 1924 and 1929. Cruz was always reluctant to reveal the exact year of her birth, but 1924, 1925, and 1929 are
the dates most often suggested. Her father, Simon Cruz, was a
railroad stoker; her mother, Catalina (Alfonso) Cruz, ran the
family household. Her family heritage was Afro-Cuban. Cruz

was the second of her parents' four children, but the household also included an extended family of ten other children. Music was an important part of the household, and both her mother and her brother Barbaro enjoyed singing.

YOUTH

Cruz grew up in the Santo Suárez neighborhood of Havana, in what she described as a "poor neighborhood." Living in a big household with an extended family of nieces, nephews, and cousins, Cruz was expected to help out where she could. Because she loved to sing around the house, she was given the task of singing lullabies to younger family members. "I would sit in a chair by their beds and begin singing them to sleep," she recalled. "But, you know, they never went to sleep. And what's more, neighbors would congregate around the door to the house."

> *Because she loved to sing around the house, Cruz was given the task of singing lullabies to younger family members. "I would sit in a chair by their beds and begin singing them to sleep," she recalled. "But, you know, they never went to sleep. And what's more, neighbors would congregate around the door to the house."*

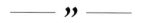

Although Cruz hoped that one day she might sing with an orchestra, like her favorite singer Paulina Alvarez, she didn't seriously think she could make singing a career. Nevertheless, she recalled that "music is what gave me the courage to fight and get out of poverty and touch the universe." As a teenager she began entering — and winning — local talent contests, which fueled her desire to sing.

Cruz's father believed that a musical career wasn't appropriate for a woman, but her mother encouraged her to pursue it. Accompanied by a female cousin, Cruz began accepting jobs around the island. At the time, many radio stations used live performances for much of their programming, so she found jobs singing on the radio. She sang for a week on Radio Progreso Cubana, then had a regular gig on Radio Unión, a station with one of Cuba's most powerful transmitters. This job lasted several months. For these early jobs, Cruz specialized in a type of song called the *pregón*. This was a traditional Cuban song which grew out of the chants and cries that street vendors used to sell their wares.

EDUCATION

Cruz graduated from the República de México school in Havana, and entered the Escuela Normal para Maestros, a school for educators. She planned to teach literature, but dropped out of the Escuela Normal when her singing career took off. She continued her education, however, by studying voice, piano, and music theory at Havana's Conservatory of Music from 1947 to 1950.

FIRST JOBS

While attending the music conservatory, Cruz continued to enter talent contests. In 1947, a local radio station sponsored a talent show

A shot of Cruz from the 1950s, when she was a singer in Cuba with La Sonora Matancera.

called "La Hora de Té." Cruz sang a romantic tango called "Nostalgia," but performed it with the slower tempo of a bolero. She won the contest, and her victory led to several offers to perform locally. "I really loved to sing," she recalled. "But I also did it because if you won, you would get a cake, or a bag with chocolate, condensed milk, ham. We were very poor. All of that came in very handy at home."

Cruz's radio appearances, combined with her musical training, led to even more work. With her family's blessing, she began performing on stage as well as radio, singing with the orchestra Gloria Matancera. She also worked with a female dance troupe, Las Mulatas de Fuego. Her job was to sing along during theatrical numbers and entertain the audience during the dancers' costume changes. This valuable experience, along with her music classes, helped Cruz polish her stage presence and prepare for new opportunities.

CAREER HIGHLIGHTS

Getting Her First Big Break

Cruz got her first big break in 1950, when Cuba's most popular dance band, La Sonora Matancera, lost their lead singer. Myrta Silva had been with the band for over 20 years, but she had decided to return to her native Puerto Rico. Cruz was hired to sing with the band in August 1950 on their weekly radio program for Radio Progreso. Although some fans of Silva complained, Cruz quickly became a valued part of the orchestra. When an American record company executive didn't want her to record with the group, the band's leader offered to repay the recording costs if it didn't sell. The executive had thought no one would want to hear a woman singing a rumba, but the record went on to become a big seller in both Cuba and the United States.

Less than six months after joining La Sonora Matancera, Cruz was regularly making records with the group. That first recording was "Cao Cao Mani Picao/Mata Siguaraya," released in early 1951. Several songs from her first years with the orchestra became standards, including "Yembe Laroco," "Yerbero Moderno," "Caramelo," "Burundanga," and "Me Voy al Pinar del Rio." Cruz and La Sonora Matancera not only performed on radio, but on television and on stage at Havana's famous Tropicana casino. They toured throughout the Western Hemisphere, from the United States and Mexico to Central and South America. They were even featured in five Mexican films, including *Affair in Havana* (1957) and *Amorcito corazón* (1961). Many critics consider Cruz's early years with La Sonora Matancera the "golden era" of her career.

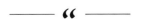

Cruz entered talent contests as a teenager, both for the opportunity to perform and for the chance to win prizes. "I really loved to sing," she recalled. "But I also did it because if you won, you would get a cake, or a bag with chocolate, condensed milk, ham. We were very poor. All of that came in very handy at home."

Leaving Cuba

In 1959, political events in Cuba would lead to a life-changing decision for Cruz. A revolutionary group led by Fidel Castro successfully overthrew the government of Fulgencio Batista. Batista had ruled Cuba as a repressive dictatorship, brutally suppressing opposition to his government. Many people had hoped Castro would create a democratic government, but instead he formed a communist state, allied to the Soviet Union (now Russia). He executed members of the Batista regime and assumed control of the media. Independent newspapers were forbidden, as was any political opposition. Castro's government also took charge of the judiciary and university system. Artistic and intellectual freedoms were severely restricted.

Many Cubans were horrified by the direction of the new government. But it was too dangerous to oppose the government, so some people chose to

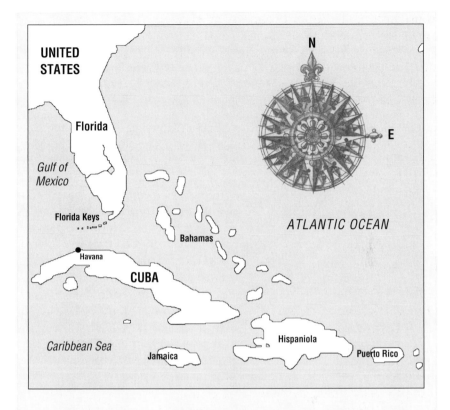

Cuban Music

Cuba in the mid-20th century was a hotbed of popular music, especially dance music. Many popular Latin dance styles grew from Afro-Cuban roots. The rumba was based on a native African dance and grew into a slower, more formal dance called the "sóón." The guaracha was a similar dance with a faster tempo. The mambo, which combined rumba with jazz swing rhythms, was popularized in Cuba in the 1940s. The cha-cha, with its distinctive three-step rhythm (the cha-cha-cha), was a slower kind of mambo. Other Latin dance styles, such as the merengue, tango, and samba, came from other countries in the Caribbean and South America, but were also popular with Cuban audiences. There were differences among the dances in rhythm and tempo (how fast or slow the music was played), but most featured Latin percussion instruments such as the maracas, the claves, the marimbola, and the drums.

leave. Many of these exiles landed in Florida, less than 100 miles north of Cuba. Others wanted to leave, but found their travel restricted by the government. Cruz and the musicians of La Sonora Matancera managed to use one of their tours to escape. Castro's government "wanted us to stay," the singer recalled. "We gave the impression we were just going on another temporary tour abroad." During this tour of Mexico in July 1960, the group announced that they were defecting—in other words, refusing to return to Cuba and renouncing their Cuban citizenship. The Cuban government retaliated by banning their music and refusing them entry to Cuba. Cruz had left her family behind, but she was never allowed into Cuba again, not even to attend her mother's funeral.

> ―― " ――
>
> *Of all the men in the band, it was Pedro Knight who attracted her attention. Not only was he a "gentleman," he honored her talent. As Cruz recalled, he was "the first to approach me and ask if I liked the music, the arrangements, and if the tempo was right for me."*
>
> ―― " ――

Cruz and the orchestra spent a year and a half in Mexico before coming to the United States in 1961. Within a year, she had become an American citizen and was appearing with La Sonora Matancera at Carnegie Hall. In 1962 she also married Pedro Knight, who played first trumpet in the band. While all the men in the band felt protective towards their female singer, it was Knight who attracted her attention. Not only was he a "gentleman," he honored her talent. As she recalled, he was "the first to approach me and ask if I liked the music, the arrangements, and if the tempo was right for me." Knight would later leave the band to become his wife's manager and musical director.

Making Her Mark in America

After moving to America, Cruz cut a deal with Secco Records. She would release more than 20 albums on that label, some with La Sonora Matancera and some without. These albums included *La Incomparable Celia* (1958); *La Reina del Ritmo Cubano* (1959); *La Tierna, Conmovedora, Bamboleadora* (1963); *Sabor y Ritmo de Pueblos* (1965); and her biggest hit for the label, *Canciones Premiadas* (1965). In 1965, after 15 years with La Sonora Matancera, Cruz decided to strike out on her own. She left the orchestra, with Knight as her manager, and also switched labels. On the Tico Records label she would record 13 albums in seven years. Some of these were solo,

La Incomparable Celia *was Cruz's first recording.*

while on several others she performed with the orchestra of Tito Puente, the noted percussionist and bandleader. These albums included *Cuba y Puerto Rico Son* (1966), *El Quimbo Quimbumbia* (1969), and *Algo Especial Para Recordar* (1972).

While Cruz made numerous records during the 1960s and early 1970s, her hard work wasn't rewarded with big sales. Rock 'n' roll was more popular with young Hispanics in America, and her music—traditional songs sung in Spanish—was considered old-fashioned. In addition, she didn't get much promotional support from her record label or from radio stations, so her music didn't reach a wide audience. Cruz sought out that audience herself, however, performing before crowds across the United States and South America. Sometimes she would give as many as six concerts in one day.

Canciones Premiadas *was Cruz's biggest hit for her first label, Secco Records.*

The musical climate took a turn for the better for Cruz in the mid-1970s. Large numbers of Caribbean immigrants came to the United States — immigrants who loved their new country but celebrated their own roots as well. New York City, in particular, had large groups of Afro-Caribbean immigrants from Puerto Rico and Cuba, and Latino culture became widespread. Immigrant musicians began setting traditional Latin dances — sambas, rumbas, cha-chas, and especially the Afro-Cuban guaracha — to a new, modern beat. The result became known as salsa music, a general term that now covers a wide variety of songs that share Latin rhythms. These salsa rhythms soon became very popular. Cruz became part of this new musical wave when she performed in the "Latin opera" *Hommy* at Carnegie Hall in 1973. This musical was a Latin-music version of the classic "rock opera"

Tommy by British rock supergroup The Who. Her part was small but memorable, and it exposed Cruz to a new, younger audience.

Reigning as "The Queen of Salsa"

In 1974, Cruz switched record labels again, signing with the Vaya label on Fania Records. She collaborated with rumba band leader and flutist Johnny Pacheco, who created updated arrangements of many of her La Sonora Matancera classics. Their first album, *Celia and Johnny* (1974), went gold, selling over half a million copies. She recorded two other albums with Pacheco, *Tremendo Cache* (1975) and *Recordando el Ayer* (1976), that continued building her popularity with Latino audiences. Then she branched out to record with the "Fania All-Stars," a group of salsa artists that included other giants of the genre, including Tito Puente, Willie Colon, and Pete "El Conde" Rodriguez. Older audiences loved hearing songs from their youth, while newer fans enjoyed Cruz's creative "scatting" — a fast-paced, improvisational singing style that reminded many critics of jazz great Ella Fitzgerald.

> *Cruz had a stage presence that was both forceful and friendly. Her rich, contralto voice was soulful and powerful, and she was a skilled improviser, able to devise rhymes on the spot. Although her booming voice could fill a room, it could also span octaves, dance quickly from note to note, and sing intricate rhythms. Not only was she a skillful singer, she was a born entertainer.*

No one knows exactly when Cruz received the label "The Queen of Salsa," but there was no question she deserved it as her career continued. One of the rare female performers in the genre, she was its most visible figure. She sold out concerts in France and Africa in the 1970s, including one in 1975 before the famous "Rumble in the Jungle" boxing match between Muhammad Ali and Joe Frazier. She topped "Best Vocalist" polls of the *New York Daily News, Billboard Magazine,* and *Latin N.Y.,* and was awarded keys to the cities of Miami, Dallas, and New York, as well as Union City, New Jersey, and Lima, Peru. In 1982 she recorded a reunion album with La Sonora Matancera, *Feliz Encuentro,* which contained mostly new material. The title track was another chart-topper for Cruz. Whether on stage in front of thousands, or in the studio making records, Cruz was always trying to please her audience.

Cruz had a stage presence that was both forceful and friendly. Her rich, contralto voice was soulful and powerful, and she was a skilled improviser, able to devise rhymes on the spot. Although her booming voice could fill a room, it could also span octaves, dance quickly from note to note, and sing intricate rhythms. Not only was she a skillful singer, she was a born entertainer. Wearing glittering, flamboyant costumes, she had a seemingly boundless energy that she shared with her audience. Dancing, joking, waving her arms, and giving her trademark call of "Azucar!" ("Sugar!"), she would leave audiences feeling she had given them everything she had to give—sometimes for as long as three hours. "It is hard to describe the dazzling energy and warmth she was able to convey to an audience," Pulitzer Prize-winning author Oscar Hijuelos wrote in the *New York Times*. "That she could create a rush to the dance floor, and yet do so while maintaining an air of intimacy and connection with her listeners, is a testament to her great personality and charisma as a performer."

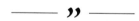

> "It is hard to describe the dazzling energy and warmth she was able to convey to an audience," Pulitzer Prize-winning author Oscar Hijuelos wrote in the New York Times. "That she could create a rush to the dance floor, and yet do so while maintaining an air of intimacy and connection with her listeners, is a testament to her great personability and charisma as a performer."

A Musical Ambassador

In the 1980s and 1990s Cruz began using her star power to spread salsa to a wider audience. She collaborated with singer David Byrne, of the avant-garde rock group Talking Heads. She also recorded or performed with pop singer Dionne Warwick, soul singer Patti Labelle, opera singer Luciano Pavarotti, and rapper Wyclef Jean, among others. For Cruz, these collaborations weren't marketing gimmicks to appeal to curious listeners—they were just new ways to express her love of music. "We've never had to attract these kids," she said of her younger fans. "They come by themselves. Rock is a strong influence on them, but they still want to know about their roots. The Cuban rhythms are so contagious that they end up making room for both kinds of music in their lives."

It wasn't just young Latinos who made her music part of their lives. Cruz performed to sold out audiences in Japan, Thailand, Morocco, Ireland, Denmark, England, Germany, and all over Latin America. She even entered the Guinness Book of World Records in 1987, when she set a record for the largest concert crowd ever. That year some 240,000 fans heard her sing in Tenerife, Spain, at the festival "El Baile del Carnaval."

Cruz appeared in the 1991 film The Mambo Kings *with Antonio Banderas and Armand Assante.*

Cruz also increased her audience through her film and television work. She made appearances in Mexican movies and "telenovelas" (soap operas) in Spanish-language roles. But in 1992 she was given a small part in the film *The Mambo Kings,* an American film about salsa music starring Antonio Banderas and Armand Assante. The director was so impressed by her acting ability that her role was expanded. Cruz understood English but wasn't very confident in her ability to speak it, so it was a great step forward. She followed *Mambo Kings* with an acting turn in another English-language movie, *The Perez Family* (1995), with Marisa Tomei and Angelica Huston.

Cruz had brought salsa music into the mainstream, and she began receiving mainstream recognition. In 1987 she was awarded a star on the Hollywood Walk of Fame. In 1990 she was awarded a special Lifetime Achievement Award from the Smithsonian Institution. She received the prestigious National Medal for the Arts from President Bill Clinton in 1994. Four years later she received a Hispanic Heritage Lifetime Achievement Award, which recognized not only her talent, but also her efforts to raise money for charities ranging from AIDS and cancer research to organizations that aid orphans and handicapped people in Central America. As for musical awards, she received some of the industry's most important honors. In 1989 she won her first Grammy Award, for the Tropical Salsa album *Ritmo en el Corazón,* which she recorded with Ray Barretto. In 1998 she received a Grammy nomination for Best Rap performance by a duo or group for a collaboration with rapper Wyclef Jean. When the Latin Grammy Awards (an international award) made their debut in 2000, Cruz won for her album *Celia Cruz & Friends.* She followed that up with another Latin Grammy the following year for her album *Siempre Viviré,* and a third in 2002 for her smash hit album *La Negra Tiene Tumbao,* which also earned her a second U.S. Grammy Award.

Although she was well past the age of retirement by the year 2000, Cruz showed no signs of slowing down. She sometimes had to trade in her six-inch heels for sneakers because of a knee problem, but she spent most of her time out on the road. When asked if she thought about retiring,

— **"** —

When asked if she thought about retiring, Cruz said: "Why should I? You would give up your career if you lost your voice for good, or if the impresarios stopped calling, or the audiences stopped coming. But as long as those things are there, I don't plan to stop. There is nothing that makes me feel better than to be with my public."

— **"** —

she said: "Why should I? You would give up your career if you lost your voice for good, or if the impresarios stopped calling, or the audiences stopped coming. But as long as those things are there, I don't plan to stop. There is nothing that makes me feel better than to be with my public." Her public felt the same way, for Cruz always tried to keep her performances fresh. "I always try to shape my repertoire around a particular audience. . . . I'm always changing my outfits, my look onstage."

A Lasting Legacy

Cruz was delighting crowds on television and in concert, from the United States to Latin America to Asia, up until the end of her life. In December 2002, she had surgery to operate on a brain tumor. The surgery did not cure her cancer, and she was in and out of the hospital several times after the operation. She still managed to finish work on her final album, *Regalo del Alma* (2003), although the operation meant she had trouble remembering lyrics. Cruz was at her home in Fort Lee, New Jersey, when she died on July 16, 2003. Tributes came in from all over the world, including from President George W. Bush in the White House. The official newspaper of Cuba's government, which never forgave Cruz for defecting, published only two paragraphs on the death of this legendary performer. But fans in Cuba and all over the world mourned her passing. Memorial services in Miami and New York City drew tens of thousands of grieving fans. Shortly after her death, the city of New York named a music high school in her honor. At the 2003 Latin Grammys, dozens of artists performed a special tribute to this influential trailblazer.

> "
>
> *For Cruz, singing was not about the sales or the awards — it was always about the music.* "When people hear me sing, I want them to be happy, happy, happy," *she once said.* "My message is always felicidad — happiness."
>
> "

Cruz's death renewed the demand for her work. Re-releases of her albums shot to the top of the Latin music charts. At the end of 2003, four Celia Cruz albums were on the Top 10 Tropical Album chart, holding the top three spots. *Billboard* magazine named her their Top Latin Albums Artist of the Year. In addition, her final recording, *Regalo del Alma,* won a 2004 Grammy Award for Best Salsa/Merengue Album. An autobiography based on 500 hours of interviews, *Celia,* was scheduled to appear in July 2004, while actress Whoopi Goldberg hoped to develop and star in a movie based on Cruz's life.

Throughout her lifetime Cruz received a multitude of awards from organizations around the world. She was given several Lifetime Achievement Awards, Hall of Fame citations, and even honorary university degrees, including one from Yale University. She was recognized by the governments of Colombia and the Dominican Republic, as well as the United States. In 1986 the National Ethnic Coalition of Organizations gave her an Ellis Island Medal of Honor. *Billboard* magazine named her to their Latin Hall of Fame in 1994, and the following year gave her a lifetime achievement award. Of the more than 70 albums she recorded, 20 were certified "gold" as selling more than 500,000 copies.

Cruz's final recording, Regalo del Alma, *won a 2004 Grammy Award for Best Salsa/Merengue Album.*

But for Cruz, singing was not about the sales or the awards—it was always about the music. "When people hear me sing, I want them to be happy, happy, happy," she once said. "My message is always *felicidad*—happiness." Her career spanned more than 50 years, and she was known throughout that time as much for her professionalism and kindness as her talent. For Cruz, music was her calling and her gift. As she said upon accepting her Hispanic Heritage lifetime achievement award: "I have fulfilled my father's wish [for me] to be a teacher, as, through my music, I teach generations of people about my culture and the happiness that is found in just living life. As a performer, I want people to feel their hearts sing and their spirits soar."

Cruz performing with her husband, Pedro Knight, in 2002.

MARRIAGE AND FAMILY

Cruz married Pedro Knight, who played first trumpet with La Sonora Matancera, on July 14, 1962. They had dated for two years before their marriage, although they had worked together for 10 years before beginning their courtship. Knight left his career with La Sonora Matancera to become Cruz's manager and musical director. Because of fertility problems the couple never had any children, which Cruz cited as her life's biggest regret. Instead, she spent time with nieces and nephews, and nurtured many young artists as well.

HOBBIES AND OTHER INTERESTS

Although she spent much of her time touring, Cruz thoroughly enjoyed spending time at home with her husband. She enjoyed cooking traditional dishes and spending quiet nights watching television. During her travels she collected recordings of local music, as well as gold coins and gold bracelets. Although Cruz's musical repertoire included sacred songs of the Afro-Caribbean faith known as Santeria, she was a practicing Roman Catholic.

Cruz was involved with several charities, including ones supporting AIDS and cancer research, an orphanage in Honduras, and a fund for the handicapped of Costa Rica. In 2002 she and her husband Pedro Knight established the Celia Cruz Foundation, which helps lower-income students study music and provides aid to cancer patients.

SELECTED RECORDINGS

La Incomparable Celia, 1958
La Reina del Ritmo Cubano, 1959
La Tierna, Conmovedora, Bamboleadora, 1963
Sabor y Ritmo de Pueblos, 1965
Canciones Premiadas, 1965
Cuba y Puerto Rico Son (with Tito Puente), 1966
Quimbo Quimbumbia (with Tito Puente), 1969
Algo Especial Para Recordar (with Tito Puente), 1972
Celia and Johnny (with Johnny Pacheco), 1974
Tremendo Cache (with Johnny Pacheco), 1975
Recordando el Ayer (with Johnny Pacheco), 1976
Celia Cruz and Willie Colon, 1977
Brillante, 1978
Feliz Encuentro (with La Sonora Matancera), 1982
The Winners (with Willie Colon), 1987
Ritmo en el Corazón (with Ray Barretto), 1988
The Best of Celia Cruz, 1992
Irrepetible, 1996
La Vida es un Carnival, 1998
Celia Cruz & Friends: A Night of Salsa Live, 2000
Siempre Viviré, 2000
La Negra Tiene Tumbao, 2001
Regalo del Alma, 2003

HONORS AND AWARDS

Ellis Island Medal of Honor (National Ethnic Coalition of Organizations): 1986
Awarded a Star on the Hollywood Walk of Fame: 1987
Grammy Awards: 1989, Best Tropical Latin Performance, for "Ritmo en el Corazón"(with Ray Barretto); 2002, Best Salsa Album, for *La Negra Tiene Tumbao*; 2004, Best Salsa/Merengue Album, for *Regalo del Alma*
Lifetime Achievement Award (Smithsonian Institution): 1990
Presidential Medal (Government of Colombia): 1990
National Medal of the Arts (National Endowment for the Arts): 1994
Named to Latin Hall of Fame (*Billboard* Magazine Awards): 1994
Casandra Award for International Artist of the Year (Dominican Republic): 1995, 1996

Lifetime Achievement Award (*Billboard* Magazine): 1995

ACE Award for "Extraordinary Figure of the Year" (Association of Entertainment Critics): 1996

Hispanic Heritage Lifetime Achievement Award (Hispanic Heritage Foundation): 1998

Latin Grammy Awards: 2000, Best Tropical Salsa Performance, for *Celia Cruz and Friends: A Night of Salsa;* 2001, Best Traditional Tropical Album, for *Siempre Viviré;* 2002, Best Salsa Album, for *La Negra Tiene Tumbao*

FURTHER READING

Books

Contemporary Hispanic Biography, Vol. 1, 2002
Contemporary Musicians, Vol. 22, 1998
Dictionary of Hispanic Biography, 1996
Latino Americans, 1999
Notable Hispanic American Women, Book 1, 1993

Periodicals

Billboard, Oct. 28, 2000, p.50
Current Biography Yearbook, 1983
Hispanic, Nov. 2002, p.54
Latin New York, Oct. 1982 (special Cruz issue)
Los Angeles Times, July 18, 2003, sec.5, p.8
Miami Herald, July 17, 2003, p.A1; July 20, 2003, p.M7
New York Times, Nov. 19, 1985, p. C17; Aug. 30, 1987, sec.2 p.14; July 23, 2003, p.A19
People, Aug. 4, 2003, p.69
Time, July 11, 1988, p.50
USA Today, July 17, 2003, p.D1

Online Databases

Biography Resource Center Online, 2004, articles from *Contemporary Hispanic Biography,* 2002; *Contemporary Musicians,* 1998; *Dictionary of Hispanic Biography,* 1996; and *Notable Hispanic American Women,* 1993

WORLD WIDE WEB SITE

http://www.celiacruzonline.com

Matel Dawson, Jr. 1921-2002

American Autoworker and Philanthropist

BIRTH

Matel Dawson, Jr., was born on January 3, 1921, in Shreveport, Louisiana. He was the son of Matel Dawson, Sr., a head cook at the Tri-State Sanitarium (now known as the Willis-Knighton Health System) in Shreveport, and Bessie Hall Dawson, a laundress. Dawson was the fifth of their seven children.

YOUTH

Dawson came from a family of humble means, but his parents were proud and hard-working. These were values that they instilled in their son. His father started out as a farmer, growing corn, cotton, and other crops. But tougher times came in the 1930s with the Great Depression. During this period of great economic hardship, many people were out of work and many families were desperately poor. During the Depression, Dawson earned extra income for his growing family by working odd jobs, including work at the state fairgrounds and as a groundskeeper. One of these jobs was being a hospital dishwasher at the Tri-State Sanitarium, and he eventually worked his way up to become head cook. Dawson's mother also earned an income by taking in other people's laundry. Because they worked so hard and remained employed even during the Depression, the family never had to go on welfare, a fact that made Dawson quite proud. "Those were tough times," he said, "but we made it. We were never on welfare and never received any food stamps."

It was Dawson's mother, Bessie, who especially taught him the value of saving. "My mother was a saving woman," he recalled. "Even if it was just two or three dollars, my mother would say 'save.'" As he also humorously noted, she had a way of making a little money stretch a long way: "She could squeeze a buffalo right off a nickel." His mother would always help out neighbors in need, even as her family struggled to get by; and she made her children promise that, when they got older, they would try to "give something back." Dawson would later make good on his promise in a big way.

EARLY MEMORIES

Even though Dawson's family was able to get by financially, living in the South during the 1930s was difficult because it was still a time of very oppressive racism. Many white people felt a deep and abiding prejudice against black people. African-Americans were often treated as inferior, and they were expected to act subservient. At that time, segregation — the separation of African-Americans and whites — was common in the South. The South was still segregated under what were called "Jim Crow" laws. These laws forced the segregation of the races and created "separate but equal" public facilities for blacks and whites in housing, schools, transportation, bathrooms, drinking fountains, and more. Although these separate facilities were called equal, in reality those for blacks were miserably inadequate. African-Americans usually attended dilapidated, impoverished schools with underpaid teachers. After leaving school, their opportunities for work were often just as limited.

This was the society in which Dawson grew up. "Back then," he recalled, "if you were walking down the sidewalk and saw a white person approaching you, you had to get off the sidewalk and let them pass by. We had separate water fountains and always had to ride in the back of the bus." This was a big reason why Dawson later left Shreveport and moved to Detroit. As he put it, "I just thought I'd be more comfortable going somewhere else."

——— " ———

EDUCATION

Dawson's parents only had a seventh-grade education, but, as he said, "they were not illiterate." They valued education, and they made sure their children attended school. Dawson went to West Shreveport Elementary School and Central High School. Unfortunately, because money was so tight, Dawson had to leave school after the ninth grade to earn money and help his family.

CAREER HIGHLIGHTS

Moving to Detroit

Dawson moved to Detroit in 1939. He had two uncles who lived and worked there, and he thought they might help him get a job. It turned out to be a wise decision. His first job was working as a laborer for the Civilian Conservation Corps (CCC). The CCC was a program created by President Franklin D. Roosevelt as part of the "New Deal." These programs helped put unemployed people to work during the Depression. But Dawson only stayed there a few months before one of his uncles, who worked for the Ford Motor Co., was able to get his nephew a job at the River Rouge plant in Dearborn, a suburb of Detroit.

"Back then, if you were walking down the sidewalk and saw a white person approaching you, you had to get off the sidewalk and let them pass by," Dawson recalled about growing up in the South. "We had separate water fountains and always had to ride in the back of the bus." This was a big reason why Dawson later left Shreveport and moved to Detroit. As he put it, "I just thought I'd be more comfortable going somewhere else."

——— " ———

Dawson was hired on September 30, 1940, to work for $1.25 an hour as a steel press operator, an unskilled starting position. But his supervisors soon saw that Dawson was an extremely hard-working and devoted employee, and it wasn't long before he became a forklift driver and rigger — a trade worker who is qualified to perform a number of skilled jobs. Things were soon looking up for Dawson: he had a good, well-paying job, and in 1942 he got married. The couple bought a house, and Dawson worked overtime shifts and weekends to earn extra pay. He would later often say how grateful he was to Ford, which he called "the greatest motor company" for being so progressive in hiring minorities. As he later recalled, "Ford always hired blacks in skill positions, even back then [when I was hired], and they had black supervisors."

> *Dawson would often say how grateful he was to Ford, which he called "the greatest motor company" for being so progressive in hiring minorities. As he later recalled, "Ford always hired blacks in skill positions, even back then [when I was hired], and they had black supervisors."*

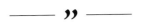

Fortunes Rise and Fall

Then, in 1956, an opportunity came along that Dawson knew he couldn't pass up. Ford offered its employees the option of investing some of their paychecks in stock. "A lot of people didn't want to take it," he recalled. "They thought [stock investment] was just for rich people." But he saw it as a great way to save and earn extra income. Most of the stocks he bought were shares of Ford Motor Co., which over time earned him an average of over 13 percent annually in interest. The money was reinvested in more stock, compounding his interest until his savings really began to grow. But even with putting part of his income into the stock market, Dawson was able to buy a house and pay off its 30-year mortgage in only six years. He also bought a Lincoln Continental for his wife, and a second one for himself.

Things seemed to be going along smoothly for Dawson until 1976, when he suffered through two emotionally traumatic events: his mother died and his wife divorced him. After 35 years of marriage, the divorce came as a particular shock. Not only was it an emotional blow, but it was also a financial blow, as his wife got the house and both cars, as well as half of his investments, in the divorce settlement. Later, he admitted that he had concentrated so much on his work, by often working weekends and never taking a vacation, that he might have neglected his marriage. "I guess I was concentrating on myself too much," he reflected.

Dawson standing in front of a photo and plaque in honor of his parents, Matel Dawson, Sr., and Bessie Hall Dawson.

Charity Becomes the Goal

After the divorce, Dawson gained a new perspective on material possessions and decided they were not so important. He moved into a one-bedroom apartment and for a long time drove a 1985 Ford Escort, which was missing its hubcaps because they had been stolen and he had never bothered to replace them. He realized that doing well for himself and his family wasn't enough and that making contributions to his community would be far more satisfying. So, in the late-1980s, after rebuilding his savings after the divorce, he began to give money to charities—first to his local church, the People's Community Church in Detroit, then to his family's old church in Shreveport. And these weren't $50 or even $100 donations, either, but very sizeable contributions that over a couple years amounted to over $100,000. He also gave money and gifts to members of his family, helping them with house payments and college, though he had always helped them out from the time he had moved to Detroit.

But Dawson wanted to do even more. He remembered how important education had been to his parents, and how he regretted not being able to finish school himself because he had had to work at a young age. So he

In 1991, Dawson made a $30,000 donation to the United Negro College Fund. Director Deborah Dolsey Diggs vividly recalled how she met Dawson as he came into the charity's office to give them the check: "He walked into the office in overalls and rubber fisherman's boots up to his knees. In his hand he held a paper bag, and in that bag was a check for $30,000."

decided he wanted to help kids get a college education. "We've got to prepare this young generation for the future," he explained. "I choose education because that's the only way we can get things done." So, in 1991, during a fundraising telethon, Dawson made a $30,000 donation to the United Negro College Fund (UNCF). UNCF director Deborah Dolsey Diggs vividly recalled how she met Dawson as he came into the charity's office to give them the check: "He walked into the office in overalls and rubber fisherman's boots up to his knees. In his hand he held a paper bag, and in that bag was a check for $30,000."

Leaving a Legacy

The giving did not stop there, not by any means. Over the years, Dawson donated $240,000 to the UNCF, $632,000 to Wayne State University in Detroit, $300,000 to Louisiana State University in Shreveport, and $150,000 to the National Association for the Advancement of Colored People (NAACP), for a total of $1,322,000. Some of this money went to specific funds. For example, $100,000 went to LSU to establish the Matel and Bessie Hall Dawson Endowed Scholarship Fund named in honor of his parents, and a scholarship fund was also set up in his name at Wayne State University. The scholarships at both universities go to deserving students regardless of race or ethnicity and pay for four years of college. Students who receive the scholarships often are surprised to learn that the money comes not from a rich corporate executive but from a humble forklift operator. Scholarship recipient Sonia Taggart, for example, once said she had assumed that the money came from "someone who would not miss the money he was giving away. Then I found out what he does, where he works, and I think that's what really floors you about him. He's so humble."

Dawson's donation made him a celebrity in Detroit, where he came to be known as the "blue-collar benefactor" and the "forklift philanthropist."

But he didn't donate his money to become famous. In fact, his supervisor at Ford didn't even know that Dawson was donating his money until he heard a story about the forklift operator on the radio. But Dawson did acknowledge that he would like to be remembered for his contributions. As he put it, "I'm not trying to impress anybody. I just want to help people, leave a legacy, and be remembered."

Working until the End

Most people who have led such a successful life would look forward to retirement and resting by the age of 65, but Dawson never had the urge to retire. He worked until the age of 81, getting up at 4:00 a.m. in the morning and arriving at the factory by 5:00 a.m. Then he would work until 3:30 or later, go home, and go to bed early. "I wouldn't know what to do if I retired," he said in 1999. "It keeps me going." He continued to save, and toward the end of his life, when he was earning over $100,000 annually including overtime, he lived on only $600 a month while socking the rest into his investments or donating it.

Dawson became wealthy not because he was a financial wizard, but because he lived frugally, worked hard, and invested carefully. Keeping his eye on newspapers and television reports, he felt that anyone could do well enough in the stock market if they were careful. "I know what's good on the market and what's not good on the market," he said. "It's just as plain as day. I'm not going to jump into something that's not established, that doesn't have a reputation." The problem for most people, he noted, is that they are too lazy or greedy and want to make their fortunes quickly. "The trouble with a lot of people is they're looking for something for nothing—and it doesn't exist," he explained. "You have to get out there and work for it. I don't play no lotto, no numbers and all that stuff; that ain't my cup of tea."

Satisfaction for Dawson came through his work and through giving, which he learned was more rewarding than vacations and material possessions. As he once said, "I've owned big

Scholarship recipient Sonia Taggart once said she had assumed that the money came from "someone who would not miss the money he was giving away. Then I found out what he does, where he works, and I think that's what really floors you about him. He's so humble."

——— " ———

*"I've owned big homes
and big cars and that
don't excite me no more.
All that material stuff
doesn't excite me no
more. . . . I just want
people to say that I
helped somebody."*

——— " ———

homes and big cars and that don't excite me no more. All that material stuff doesn't excite me no more. . . . I just want people to say that I helped somebody." Looking back, he believed that his parents would have been proud of what he had done for others: "I'm on a mission fulfilling my parents' dreams. They wanted us to be something in life and stand for something."

Dawson died of a heart attack on November 2, 2002, in Highland Park, Michigan, at the age of 81. Two of his siblings, Luella Fuller and Clyde Dawson, survived him. He may have died in a humble one-bedroom apartment with few possessions to his name, but his legacy of giving and his belief in education lives on. In his will, he left his estate to the United Negro College Fund, which continues to use the money to help those in need achieve their dreams.

MAJOR INFLUENCES

Besides his parents, who taught him the values of saving and an education, Dawson greatly admired two American leaders: Franklin Delano Roosevelt and Reverend Martin Luther King, Jr. Roosevelt, he said, "gave the whole country a new start"; and King "gave black people hope when there wasn't none." King's example was particularly inspirational to him when it came to his spirit of giving. He once remarked, "Like Dr. King said, 'If I can help somebody, then my living will not be in vain' — that's how I want to be remembered."

MARRIAGE AND FAMILY

Dawson married Herneta Alberta Davis on February 21, 1942. The couple had a happy marriage for many years, but it ended in divorce in 1976. They had one daughter, JoAnn Dawson-Agee.

MEMORABLE EXPERIENCES

After word got out about Dawson's many charitable contributions, he was invited to appear on television shows and at public events. For example, in 1991 he was Grand Marshall at the city of Highland Park's Michigan Week parade. He appeared on the Oprah Winfrey show and other television programs, and during the Clinton administration, he was invited to the White House. Dawson enjoyed these events, which were his only indulgences in life besides the Burberry suits he liked to wear during church and college visits.

HONORS AND AWARDS

Michiganian of the Year: 1990
Outstanding Philanthropy Award (National Society of Fund Raising Executives): 1995
International Heritage Hall of Fame Honoree: 1996
Equal Opportunity Day Community Hero Award (National Urban League): 1996
Ossian Sweet Award: 1997, for donating to the United Negro College Fund
Living Legacy Award: 1997
Trumpet Award (Turner Broadcasting System): 1998

FURTHER READING

Books

Contemporary Black Biography, Vol. 39, 2003
Who's Who among African Americans, 2003

Periodicals

Black Enterprise, Mar. 2000, p.97; Feb. 2003, p.65
Detroit News, Nov. 7, 2002, p.2
Ebony, Oct. 1996, p.62
Jet, Jan. 31, 1994, p.23; Apr. 21, 1997, p.22; Dec. 29, 1997, p.61
Los Angeles Times, Nov. 8, 2002, p.B14

New York Times, Nov. 13, 2002, p.B10
People, June 7, 1999, p.103
Time, July 19, 1999, p.6

Online Articles

http://www.freep.com
   (*Detroit Free Press,* "An Unlikely Benefactor: A Forklift Operator's Frugal
   Life Lets Him Donate More than $1 Million toward Education," April
   25, 2001; "Matel Dawson Jr.: Forklift Operator Gave $1 Million," Nov. 5,
   2002)
http://www.media.wayne.edu/iws.back.issues/cn_11_14_02/Dawson.html
   (*Wayne State University,* "Wayne State Benefactor Matel Dawson Jr. Dies
   at 81," Nov. 14, 2002)

Online Databases

Biography Resource Center Online, 2003, articles from *Contemporary Black
Biography,* 2003, and *Who's Who among African Americans,* 2003

THE DONNAS

Brett Anderson (Donna A.) 1979-
Torry Castellano (Donna C.) 1979-
Maya Ford (Donna F.) 1979-
Allison Robertson (Donna R.) 1979-

American Rock Group

EARLY YEARS

The hard rock, all-female group known as The Donnas includes four young women who have been friends since elementary school: vocalist Brett Anderson (Donna A.), born on May 30, 1979; drummer Torry Castellano (Donna C.), born on

January 8, 1979; bassist Maya Ford (Donna F.), born on January 8, 1979; and guitarist Allison Robertson (Donna R.), born on August 26, 1979. (Castellano and Ford share the same birthday by coincidence; they are not twins.)

———— " ————

"Maya and I were playing bass and guitar together early on," says Robertson. "We thought about having a band, but we really didn't have any friends to round one out. It was impossible finding people that knew how to play. Then we thought of the idea of asking people to learn how to play drums and sing so we could eventually form a band. It wasn't a plan to control the world and be big superstars. It was started as kind of a joke on the other bands in our school — which, in our town, were all formed by these popular, blond rich guys trying to be like Nirvana."

———— " ————

Little has been reported about the individual members' childhoods or parents. Allison Robertson is the only one whose parents had experience in the music business — her father, Baxter, is a guitarist, songwriter, and session recording artist. All four girls grew up in Palo Alto, California, near San Francisco, otherwise known as the Bay Area.

FORMING THE BAND

The girls all attended school in Palo Alto, where they all knew one another and were friends. By the eighth grade at Jordan Middle School, Robertson (guitar) and Ford (bass) already had an interest in playing rock music. "Maya and I were playing bass and guitar together early on," says Robertson. "We thought about having a band, but we really didn't have any friends to round one out. It was impossible finding people that knew how to play. Then we thought of the idea of asking people to learn how to play drums and sing so we could eventually form a band. It wasn't a plan to control the world and be big superstars. It was started as kind of a joke on the other bands in our school — which, in our town, were all formed by these popular, blond rich guys trying to be like Nirvana." The middle school had a lunchtime performance opportunity at which many of the school's "boy bands" would play. "The cool thing was to be in bands," said Ford, "so they were all going to play. And there weren't any girl bands playing so we decided to play the show."

From left: Donna F. (Ford), Donna C. (Castellano), Donna R. (Robertson), and Donna A. (Anderson).

Robertson and Ford had heard Anderson singing in the hallways and asked her to be part of the band, and they also asked their friend Torry Castellano if she'd be interested in learning to play the drums. "I had never played drums before," said Castellano. "And Donna R. and Donna F. had only been playing guitar and bass for two months or something. And Donna A. had never sung before in front of people. So a month before the show, we were just like, 'All right let's just do it.' So we practiced and practiced and practiced." Castellano rented a drum kit and learned to play. But it was set up backwards, which she only found out after some of the boys made fun of her.

Screen

The band's first public appearance was at Jordan Middle School's "Day on the Green" on June 8, 1993. They played four "cover" tunes (songs written and performed by others) by The Muffs, Shonen Knife, and Syndicate of Sound. "We didn't have time to learn how to play *and* write songs, you know?" said Castellano.

"We didn't want people to make fun of us because they already made fun of us," guitarist Robertson remembers. "Obviously, news would travel fast that these geeks were gonna form an all-girl band. So in trying to come up with a name, we, like, searched the dictionary for something you couldn't make fun of." They settled on "Screen," a name that wouldn't necessarily mean anything—or provide a reason for anyone to tease them. Other bands appeared under the names "Invisible Purple Butterflies" and "Verbal Constipation."

> "We didn't want people to make fun of us because they already made fun of us," Robertson remembers. "Obviously, news would travel fast that these geeks were gonna form an all-girl band. So in trying to come up with a name, we, like, searched the dictionary for something you couldn't make fun of." They settled on "Screen," a name that wouldn't necessarily mean anything.

Reaction from their fellow students was not positive. Despite the comical names of the other bands appearing, the audience found ways to make fun of the newly formed Screen: "Screen? I oughta screen your calls," or "You should be Screen and not heard," and "Screen? What a stupid name! How about the Hockey Pucks?" "From then on, we were lepers," recalls Ford. "Everyone thought we were big weirdos — Satan worshipers, drug addicts, lesbians." Anderson remembers, "It was like, 'Okay, you're never, ever going to be popular.' But it wasn't that much of a gamble. We already didn't have friends."

Ragady Anne

The girls spent the following summer practicing hard in the Castellano garage and writing their own songs, in addition to learning more cover tunes. The first song they wrote was "Tammy the New Feminist," which made fun of the type of girl they thought many of their peers thought they were.

When they entered Palo Alto High School in the fall of 1993, they'd changed the band's name to Ragady Anne. Despite the name change, the teasing only seemed to get worse. "We'd be walking to class and the singer in this band called Smiley Face—he was popular and had a really big ego—would follow us around going, 'Ragady Anne! I love Ragady Anne! I looooove them! They're so awesome," says Robertson. "He'd be screaming it behind us."

The reaction of others only served to motivate the young musicians. "We dealt with so many people hating us that it really brought us together," remembers bassist Ford. "If one of us had gotten sick of being in the band, there wasn't really anything else to do or anybody else to be friends with." They kept practicing, writing songs, and performing whenever they had the chance. Their second public performance was as Ragady Anne on November 6, 1993, at a "battle of the bands," at which, according to the band's web site, they "blew everybody off the stage." They also participated as Ragady Anne in a Christmas Benefit, a food and toy drive for disadvantaged families in the Bay Area (the band continues to participate every year). They released a 7" vinyl record with independent recording label Radio Trash, which included a single called "Freakshow" about breakfast cereal.

During this time the members of the band began listening to and performing the music of harder rock bands that were popular in the late 1970s and 1980s, including Kiss, AC/DC, Metallica, and Motley Crue. To reflect this new edge in their repertoire (and because there were already other bands named "Ragady Anne"), the girls chose a new name: "The Electrocutes."

The Electrocutes and The Donnas

As the band's musical style began to solidify, others began to notice them. They caught the attention of Bay Area promoter Mark Weiss, who gave the band one of their earliest professional gigs. "They weren't faking anything; they were just being themselves," Weiss said. "They were unconscious of how good they were." Singer Anderson describes the music of The Electrocutes as "speed metal." She said, "The Electrocutes were kind of confusing and enigmatic; we understood it but nobody else did."

Soon, another opportunity emerged with Darin Rafaelli, a local musician, songwriter, promoter, and owner of a small independent label. He heard the girls play live and asked them if they'd like to be part of a project he'd conceived for his Super**Teem record label. "He was like, 'Yeah, you guys are great. I've been looking for a girl band. Do you guys want to play some

> ""
>
> *"From then on, we were lepers," recalls Ford. "Everyone thought we were big weirdoes — Satan worshipers, drug addicts, lesbians." Anderson remembers, "It was like, 'Okay, you're never, ever going to be popular.' But it wasn't that much of a gamble. We already didn't have friends."*
>
> ""

Their first CD, The Donnas, *was released on an independent label.*

rock songs, rock 'n' roll?' We were like, 'OK, whatever, that sounds cool.'" Rafaelli had written some songs for an all-girl band and needed a group to perform them. The music was less edgy than the hard-driving music the Electrocutes had been performing, and the band's name didn't quite fit what has been described as the "bubble gum punk" music written by Rafaelli.

The name "The Donnas" came about when the band manager was doodling on a McDonald's "Happy Meal" box. But the name was also a nod to the influence of a 1970s and 1980s punk rock band, The Ramones. The members of the Ramones (Joey, Dee Dee, Johnny, and Marky) all claimed to share the same last name. Instead of having the same last name, however, The Donnas would each have the same first name, using the first letter of their actual last names to differentiate them. It was a gimmick, and calling the Rafaelli project The Donnas enabled the band to continue playing and writing as The Electrocutes.

"We always thought of The Electrocutes as our artistic outlet, our baby, you know. And then The Donnas was just a side project," said Anderson. While the girls wrote and recorded with Rafaelli as The Donnas, they continued playing live as The Electrocutes. "It was kind of fun, because we really took The Electrocutes seriously, but with the Donnas, we could just eat tacos and write a song in a few minutes and that was it," says drummer Castellano.

Their First Release: *The Donnas*

The Donnas released three singles and one album with Rafaelli's Super** Teem label. Their first album, called *The Donnas*, was recorded in a single day and released in January 1997. "It was always a joke for us," said guitarist Robertson. "Not a bad joke, but, like a fun joke—this fake band that was from South City and wore matching outfits. It was kind of silly. We didn't think people would really buy into it."

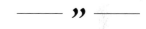

"It was kind of fun, because we really took The Electrocutes seriously, but with the Donnas, we could just eat tacos and write a song in a few minutes and that was it," says drummer Castellano.

The group's dual public images soon offered some interesting ironies. The Electrocutes were a hard-driving speed metal act and The Donnas were a pop-punk outfit. As The Electrocutes, they would publicly slander The Donnas as a "goody goody" band. Among other things, The Donnas would wear matching T-shirts with the band's name on it, which the girls considered part of the joke. Once, they even performed live on a radio show, as the two different bands. "Because you couldn't see us, it was a good little joke."

But The Donnas were catching on faster than The Electrocutes—even as far away as Japan. In the spring of 1997, during the girls' senior year at Palo Alto High School, they got their first taste of rock and roll stardom. The owner of a record store in Tokyo invited them to come and play and offered to pay for it. "This guy owned a tiny little record store in Tokyo—I'm talking the size of someone's bathroom—crammed with records," remembers Robertson. "He carried our albums and they were selling like hotcakes. . . . We stayed in his friend's house and slept on the floor, freezing. But once we got to the shows, they were all jam-packed. That was the first time we ever saw a group of people singing our lyrics."

American Teenage Rock 'n' Roll Machine

When it became time to think about recording a second album, the band members agreed they wanted to exert more creative control and to rely less upon the direction of Rafaelli. Some have compared the influence of the older Rafaelli (in his mid-30s) to that of a "Svengali," essentially a puppet-master who controlled them from behind the scenes. Others have compared him to famed rock and roll producer Phil Spector (The Kinks, The Ramones, and many others), who controlled every detail of a band's sound. But band members describe the relationship differently. "We were writing songs before we ever met Darin, so it's not like we started playing and someone else was writing our songs," says Anderson. "Then we met him and started making this kind of music and after awhile, no one was taking us seriously because they saw him and immediately went, oh, they're not really friends, he's telling them what to do, he's the Svengali/ Phil Spector to their puppets — as if there wasn't a possibility for anything else to happen!"

> "I thought they were so cool," said Lookout co-owner Molly Neuman. "It was extremely charming to see these 17-year-old girls singing these funny, catchy, one-and-a-half minute songs."

For their next album, *American Teenage Rock 'n' Roll Machine*, the girls decided not to rely solely on Rafaelli for all the material. Instead, they contributed four songs they originally wrote without Rafaelli for The Electrocutes. Among these songs were "Looking for Blood," "You Make Me Hot," and "Speed Demon." As Anderson says, "We finally just merged them together, so instead of saving all of our ideas for the Electrocutes, we used them for the Donnas." But they also continued occasionally co-writing with Rafaelli and performing his songs.

In the summer of 1997, the year the girls graduated from high school, they were approached by the independent punk rock label Lookout — whose signed bands included Green Day and Rancid. The girls had not entirely given up on The Electrocutes as a concept, but the label was more interested in The Donnas. "The Donnas had a bigger profile," said Lookout co-owner Molly Neuman. "I thought they were so cool. It was extremely charming to see these 17-year-old girls singing these funny, catchy, one-and-a-half minute songs."

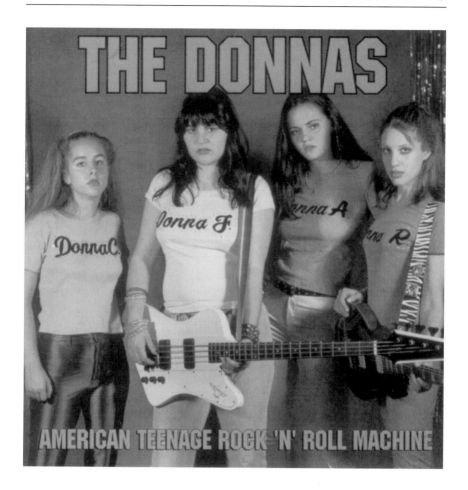

Lookout signed the band to a recording contract and produced their second album, *American Teenage Rock 'n' Roll Machine*. According to guitarist Robertson, "The first album sounds garagey and was recorded in one day. *Rock and Roll Machine* was recorded in two days. In a studio." The new album, released in 1998, received favorable press, and the band was offered the opportunity to go on tour. But by then the girls, recently graduated from high school, had all headed off for college.

EDUCATION

Even while the band was in their intensely active formative phase, they made their school work a priority. "Our high school was a really good high school—everyone did well," says bassist Ford. "We're all smart, and it wasn't hard to do really well. Also, if you do well in school then your parents worry about you less, you can stay out later. They trusted us more." All four young women graduated from Palo Alto High School in 1997.

That fall, despite the success of the band so far, all four started college. Ford and Robertson went to the University of California at Santa Cruz, Anderson to the University of California at Berkeley, and Castellano went to New York University. But they had just signed a contract with a label that had done well for other bands, and the college experiment did not last long. They dropped out of school, and The Donnas were soon reunited. "It was like, 'yeah, I'd much rather hang out with these people rather than all these stupid new people in college,'" recalls Robertson.

CAREER HIGHLIGHTS

Breaking Away

The collective decision of Anderson, Castellano, Ford, and Robertson to leave college was a turning point in their pursuit of a career in the music business. As they got down to touring and writing and practicing, the group decided to break from Rafaelli and go it alone. "We didn't want to be stuck in some band where some dude wrote the songs for us," said guitarist Robertson.

Other members of the band describe the parting in more diplomatic terms. "People didn't really understand that it was just, like, five friends writing songs together and stuff," says drummer Castellano. "They kind of had this idea of this older guy/younger girl thing where he had all the control, which is not true at all. And I think he was kind of tired of people perceiving it that way and so were we. You know, we'd been a band for, like, three years before we even met him, so we wrote a lot of songs before we even met, and we kind of wanted to just go back to writing by ourselves."

Singer Anderson credits Rafaelli with helping them to write songs that would sell. "I think his biggest contribution is that he taught us, like, how to keep songs simple enough for people to latch onto them," she said. "We were into our [instrumental] abilities so much that the songs were inaccessible."

Get Skintight

In 1998, The Donnas toured extensively by van and bus to support their first two albums. At the same time, they wrote and perfected the sound they wanted for the third album, which was to be called *Get Skintight*. For this album, they decided to spend a little more time in the studio and used

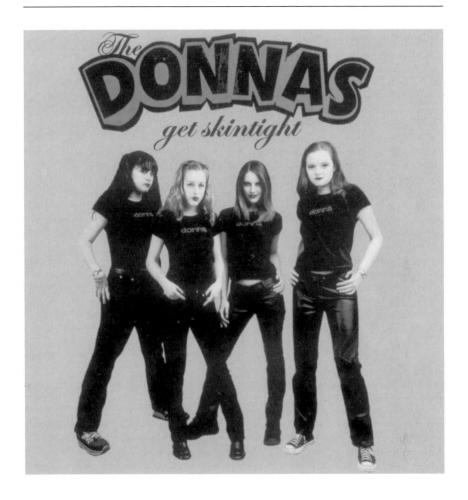

producers Jeff and Steve McDonald, who'd produced the Los Angeles-based punk group Red Kross. The McDonald brothers had seen The Donnas perform live and talked their way into letting them produce the upcoming CD.

"This time," says Castellano, "We had 10 days, so we did a lot of different takes, even if we did it perfect the first time." *Get Skintight* was released in 1999 and included rocking songs like "Get Out of My Room," "Hot Boxin'," "Doin' Donuts," and a cover of metal band Motley Crue's "Too Fast For Love."

Other highlights of the band's early days as full-time professionals were opening for the glam-metal rockers Cinderella in Las Vegas and veteran rocker Joan Jett in New York City. They also appeared in two teen films,

Jawbreaker and *Drive Me Crazy*. For *Drive Me Crazy*, the band had to play a cover of REO Speedwagon's "Keep On Lovin' You," a ballad they detested. The film's producers wanted The Donnas to play something softer than their usual fare. "We got tricked into doing it," said Ford. "We wanted to do Bon Jovi or Guns 'n' Roses, and then they just made us play that. We were, like, 'We'll do anything else!'" They also covered the Kiss 1970s hit "Strutter" for the film *Detroit Rock City*, which was produced by Kiss bassist Gene Simmons.

The Donnas Turn 21

By this point, the band members were growing up. The first three albums were largely about being high school girls. But their fourth album, *The Donnas Turn 21*, released in 2001, was about becoming young women, with a lot of humor woven in. "We just write about having fun," Anderson said in an interview at that time. "We'll be doing that until we're 31. We have more to write about now, we travel a lot, we meet more guys, y'know? I think touring is a lot more eventful than high school."

Many of the songs reflected the band's growing emotional and sexual maturation. Despite the suggestiveness of some of the lyrics, there is none of the blatant lewdness that can be found in much of today's popular music. And music reviewers praised the band's improved musical ability and their more polished sound. "Our sound's changed a lot," said Anderson at the time of the CD's release. "We used to sound like a really garage band, it's just that the recordings early on were so terrible. Production-wise the new album sounded so much better than *Get Skintight.*"

The Donnas were enjoying a certain amount of notice from regional fans and critics, but they hadn't yet received national attention. Their manager, Molly Neuman, who was also co-owner of the independent label Lookout, began helping the band make the next big step. Drummer Castellano put it this way: "There's only so far you can go on an independent label. It would have been nice to be on Lookout forever, but there's no way that you're going to get very far on the radio with an independent label."

The Donnas Turn 21 *was about becoming young women, with a lot of humor woven in. "We just write about having fun," Anderson said. "We'll be doing that until we're 31. We have more to write about now, we travel a lot, we meet more guys, y'know? I think touring is a lot more eventful than high school."*

Hitting the Big Time: *Spend the Night*

For their fifth album, the band and manager Neuman agreed that it was time to sign to a major label. Atlantic Records saw the band's potential and had much more to offer in terms of promotional support and distribution than the independent Lookout label. There was some fear, though, among band members that they might lose some of what they enjoyed at Lookout—an attentive staff, complete artistic control, and enthusiasm for everything the band did.

153

"It's a nurturing feeling when the people putting out your album are really excited about it," said Robertson, about the transition from an "indie" label to a corporate giant like Atlantic. "It's kind of nice to feel that here as well. The stress came with the recording. There were a lot of different opinions on how it should be recorded, where it should be recorded, who should produce it. We thought we were going to be able to do it the way we always do it. Then we kind of panicked, we were afraid the songs wouldn't come out the way we had written them," she said. They were able to bring in the producer they wanted, Robert Shimp, and together with him they worked on demos (practice recordings) of all the songs before actually recording the album. Gradually the band began to appreciate the benefits of additional input from other recording professionals brought in by Atlantic. "You don't need someone telling you what to do, but you do need more checks and balances," said Robertson.

On one point, though, The Donnas stood their ground. The Donnas strongly opposed using high technology studio techniques that would have resulted in what they felt was not their true sound. Guitarist Robertson is adamant about not doing anything in the studio that can't be reproduced onstage. "Nobody ever forces anything on us," she says, "but occasionally someone will say something to the effect of 'Maybe it could use a little extra guitar here,' or 'What about these vocals? Maybe you should add some harmonies' — stuff like that. But we're a band with one guitar and one vocalist, and we have to be conscious of that, or we'll end up with this big slick project that we then have to take out on the road. . . . We're always asking ourselves, 'Will it hold up onstage?'" Singer Anderson agrees: "Touring, you learn a lot about your instrument, what you can and can't do. We're very strict about only writing things that we can pull off really tight live. We don't want anything to sound better on the album than it does on stage."

> **"**
>
> *"Nobody ever forces anything on us," Robertson says, "but occasionally someone will say something to the effect of 'Maybe it could use a little extra guitar here,' or 'What about these vocals? Maybe you should add some harmonies' — stuff like that. But we're a band with one guitar and one vocalist, and we have to be conscious of that. . . . We're always asking ourselves, 'Will it hold up onstage?'"*
>
> **"**

The Donnas pose in downtown San Francisco. From left: Donna R. (Robertson), Donna A. (Anderson), Donna C. (Castellano), and Donna F. (Ford).

The band's sense of their own identity as a group, coupled with Atlantic's production and promotional savvy, has spelled success for The Donnas so far. Their transition to a major national label brought them this kind of review from *Rolling Stone* reviewer Michael Ansaldo:

> From the first seconds of *Spend the Night's* feral opener, "It's on the Rocks," it's clear that the major-label jump has done nothing to soften the group's edges. Tracks like "Take it Off," "Too Bad About Your Girl," and "Take Me to the Back Seat" rock with the same exaggerated badness as their first four albums. If anything the big-budget production fully reveals the rock chops that previous releases only hinted at, and *Spend the Night* boasts a sonic punch that places it confidently between AC/DC's *Powerage* and Judas Priest's *British Steel* on your CD shelf.

Suddenly the band was enjoying a lot of success. Their new album began getting positive reviews, their songs "Take it Off" and "Who Invited You" began getting radio air play, and the band began getting invitations to appear as musical guests on the "Tonight Show with Jay Leno" and "Saturday Night Live." Their video production of "Take it Off" was in rotation on MTV, and they appeared in a Budweiser commercial.

In early 2003, the band launched a tour as the headliner, no longer as the opening band. "We have so many things planned," said drummer Castellano, "and so many things are happening that we have to concentrate on what's happening right now. I think you have to kind of look at the big picture, but also it can get a little overwhelming, so you have to look at what's right in front of you. I think you have to just keep on going."

> **"We know each other better than we know ourselves," Anderson said. "We know when to leave each other alone and when we need each other. When we're on the bus and one of us seems irritable, that's when we give her space. We try not to press each other. It's just common courtesy. We try to respect each other."**

Their recent stardom has been hard won, with ten years of ups and downs holding The Donnas together. "We know each other better than we know ourselves," Anderson said. "We know when to leave each other alone and when we need each other. When we're on the bus and one of us seems irritable, that's when we give her space. We try not to press each other. It's just common courtesy. We try to respect each other." Anderson says the respect comes from "knowing that everyone in the band is important, irreplaceable. When you realize that, respect is easy. And you know what? We like each other too."

The Image of the Band

With the popularity the band has earned in recent years has come the challenge of dealing with their public image and how that matches their real lives. "I feel sometimes we have people fooled, because part of The Donnas is that it's larger than life and it has nothing to do with what we're like in person," Robertson says. "I think people would be sad to find out that when I'm not on tour I hang out at my house—I'm a total homebody." Castellano comments about the hard-work side of being in the band: "Sometimes people think that we are just wild and crazy, that we never have to be responsible, we never have to take anything seriously and this isn't a job. So, that's hard to hear too, because we do put a lot of hard work

into it. We try hard to play the best we can every night, and we do have to do lots of interviews and meetings and crazy business stuff."

In terms of their physical appearance, The Donnas prefer a straight-ahead approach that is consistent with their approach to rock music. "We don't get the free clothes or borrow stuff because we don't have a stylist," Robertson says. In fact, during one photo shoot for a magazine the publication's stylist insisted she wear what she calls "a turquoise fur pimp coat, something that Kid Rock or Poison's Bret Michaels or Ludacris would wear—but not me. It's my life and my body." She dug her heels in and refused to wear the outfit: "You either have to go with the flow and be bummed later when you see the picture . . . or stand your ground and people might end up saying you're hard to work with."

Publicly, at least, The Donnas prefer the grungy, garage band look, including T-shirts, jeans, and messy hair. "I wash my hair like four times a month

———— " ————

Reflecting on the band's recent status as a rock and roll force on the national scene, Ford makes a statement that recalls their early days at Jordan Middle School in Palo Alto: "I feel like we don't fit in. I don't think we want to be women in rock. We just want to be rock."

———— " ————

but not necessarily once a week," says Robertson. Bassist Ford echoes the sentiment, saying, "I like having my hair in my face when I rock out. I can't have a ponytail." Of the band's image, Ford says, "I don't think we're that made up. In every picture, we're in jeans, but we don't have a really polished, made-up image at all."

Reflecting on the band's recent status as a rock and roll force on the national scene, Ford makes a statement that recalls their early days at Jordan Middle School in Palo Alto: "I feel like we don't fit in. I don't think we want to be women in rock. We just want to be rock."

MAJOR INFLUENCES

The first major influences on The Donnas were bands that were receiving a lot of radio play while the band was first forming, like R.E.M. and XTC. Guitarist Robertson says, "If you can imagine the biggest, weirdest R.E.M. fans, that was me and Maya [Ford, bassist] before we formed our band."

When they entered high school, however, they began listening to and playing covers of earlier rock and roll music, including The Ramones, and especially metal bands like Alice Cooper, Kiss, Cinderella, AC/DC, Cheap Trick, and Motley Crue. The Donnas also mention the influence of prominent female-fronted bands of the same era, including Chrissie Hynde and The Pretenders and Deborah Harry and Blondie.

MARRIAGE AND FAMILY

Only one of The Donnas, Allison Robertson, is married. Her husband is Robert Shimp, who produced *Spend the Night*. The other members date and often have steady boyfriends. None of the band members have any children, though.

"You know, when we really like a boy, we get really excited," says drummer Castellano. "We all have different kinds of guys that we like. We may all think one guy is really cute and agree on it and everything, but we don't ever compete."

Their social lives revolve around one another and their families, who remain the band's biggest fans. "We'll be getting ready to go out to dinner," says Ford, "and my parents will be wearing Donnas T-shirts and I have to ask them to change. They're super excited about it."

HOBBIES AND OTHER INTERESTS

It would be safe to say that the common interest all four women share is a love for rock and roll. But they still have other interests as well. For example, in May 2003, The Donnas celebrated their tenth anniversary together as a band. They were on tour in Japan at the time. They took the opportunity to celebrate their big day together at Tokyo Disney. "I know, I know, I know," laughed Robertson, "We're total cornballs. We're the kind of people who would go there anyway, but going there on a big occasion, that's our style."

The band's official web site lists some of the group's individual interests. Brett Anderson, vocalist, enjoys making lasagna. Torry Castellano, drummer, likes "playing drums, hanging out, watching movies, and shopping." Donna Ford, bassist, claims her hobby is drawing pictures of Richard Nixon. And guitarist Allison Robertson enjoys collecting toys and shopping.

RECORDINGS

The Donnas, 1998
American Teenage Rock 'n' Roll Machine, 1998
Get Skintight, 1999
The Donnas Turn 21, 2001
Spend the Night, 2002

FURTHER READING

Books

Contemporary Musicians, Vol. 33, 2002

Periodicals

Boston Herald, Feb.7, 2003, p.S25
Denver Post, Feb. 21 2003, p.FF3
New York Post, Feb. 7, 2003, p.58
New York Times, Nov. 24, p.L4
New Yorker, Apr. 2, 2001, p.96

Online Articles

http://onstagemag.com/ar/performance_bashing_night_away/index.htm
   (*Onstage*, "Bashing the Night Away," May 2003)

Online Databases

Biography Resource Center Online, 2004, article from *Contemporary Musicians,* 2002

ADDRESS

The Donnas
Atlantic Records
9229 Sunset Boulevard
Los Angeles, CA 90069

WORLD WIDE WEB SITE

http://www.thedonnas.com

Tim Duncan 1976-

American Professional Basketball Player for
the San Antonio Spurs
NBA Most Valuable Player in 2002 and 2003

BIRTH

Victor Theodore Duncan was born on April 25, 1976, on the
island of St. Croix in the United States Virgin Islands, located
in the Caribbean. His father, William Duncan, was a mason
and also operated a hotel and worked at an oil refinery. His
mother, Delysia Bryan Duncan, better known as Ione, worked

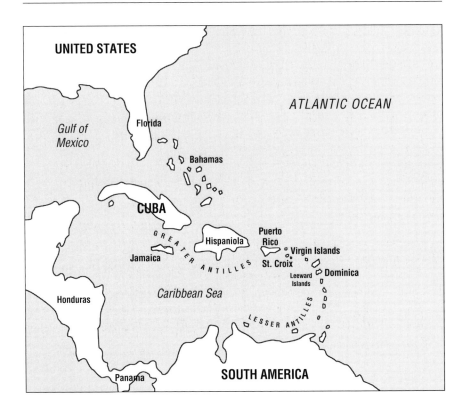

as a midwife—a person who assists mothers when they give birth. Tim has two older sisters, Cheryl and Tricia, and three half-brothers, William, John, and Scott.

YOUTH

The Virgin Islands are made up of 100 or so small isles in the Caribbean Sea. They lie about 1,100 miles southeast of Miami, Florida. The United States purchased several of the islands in 1917, including St. Croix—Duncan's home. These became known as the United States (or U.S.) Virgin Islands. This means that Duncan grew up as a United States citizen, even though he lived far away from the U.S. mainland.

In many ways, St. Croix is similar to the United States. It receives many of the same television shows, and kids often dress in T-shirts and shorts. The climate and scenery are quite different, however. Like other islands in the Caribbean, St. Croix is beautiful and tropical. It's surrounded by warm water and has lots of beaches and palm trees. Given these surroundings, it's not surprising that Duncan's first sport was swimming rather than basketball. What is surprising is that he didn't do much of his swimming in the ocean. Duncan was afraid of sharks, so he preferred to swim in pools. Fortunately, that's where the races were held. He began swimming in meets at a young age, following in the wake of his older sisters, who were both strong swimmers. In fact, Tricia was so good that she swam in the 1988 Olympics as a member of the Virgin Islands team.

A big reason for the success of Tim and his siblings was that their parents were very involved in their sporting activities, especially their mother, Ione. She was always there to show her support—and when Ione gave you support, *everybody* heard it. "Every meet she was the loudest parent there," Tim remembered. "Somehow I could always pick out her voice yelling over everybody else." She had a say-

Duncan's parents were very involved in their sporting activities, especially his mother, Ione. She was always there to show her support—and when Ione gave you support, **everybody** *heard it.* "Every meet she was the loudest parent there," Tim remembered. "Somehow I could always pick out her voice yelling over everybody else."

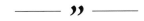

ing that she used to motivate her children: "Good, better, best. Never let it rest. Until your good is better, and your better is best." By the time he was 13 years old, Duncan was getting closer to being the best: he was rated among the top swimmers in the United States in his age group for the 400-meter freestyle. It was thought he might be able to compete in the Olympics as early as the 1992 summer games.

The Storm Hits

Age 13 turned out to be Tim Duncan's unlucky year. A few months after he became a teenager, he was introduced to one of the biggest dangers in the Caribbean: a hurricane. In September 1989, Hurricane Hugo bore down on St. Croix. His family took shelter in their home and hoped for the best. "It was very scary," Duncan recalled in *Tim Duncan: Tower of Power.* "You could hear trees snapping. I had never experienced anything like that." The Duncans' house came through the storm fairly well, but that wasn't true of the rest of island. Roofs were ripped from houses. Boats were tossed onto the land. And the pool where Duncan's swim team trained—the only suitable one on the island—was totally destroyed. His team moved their practices to the ocean. Duncan was still afraid of sharks, and he found it difficult to swim well in the open sea. His interest in the sport began to fade.

But an even worse catastrophe had begun in the months before the hurricane arrived. Duncan's mother had been diagnosed with breast cancer. She began chemotherapy treatments immediately, but they were delayed after the hospital was damaged by the storm. By the following spring her condition had grown worse. In April 1990, the day before Duncan's 14th birthday, she died. Without the woman he called his "number one fan," Duncan became even less interested in swimming, and he gave up the sport. "The hurricane broke Tim's routine by taking away our pool," his sister Tricia said in *Sports Illustrated*. "Then when Mom passed, he lost his motivation."

Fortunately, there was another sport that helped take his mind off his grief. The year before, Tim's sister Cheryl, who had married and moved to Ohio, had sent a basketball hoop and backboard to her brother as a present. His father had set it up, but it wasn't until after Ione's death that Duncan began to concentrate on the game. A big reason for his interest was that Cheryl and her husband, Ricky Lowery, had moved back to St. Croix to help out after Ione had died. Lowery had played college basketball in Ohio, and he began to work with Duncan on the basic skills. "You could just tell this kid was a ballplayer," Lowery later said. "First starting out, he was a bit awkward, but he caught on quickly." Lowery and Duncan spent long hours playing one-on-one games, with Lowery giving Duncan a crash course in hoops. "I wanted to make sure he learned the game right. I spent a lot of time with him on a personal basis, getting him ready for the next level."

> "
>
> *"You could just tell this kid was a ballplayer. First starting out, he was a bit awkward, but he caught on quickly," said his brother-in-law, Ricky Lowery, a former college player. "I wanted to make sure he learned the game right. I spent a lot of time with him on a personal basis, getting him ready for the next level."*
>
> "

EDUCATION

When she was alive, Ione Duncan made sure her children applied themselves to their studies as well as their sporting events. Tim's sister Tricia remembers that her brother "used to make high honors all the time" in his schoolwork. He was even allowed to skip a grade during elementary school. As a result, Duncan was a year younger than his classmates from that point on. He began high school at St. Dunstan's Episcopal at age 14, the same year that he took up basketball. Even though he had only been seriously playing the sport for a few months, he made the team.

Duncan's athletic abilities were aided by his height—at age 14 he was already six feet tall and still growing. He played guard during his freshman season. Two years later and nine inches taller (and *still* growing), Duncan was the team's center. Local papers began to cover his games, and he drew the attention of some college recruiters. But few universities hear about promising players in the Caribbean, so only a few schools showed interest in Duncan. Providence College offered him a scholarship, then changed their mind and withdrew it.

Fortunately, a tour of rookie NBA players paid a visit to St. Croix before Duncan's senior year in high school. Duncan got a chance to match up against rising star Alonzo Mourning in a game, and Duncan did very well. News of the performance soon reached Dave Odom, head coach at Wake Forest University in Winston-Salem, North Carolina. Odom soon made a trip to St. Croix and got to see Duncan play in an informal outdoor game. Informal or not, it allowed the Wake Forest coach to see what Duncan could do on the court. He made a scholarship offer, and a month later Duncan accepted. He was about to move from a small Caribbean island to a major university in a large North Carolina city. And he was about to test his skills against the best amateur players in the world.

Duncan attended Wake Forest University from 1993 to 1997. There, he spent time on the basketball court with the Demon Deacons and also spent time in classes, majoring in psychology. Though he wasn't a star student, he maintained a 2.7 grade-point average. He completed his studies in the spring of 1997, earning a bachelor's degree.

CAREER HIGHLIGHTS

Duncan's career really began as a college student at Wake Forest. When he began his first season with the Demon Deacons (1993-94), Coach Odom didn't expect him to play much. But then two other players became ineligible, so Duncan became the starting center. He was certainly big enough to fill the position: during his college years, he reached his full seven-foot height.

During his sophomore year at Wake Forest, Duncan and the Demon Deacons lost to Oklahoma in the NCAA tournament, March 1995.

No one knew much about him at the beginning. Most fans focused on Randolph Childress, Wake Forest's star player. Early in the season, Duncan simply played and learned, but soon he started to show his stuff. He averaged 10 rebounds and almost 10 points a game and set the school record for the number of blocked shots in a season. He had become an important player much sooner than anyone expected. "He has made us a completely different team," Odom said. With Duncan's help Wake Forest made it to the NCAA tournament, but they were eliminated after losing their second game.

Off the court, Duncan settled into life at the university. When he first arrived, many of the people he met had never heard of the Virgin Islands. Sometimes they asked funny questions about Duncan's home. One woman even wondered if people wore clothes on St. Croix. Duncan soon made friends, however, and began to enjoy life in Winston-Salem.

Sophomore Sensation

At the beginning of Duncan's second college season (1994-95), Wake Forest wasn't expected to do well against its rivals in the Atlantic Coast Conference (ACC). But the play of Duncan and Randolph Childress made the Demon Deacons strong contenders. At the close of the regular season, Wake Forest claimed the ACC championship. The team then entered the NCAA tournament, where they won two

> **"**
>
> *After his sophomore year, everyone began to wonder if Duncan would turn pro and move to the NBA. But Duncan wasn't hoping for a big payoff—at least not yet. "To be honest, I'm not looking too far ahead," he explained. "I mean, I've thought about the pros, obviously. But not to the extent that it would happen this year. I'm not going anywhere this year."*
>
> **"**

games before being beaten by Oklahoma State. It had been a surprisingly good year for the team and an amazing year for Duncan. He had upped his numbers, averaging 16.8 points and 12.5 rebounds per game. He also proved himself an outstanding defensive player who could force opponents to alter their attack.

His performance caught the attention of the basketball world. Jerry West, the general manager of the Los Angeles Lakers and former pro superstar, was one of several people who called Duncan the best college player in the country. Suddenly, everyone began to wonder if Duncan would turn professional and move to the National Basketball Association (NBA). Because NBA players can earn enormous amounts of money, many promising college players decide to turn pro before they have completed the full four years of college ball. Duncan, however, wasn't hoping for a big payoff—at least not yet. "To be honest, I'm not looking too far ahead," he explained. "I mean, I've thought about the pros, obviously. But not to the extent that it would happen this year. I'm not going anywhere this year."

He made the same choice one year later, following his junior season. Many people were amazed that Duncan could turn down the millions that the pros were offering, but he had his reasons. The biggest was a vow he had made years before. "I promised my mother when she was dying that I would graduate and I will carry that promise out," he told one journalist. Another factor was his age. Even after three years in college, Duncan was still only 20. "I just felt too young to be in the NBA," he said. "I was not ready." He was also enjoying his time at a student. "The truth is, he loves college," his coach said. "He loves hanging out with people his own age."

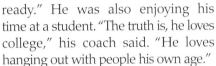

> Many people were amazed that Duncan could turn down the millions that the pros were offering, but he had his reasons. The biggest was a vow he had made years before. "I promised my mother when she was dying that I would graduate and I will carry that promise out," he told one journalist.

Taking the Heat

In his junior and senior years, Duncan faced new challenges. After Randolph Childress graduated, Duncan had to become the team's leader. Also, teams were able to double- and triple-team him because they no longer had to worry about the high-scoring Childress. Despite the added pressure, Duncan was able to adjust and improve his game, and his statistics got better and better. He averaged 20.8 points and 14.7 rebounds in his final year.

As he became more famous, Duncan had to deal with greater expectations and more demands from fans and reporters. Many players, especially young ones, have trouble dealing with this attention. Perhaps Duncan did, too, but you would never know it from his behavior. He almost always spoke quietly and appeared calm—even while on the court. His teammates nicknamed him Spock, after the "Star Trek" character who shows no emotion.

Some people mistook his reserved behavior as a sign of boredom and thought that he sometimes wasn't interested in the game. Duncan was well aware that some people criticized his intensity, but—not surprisingly—he didn't get too excited about it. "It's just how I was brought up," he

Duncan stretches for the ball over Chris Alexander (#30) of the Virginia Cavaliers, March 1996.

said. "It's my personality, and it carries onto the court. But I don't see myself as laid back as people say. Once I'm out there, I want to play. I'm excited to play."

Duncan was also excited to win a national championship with Wake Forest, but it was not to be. In his junior year (1995-96), the Demon Deacons won their second consecutive ACC tournament. But their season ended in the NCAA tournament, when the University of Kentucky beat them soundly, 83-63. In his senior year (1996-97), they made it to the second round of the NCAAs but lost to Stanford. Duncan was disappointed with the losses, but he knew he had a big future in front of him. As he left Wake Forest in the spring of 1997, he waited to hear where he was going to play pro ball.

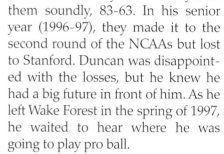

Some people mistook Duncan's reserved behavior as a sign of boredom and thought that he sometimes wasn't interested in the game. "It's just how I was brought up," he said. "It's my personality, and it carries onto the court. But I don't see myself as laid back as people say. Once I'm out there, I want to play. I'm excited to play."

Going Pro

The San Antonio Spurs made Duncan the first choice in the 1997 NBA draft. His initial contract paid him $10 million dollars over three years. In joining the Spurs, he became a teammate of David Robinson, one of the top centers in the NBA. Nicknamed "the Admiral" (because he had attended the U.S. Naval Academy and served in the U.S. Navy), Robinson was a seasoned veteran who had spent seven years in the league. Even before official training began for the 1997-98 season, Robinson invited Duncan to his home in Colorado so that they could start getting ready for the season.

The two talented big men made San Antonio a team to be reckoned with, and Duncan quickly got the attention of his opponents. Following a preseason game against the Houston Rockets, Charles Barkley said that "I have seen the future, . . . and it wears No. 21"—a reference to Duncan's jersey numeral.

Duncan was officially listed as the Spurs' power forward, with Robinson as the center. During their first season together, Robinson gave Duncan pointers on the players he would face each night. Though Robinson was the more experienced NBA player, he admitted that he admired Duncan's maturity and patience. "Tim brings that calm perspective to things," Robinson told *Sports Illustrated*. "You don't often say this about a rookie, but he's got a lot of wisdom." Duncan dismissed such compliments. "I'm a kid. Corny as that sounds, that's what I am." He certainly had his share of toys: when the team went on the road, Duncan carried his own video-game system with him, so he could play in his hotel room.

Nicknamed "The Twin Towers" and "The Swat Team" (for their shot-blocking abilities), Duncan and Robinson made the Spurs into contenders. (The season before Duncan's arrival, with Robinson

Number one — Duncan poses after being selected by the San Antonio Spurs as the first pick overall in the 1997 NBA draft.

injured, the Spurs had won only 20 games.) In the 1998 NBA playoffs, the Spurs were eliminated by the Utah Jazz in the conference semifinals, but the season had been a big success for Duncan. He was named the NBA Schick Rookie of the Year and the *Sporting News* Rookie of the Year, and he was the only first-year player to make the All-Star team.

A Year to Remember

The start of the following season (1998-99) was delayed because of a labor dispute between NBA owners and players. Once games resumed, the Spurs took a few weeks to get themselves together. Then they started winning. Robinson and Duncan honed their attack, with Duncan becoming the higher scorer. The regular season closed with San Antonio winning 31 of their final 36 games. They hit the playoffs in high gear and never slowed down. After winning their series against the Minnesota Timberwolves, the Spurs took on the Los Angeles Lakers, who were led by Shaquille O'Neal and Kobe Bryant. The Spurs took the Lakers apart, sweeping the series in four games. In Game Three, Duncan scored 37 points.

Next, San Antonio swept the Portland Trailblazers to advance to the NBA Finals against the New York Knicks. The series opened in San Antonio, where Duncan put on a show for the hometown fans. He scored 33 points

*Duncan grabs a rebound during the NBA finals against the
New York Knicks, June 1999.*

on the way to a convincing Spurs win. The rest of the series was pretty much the same. The Knicks managed to win Game Three, but otherwise San Antonio dominated. Duncan was the most dominant of all: he averaged 27.4 points a game in the series. When the buzzer sounded in Game Five, the San Antonio Spurs were the 1999 World Champions. In just his second year in the pros, Duncan had helped lead his team to the top. He was named Most Valuable Player in the Finals and placed third in voting for the season MVP.

Winning and Joking

Duncan had proven himself a winner and one of the best players in the game. Still, sports writers often focused on his apparent lack of emotion. As in his college days, some suggested that he was indifferent — that he didn't care if his team won or lost. Duncan didn't agree with these opinions. In an article for *Sport* magazine that he wrote himself, he explained that his composure was an important part of his game. "Emotions must not always be shown. If you show excitement, then you may also show disappointment or frustration. If your opponent picks up on this frustration, you're at a disadvantage. I make sure my opponents don't know what's going on in my head." His teammates certainly didn't have any problem with Duncan's commitment: "There is nobody more focused or fiercer than Tim when it comes to basketball," said Spurs forward Mario Elie.

> *"Emotions must not always be shown," Duncan once said in explaining how his composure was an important part of his game. "If you show excitement, then you may also show disappointment or frustration. If your opponent picks up on this frustration, you're at a disadvantage. I make sure my opponents don't know what's going on in my head."*

Though he may be very focused on the court, Duncan likes to have fun off of it. "Life is too short to be serious all the time," he wrote. That may explain why he likes to wear his practice shorts backwards and why he likes to play pranks and jokes. Duncan's friend and teammate Antonio Daniels said he is a practical joker but "not a very good one." Daniels also said his friend's jokes were "cheap-shot humor. But it's funny." Will Perdue, another teammate, said that there is definitely one thing that makes Duncan get

Duncan (# 21), Robinson (# 50), and their teammates celebrate after defeating the New York Knicks 78-77 in Game 5 of the NBA Finals, 1999.

excited: "kicking somebody's behind in Sony PlayStation. He does take a lot of pride in that."

Hurting and Healing

As the 1999-2000 season opened, the Spurs had a good chance to repeat as champions. Everything changed on April 11, however. In a late-season game against Sacramento, Duncan tore the cartilage in his knee. It was a serious injury that ended his season. The Spurs had already qualified for the playoffs, but with Duncan on the bench they were eliminated in the first round.

The injury proved doubly disappointing for Duncan because it forced him to withdraw from the U.S. Olympic basketball team that was set to compete in the 2000 summer games in Sydney, Australia. He had played with the national team in previous tournaments and was looking forward to trying for the gold medal that he had dreamed about during his years as a swimmer. In late May, Duncan underwent knee surgery to repair the damaged cartilage, then worked on getting himself back into shape.

On top of everything else, Duncan had a big decision to make in the summer of 2000. His initial contract with San Antonio had ended, and he was now a free agent who could sign with any NBA team. Even with his injury, he was one of the most desirable players in the league. The Orlando Magic did their best to convince Duncan that he should join their team. They flew him and his girlfriend Amy Sherrill to Florida, gave them private tours of Disney World, and introduced them to local resident Tiger Woods. San Antonio wasn't giving up without a fight, though. They did their best to convince Duncan that he should remain a Spur. In the end, Duncan agreed. He re-signed with San Antonio. "Orlando had a lot to offer," he said after making his choice, but he added that "when it came down to it, I just like what I had here."

Teammate Will Perdue said that there is definitely one thing that makes Duncan get excited: "kicking somebody's behind in Sony PlayStation. He does take a lot of pride in that."

It took some time for Duncan to get back in top form after his injury. By the second half of the 2000-01 season, however, he was again one of the best in the league. In the regular season, the Spurs won more games than any other team in the NBA and had hopes of regaining their championship. Then, in the Western Conference Finals, they met the Los Angeles Lakers. Over the previous two years, the Lakers had become the most powerful team in the league and had won the NBA crown the previous season. The Lakers finished off the Spurs in four straight games, bringing San Antonio's season to a disappointing close.

Talking and Teaching

The Spurs were forced to make some adjustments the following season (2001-02). David Robinson was burdened by injuries and struggled with his performance. This put more pressure on Duncan, both as a player and as the team's leader. He responded to both challenges. Spurs forward Malik Rose remarked that "this season [Duncan's] always talking, teaching, communicating. He's always trying to get us pumped up." Duncan also had one of his best years as a performer, scoring an amazing 2,089 points and hauling down 1,042 rebounds.

As the team entered the playoffs, Robinson was out of the lineup with a strained back. Then, in the midst of the Spurs' first-round series against Seattle, Duncan faced a new challenge. His father died at age 71, after battling cancer for several years. Duncan flew to St. Croix to be with his family. This caused him to miss one playoff game — a game that the Spurs lost. Upon his return, however, they won the final game of the series to advance to the next round. There, the defending champion Lakers awaited them once again. The teams split the first two games, but then Los Angeles took control. The Lakers finished off the Spurs, then went on to claim their third championship. Duncan's great season hadn't gone unnoticed, however. He was named the NBA's most valuable player in 2002.

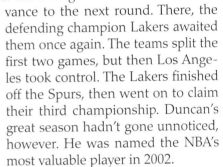

"Dave has taught me a lot about being a being a leader, being a winner, and about doing things the right way, with some dignity," Duncan said of his friend and teammate. "I have been very fortunate to have been able to play with him from the beginning."

The Admiral's Last Voyage

David Robinson announced that the 2002-03 season would be his last. After a long and distinguished career, the injuries were catching up with him. Still, he was expected to be a valuable asset for the Spurs in his final year, and he had certainly been an influence on Duncan's development as a professional player. "Dave has taught me a lot about being a being a leader, being a winner, and about doing things the right way, with some dignity," Duncan said of his friend and teammate. "I have been very fortunate to have been able to play with him from the beginning."

To make the Admiral's last voyage a memorable one, the Spurs played some great basketball. They finished the regular season with 60 wins, tying Dallas for the best record in the league. In the playoffs, the Spurs dispatched the Phoenix Suns, then squared off against the Lakers once more. This time, things were different. With the series even at two games apiece, Duncan scored 27 points in Game Five to put San Antonio up three games to two. In Game Six he was even better, scoring 37. The Spurs sent the

*Robinson and Duncan pause for a hug in the closing minutes of the
Spurs 88-77 win over the New Jersey Nets, June 2003.*

Lakers packing and moved on to the Western Conference Finals, where
they beat the Dallas Mavericks four games to two.

That brought the team to the NBA Finals, where their opponents were
the New Jersey Nets. It was a tough defensive series marked by low
scores and missed shots. While most of the other players struggled to put
points on the board, Duncan was as consistent as usual: he averaged 24.2
points a game. The Spurs battled to a three-games-to-two advantage in
the series. With a win in Game Six, they could become champions, but the
game was a tough one. They found themselves trailing by nine points
with only nine minutes to go. Then, in a thrilling rally, they scored 14
unanswered points and put the Nets away. Duncan had his second NBA
Championship in five years and his second series MVP award. Also, for

the second year in a row he was voted the most valuable player in the NBA. Yet another honor came in December 2003, when Duncan and David Robinson were named Sportsmen of the Year by *Sports Illustrated*.

Going for Gold

Following the 2002-03 season, Duncan was again eligible to become a free agent. This time, however, there was less indecision about staying with the Spurs. He inked a seven-year deal with San Antonio worth $122 million. With his pro future settled, Duncan could concentrate on playing basketball on a different level: he joined Team USA at a qualifying tournament in Puerto Rico, where the team earned the right to participate in the 2004 Olympics. Barring another injury, Duncan will get his shot at a gold medal at the summer games in Athens.

———  ———

If Duncan bragged about his abilities more, some say, he could be a bigger star. Duncan refuses to play that part. "Everything I do is basic, and that doesn't sell," he claimed. "I don't have the icing. My icing is, I just want to win."

——— **"** ———

Whether or not he wins gold, Duncan is recognized as one of the top players in the NBA and has even earned comparisons to such legends as Michael Jordan. Many sports writers have suggested that he may be too quiet for his own good. If he bragged about his abilities more, some say, he could be a bigger star. Duncan refuses to play that part. "Everything I do is basic, and that doesn't sell," he claimed. "I don't have the icing. My icing is, I just want to win."

MARRIAGE AND FAMILY

Duncan married his longtime girlfriend Amy Sherrill on July 21, 2001. The two had met when they were students at Wake Forest, where Sherrill had majored in health and exercise sciences. They have two Labrador retrievers, Zen and Shadoe, and a cockapoo named Nicole.

HOBBIES AND OTHER INTERESTS

Duncan has been a video-game fanatic for many years. He also likes to watch movies and surf the Internet. Another of his hobbies is collecting knives and swords. He's especially proud of the Japanese samurai sword that he owns. Both Duncan and his wife, Amy, spend a lot of time raising

money for charities. Some of this work is carried out through the Tim Duncan Foundation, an organization that provides funding to non-profit groups in education, health, and youth sports. Amy serves as the foundation's executive vice president. They also raise money to fight against the two diseases that claimed Duncan's parents — breast cancer and prostrate cancer. He and Amy host a celebrity-bowling event each year with the proceeds going to a variety of cancer-related causes.

HONORS AND AWARDS

NCAA Defensive Player of the Year: 1994-97
NABC National Defensive Player of the Year: 1995-1997

College Basketball Player of the Year: 1996-97
Associated Press All America First Team: 1997
Associated Press National Player of the Year: 1997
John R. Wooden Award for Outstanding College Basketball Player in the
    United States (Los Angeles Athletic Club): 1997
Naismith Basketball Award for Men's College Player of the Year (Atlanta
    Tipoff Club): 1997
National Association of Basketball Coaches National Player of the Year:
    1997
U.S. Basketball Writers National Player of the Year: 1997
All NBA First Team: 1998-2003
NBA All-Rookie First Team: 1998
NBA Schick Rookie of the Year: 1998
NBA All Star: 1998, 2000-2003
Sporting News Rookie of the Year: 1998
NBA All-Defensive First Team: 1999-2003
NBA Finals Most Valuable Player: 1999, 2003
NBA All-Star Game Co-Most Valuable Player: 2000
NBA Most Valuable Player: 2002, 2003
IBM Award: 2002, for all-around contribution to team's success
Basketball Digest Player of the Year: 2001-2002
Sporting News Player of the Year: 2001-2002 and 2002-2003.
Sports Illustrated Sportsman of the Year: 2003 (co-winner with David
    Robinson)
USA Basketball Male Athlete of the Year: 2003

FURTHER READING

Books

Byman, Jeremy. *Great Athletes: Tim Duncan,* 2000
Contemporary Black Biography, Vol. 20, 1998
Sports Stars, Series 5, 1999
Stewart, Mark. *Tim Duncan: Tower of Power,* 1999
Who's Who among African Americans, 2003

Periodicals

Basketball Digest, Summer 2002, p.26
Current Biography Yearbook, 1999
Los Angeles Times, Dec. 6, 1995, p.C1; Nov. 13, 1997, p.C1
New York Times, June 25, 1996, p.B15; Mar. 31, 1998, p.C2; June 20, 1999,
    sec. 8, p.3

Philadelphia Inquirer, Mar. 22, 1995, p.D1
Sport, July 1997, p.34; Mar. 1999, p.34; Oct. 1999, p.86
Sporting News, June 23, 2003, p.10; Nov. 10, 2003, p.20
Sports Illustrated, Nov. 27, 1995, p.78; Feb. 17, 1997, p.28; Nov. 24, 1997,
    p.58; May 31, 1999, p.48; July 7, 1999, p.77; May 20, 2002, p.42; Dec. 15,
    2003, pp.58 and 66
USA Today, Jan. 29, 2003, p.C1
Washington Post, Jan. 13, 1996, p.F1

Online Databases

Biography Resource Center Online, 2004, articles from *Contemporary Black Biography*, 1998; *Sports Stars*, 1999; and *Who's Who among African Americans*, 2003

ADDRESS

Tim Duncan
San Antonio Spurs
One SBC Center
San Antonio, TX 78219

WORLD WIDE WEB SITES

http://www.nba.com
http://www.slamduncan.com

Shirin Ebadi 1947-

Iranian Lawyer and Human Rights Advocate
Winner of the 2003 Nobel Peace Prize

BIRTH

Shirin Ebadi (pronounced shih-REEN eh-BAH-dee) was born
in 1947 in the town of Hamadan, 180 miles southwest of Tehran, the capital of Iran. Her mother was Minu (sometimes
spelled Mino or Minoo) Yamini (also listed as Amidi), and her
father was Muhammad-Ali Ebadi, a lawyer and law professor.
She has a brother named Jafar. Ebadi grew up speaking the

Farsi language, also known as Persian, which is written in the Arabic alphabet. When words are translated from Farsi to English, there can be several different spellings.

BACKGROUND ON IRAN

Ebadi was certainly affected by the many changes her country experienced throughout the 1900s. Once known as Persia, Iran has long been an important and influential part of the Middle East. The discovery of the country's vast oil reserves in the early 1900s made it even more important. World powers such as Russia, Great Britain, and the United States all kept a close eye on events in Iran. All of them wanted to have access to its rich resources.

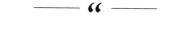

Another important factor in Iran's history is that it is an Islamic country—most people are Muslims who follow the religion of Islam. Up until the early 1900s, Muslim religious figures, or clerics, were very powerful because they administered the laws of the country. In fact, Ebadi's grandfather was a religious judge.

Historically, women faced many restrictions in Iran. For instance, they did not leave their homes very often, and when they did, they were expected to keep their faces covered with a veil. Very few women got an education or held jobs outside the home. These restrictions were found in many countries in the Islamic world in the early 1900s and even today.

The Pahlavis and Modern Iran

This system changed in the 1920s, after Reza Shah Pahlavi took control of the country in a military coup. This began the long reign of the Pahlavi

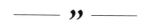

dynasty. Reza Shah himself ruled Iran until 1941, and his son, Muhammad Reza Shah Pahlavi, ruled from 1941 to 1979. The Pahlavis introduced modern, Western-style laws and reduced the influence of the Muslim clerics in the areas of education and legal proceedings. Iran remained an Islamic country, but religious figures had less say in governmental and social policy.

The Pahlavis made other changes, as well. Previously, women had faced many restrictions. For instance, they did not leave their homes very often, and when they did, they were expected to keep their faces covered with a veil. Very few women got an education or held jobs outside the home. These restrictions were found in many countries in the Islamic world in the

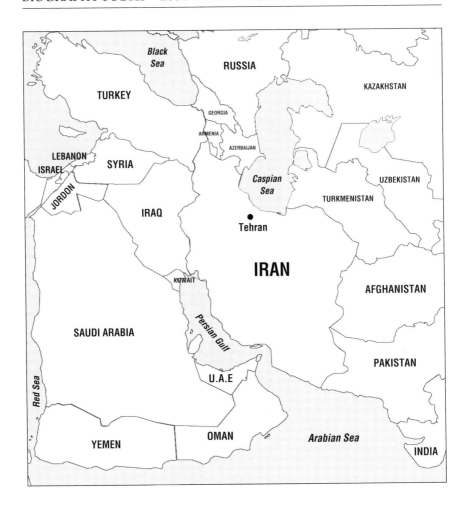

early 1900s, and some nations still observe these practices today. Some Muslims—though certainly not all of them—believe that women should not have a large public role in society. They interpret certain passages in the Koran (the Muslim holy book) to mean that women should be subservient to men and that women should keep their faces and bodies well covered when away from home.

The Pahlavis discouraged these practices. Under their rule, girls were allowed to attend school and women were allowed more freedom in where they went and what they wore. This made Iran one of the most progressive countries in the Middle East. While the Pahlavis introduced some social freedoms, they did not promote political freedom. Both father and son were absolute rulers who crushed political dissent.

EBADI'S YOUTH

Under the Shah, Ebadi's father, Muhammad-Ali Ebadi, became a well-respected figure in Iran's modernized legal system. He wrote a famous textbook on commercial law that is still in print. At the time of Shirin's birth, the family lived in Hamadan, but when she was six months old, they moved to Tehran, the capital and largest city in Iran.

In the early 1960s, when Ebadi was a teenager, new laws were passed that gave women even more freedom. They won the right to vote and to hold political office, and they gained greater rights in attaining divorces (though still less than those granted to men). It also became more common for women to drive cars and hold jobs. While such freedoms are taken for granted in many countries, they are rare in parts of the Islamic world. Even today, such countries as Saudi Arabia enforce strict rules that prevent women from traveling by themselves or even speaking with a man to whom they are not related.

In the early 1960s, when Ebadi was a teenager, new laws were passed that gave women more freedom. They won the right to vote and to hold political office, and they gained greater rights in attaining divorces.

EDUCATION

The 1960s were also a time when large numbers of Iranian women began attending universities. When she was old enough, Ebadi joined them. She enrolled at the University of Tehran and studied law, following in her father's footsteps. She graduated with her degree in 1971.

CAREER HIGHLIGHTS

Becoming a Judge

After finishing school, Ebadi quickly became an important figure in the legal system. In 1975, just four years after leaving the university, she became the first female judge in Iran. Her official title was President of the City Court of Tehran. Other women soon assumed important judicial positions throughout the country. With such moves, the government of Muhammad Reza Shah Pahlavi showed that it was still dedicated to expanding the rights of women.

But by the late 1970s, the Shah's government was in trouble. Many Iranians were opposed to the lack of political freedom. In addition, conservative religious figures resented the liberal social reforms instituted by the Pahlavis. In late 1978, the events began to unfold that became known as the Iranian Revolution. Widespread demonstrations, strikes, and riots took place throughout the country. Unable to restore order, the Shah left the country in January 1979. A Muslim opposition leader, Ayatollah Ruhollah Khomeini, returned to Iran and played a key role in establishing a new government. In April 1979, the Islamic Republic of Iran was established.

From Judge to Clerk

In the beginning, Ebadi supported the revolution. She joined the strike committee of the Ministry of Justice and hoped the nation's new government would make Iran a place of greater political and legal freedoms. But that was not to be. The new government became dominated by Muslims who favored a very conservative form of Islamic belief. Sometimes known as "hard-liners," these figures favored more power for religious clerics. They also set about repealing some of the country's progressive reforms — especially those that granted more freedom for women.

Ebadi was soon notified that she could no longer be a judge. She was told that women were too emotional to be deciding legal cases. She was instead given the lowly rank of legal assistant and forced to perform clerical duties at the Ministry of Justice. She later compared this experience to that of making "the president of a university into a janitor."

Over the next few years, the government enacted more legal and social changes that fit its conservative vision. In seeking to undo some of the reforms of the pre-revolutionary period, the powerful religious clerics passed a number of laws that gave men certain privileges in the legal system. The hard-liners also turned against foreign powers that had supported the Shah, especially the United States. The government's anti-American sentiment inspired a group of radical Iranian students to seize the U.S. embassy in Tehran in late 1979. They took 52 Americans as hostages and held them for more than a year.

A Proud Iranian

Many Iranians who did not agree with the conservative reforms chose to leave the country. Ebadi was not happy with being removed as judge, and she did not like the loss of political and social freedoms then taking place. Still, she decided to remain in Iran. As she explained in an article in *The Times* (London, England), "I'm proud to be Iranian and I'll live in my country as long as I can."

After finishing school, Ebadi quickly became an important figure in the legal system. In 1975, just four years after leaving the university, she became the first female judge in Iran. Her official title was President of the City Court of Tehran.

Ebadi continued to work at the Ministry of Justice until 1984, when she was given the opportunity to take an early retirement. She then joined a law firm, but her involvement in legal cases could only go so far: at that time, women lawyers were prevented from performing many duties. Still, she continued to work on legal issues: she began teaching law at Tehran University and served as a consultant to businesses.

In the early 1990s, women were again allowed to work as fully practicing lawyers, so Ebadi opened her own law office. This allowed her to use her legal skills to help those she felt were being mistreated by the Iranian justice system. She soon became well known for defending the rights of women and children. Because many of her clients were poor, she often received no pay for her work.

Fighting the System

Several of Ebadi's cases focused public attention on laws that had been enacted since the 1979 revolution. For instance, the Iranian legal code considers the life of a male to be twice as valuable as the life of a female. Also, in many cases the divorce laws automatically give the father custody of children, regardless of other circumstances. There is even an Iranian law that states that a father can't be convicted of murdering his children. Ebadi's court battles didn't succeed in changing these laws, but they did make Iranians more aware of the extreme measures sponsored by the hard-liners. "All these laws were written after the 1979 revolution," she explained. The conservatives who wrote the laws intended to promote Islamic values, but Ebadi believes that they were misguided. "The problem is that our laws come from a wrong interpretation of Islam," she said.

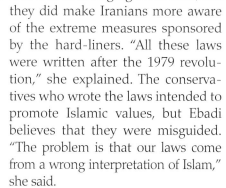

The Iranian legal code includes many laws that place a higher value on men than on women. "All these laws were written after the 1979 revolution," she explained. The conservatives who wrote the laws intended to promote Islamic values, but Ebadi believes that they were misguided. "The problem is that our laws come from a wrong interpretation of Islam," she said.

In addition to her court cases, Ebadi established the Society for the Protection of the Rights of the Child, an organization that pursues a range of child-welfare issues. She also wrote books. Some focused attention on the mistreatment of children; others addressed Iran's record on human rights. Like many others around the world, Ebadi believes that there are certain rights that every human is entitled to, including democracy, equal treatment under the law, and freedom of speech.

Also, she feels that religion—including her own Islamic faith—should not be used as a reason to deny basic human rights. She has often stated her belief that "there is no difference between Islam and human rights." By this she means that one can faithfully follow the Muslim religion and still uphold such ideals as equal rights. In her opinion, those Muslims that take a more extreme view—claiming men are superior to women, for instance—are misreading the Koran.

Ebadi is shown speaking below portraits of Iran's leaders (left to right): Mohammad Khatami, President of Iran; Ayatollah Ruhollah Khomeini, the late founder of the Islamic Republic of Iran; and his successor, Ayatollah Ali Khamenei, Supreme Leader of Iran.

Deadly Politics

By the late 1990s it appeared that a growing number of Iranians opposed the hard-liners. In 1997, Mohammad Khatami was elected president. Though he is a Muslim cleric, Khatami is part of the reform movement in Iran. The reformers seek to undo the more extreme laws put in place by the conservatives. In winning his victory, Khatami received a lot of votes from women, many of whom felt that they were being treated unfairly by the country's laws. As Ebadi often points out, women play a very important role in Iranian society. More women than men attend Iranian universities, and women account for three out of every ten workers in the country. Khatami and other reform-minded politicians have continued to receive a lot of support from Iranian voters. The majority of elected officials in Iran's parliament are reformers.

Yet the reformers have not had a lot of success in changing things in Iran. This is because the Iranian political system is not completely controlled by elected officials. There are many powerful figures who are not chosen by voters, and many of them are hard-line conservatives. The most powerful is Ayatollah Ali Khamenei, the country's Supreme Leader. In addition, con-

Ebadi is shown here with a representation of the scales of justice.

servatives exert a lot of control over the country's justice system and the powerful Guardians Council. After President Khatami's election, the struggle between the conservatives and the reformers intensified. The battle soon turned deadly.

In 1998, a number of reformers were beaten, kidnaped, and killed by conservative vigilante groups. Ebadi became involved in the case of a husband and wife who had been stabbed to death in their home. Both were outspoken critics of the hard-liners. While conducting her investigation, she was contacted by two men who said they had been members of a vigilante group. More importantly, the men said that the attacks had been ordered by hard-line politicians. This was startling news because it linked the attack to conservative members of the Iranian government. Ebadi videotaped the men's confessions, then gave the tape to the government. Later, the tape was widely distributed in Iran and caused a political scandal that forced a high-ranking government official to resign.

In 1999 the political turmoil led to student riots in which several people were killed. Again, Ebadi got involved. She represented the family of one of the protestors who died in the riots and called for a thorough investigation of events surrounding the disturbances.

Dangerous Work

Ebadi soon learned that her work could get her in trouble. In 2000, she was charged with insulting public officials. This accusation was caused by her involvement in the videotaped confessions of the vigilantes. Ebadi denied that she had done anything wrong, but she was arrested and held in Evin Prison in Tehran. Evin Prison is infamous because many of those who are jailed for opposing the Iranian government are held there. Some have died under mysterious circumstances while in custody. Ebadi was placed in solitary confinement, and she found the conditions very difficult. She suffered from extreme back pain while locked up but did her best not to show her jailers any weakness. "I try not to complain," she later wrote. After three weeks, Ebadi was released from the prison, but she still had to face the charges in court. She was convicted in a closed hearing and was banned from practicing law for five years. This sentence was later suspended.

Ebadi's jail term and temporary ban showed that her work carried some real risks. But there was an even larger danger: someone might try to kill her. This became very clear when her name appeared on a list of political enemies compiled by the Iranian Intelligence Ministry. It showed that some members of the government considered her a serious threat. Despite the danger, Ebadi continued her work. "Any person who pursues human rights in Iran must live with fear," she said. "It comes to you like hunger, you don't have a choice. But I have learned [to] not let it interfere with my work." Her husband, quoted in *Time*, confirmed that she was aware of the threats: "She was worried, but she didn't let that stop her. . . . She is very brave."

> "
>
> *"Any person who pursues human rights in Iran must live with fear," Ebadi said. "It comes to you like hunger, you don't have a choice. But I have learned not [to] let it interfere with my work."* Her husband, quoted in **Time**, *confirmed that she was aware of the threats: "She was worried, but she didn't let that stop her. . . . She is very brave."*
>
> "

In the early 2000s, Ebadi found new ways to further the cause of human rights. She joined with other activists to establish the Center for the Defense of Human Rights. The organization provides legal help for families of journalists and students who had been imprisoned for speaking out against the government. She also continued to make public speeches and to attend human-rights conferences. In October 2003 she went to Paris, France, to attend a conference on Iranian films and human rights. When it was over, she prepared to return to Iran. But before she left she received a telephone call with some big news.

The Nobel Peace Prize

The caller informed Ebadi that she had won the Nobel Peace Prize. "I'm shocked," she said shortly after receiving the news. Later, in an interview with Amir Taheri in the *Weekly Standard*, she stated that "I did not even know my name had been put forward for a Nobel." Among the most prestigious awards in the world, the Nobel Prizes are awarded annually in a number of fields, including economics, literature, physics, chemistry, and physiology or medicine. The Peace Prize is awarded to a person or persons who has made a significant contribution to world peace, usually through politics or diplomacy. Ebadi's win was a surprise to many observers — Pope John Paul II had been considered the most likely person to win the prize in 2003. In the official announcement, the Nobel Committee (based in Norway) commended Ebadi:

> As a lawyer, judge, lecturer, writer, and activist, she has spoken out clearly and strongly in her country, Iran, and far beyond its borders. She has stood up as a sound professional, a courageous person, and has never heeded the threats to her own safety. . . . . Ebadi is a conscious Moslem. She sees no conflict between Islam and fundamental human rights. It is important to her that the dialogue between the different cultures and religions of the world should take as its point of departure their shared values. It is a pleasure for the Norwegian Nobel Committee to award the Peace Prize to a woman who is part of the Moslem world, and of whom that world can be proud — along with all who fight for human rights wherever they live.

———— **"** ————

"It's not easy to be a woman today in Iran, because they have laws that are against the rights of women. . . . This prize gives me the energy to continue my fight." In an interview with Norwegian television reporters, Ebadi called the award "very good for human rights in Iran, especially for children's rights in Iran. I hope I can be useful."

———— **"** ————

In addition to giving Ebadi worldwide acclaim, the prize offered money: the Nobel committee awarded her $1.3 million, which will be a big help in furthering her work. She was the first Iranian and only the 11th woman to receive the prize in its 102-year history. She was also the first woman from the Muslim world to win this prestigious award.

After hearing the news, Ebadi delayed her return to Iran and remained in Paris so that she could field questions from reporters. At her first press conference she said "it's not easy to be a woman today in Iran, because they have laws that are against the rights of women. . . . This prize gives me the energy to continue my fight." In an interview with Norwegian television reporters, she called the award "very good for human rights in Iran, especially for children's rights in Iran. I hope I can be useful."

A Controversial Winner

The Paris press conference became a source of controversy. In Iran, when women appear in public they are forced to wear a *roosari*, a type of head covering. But at the Paris press conference, Ebadi was bareheaded. Upon seeing the tape, conservative observers in Iran complained that she wasn't a devout Muslim. Ebadi later explained that she obeys the laws of Iran while in Iran but not elsewhere. In the *Weekly Standard* interview, she commented that "instead of telling girls to cover their hair, we should teach them to use their heads."

Ebadi poses with her Nobel Peace Prize diploma.

Iranian hard-liners had more to complain about. They were unhappy that one of their most vocal critics had received such a prestigious award, so they argued that the Nobel was made for "political" reasons. They suggested that the Norwegian judges had chosen Ebadi because the Europeans wanted to embarrass Iran's devout Muslim leaders. Such reaction from Iranian conservatives was expected, but observers were more surprised when President Khatami, a moderate politician, also downplayed the award. "The Nobel Peace Prize is not very important," the president told a journalist, "the ones that count are the scientific and literary prizes." Khatami also warned Ebadi that she shouldn't let anyone "exploit her success." These comments were viewed as proof that the president was afraid to congratulate Ebadi for fear of angering the conservatives.

A Hero's Welcome

Perhaps the president wasn't excited about Ebadi's prize, but other Iranians certainly were. When she flew back to Tehran a few days after the award was announced, thousands of supporters greeted her at the airport. The majority of them were women, and many of them wore white *roosaris* in opposition to the black scarves preferred by the authorities. "This prize

Ebadi gives her Nobel Peace Prize lecture, 2003.

is not only for me, but for all those in favor of peace, democracy, human rights, and legality," Ebadi told the crowd. At a press conference a short time later, she said that the Nobel "put a heavy burden on my shoulders," but she had her own warning for those that oppose her: "I will not reduce my activities, I will increase them."

Ebadi also had a message for foreign governments that seek changes in Iran. While she is in favor of reforming her country's government, she insists that Iranians direct the changes. "The fight for human rights is conducted in Iran by the Iranian people, and we are against any foreign intervention in Iran." Her comments were aimed primarily at the United States, which had invaded neighboring Iraq in March 2003. Some people believe that the U.S. will put more political pressure on Iran and may even threaten military force. That is something that Ebadi clearly opposes. "America should not interfere in the domestic affairs of any country, including Iran," she said in an interview. "America should be aware that human rights cannot be exported with bombs and bullets."

> *"America should not interfere in the domestic affairs of any country, including Iran," Ebadi said in an interview. "America should be aware that human rights cannot be exported with bombs and bullets."*

Ebadi is also against violence by Iranians, including violent protests against the government. "There can be no place for disturbances or rioting or destruction," she said. Instead, she seeks peaceful change. Some of her supporters felt that the best way to achieve such a change was to make Ebadi into a politician. They began urging her to seek public office, telling her that she now had enough prestige to lead an opposition political party. Ebadi refused. "I never want to be or will be part of government," she said. "I will always be what I have been — a defender and spokesperson for the weak."

New Challenges

In early November 2003, Ebadi announced that she would assist in a new court case. It involves the death of Zahra Kazemi, a Canadian photojournalist of Iranian descent. Kazemi had gone to Tehran to work on a story about the Iranian justice system. She was arrested for taking photographs outside Evin Prison and then died from a blow to the head while in custody. Her family is seeking to punish those responsible.

Ebadi celebrates with her daughter, Narguess Tavassolian, who is a law student in Tehran.

In early 2004, as the country prepared for parliamentary elections, a new political controversy erupted. Hard-line government officials banned thousands of reform candidates who were seeking office, declaring them unsuitable because they did not respect Islam and the Iranian constitution. With the reformers off the ballot, the conservatives won many seats and became the majority party in Parliament. Many Iranians believed that banning reform candidates was unfair. Ebadi was one of many who protested the action by refusing to take part in the voting. "Human rights don't have any meaning without democracy," she said. "Democracy is also based on free elections. And free elections means you can vote for anyone you want to."

Ebadi has received death threats since winning the Nobel, and bodyguards have been assigned to help protect her. Still, she remains dedicated to her mission. She believes that new reforms will take place in Iran because the country is ready for them. "In every society there comes a time when people want to be free," she said in the *Sunday Times* (London). "That time has come in Iran." She feels her Nobel Prize will help inspire others who seek change. "The prize will give more confidence to people who support democracy and human rights. More people will want to join the struggle. And whenever a majority demands change, change will happen."

MARRIAGE AND FAMILY

Ebadi is married to Javed Tavassolian, an electrical engineer. She has two daughters: Negar, who is doing post-graduate work in engineering in Montreal, Canada, and Narguess, who is studying law in Tehran.

WRITINGS

The Rights of the Child: A Study of the Legal Aspects of Children's Rights in Iran, 1994 (nonfiction)
History and Documentation of Human Rights in Iran, 2000 (nonfiction)

—— **"** ——

"The prize will give more confidence to people who support democracy and human rights. More people will want to join the struggle. And whenever a majority demands change, change will happen."

—— **"** ——

HONORS AND AWARDS

Human Rights Watch Award: 1996
Rafto Prize (Thorolf Rafto Foundation for Human Rights): 2001
Nobel Peace Prize: 2003, "for her efforts for democracy and human rights"

FURTHER READING

Periodicals

Baltimore Sun, Jan. 28, 1998, p.A1
Christian Science Monitor, Oct. 15, 1999, p.1; Oct. 17, 2003, p.11; Dec. 12, 2003, p.1
Guardian (London), Oct. 11, 2003, p.21; Oct. 13, 2003, p.17; Oct. 15, 2003, p.16
Independent (London), Dec. 24, 1997, p.8; Oct. 11, 2003, p.5
International Herald Tribune (Paris), Oct. 11, 2003, pp.1 and 7
Maclean's, Nov. 17, 2003, p.81
New York Times, Oct. 11, 2003, pp.A1 and A6; Dec. 11, 2003, p.A20
Time, Oct. 20, 2003, p.39
The Times (London), Oct. 11, 2003, pp.7 and 29
San Francisco Chronicle, Oct. 29, 2003, p.A2
Seattle Times, Dec. 1, 1996, p.A25
Sunday Times (London), Oct. 19, 2003, p.7
Washington Post, Nov. 22, 1996, p.A42
Weekly Standard, Nov. 3, 2003, p.22

Other

60 Minutes, "Iran versus Iran," May 10, 1998 (transcript of television broadcast)

All Things Considered, "Hope That the Awarding of the Nobel Peace Prize to an Iranian Human Rights Activist Will Revitalize the Reform Movement Inside the Country," Nov. 5, 2003 (transcript of radio broadcast)

ADDRESS

Shirin Ebadi
Iranian Children's Rights Society
PMB #220
27881 La Paz, Suite G.
Laguna Niguel, CA 92677

Shirin Ebadi
Law Firm of Shirin Ebadi
No. 19 Street 57
Seied Jamal eldin Asad Abadi Ave.
Tehran 14349, Iran

WORLD WIDE WEB SITE

http://www.nobel.se

Carla Hayden 1952-

American Librarian
Director of the Enoch Pratt Free Library in Baltimore
and Former President of the American Library
Association

BIRTH

Carla Hayden was born in Tallahassee, Florida, on August 10,
1952. Her parents were Bruce Hayden, Jr., and Colleen (Dowl-
ing) Hayden. Her father played the violin and taught music,
while her mother played piano and later worked for the city of
Chicago.

YOUTH

Carla Hayden is a private person who rarely talks about her childhood. She was born in Tallahassee while her father was teaching at Florida A&M University, but the family soon moved to New York City so he could play with the jazz musician Cannonball Adderly. Since both of her parents were musicians, Carla grew up enjoying music. "I have fond memories of sitting under a piano reading books while my parents practiced," she recalled.

After her parents divorced, Carla moved with her mother to Chicago, where she spent most of her youth. She loved to read as a child, especially the Nancy Drew mystery series and historical romances. Her favorite book was *Bright April,* by Marguerite DeAngeli, which tells the story of a young African-American girl's first encounter with racism in her local Brownie troop. "I love it to this day," she stated. Thanks to her love of books, Carla felt drawn to the library from an early age. "I still remember the first time my mother took me to a library," she noted. "There was something magical about those books." Although the idea of becoming a librarian appealed to her, she remembered hearing her grandmother say that it could not possibly be a very exciting career choice.

> ――― " ―――
>
> *"I still remember the first time my mother took me to a library,"* Hayden noted. *"There was something magical about those books."*
>
> ――― " ―――

EDUCATION AND FIRST JOBS

Hayden attended Roosevelt University in Chicago. After graduating with a bachelor of arts degree in 1973, she went to work as a children's librarian in the Chicago Public Library. She was inspired by one of her colleagues there, a woman who "wore jeans, had frizzy hair, and got down on the floor to talk with kids." This woman's hands-on approach to the job convinced Hayden to build a career as a librarian. She continued her education at the University of Chicago's Graduate Library School, earning a master's degree in library science in 1977. Two years later, she was promoted to young adult services coordinator at the Chicago Public Library.

In 1982 Hayden left her job to become library services coordinator at Chicago's Museum of Science and Industry. She also began working on her Ph.D. (doctorate) in Library Science at the University of Chicago. Upon earning her doctorate in 1987, she left her job at the museum to teach at the University of Pittsburgh's School of Library and Information Science. In May 1991 she returned to the Chicago Public Library as its first deputy commissioner and chief librarian — the library's second-highest position.

CAREER HIGHLIGHTS

Although Hayden was happy to be back working at her hometown library, she began to feel restless after spending a year as second-in-command. The library's top position was open, but the board of trustees could not seem to decide on a candidate to fill the job. Meanwhile, Hayden heard about another interesting job opening at the Enoch Pratt Free Library in Baltimore, Maryland. The Enoch Pratt was the first public library system to be established in the United States, but it had fallen on hard times due to budget cutbacks and declining circulation at many of its branches. Although Hayden had been raised and educated in Chicago, the challenge of saving an old and once-glorious library was one she could not pass up. "It was a tough decision," Hayden recalled, "but Baltimore had a real appeal to me."

Just as the board of trustees at Enoch Pratt was celebrating Hayden's decision to accept the job, Chicago Mayor Richard Daley announced that she had been appointed to the top job at the Chicago Public Library. Daley had heard that Hayden was considering a job elsewhere. He thought that if he acted quickly enough and gave her the highly paid job she had been waiting for, he could persuade her to stay. Unfortunately, Daley's announcement was released to the press without being cleared by Hayden, resulting in an embarrassing mix-up. The Chicago offer also came too late to change her mind. Hayden accepted the Enoch Pratt job and moved to Baltimore in July 1993.

A Library with a History

The Enoch Pratt Free Library was established in 1882 by Enoch Pratt, a young man from Massachusetts who had come to Baltimore as an iron merchant. Pratt soon formed his own company, E. Pratt & Bros., which became a major force in the railroad and steamboating industries as well as other business ventures. By the time he was ready to retire, Pratt was a very wealthy man who wanted to do something for the city that had provided him with so many opportunities.

Pratt gave Baltimore money to establish a central library with four branches scattered throughout the city. "My library," he said, "shall be for all, rich and poor, without distinction of race or color." Pratt made it clear that although the library system would be owned by the city of Baltimore, its operation would be guided by a board of trustees separate from city government. The

Throughout her career as a librarian, Hayden has emphasized the importance of providing resources for students.

result became a model for city public libraries throughout America. It even inspired Pittsburgh industrialist Andrew Carnegie to begin his famous library-building program in the early 20th century.

The Enoch Pratt Free Library had flourished for more than 100 years, but by the time Hayden took over it was facing some serious problems. For example, some of the 28 branch libraries were housed in 19th-century buildings that needed expensive repairs. In addition, a 30 percent decline in Baltimore's population meant that the branches in several city neighborhoods did not see much use. Finally, the city of Baltimore had not increased its contribution to the library's budget in a number of years.

Immediately after taking the director position, Hayden came up with a plan to improve the library's financial situation. She persuaded the city to increase the library's budget, and she also started raising money from grants and private sources. But Hayden knew that she would also have to make some unpopular changes. She wanted the libraries to be open on Saturdays—something that staff members often resisted. In order to afford this change, she closed the branches during "quiet times" when not many people used them. Even more controversial was her decision to close several of the branches so that the money saved could be put toward making improvements elsewhere.

According to former American Library Association President Peggy Sullivan, closing branch libraries is normally considered "the quickest way for a director to ruin his or her career." As expected, many people in Baltimore were upset about Hayden's actions, even though she emphasized that her decisions on which branches to close were made on the basis of their location, number of visitors, and the condition of their buildings. Some critics also complained that closing the branch libraries took away a "safe haven" for many of the city's children. Hayden countered some of this criticism by pointing out that the money saved would enable her to build four large regional libraries and expand the central library to make its collections more accessible to the public.

Turning the Library into a Community Resource

Once she had the library system's financial problems under control, Hayden wasted no time in reorganizing it and instituting several long-overdue changes. She created an Information Access Division to run "Sailor," an electronic network that serves public libraries and their users throughout the state of Maryland. Sailor proved extremely popular and eventually received about 30,000 hits per day. Hayden also turned the library into the city of Baltimore's electronic information provider, setting up electronic kiosks in grocery stores and malls that people could use to gain access to the library's collections.

Hayden also instituted several programs directly aimed at children and young adults. She implemented an electronic literacy program for the city's at-risk children and set up a multimedia center to provide homework as-

Hayden introduced a variety of programs for children after taking the reins at Baltimore's Enoch Pratt Free Library.

sistance, computer training, and college counseling to middle and high school students. She also replaced the library's bookmobile, which spent most of its time in the shop being repaired, with an entire fleet of vehicles that could bring books and library services to summer camps, recreation centers, day care facilities, and apartment complexes for the elderly.

Not all of Hayden's ideas have been high-tech in nature, however. For example, she used an innovative idea to eliminate security concerns at the central library. Some patrons felt uncomfortable about dropping their children off at the library because there was a soup kitchen serving homeless people across the street. Remembering Enoch Pratt's original vision of a library that is open to everyone, Hayden solved the security problem by instituting a "Coffee for Cops" program, in which local police officers could drop by any time and use a special area of the library as their "office" when they were on patrol. Parents and their children felt much more comfortable about using the library when they routinely saw police officers sitting in the facility filling out paperwork.

President of the ALA

Hayden had been an active member of the American Library Association (ALA) throughout her career. Founded in 1876, the ALA is a professional organization for librarians, with 65,000 members around the country. Her achievements as director of Enoch Pratt brought her a certain amount of renown in her field. In fact, her stature enabled her to win election as president of the ALA for 2003-2004. She became only the second African-American woman to hold the prestigious position.

Upon assuming the presidency of the ALA on June 24, 2003, Hayden said that one of her highest priorities would be to ensure equity of access in libraries. "Equity of access is not only one of the basic tenets of our profession but it encompasses all of our basic and pressing contemporary concerns as well," said Hayden. "We need to recommit ourselves to the ideal of providing equal access to everyone, anywhere, any time, and in any format, particularly those groups who are already underserved, such as residents of rural and urban America, minorities, senior citizens, and the handicapped."

— **"** —

"We need to recommit ourselves to the ideal of providing equal access to everyone, anywhere, any time, and in any format, particularly those groups who are already underserved, such as residents of rural and urban America, minorities, senior citizens, and the handicapped."

— **"** —

As ALA president, Hayden did not shy away from taking strong public stances on issues she thought were important. For example, she became a vocal critic of the Patriot Act, a piece of legislation passed by Congress following the terrorist attacks against the United States on September 11, 2001. The Patriot Act gave the federal government broad powers to investigate the activities of suspected terrorists. For example, it lowered the legal standards federal investigators needed to meet in order to monitor people's Internet use and cell phone conversations. The Patriot Act also allowed the U.S. government to force suspected terrorists to leave the country and to take control of money and property that might be used to finance terrorist activities.

Hayden and many fellow librarians objected to a specific provision of the Patriot Act — Section 215 — which granted federal investigators access to the library records of individual patrons. The law required libraries and bookstores to provide information about individuals' reading habits to government officials. But it also placed a gag order on librarians and booksellers, preventing them from publicly disclosing that they had been contacted under the Patriot Act. As the president of ALA, Hayden spoke out against the provisions of Section 215. She claimed that the law intruded on library patrons' right to privacy and prevented libraries from serving their intended function in American society. "Now, more than ever, libraries worldwide represent a calming sanctuary during tumultuous times and a place of opportunity and enjoyment," Hayden stated in *American Libraries* magazine. "Yet the unifying factor is the ability to inquire and to receive service without fear of reprisal and with a measure of privacy. When that ability is threatened, we have an obligation to question how intrusions into the basic rights of our patrons will inhibit their use and ultimately invade the public's right to know."

"Now, more than ever, libraries worldwide represent a calming sanctuary during tumultuous times and a place of opportunity and enjoyment," Hayden stated in American Libraries *magazine. "Yet the unifying factor is the ability to inquire and to receive service without fear of reprisal and with a measure of privacy. When that ability is threatened, we have an obligation to question how intrusions into the basic rights of our patrons will inhibit their use and ultimately invade the public's right to know."*

U.S. Attorney General John Ashcroft dismissed Hayden's criticism of the Patriot Act. He accused the ALA of exaggerating the government's interest in the library records of ordinary people. "The fact is, with just 11,000 FBI agents and over a billion visitors to America's libraries each year, the Department of Justice has neither the staffing, the time, nor the inclination to monitor the reading habits of Americans," he stated. Ashcroft also warned the ALA that their negative comments about Section 215 of the Patriot Act could trigger "baseless hysteria," a comment that angered many librarians. But he later called Hayden personally to reassure her that he would at least make public a report to Congress about how often library records were actually searched.

Another law that Hayden opposed was the Children's Internet Protection Act (CIPA). This law said that libraries that provided their patrons with

As president of the ALA, Hayden emphasized equity of access to library resources and the preservation of privacy rights.

Internet access were required to install filters designed to prevent schoolchildren from accessing pornography and other inappropriate information online. Such filters did not always work properly. For example, they were criticized for occasionally restricting access to information about legitimate research topics, like breast cancer. Still, libraries that did not install the filters stood to lose government funding.

Believing that such restrictions placed an unconstitutional limit on the freedom of speech, Hayden and the ALA took the case all the way to the U.S. Supreme Court. But the Court ruled against the ALA, saying that the law was constitutional as long as the filters could be disabled upon request by adult library users. Hayden was disappointed with the Supreme Court decision, which she worried "could result in ignorance about a life-threatening disease or leave teenagers with unanswered questions about their physical and mental development." She pointed out that disabling filters is both time-consuming and expensive, and that libraries that could afford to do without government assistance would probably decide not to install the filters in the first place.

Recent Achievements

In March 2004 the Enoch Pratt Free Library opened a $15 million, four-story annex—its first major expansion after closing one-fourth of its 28 branch libraries between 1997 and 2001. The new annex is designed to give the public more access to its special collections, which include materials relating to Baltimore newspaper essayist H.L. Mencken and an extensive African-American collection. On a separate floor is the Maryland Reading Room, where patrons can find 19th-century books, maps, postcards, and pamphlets about the state. The annex even contains a "cybercafe," which reflects the widespread trend toward relaxing rules against bringing food and drinks into libraries. "I want very much to be a part of the story of the Enoch Pratt Free Library," Hayden stated. "I only hope I'll know when it is time for me to get off the stage."

> "*While we face many challenges [as librarians], I see a profession that is progressively more vibrant and visible than at any time I can recall in my professional career,"* Hayden said. *"Libraries have become so high-profile and library workers and supporters so increasingly vocal that we are making waves across the nation."*

In July 2004 Hayden completed her one-year term as president of the ALA. She was succeeded by Carol A. Brey-Casiano, executive director of the El Paso (Texas) Public Library. Upon completing her term as president, Hayden stated that her year at the organization's helm had been an uplifting and inspiring one for her personally. "While we face many challenges [as librarians], I see a profession that is progressively more vibrant and visible than at any time I can recall in my professional career," she wrote in *American Libraries.* "Libraries have become so high-profile and library workers and supporters so increasingly vocal that we are making waves across the nation. During my college and university campus visits, I became reassured about the future due to the commitment and passion of library school students. . . . I sincerely appreciate the opportunity to serve the membership and represent the Association. My faith in our work has been strengthened and reinforced. I look forward to continuing our efforts to ensure equity for everyone @ the library."

HONORS AND AWARDS

Black Achievers Award (YMCA): 1984
Librarian of the Year (*Library Journal*): 1995

Hayden celebrates with Maryland Congressman Elijah E. Cummings after she received the 2003 Ms. *magazine Woman of the Year Award.*

Torch Bearer Award (Coalition of 100 Black Women): 1996
Andrew White Medal (Loyola College): 1997
President's Medal (Johns Hopkins University): 1998
Women of the Year (*Ms.* Magazine): 2003

FURTHER READING

Books

Notable Black American Women, 2002
Who's Who Among African-Americans, 2003

Periodicals

American Libraries, Sep. 2003, p.5; Nov. 2003, p.5; May 2004, p.5; June/July
    2004, p.5
Baltimore Sun, Aug. 11, 1996, p.J1; July 20, 2001, p.B1; May 11, 2002, p.A1;
    Mar. 14, 2004, p.B1
Black Collegian, Oct. 2003, p.40
Christian Science Monitor, Sep. 8, 2003, p.11

Library Journal, Jan. 1996, p.36
Ms., Winter 2003/2004, p.45
Newsday, Sep. 17, 2003, p.A35

ADDRESS

Carla Hayden
Enoch Pratt Free Library
400 Cathedral Street
Baltimore, MD 21201-4484

WORLD WIDE WEB SITE

http://www.ala.org

Ashton Kutcher 1978-

American Actor and Producer
Stars in the Fox TV Sitcom "That '70s Show" and
Produced and Starred in the MTV Reality Show
"Punk'd"

BIRTH

Christopher Ashton Kutcher was born on February 7, 1978, in Cedar Rapids, Iowa. Known as Chris to his family and friends, he was born five minutes before his fraternal twin, Michael. Chris was born healthy, but Michael spent his first three months in an incubator and was diagnosed with mild cerebral palsy, a disability caused by damage to the brain at the time of birth.

The twins completed the family of Larry and Diane Kutcher, who already had a three-year-old daughter, Tausha. Larry and Diane supported their family by working on factory assembly lines. Larry worked on the Fruit Roll-Ups assembly line for General Mills, and Diane worked on the Head & Shoulders shampoo line for Procter & Gamble. Larry and Diane divorced in 1991, but they didn't let their differences affect their children. Kutcher praised his parents, saying "My parents are so cool. They couldn't have handled it better."

YOUTH

Not long after his parents' divorce, Kutcher's brother, Michael, nearly died at age 13. Michael suffered from cardiomyopathy, a viral infection of the heart that can be fatal, and he received a heart transplant. During the critical hours before his transplant, Kutcher never left his brother's side. "We fought and argued all the time as kids, but after [the transplant] we bonded completely and we're the best of friends," Kutcher said. His brother became a huge source for his drive in life. "After seeing all that he went through, there's no mountain I can't climb. His courage is really inspirational and brought me very close to God and my spirituality. It's not something that you want to experience, but we all got the best out of it."

Chris has always been the more lively of the twins. High school acquaintance Joy Janda Curfman once said that "What Chris has, Mike lacks. . . . Chris was always the class clown, he wanted a lot of attention, and he got it. He always acted off the wall and did crazy stuff." But after Michael's heart transplant, Chris's antics became "at some level . . . a way of lightening the mood with his brother," Curfman added.

> "We fought and argued all the time as kids, but after [the transplant], we bonded completely and we're the best of friends," Kutcher said about his brother, Michael. "After seeing all that he went through, there's no mountain I can't climb. His courage is really inspirational and brought me very close to God and my spirituality. It's not something that you want to experience, but we all got the best out of it."

Kutcher's love of attention led him to try out for a junior high school play. He loved the stage and discovered that he "got such an adrenaline rush when I was onstage. I felt like a rock star." He played the thief in the seventh-grade production of *The Crying Princess and the Golden Goose.* The experience set in motion Kutcher's desire to be a movie star, and he continued to act in plays and musicals throughout his school years.

In 1993 Diane moved with her children from Cedar Rapids to Homestead, Iowa, a small farming community with a population of 100. There she built a house on a 300-acre farm with Mark Portwood, a construction worker whom she married in 1996. After the move, Kutcher dove head first into school activities. He played football, ran track, wrestled, sang in the jazz choir, joined the science, thespian, and Spanish clubs, and was a member of the National Honor Society. After school hours he and his friends made their own fun, horsing around together in Iowa's vast, remote cornfields. Kutcher especially liked hunting and racing snowmobiles.

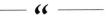

> *Joy Janda Curfman, a high school acquaintance, once said that "Chris was always the class clown, he wanted a lot of attention, and he got it. He always acted off the wall and did crazy stuff." But after Michael's heart transplant, Chris's antics became "at some level . . . a way of lightening the mood with his brother."*

But small-town life also included a lot of plain hard work. Kutcher learned from an early age the value of hard work and eagerly sought out jobs for extra money. He spent a lot of his time with animals, especially herding cattle with wranglers. He noted that "When you live in the country you can always find something to do. So you kind of pop from job to job, whether it's cutting the nuts off cattle one day or baling hay the next." To earn money during the winter Kutcher skinned deer at a local butcher shop when he was 17. "That was really crappy," he recalled. "It was really cold and I had to work outside so the meat would stay frozen. Plus you had to spray the deer down with a hose, so you'd wind up completely soaked, and then your clothes would freeze."

Costly Mistakes

Kutcher admits to having made some mistakes in his teens. One particularly stupid stunt involved his arrest at age 18. One night, after saying

213

goodnight to his girlfriend and her father, who was the high school principal, Kutcher and his cousin broke into their high school. Police apprehended them by 3:00 a.m. Kutcher found himself in police custody and in the difficult position of having to explain himself to his girlfriend's father and his own family. He spent the night in a jail cell because his stepfather refused to pay his bail.

A felony charge of third-degree burglary was placed on his record. Although his crime could have carried a jail sentence, Kutcher instead was sentenced to 180 hours of community service and three years of probation. The stunt also cost him his girlfriend and a lead role in the high school production of *Annie,* for which he had already shaved his head in preparation for his part as Daddy Warbucks. His criminal record haunted him years later when the requirements of his probation forced him to plead with a judge to leave Iowa in order to pursue a modeling career. By 2003 Kutcher's record had been expunged, or erased; he was no longer a felon and could finally vote.

> ——— *««* ———
>
> *Kutcher dreamed of becoming a professional actor, but he had real doubts about his abilities. "I was never the star of my high-school plays. My private feeling was, 'You can't even get the lead when there are 52 people in your class. How are you possibly going to go to Hollywood?'"*
>
> ——— *»»* ———

EDUCATION

Despite his troubles with the law during his senior year, Kutcher finished high school in 1996 and entered the University of Iowa as a biochemical engineering student. Although he still wanted to become an actor, he had no idea how to make his dream come true. "I realized that unless I left for California, there wasn't anywhere for me to go with the acting. I couldn't afford to move that far, so I decided to go to school and become a genetic engineer." His interest in biochemical engineering was based on his concern for the health of his twin brother; he wanted to find a cure for cardiomyopathy, the disease that had nearly taken his brother's life.

Even as Kutcher pursued his engineering courses, he never lost his desire to act. He carried his dream with him in his wallet; on a small piece of paper Kutcher had written his goal of going to Hollywood to become an actor. But he had real doubts about his abilities. "I was never the star of my high-school plays. My private feeling was, 'You can't even get the lead

The cast of "That '70s Show."

when there are 52 people in your class. How are you possibly going to go to Hollywood?'" Despite his doubts and other obstacles, he decided to quit college and try to become an actor. He packed a bag of gear and started walking to the airport, which was about 30 miles away. He made it about 20 miles but detoured to his mother's house. She drove him back to school, where he finished the semester.

FIRST JOBS

Soon after Kutcher's first attempt to get to Hollywood, a modeling agent approached him and suggested that he enter a statewide modeling competition. "Whoa, do guys even do that?" he wondered. In Homestead men became farmers or factory workers, not models. The only male model he knew of was Fabio, and Kutcher wasn't anything like this muscular model with tanned skin and flowing blond hair. He said he "figured it was a scam," but entered on the urging of a friend.

To his surprise, Kutcher won the Fresh Faces of Iowa modeling contest in 1997 and a trip to the International Modeling and Talent Association's convention in New York. At the convention, a modeling agent noticed him and soon Kutcher had an appointment with talent manager Stephanie Simon. Kutcher immediately impressed Simon. "The second I met him, I just knew," she said. "I knew he was going to be huge. I told him on the spot, 'You're moving to New York' — and he did." Within days, Kutcher began modeling for top designers on runways in New York, Milan, Paris, London, and other parts of the world.

Because there were several other models named Chris at the agency, Kutcher opted to use his middle name, Ashton. Although all his friends and family in Iowa still call him Chris, Ashton Kutcher is the name he uses for the rest of the world.

> **"**
>
> *When talent manager Stephanie Simon first met Kutcher, she was immediately impressed. "The second I met him, I just knew," she said. "I knew he was going to be huge. I told him on the spot, 'You're moving to New York' — and he did."*
>
> **"**

Within a year modeling led to acting. Kutcher flew to Los Angeles to test for a television pilot. Though he didn't get that role, he also tested for two others. One part was for an NBC drama called "Wind on Water," and the other was for a Fox sitcom called "That '70s Show." He was offered both roles within hours. He chose to sign for the role of Michael Kelso on "That '70s Show." Kutcher was about to realize his dream.

CAREER HIGHLIGHTS

"That '70s Show"

"That '70s Show" is a sitcom about six teenage friends growing up together in a Wisconsin suburb during the mid-1970s. The series is a nostalgic look at a time when the roles of women, men, and even families were changing in America. The main character of the show is Eric Forman (played by Topher Grace), a likable young man who struggles for independence from the authority of his parents, Red (Kurtwood Smith) and Kitty (Debra Jo Rupp). His family is conservative and solid.

Eric and his group of teenage friends spend most of their time hanging out in Eric's basement talking about their lives. This group includes Donna Pinciotti, Steven Hyde, Fez, Jackie Burkhardt, and Michael Kelso. Donna (Laura Prepon) is Eric's bright, even-tempered girlfriend and next-door neighbor whose parents experiment with every fad and are much more

liberal than the Formans. Hyde (Danny Masterson) lives with Formans, who took him in after his single mother abandoned him. He is a skeptical kid with a dry sense of humor who believes conspiracy theories about big business taking over the world. Fez (Wilmer Valderrama) is a foreign exchange student who is eagerly soaking up American culture. Kelso (Ashton Kutcher) is a good-looking, goofy teenage boy whose gullibility gets him into very funny situations, especially with Jackie (Mila Kunis), his beautiful and spoiled on-again, off-again girlfriend.

The sitcom pokes fun at such 1970s fads as bell bottoms, glam rock music, and polyester clothing, while offering keen insights into the decade's practices and beliefs. Although each episode centers around the comic mishaps of the teenagers, the show also tackles such difficult subjects as open marriages, recreational use of drugs, sex before marriage, and feminism. Kutcher said "The show's writers have nailed what it's like to be a restless Midwestern teen." Since its debut in 1998, the show hit a nerve with the public and critics alike and has become a huge popular success. By now, of course, the group has finished high school and started to grow up, but they still remain best friends.

"I can't begin to tell you what a pleasure it is working on ['That '70s Show']," Kutcher said. "I can't get enough of it. It's kind of sick, really."

"That '70s Show" opened up a new world for Kutcher. He dove into his role as Michael Kelso, playing the teenage character as a simple boy who thinks mostly about girls. Kutcher's work on the show confirmed his love of acting. "I can't begin to tell you what a pleasure it is working on that show," he said. "I can't get enough of it. It's kind of sick, really." The character provided a platform for Kutcher's comic talent, but also showed him to be a good-looking, kindhearted guy. Viewers responded to his quirky character and clamored for news about the actor's personal life. After the first season of "That '70s Show," Kutcher had become a teenage heartthrob. *Seventeen* magazine named him "TV's Hottest New Hunk," and *TV Guide, People,* and *US* magazines featured stories about him. While fans swooned over Kutcher, agents vied to cast him in movies.

Becoming a Film Star

Kutcher welcomed the attention and the opportunities for more work. While continuing to work on "That '70s Show," he also began pursuing movie roles. After a few smaller parts, he landed a starring role in the comedy *Dude, Where's My Car?* (2000), which earned him a nomination at the MTV awards in 2001 for Breakthrough Male Performance. In the movie he plays Jesse Richmond, a character very similar to Michael Kelso from "That '70s Show." Jesse and his friend Chester Greenburg, played by Seann William Scott, wake up after a night of partying to discover Jesse's car is missing. Unable to remember what happened to the car, the two try to retrace their steps from the night before. As they search for the car, they en-

Kutcher and Seann William Scott search for their
missing car in Dude, Where's My Car?

counter a number of comic obstacles, including their angry girlfriends, a street gang, a stripper, a cult looking for space aliens, and actual space aliens. Although serious critics ignored the film, viewers enjoyed the wacky, oddball antics of Kutcher and Scott. *Dude, Where's My Car?* became a success at the box office, where it grossed over $46 million.

Kutcher followed this box office hit with a number of other movies, including the western *Texas Rangers* (2000). Set in Texas in 1875, *Texas Rangers* tells the story of a small group of men who band together to battle outlaws in their rugged homeland. Dylan McDermott plays the leader of the Rangers, an unusual mixed group of young adult orphans and older American Civil War veterans, played by actors James Van Der Beek, Ashton Kutcher, Randy Travis, Usher Raymond, and Robert Patrick. *Texas Rangers* tried to capture the essence of old-time western films, but many said it missed the mark. While the story was packed with action, the movie left both viewers and critics wondering why the story and the characters had so little to offer. Kutcher's character in *Texas Rangers* provided comic relief, but wasn't as funny or endearing as Kelso from "That 70's Show."

Kutcher (left), Usher (center), and James Van Der Beek (right) in a scene from Texas Rangers.

Kutcher and Brittany Murphy in Just Married.

Kutcher had another box office success with the romantic comedy *Just Married* (2003), co-starring Brittany Murphy. The story features Tom and Sarah, a young couple who marry against the wishes of Sarah's family and friends. The movie follows the couple on their honeymoon in Europe as they encounter a series of comic mishaps, from a giant roach crawling in their bed to the attempts of Sarah's ex-boyfriend, sent by her scheming parents, to ruin their marriage. Kutcher portrayed Tom much like a grown-up Kelso, with slapstick comedy and silly facial expressions. The humor in the film was lost on film critics, but viewers pushed it to the top of the box office list. Within weeks of its opening, *Just Married* took in $18 million at the box office and edged *The Lord of the Rings: The Two Towers* from the top spot on the list.

Kutcher played another naïve young man in the romantic comedy *My Boss's Daughter* (2003). Tom (played by Kutcher) is a researcher at a Chicago publishing company. He finds himself overwhelmed as he spends a night trying to look after his boss's house and prized pet owl while a stream of unusual, uninvited houseguests threaten the order of the house and derail his attempts to win over his boss's daughter Lisa (played by Tara Reid). The film is packed with the wild antics of the unusual guests, but the movie didn't win the hearts of either critics or most viewers.

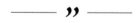

While filming Just Married, *Kutcher said he "would work from about eight o'clock in the morning until four in the afternoon on the TV show, and then from four-thirty in the afternoon until four in the morning on the movie, and I would take 15-minute military naps during the day to keep going."*

Kutcher's work in film and on TV earned him a reputation as a hard working actor. While filming *Just Married,* Kutcher said he "would work from about eight o'clock in the morning until four in the afternoon on the TV show, and then from four-thirty in the afternoon until four in the morning on the movie, and I would take 15-minute military naps during the day to keep going." Director of *Texas Rangers* Steve Miner said that Kutcher "just doesn't stop. . . . I wanted to hook up a cable to him to harness some of his energy—it would save on generator costs." Combined, his hard work and his public appeal make Kutcher an actor popular with directors and viewers alike.

Kutcher and Justin Timberlake in a scene from "Punk'd."

"Punk'd"

Kutcher cemented his reputation for hard work by landing his own television series on MTV in 2003. His show, "Punk'd," was a reality-based comedy show in which Kutcher and others played practical jokes on celebrities. In each episode, "Punk'd" cast members used a hidden camera set-up while trying to put television and film stars in awkward and humiliating situations. But these situations seemed so genuine that the celebrities fell for the bait and believed it was real. Kutcher narrated the action from behind the scenes and always revealed the joke to the stars in the end.

In one episode, for example, the "Punk'd" cast members fooled teen actor Hilary Duff (star of the popular television show "Lizzy McGuire") into thinking she was taking a normal driving test. The camera followed Duff's reaction as her instructor offered bad driving advice, leapt from the car to fight with another driver, and eventually ran off, leaving Duff to fend for herself as a man tried to steal the car she was driving. Before any real damage was done, Kutcher appeared, much to Duff's relief. In another episode, Justin Timberlake was devastated when he found fake IRS (Internal Revenue Service) agents confiscating his house, possessions, and pets. A few of the other stars who have been "punk'd" include Kelly Osbourne, daughter of the rock star Ozzie Osbourne, Frankie Muniz, star of

"Malcolm in the Middle," singers Usher, Pink, and Mandy Moore, rappers Missy Elliott and OutKast, and Kutcher's costar from "That '70s Show," Wilmer Valderrama.

"Punk'd" aired for two seasons on MTV. Then in December 2003, Kutcher announced that he was ending the show. "We have had an incredible time doing the show," he announced, "and have decided to stick with the old adage of 'leave em wanting more.'" Lois Curren, an MTV executive in charge of series development, said that "Today is a sad day for MTV, but probably a happy day for Hollywood. Celebrities can rest a little easier knowing that the Punkings have ceased." Beyonce Knowles was the final victim, when she appeared at a charity Christmas event for young orphans. She tried to place a star on top of the Christmas tree, the tree fell on top of the presents and crushed them, and Beyonce was convinced that she had ruined it for the young orphans, who of course were already in on the joke. Still, many wondered if perhaps the announcement was itself a joke and if Kutcher planned to resume the show later.

———— " ————

In December 2003, Kutcher announced that he was ending "Punk'd." "We have had an incredible time doing the show," he announced, "and have decided to stick with the old adage of 'leave em wanting more.'"

———— " ————

A Bright Future

Along with his work on "That 70's Show," Kutcher continues to act in and produce movies. His most recent project is the production of and starring role in *The Butterfly Effect* (2004). The movie is based on a scientific argument called the "butterfly effect," which explores how seemingly small changes in one part of the world might have a huge impact on another. The phrase refers to an idea based on chaos theory of cause and effect, that a butterfly flapping its wings in one part of the world could set off climactic changes that would result in a tsunami somewhere else. In this sci-fi thriller, Kutcher plays a tormented young man who, while attempting to deal with hurtful childhood memories, discovers how to travel back in time. As he alters his own history, he discovers that he has also changed his future. This more serious and dramatic role was a big shift for Kutcher, and he took his part in the film very seriously. "I don't think people think I can handle a dramatic movie. So I want to be good. No, I want to be great," Kutcher said. Unfortunately, most critics and even his fans faulted

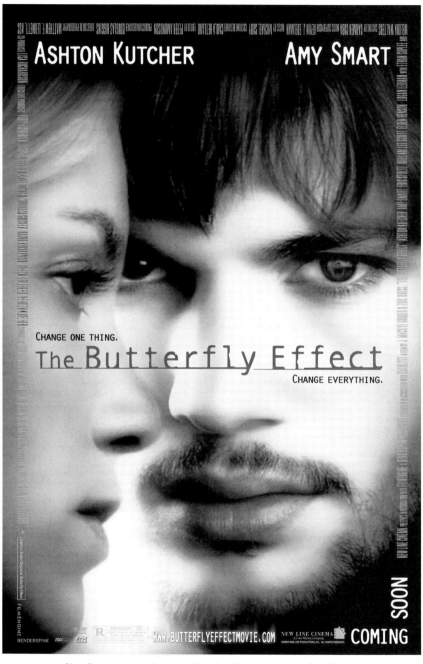

Kutcher stars as Evan in the thriller The Butterfly Effect.

the movie as pretentious and muddled and disparaged his acting as inept, and it was a flop at the box office.

Still, Kutcher's future looks very promising. He is in the center of the public eye, being voted "Hottest Bachelor" by *People* magazine readers in 2003, and he has many fans who enjoy his more light-hearted TV shows and movies. About his life, Kutcher notes that "I don't believe good things come to those who wait. I believe that good things come to those who want something so bad, they can't wait."

HOME AND FAMILY

Kutcher moved to Los Angeles when he began working on "That '70s Show" in 1998. Although he misses his family, he often returns to visit them in Iowa. His twin brother works at an insurance company and his sister teaches art at an elementary school.

Kutcher has never married, but he has had a series of high profile romances since entering show business. He has also been romantically linked with his co-stars on several projects, including Brittany Murphy from *Just Married* and Amy Smart from *The Butterfly Effect*. But it is his relationship with the actress Demi Moore that has created the biggest media stir. Moore was the highest-paid female actor in Hollywood when she dropped her high-profile life in 1998 to raise her three children in Idaho. Reports that Kutcher and Moore were dating coincided with his rapid rise to fame and her return to movies after a five-year break. The 15-year age difference between Kutcher and Moore has inspired much curiosity and gossip about the relationship. In Hollywood, it is not unusual for women to date older men, but it is very unusual for men to date older women. Some skeptics wonder whether Kutcher and Moore's romance is real or only a publicity stunt to fuel their careers. Only time will tell.

> " *About his life, Kutcher notes that "I don't believe good things come to those who wait. I believe that good things come to those who want something so bad, they can't wait."* "

MEMORABLE EXPERIENCES

In 2003 Kutcher came face to face with his own fame. While driving by the 20th Century Fox lot, he and his friends noticed his face on a billboard advertising the movie *Just Married*. They pulled over to take a picture. "So I'm standing there like, 'This is ridiculous. I've made it,'" Kutcher said. "And this girl pulls up and looks at the billboard, looks at me, and starts laugh-

—— " ——

To spur him to do more with his life, Kutcher taped a piece of paper to his phone on which he wrote "Dream Bigger." "So, if you see a guy standing in front of his own movie poster," Kutcher jokes, "that's me, trying to think of a dream that's bigger than my billboard."

—— " ——

ing hysterically. Because I was standing there looking at my own billboard thinking, 'Wow.'" Kutcher added, "It's the most bizarre thing in the world when your dreams become reality." To spur him to do more with his life, Kutcher taped a piece of paper to his phone on which he wrote "Dream Bigger." "So, if you see a guy standing in front of his own movie poster," Kutcher jokes, "that's me, trying to think of a dream that's bigger than my billboard."

HOBBIES AND OTHER INTERESTS

Kutcher loves collecting hats, including the trucker hats he wore on his MTV show "Punk'd." He is a good cook himself, but ranks his mom's enchiladas as his favorite food. Kutcher doesn't "think you can live a good life without a dog," and he owns a black lab named Willy Wonka and a golden retriever named Mr. Bojangles. An excellent carpenter, he built his own earthquake-proof deck and is redecorating his home.

Despite his stardom, Kutcher hasn't forgotten his commitment to help his brother and others with diseases. He's recorded public announcements for and donated money to health-related charities.

SELECTED CREDITS

Television Series

"That '70s Show," 1998-
"Punk'd," 2003 (co-creator, executive producer, and host)

Movies

Coming Soon, 1999
Down to You, 2000
Reindeer Games, 2000
Dude, Where's My Car? 2000
Texas Rangers, 2001

Just Married, 2003
My Boss's Daughter, 2003 (co-producer and actor)
Cheaper by the Dozen, 2003
The Butterfly Effect, 2004 (co-producer and actor)

HONORS AND AWARDS

Teen Choice Awards: 2003 (four awards), Best TV Actor in a Comedy, for "That '70s Show"; Reality/Variety TV Host and Reality Hunk, for "Punk'd"; Male Hottie

FURTHER READING

Books

Contemporary Theatre, Film and Television, Vol. 39, 2002
Krulik, Nancy. *Second to None: Superstars on the Rise,* 2000

Periodicals

Cosmopolitan, Feb. 2001, p.174; Apr. 2003, p.138
Des Moines Register, Jan. 24, 1999, p.E1; Feb. 3, 2001, p.1; July 4, 2003, p.1 (Iowa Life section)
GQ, Mar. 2000, p.341
InStyle, Feb. 2003, p.121
Interview, Mar. 2000, p.70
Los Angeles Times, June 20, 1998 p.F1; Aug. 10, 2003, p.E1
Louisville (Ky.) Courier-Journal, July 25, 2003, p.C1
New York Post, Mar. 17, 2003, p.79
People, Nov. 2, 1998, p.75; June 16, 2003, p.108; June 30, 2003, p.60
Premiere, Aug. 2000, p.74
Rolling Stone, May 29, 2003, p.44
Seventeen, Feb. 2003, p. 84
Teen, Sep. 2000, p.64
Teen People, July 30, 2003, p.14
USA Today, Dec. 11, 1998, p.E12
Washington Post, Feb. 6, 2000

Online Articles

http://www.eonline.com/Features/Features/Kutcher/
(*Eonline.com,* "How That Kutcher Dude Went from a Nobody to A-List Gossip Bait in No Time Flat," June 27, 2003)

http://abcnews.go.com/sections/Entertainment/SciTech/ashton_kutcher_
    040123-1.html (ABC News, "Dude, Where's My Joke? Kutcher Yearns to
    Be Taken Seriously," Jan. 23, 2004)

Online Databases

Biography Resource Center Online, 2004, article from *Contemporary Theatre,
Film and Television,* 2002

ADDRESS

Ashton Kutcher
Endeavor Talent Agency
9701 Wilshire Blvd., 10th Floor
Beverly Hills, CA 90212

WORLD WIDE WEB SITES

http://www.that70sshow.com
http://www.mtv.com
http://www.butterflyeffectmovie.com

Lisa Leslie 1972-

American Professional Basketball Player with
the Los Angeles Sparks
Led the Sparks to Two Consecutive WNBA
Championships
Two-Time Winner of Olympic Gold Medals in
Women's Basketball

BIRTH

Lisa Deshaun Leslie was born on July 7, 1972, in Los Angeles,
California. Her father, Walter Leslie, left the family when she
was very young. She rarely saw him during her childhood, and

he died when she was 12 years old. Her mother, Christine Leslie, was a postal worker who later bought an 18-wheeled truck and became a cross-country truck driver. She raised Lisa and her two sisters—Dionne, who is older, and Tiffany, who is younger—as a single mother. In 1995 Christine Leslie married Thomas Espinoza, a mechanic, and Lisa gained four younger stepbrothers.

YOUTH

Growing up, Leslie lived in several different parts of the Los Angeles area, including Carson, Compton, Gardena, and Inglewood. Money was always tight during her childhood, as her single mother struggled to make ends meet on her salary as a postal worker. Christine Leslie eventually decided to launch a new career as a truck driver. She sold the family home and used the money to buy an 18-wheeler. "We had no money and we could have gone on welfare, but my mom wanted to do something she was proud of," Lisa recalled. "She sat us down and said, 'This is what I've got to do. I'm going to buy a truck and learn how to drive it. It's going to take time for me to pay it off and get a local route. I need you kids to give me five years.'"

During the school year, Leslie and her sisters lived with relatives while their mother hauled goods back and forth across the country. Christine Leslie only managed to come home for a few days each month, and Lisa missed her terribly while she was away. "There were some sad times," she noted. "Mom had to travel so far and so long. But we understood she had to do it. It made me mature really fast. I had so much to do." In the summertime, Lisa and her sisters often accompanied their mother on the road, traveling to cities all around the country. They helped plot out routes on maps, showered at truck stops, and slept in the cab of their mother's rig. The sleeping compartment was only 36 inches wide, Lisa recalled. "All of us would jam in there. We had to hold on to each other. That helps us now. We all hold on to each other in a lot of ways."

Even as a little girl, Leslie was exceptionally tall. The daughter of parents who were both six feet, three inches tall, Lisa was taller than her second grade teacher. She stood six feet tall by the time she was 12 years old, and she reached her full adult height of six feet, five inches during high school. Other kids teased her about her height throughout her adolescence. "They called me Olive Oyl, they called me all sorts of things," she remembered. "The grown-ups mostly thought my height was beautiful, but the kids gave me a hard time." Fortunately, Leslie had a tall female role model in her very own home. "The closer I got to my mother's height, the more beautiful I felt," she noted. "She raised me to be confident and hold my head up."

Because of her height, people always assumed that Leslie played basket-ball. She actually resisted playing the sport for many years because so many people asked her about it. "I hated the association with basketball because I was so tall," she admitted. "I got so sick of everyone asking me. I developed this real bad attitude toward sports, especially basketball." Finally, a junior high classmate convinced her to try out for the school team. Leslie soon discovered that she could have an impact on the court without even trying. "We went 7-0," she remembered of her first season on the junior high team. "They'd throw me the ball, I'd catch it and make a layup. That's all I could do. I told the coach, 'If I fall down, I'm quitting.' And I didn't want to break a sweat. I hated to sweat. I was so prissy."

But Leslie became much more serious about basketball the following year. "I just changed my whole attitude," she admitted. "I guess it was my destiny but I never knew it." She credits an older cousin, Craig Simpson, with helping her improve her strength and conditioning. "Working with my cousin is how I got my skills. I told him I liked basketball, and that was it," she related. "My cousin made me do push-ups and sit-ups and then we'd work on my shots. I think it was at that point I learned how hard you had to work to get from one level to the next." Playing pick-up basketball games with Simpson and other boys also brought out Leslie's competitive instincts.

> "
>
> *Leslie credits an older cousin, Craig Simpson, with helping her improve her strength and conditioning. "Working with my cousin is how I got my skills. I told him I liked basketball, and that was it," she related. "My cousin made me do push-ups and sit-ups and then we'd work on my shots. I think it was at that point I learned how hard you had to work to get from one level to the next."*
>
> "

While still a student at Morningside High School, Leslie scored 101 points in the first half of a basketball game on February 8, 1990. The opposing team, South Torrance High, walked off at half time.

EDUCATION

By the time Leslie entered high school, her mother had secured a local truck route and settled the family in Inglewood. Leslie attended Morningside High School, where she earned a 3.5 grade-point average and was elected class president three times. She was also the starting center for the girls' varsity basketball team from the time she was a freshman. She led the Monarchs to a 125-9 record and two California state championships during her four-year high school career, averaging 26.9 points, 15 rebounds, and 6.9 blocked shots per game. She finished her career with 2,896 points (which ranked second in California girls' high school history) and set a new state record with 1,705 rebounds. She also played volleyball and competed in track, winning the state title in the high jump with a leap of 5 feet, 5 inches during her senior year.

During her junior year in 1989, Leslie became the first girl to dunk a basketball in a high school game (and only the second woman ever to dunk in competition). She learned that she could dunk by accident while she was fooling around with a tennis ball during track practice. "I started my attack, taking steps like boom, boom, boom. I was driving really hard with my knee in the air. And then I dunked it," she remembered of that day. "The track coach was like, 'What was that?' I dunked it so hard, with so much authority, he yelled for somebody to get a volleyball and told me to do the exact same thing and think about the high jump. I ran my approach and I dunked the volleyball. Then I got a basketball. I backed up again and dunked it. And I've been dunking ever since."

Leslie's dunk received notice in newspapers across the country. Yet she insisted that it was not a big deal to her. "Dunking is something that guys care more about than girls," she noted. "There's something about jumping that seems to fascinate guys. Girls are more like, as long as the ball goes in, who cares how you got it there?" During her senior year, however, Leslie enjoyed entertaining her fellow students by performing dunks during school pep rallies.

Perhaps the most notable feat of Leslie's high school basketball career came during her senior year. The Morningside girls' basketball team had a longstanding tradition of helping a senior captain to score as many points as possible during her last regular-season home game. In Leslie's last home game of 1990, she took full advantage of this tradition. As the game unfolded against a completely overmatched team from South Torrance High School, Leslie's teammates fed her the ball repeatedly. Leslie scored 49 points in the first quarter and 52 in the second for a total of 101 at halftime. She

"Dunking is something that guys care more about than girls," Leslie noted. "There's something about jumping that seems to fascinate guys. Girls are more like, as long as the ball goes in, who cares how you got it there?"

seemed certain to break the all-time single-game national high-school scoring record of 105 points set by former star and current NBA commentator Cheryl Miller. But several South Torrance players had fouled out or been injured during the first half, and the opposing coach refused to play the second half. He decided to forfeit the game rather than force his team to endure further embarrassment. Leslie was disappointed that she was denied an opportunity to see how many points she could have scored. "Anyone that can count knows that I would have had [the record]," she said afterward. "They just shortened the game. I feel that I have the record."

Leslie's 100-point game received coverage in the national news as well as *Sports Illustrated.* She went on to be named Naismith National Prep Player of the Year for 1990. By the time she graduated from high school later that year, she was widely considered to be the best girls' high school player in the country. She was heavily recruited by every major college basketball program, but she ultimately decided to remain close to home and attend the University of Southern California (USC) so her mother could watch her play. Leslie balanced her school work with her time playing basketball with the USC Trojans, graduating from USC in 1994 with a bachelor's degree in communications. She returned to school in 2002 to begin working toward a master's degree in business administration.

CAREER HIGHLIGHTS

College — USC Trojans

Leslie's basketball career really began while she was in college. When she entered USC in the fall of 1990, the women's basketball team was in a rebuilding phase. The Trojans had posted a disappointing 8-19 record the previous year, but they had recruited several promising young players in addition to Leslie. Leslie turned in an outstanding freshman season, averaging 19.4 points and 10.0 rebounds per game to lead all freshmen in the nation in both categories. She also became the first freshman ever named to the All-Pacific 10 (Pac 10) Conference Team. But Leslie did encounter some problems defending against stronger, more experienced players. In fact, she set a school record for most personal fouls in a season. "I think it was a revelation to Lisa that there were weaknesses in her game that other people could exploit," said USC Coach Marianne Stanley. Although the Trojans received an invitation to the National Collegiate Athletic Association (NCAA) tournament, they lost in the early rounds.

Leslie continued her strong performance as a sophomore, averaging 20.4 points and 8.4 rebounds per game. She was named All-Pac 10 for the second time and also received first-team All-American honors. USC advanced to the regional finals of the 1991-92 NCAA tournament before being eliminated. As a junior Leslie averaged 18.7 points and 9.8 rebounds per game, which helped her earn all-conference and All-American honors once again. USC made the NCAA tournament for the third straight year, only to fall once again in an early-round contest.

Leslie averaged a career-best 21.9 points and 12.3 rebounds per game during her senior season in 1993-94. USC posted a 26-4 record and advanced to the regional finals of the NCAA tournament, where they were knocked out by Louisiana Tech. Still, Leslie's strong performance garnered a number of prestigious awards. She was named all-conference for the fourth straight year and earned All-American honors for the third consecutive season. She also received the NCAA National Player of the Year and Naismith College Player of the Year awards for 1994.

Leslie drives to the basket while playing for the USC Trojans against the UCLA Bruins, 1993.

By the end of her four years at USC, Leslie's career totals of 2,414 points, 1,214 rebounds, and 321 blocks all ranked as new Pac 10 records. Leslie took enormous pride in her college accomplishments, and she enjoyed her reputation as one of the country's best female players. When she graduated in 1994, though, no professional women's basketball league existed in the United States. As a result, she set her sights on representing her country in international competition. "A lot of coaches have said I have the potential to be the kind of player who can help women's basketball reach more people," she stated. "I think we do need that one star that even people who aren't familiar with the game can recognize. It not only gets the attention of the public, it gets the attention of the kids who will grow up to be the next superstars."

> "*A lot of coaches have said I have the potential to be the kind of player who can help women's basketball reach more people,*" *Leslie said.* "*I think we do need that one star that even people who aren't familiar with the game can recognize. It not only gets the attention of the public, it gets the attention of the kids who will grow up to be the next superstars.*"

U.S. National Women's Basketball Team

By the time Leslie graduated from USC in 1994, she had already gained a great deal of experience in international competition. As a junior in high school, for example, she represented the United States at the 1989 Junior World Championships. Two years later, as a freshman in college, she helped the U.S. team clinch a gold medal at the World University Games. Leslie was the youngest player invited to try out for the U.S. Olympic Team in 1992. As the last player cut from the roster before the Games, she narrowly missed achieving her dream of playing in the Olympics. Later that year she became a member of the World Championship qualifying team. Her performance in that competition earned her the honor of being named USA Basketball Female Player of the Year for 1993.

Leslie also helped the U.S. National Women's Basketball Team earn a gold medal at the 1994 Goodwill Games. She was virtually unstoppable in the tournament, making an amazing 72 percent of her shots from the field. Later that year, Leslie and her American teammates competed for the World Championship in Spain. They were deeply disappointed when they lost in the semifinals of the tournament and had to settle for a bronze medal. "That left a bad taste in our mouths," Leslie recalled.

In the fall of 1994, Leslie signed a contract to play professional basketball for the Sicilgesso team in Alcamo, Italy. She became a star of the European basketball league, averaging 22.6 points and 11.7 rebounds per game. She also grew more aggressive and confident with each passing week. "I just got stronger, and that changed my game mentally more than anything," she explained. "For the first time, I could move big people around. All my life I'd heard people talking about my 'potential' in basketball. In Italy, for the first time, I understood what all that meant. When I got stronger, I could play very well against bigger, older, and more experienced players." Still, Leslie did not enjoy the experience of playing in Italy. "It's hell being overseas," she admitted. "It's lonely." As a result, she ended her contract with Sicilgesso after one season and returned to the United States.

In 1995 Leslie competed for a roster spot on the U.S. Olympic Team that would compete in the 1996 Summer Olympic Games in Atlanta, Georgia. She was one of 12 players selected from among the top 60 female basketball players in the country. The impressive roster included legends like Katrina McClain and Teresa Edwards, as well as young NCAA stars such as Rebecca Lobo, Sheryl Swoopes, and Dawn Staley. "Atlanta will be an opportunity for us to go down in history as one of the greatest teams ever," Leslie declared. "It'll be a showcase for us as role models—not only for girls who play basketball but for women in general."

In preparation for the 1996 Olympics, the U.S. National Women's Basketball Team played an intense and grueling schedule. Over the course of a year, they traveled over 100,000 miles and played 52 games on four continents. The American women went undefeated in their Olympic warmup games. Leslie contributed 17.4 points and 7.0 rebounds per game to lead the team in both categories.

The U.S. team continued its dominance during the Olympic tournament, winning six straight games to reach the gold-medal match. Leslie led the team with 19.5 points and 7.3 rebounds per game, and she set a new Olympic single-game record by scoring 35 points against Japan. Leslie also showed her mettle in the gold medal match against a tough Brazil team. She played poorly in the first half of the game, but she came back strong in the second half to score 29 points on 12 of 14 shooting. The U.S. team won the game 111-87 and claimed the Olympic gold medal. Afterward, some observers claimed that the American team was the best in the history of women's basketball. Best of all, their success generated a great deal of interest in the sport. "We accomplished what we set out to do," Leslie stated.

*Leslie leaps to the basket while playing for the U.S. national team
in the 1996 Olympics.*

"We tried to get women's basketball to the next level. Our game speaks for itself, but now our names are in the public eye and that's the thing that took the NBA from one level to the next."

WNBA — Los Angeles Sparks

After achieving her dream of winning an Olympic gold medal, Leslie thought about taking a break from basketball. "I played 10 years straight to be an Olympian," she explained. "I'm tired." She decided to pursue a career as a fashion model, even going so far as to sign a contract with the prestigious Wilhelmina modeling agency. But Leslie was lured back to basketball a short time later by the formation of two women's professional basketball leagues in the United States. The first of these leagues was the American Basketball League (ABL), which formed in 1996. Due to poor planning and recruiting, however, it failed after three seasons. The second and more successful league, the Women's National Basketball Association (WNBA), was formed in 1997.

The WNBA enjoyed financial support from the NBA, the popular men's professional league. The league also attracted more fans by scheduling its games during the summer, when NBA and college basketball teams did not play. The WNBA started out with eight teams based in major cities

*" *

"We accomplished what we set out to do," Leslie said about winning the gold medal at the 1996 Olympics. "We tried to get women's basketball to the next level. Our game speaks for itself, but now our names are in the public eye and that's the thing that took the NBA from one level to the next."

" "

across the United States. Most of these teams built their rosters around key players from the gold-medal winning U.S. Women's Olympic Basketball Team, like Leslie, Rebecca Lobo, and Sheryl Swoopes. Leslie, for example, signed a contract to play for the Los Angeles Sparks, based in her hometown. "I'm excited to have the opportunity to continue my basketball career in the United States, especially in Los Angeles," she stated.

The WNBA completed its first season in the summer of 1997. Leslie immediately established herself as one of the league's premier players. She led the league in rebounding (with an average of 9.5 per game), ranked second in blocked shots (2.1 per game), and finished third in scoring (15.9 points per game). In recognition of her performance, she was named to the All-WNBA first team at the conclusion of the season. Despite Leslie's heroics, however, the Sparks posted only a 14-14 record and they failed to make the playoffs.

In 1998 the WNBA expanded to include two more teams and extended the season to 30 games. The Sparks finished with a disappointing 12-18 record, but Leslie once again ranked among the league leaders in several statistical categories. She led the WNBA in rebounds with 10.2, ranked second in blocks with 2.1, and finished third in scoring with 19.6. Due to her team's poor performance, however, she was only selected to the All-WNBA second team.

———— 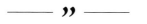 ————

Leslie was devastated by the loss when her team was swept in the 2000 conference finals. "She came home, went to her room, and cried her heart out," her mother recalled. "We were going to have lots of friends and family over for dinner because we all wanted to tell Lisa how well she had done and how proud we were of her. But Lisa said, 'Mom, I need to be alone right now. It hurts too much.'"

———— 〟 ————

The WNBA added two more teams and expanded to a 32-game schedule for the 1999 season. The league also held its first All-Star Game that year. Leslie played center for the Western Conference and was named most valuable player of the game. "I felt really honored to have this award," she stated. "I thought the crowd was great. They got me totally fired up and the atmosphere was awesome."

The Sparks played inconsistently for much of the 1999 season but finished strong for a 20-12 record. Although Leslie's personal statistics declined to 15.6 points, 7.8 rebounds, and 1.5 blocks per game, she was pleased about her team's improved performance. The Sparks won their first playoff series and advanced to the conference championship, where they faced the two-time defending WNBA champion Houston Comets. Leslie and her teammates played well but lost the series, two games to one. "I think this Comets team knows that they just went through the best team in the WNBA and I wish them the best of luck," Leslie said afterward. Houston went on to win its third consecutive WNBA title.

As the 2000 WNBA season began, Leslie vowed to bring home a championship ring. She contributed 17.8 points, 9.6 rebounds, and 2.3 blocks per game to help her team post the best record in the league at 28-4. The

Leslie grabs a rebound during a 1997 WNBA game.

Sparks' amazing regular season performance gave them home-court advantage in the playoffs, but they were not able to capitalize on it. The promising season ended in heartbreaking fashion when Los Angeles was swept in the conference finals by Houston. Leslie was devastated by the loss. "She came home, went to her room, and cried her heart out," her mother recalled. "We were going to have lots of friends and family over for dinner because we all wanted to tell Lisa how well she had done and how proud we were of her. But Lisa said, 'Mom, I need to be alone right now. It hurts too much.'"

Winning Two WNBA Championships

Leslie did not wallow in her disappointment over the Sparks' 2000 season. Instead, she decided to do her part to help prepare the team for the 2001 campaign. She hired a personal trainer and began working out twice a day. She also performed drills with the Sparks' new head coach, former Los Angeles Lakers star Michael Cooper. "I watched tapes of last year's conference finals and decided I had to become more aggressive and more mentally tough," she explained. "I also wanted to improve my passing, my shooting percentage, and my ability to drive and dribble, left and right. I wanted to solidify my post game, too. It was time to make an investment in myself."

A smiling Leslie shows off her trophy after the Sparks won the 2001 WNBA championship.

Leslie's hard work paid off during the 2001 WNBA season. Many observers claimed that she transformed herself into the most dominant player in the league. Leslie averaged 19.5 points, 9.6 rebounds, and 2.29 blocked shots per game to lead the Sparks to an amazing 34-5 record. "I call her The Package now," said Sparks assistant coach Glenn McDonald. "She can shoot the jumper, she can run the lane, she can shoot the hook, she can shoot the three [point shot]. She does everything." Opposing coaches, meanwhile, admitted that defending against Leslie was a big challenge. "In the past, physical play may have distracted her or officiating might take her out of her game," said Charlotte Sting Coach Anne Donovan. "But this year she was very focused, never distracted, always confident and poised and always showed great leadership with the Sparks. Her game was at her peak."

The Sparks advanced through the playoffs to the WNBA Finals, where they defeated the Charlotte Sting in a two-game sweep. Leslie scored 24 points, grabbed 13 rebounds, blocked 7 shots, and added 6 assists in the final game. She was named Most Valuable Player of the regular season, the All-Star Game, and the championship series — thus becoming the first WNBA player to win all three awards in a single season. Afterward, Cooper called it "one of the best [seasons] I've ever seen by a professional athlete playing basketball. From training camp to the final day, she got on a roll and then went to another level whenever we needed to win. And not only did she go up, she made everybody on the team go up." For her part, Leslie was thrilled with the results of the season. "I'm not sure I'd call this championship getting the monkey off my back," she stated. "What I did was find the heart I needed to win the big games, and that feels great."

As the 2002 season got underway for the reigning WNBA champs, opposing teams focused solely on stopping Leslie. She faced double- and triple-team defenses all year, which caused her statistics to decline to 16.9 points, 10.4 rebounds, and 2.9 blocks per game. But she still managed to accomplish some impressive feats. On July 30, 2002, Leslie became the first woman ever to dunk a basketball during a professional game. A short time later, Leslie became the WNBA's all-time leading scorer as well as the first player in the league to score 3,000 points in her career. Even more satisfying for Leslie, the Sparks earned the best record in the western conference and defeated the New York Liberty to claim their second consecutive WNBA title. Once again, Leslie was named Most Valuable Player of the championship series.

The Sparks started off strong in 2003, posting a 15-3 record during the first half of the season. But Leslie injured her knee in the All-Star Game and was forced to sit out the next 11 games. The Sparks struggled without their star center, posting a 4-7 record and dropping out of first place in the Western Conference. After Leslie returned to the lineup, however, the Sparks won their remaining five games to finish with a 24-10 record for the year. Leslie, meanwhile, finished the season with her usual dazzling numbers, contributing 18.4 points, 10.0 rebounds, and 2.74 blocks per game. After defeating the Sacramento Monarchs in the conference finals, the Sparks seemed poised to win their third straight WNBA crown.

> "
>
> *Leslie was thrilled with the results of the 2001 season. "I'm not sure I'd call this championship getting the monkey off my back. What I did was find the heart I needed to win the big games, and that feels great."*
>
> "

The Sparks' opponent in the WNBA finals was the Detroit Shock, a young team that had earned the best overall record in the league in 2003 after posting the worst overall record the previous year. Leslie and her teammates used their playoff experience to trounce the Shock in the first game in Los Angeles. Leslie contributed 23 points, 12 rebounds, and 3 blocks in that contest. But the series moved to Detroit for the two remaining games. The Sparks suffered a heartbreaking one-point overtime loss in game 2. This set the stage for the deciding game 3, which was played before a WNBA-record crowd of 22,076 people. The Shock controlled Leslie with stifling defense, and she fouled out in the final minutes after scoring only 13 points. The Shock won the game and the WNBA title, denying Leslie and the Sparks a three-peat. "I would have to say this is probably the most physical game I've ever played in my life, these last two games," Leslie said afterward. "I guess I have the bruises on my face to show it."

Two New York Liberty players can't stop Leslie during this 2003 game in Madison Square Garden.

Making an Impact on the Game

Over her six-year WNBA career, Leslie has averaged 17.6 points, 9.5 rebounds, and 2.27 blocked shots per game. Her fluid play has earned her the nickname "Smooth," and her competitive nature and well-rounded game have won over legions of fans. In fact, her number 9 Sparks jersey is the top seller in the WNBA. Of course, as one of the superstars of the league, Leslie is often the focus of boos from fans of opposing teams.

Throughout her outstanding WNBA career, Leslie has also continued to represent the United States in international women's basketball. In 1998 she led the American team to a gold medal in the World Championships. Her contributions of 17.1 points and 8.8 rebounds per game earned her USA Basketball Female Athlete of the Year honors for 1998. In 2000 Leslie won a second gold medal at the Olympic Games in Sydney, Australia. She averaged 15.8 points and 7.9 rebounds per game during the Olympic tournament. In 2002 Leslie helped the American team repeat its gold-medal performance at the World Championships. She was named Most Valuable Player of the tournament in recognition of her stellar play.

All of these accomplishments have elevated Leslie to the pinnacle of her sport and made her a role model for countless young women. By combining toughness and skill with femininity and flair, Leslie has helped increase the visibility and popularity of women's basketball. "When I'm playing, I'll sweat and talk trash. However, off the court I'm lipstick, heels, and short skirts. I'm very feminine, mild-mannered, and sensitive," she explained. "I'd definitely like some little girl to be looking at me as someone who's a woman, intelligent, attractive, and an athlete."

As much as she has done for her sport, Leslie expresses appreciation for the opportunities basketball has given her. "I always wonder what would have happened to me if I hadn't picked up that ball [in junior high]," she noted. "I might be working at a McDonald's. I might be at a local junior college. I don't know. Basketball's done a lot for me. Put me through college and let me go around the world."

Leslie hopes to take advantage of her time in the spotlight to influence the lives of young people. "Everything in my life is a blessing," she stated. "Right now I'm in that window of opportunity. I might be hot, people know my name. But that window only stays open for a short period of time. When it closes, it will be someone else's turn. I understand that while the window is open, I give all I can. I do the autographs, smile at people, try to touch lives in the ways I can. There are many things I like to do in life, but I recognize that while the attention is on me, people are listening. So I have to use my ability to hopefully help some kids want to set goals and do something with their lives."

> **By combining toughness and skill with femininity and flair, Leslie has helped increase the visibility and popularity of women's basketball. "When I'm playing, I'll sweat and talk trash. However, off the court I'm lipstick, heels, and short skirts. I'm very feminine, mild-mannered, and sensitive," she explained. "I'd definitely like some little girl to be looking at me as someone who's a woman, intelligent, attractive, and an athlete."**

Leslie plans to continue her WNBA career for several more years. She has also been selected for the U.S. Olympic Women's Basketball Team that will compete in 2004 in Athens, Greece, and she hopes to add a third gold medal to her trophy case at that time. "Overall, in regards to my career, I have fulfilled a lot of the goals I have set," she noted. "But even when I found myself the best at certain levels—whether high school, college, or the pros —there is always something I could learn and do better. That's my attitude. The day I stop doing that is the day I'm going to be done."

> *"Overall, in regards to my career, I have fulfilled a lot of the goals I have set," Leslie noted. "But even when I found myself the best at certain levels—whether high school, college, or the pros— there is always something I could learn and do better. That's my attitude. The day I stop doing that is the day I'm going to be done."*

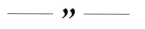

HOME AND FAMILY

Leslie, who is single, earns well over $1 million per year from her WNBA salary and endorsements. She lives in a large, split-level home in Los Angeles with a view of the ocean. She shares her home with a pit bull puppy named Lennox. Leslie remains very close to her mother, who lives nearby in a home that was a gift from her daughter.

HOBBIES AND OTHER INTERESTS

Leslie enjoys playing cards and board games in her spare time. Since 1996, when she signed a contract with the prestigious Wilhelmina agency, she has also enjoyed a second career as a fashion model. She has appeared in a number of national magazines and has walked the runway at several fashion shows. "I love all types of modeling, whether it be on a runway in front of hundreds of people, or the photo shoot where it's just me and the photographer," she explained. "It gives me a chance to let people know that there's much more to Lisa Leslie. I also like to show girls that you can be tough and feminine, too."

Leslie hopes to become a sportscaster when her basketball career is over. To that end, she has provided color commentary for USC basketball games and worked as a correspondent for "NBA Inside Stuff." She has also tried her hand at acting, appearing as a guest star on such TV shows as "Moesha," "Hang Time," "Sister Sister," and "Who Wants to Be a Millionaire?"

Leslie enjoys the moment, after winning a gold medal with Team USA in the 2000 Olympics.

Leslie is very active in charity work, particularly for causes that serve children. She works with several programs designed to raise the self-esteem of young girls, and she personally sponsors six foster children. She is also a national spokesperson for the Big Brothers/Big Sisters organization. "I think it's very important that kids have role models to look up to," she noted. "My mom made sure that I was raised properly and was given all the support I needed. Big Brothers/Big Sisters of America is focused on providing youth with the necessary support when they can't receive it at home." Leslie is a board member of her church, and she also has donated money to help her former high school improve its athletic facilities.

247

HONORS AND AWARDS

High School All-American: 1989, 1990
Naismith Prep Player of the Year: 1990
Pacific 10 Conference Freshman of the Year: 1990-91
NCAA Women's Basketball Freshman of the Year: 1990-91
All-Pacific 10 Conference: 1990-91, 1991-92, 1992-93, 1993-94
NCAA All-American: 1991-92, 1992-93, 1993-94
NCAA National Player of the Year: 1993-94
Naismith College Player of the Year: 1993-94
USA Basketball Female Athlete of the Year: 1993, 1998, 2000
Women's Basketball World Championship: 1994, bronze medal; 1998, gold
    medal; 2002, gold medal
Olympic Women's Basketball: 1996, gold medal; 2000, gold medal
All-WNBA: 1997, 2000, 2001, 2002, 2003
WNBA All-Star: 1999-2003
WNBA All-Star Game Most Valuable Player: 1999, 2001, 2002
WNBA Most Valuable Player: 2001
WNBA Championship Most Valuable Player: 2001
WNBA Championship: 2001, 2002 (with Los Angeles Sparks)
Team Sportswoman of the Year (Women's Sports Foundation): 2001
ESPY Award as Best WNBA Player: 2002
Women's Basketball World Championship Most Valuable Player: 2002
Most Outstanding High School Girls Basketball Player of the Past 20 Years
    (*USA Today*): 2002

FURTHER READING

Books

Corbett, Sara. *Venus to the Hoop: A Gold Medal Year in Women's Basketball,*
    1997
Kelley, Brent. *Lisa Leslie,* 2001 (juvenile)
Ponti, James. *WNBA: Stars of Women's Basketball,* 1998
Stewart, Mark. *Lisa Leslie: Queen of the Court,* 1998
VanDerveer, Tara. *Shooting from the Outside: How a Coach and Her Olympic
    Team Transformed Women's Basketball,* 1998
Who's Who in the World, 2003

Periodicals

Cleveland Plain Dealer, Aug. 4, 1996, p.D11; Feb. 7, 1997, p.D5
Current Biography Yearbook, 1998

Detroit News, Sep. 17, 2003, p.E6

Los Angeles Times, Jan. 12, 1989, Sports sec., p.12; June 21, 1997, Sports sec., p.3; Aug. 8, 1999, Magazine sec., p.10; Aug. 25, 2001, p.D1; May 14, 2002, p.D1; Aug. 1, 2002, p.D1; Sep. 17, 2003, Sports sec., p.1

Ms., Dec. 2002/Jan. 2003, p.49

New York Times, Dec. 5, 1993, sec. 8, p.8; July 11, 2003, p.D5

People, Aug. 19, 1996, p.42; June 30, 1997, p.109

Sport, July 1997, p.46

Sports Illustrated, Feb. 19, 1990, p.30; Dec. 3, 1990, p.92; Nov. 25, 1991, p.78; Sep. 10, 2001, p.46; Sep. 1, 2003, p.6

Sports Illustrated Women, May/June 2002, p.86

Vogue, May 1996, p.288

Women's Sports and Fitness, Nov./Dec. 1996, p.50

USA Today, May 1, 2002, p.C7

Online Articles

http://www.usolympicteam.com/10_questions/071702basketball.html
 (*USA 2002,* "Ten Questions for Basketball's Lisa Leslie," July 17, 2002)
http://www.detnews.com
 (*Detroit News,* "Shock Defense Stymies Leslie," Sep. 17, 2003)

Online Databases

Biography Resource Center Online, 2003, article from *Notable Sports Figures,* 2003

ADDRESS

Lisa Leslie
Los Angeles Sparks
555 North Nash Street
El Segundo, CA 90245

WORLD WIDE WEB SITES

http://www.wnba.com
http://www.usabasketball.com
http://www.usolympicteam.com

LINKIN PARK

Chester Bennington 1976-
Rob Bourdon 1979-
Brad Delson 1977-
Dave Farrell (Phoenix) 1977-
Joe Hahn 1977-
Mike Shinoda 1977-

American Rap-Rock Band

EARLY YEARS

The rap-rock group known as Linkin Park includes six members: Chester Bennington (singer); Rob Bourdon (drums);

Brad Delson (guitar); Dave Farrell, who is known as Phoenix (bass); Joe Hahn (DJ); and Mike Shinoda (rapper).

The connections among the group's members reach all the way back to their student days. Delson and Shinoda have known each other since junior high school, while Shinoda met Hahn at the Art Center College of Design in Pasadena. Phoenix was Delson's roommate in college, and Bourdon, who also attended the Art Center College of Design, first met Delson when he was in high school. At least part of the band's success can be attributed to how well and how long most of them have known each other, and to the goals and values they share.

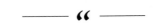

Brad Delson

Brad Delson was born in Los Angeles on December 1, 1977. He began studying the guitar in elementary school, and in seventh grade he met Mike Shinoda. After graduating from Agoura High School, where he met future band member Rob Bourdon, he went to the University of California at Los Angeles (UCLA), where he majored in communications. He divided his time at college between studying, writing songs with Shinoda, and serving as an intern at Zomba Music, where he learned all about what it takes for an artist or a band to get a recording contract. This experience would prove valuable later on, when Delson and his own band were trying to attract the attention of a major recording label.

Delson seriously considered applying to law school, but by the time he graduated from UCLA he had already gotten together with his roommate, Dave Farrell (Phoenix), and his childhood friend Mike Shinoda to form a group called Xero. Rather than pursuing a career as a lawyer, he decided to stick with the band and see what happened. "I'm glad I took the risk," he says.

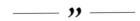

Delson seriously considered applying to law school, but by the time he graduated from UCLA he had already gotten together with his roommate, Dave Farrell (Phoenix), and his childhood friend Mike Shinoda to form a group called Xero (pronounced "Zero"). Rather than pursuing a career as a lawyer, he decided to stick with the band and see what happened. "I'm glad I took the risk," he says, although it wasn't easy for him to be unemployed while his friends moved on to careers or graduate school.

———— *"* ————

In 1991 Shinoda attended a rock concert featuring the metal band Anthrax and the rap group Public Enemy. "It was the first concert I'd ever been to, and it was this mixing of all these different types of music," he explains. "They played 'Bring the Noise' at the end of the show, and that left a mark on me. I always wanted to do something that mixed these styles of music."

———— *"* ————

Mike Shinoda

Michael Kenji Shinoda was born in Los Angeles on February 11, 1977, a second-generation Japanese-American whose father had spent time in a U.S. internment camp during World War II. At that time, the United States was at war with Japan. Some Americans worried that Japanese and Japanese-American people living and working in the U.S. might be traitors who would sabotage the American war effort—even though most of them, like Mike's father, thought of themselves as loyal Americans. In 1942 President Franklin Delano Roosevelt ordered that people of Japanese descent should be evacuated from the West Coast, and about 120,000 people were confined to these camps until the war was over. About two-thirds of them were native-born American citizens. They were forced to sell their homes and were sent to live in camps surrounded by barbed wire.

Born years later, Mike Shinoda avoided these hardships. He developed an early interest in music after he started taking piano lessons when he was six. "At first I went because my mom told me to—I wasn't all that excited about it," he says. "Eventually, though, I got really into it." He played mostly classical music until he was 13. Then he told his piano teacher that what he really wanted to play was jazz, blues, and even hip-hop. Because she didn't have any training in this kind of music, she suggested he buy a keyboard and try to teach himself. "I got a sampler," he recalls, "started making beats and playing around with . . . digital-based music."

As a junior high school student, Shinoda was interested in art, computers, and hip-hop. He would practice rapping by listening to Run DMC, LL Cool J, Grandmaster Flash, and others. Soon he was making up his own raps and performing them for his friends at school. Then in 1991 Shinoda attended a rock concert featuring the metal band Anthrax and the rap group Public Enemy. "It was the first concert I'd ever been to, and it was this mixing of all these different types of music," he explains. "They played

'Bring the Noise' at the end of the show, and that left a mark on me. I always wanted to do something that mixed these styles of music." Soon afterward, he got together with his childhood friend Brad Delson and began writing songs.

After graduating from Agoura High School with Delson, Shinoda majored in illustration at the Art Center College of Design in Pasadena, where he met Joe Hahn and Rob Bourdon. They joined with Shinoda and Delson to form Xero. Mike remembers how exhausting it was to balance his schedule as an art school student with his budding career as a musician: "I'd do classes from nine to four, four to seven, and seven to ten at night. I'd go from there to band practice in Hollywood for two or three hours, then all the way back to my parents' house and work on paintings until I couldn't do it anymore. Then I'd get up in the morning and do it all again." But his hard work paid off, and he graduated from college.

Phoenix

Phoenix was born David Farrell in Massachusetts on February 8, 1977. He studied classical violin for nine years and also played the cello when he was growing up. "There's a huge advantage to having played an instrument when I was younger," he admits, "not only in terms of dexterity, but in having a basis in music theory and developing an ear for music. You can learn a ton about composition and structure from Mozart."

After graduating from high school he went to UCLA, where he was Brad Delson's roommate and majored in philosophy. By the time he earned his bachelor of arts degree (B.A.) in 1999, he was being called "Phoenix," a nickname that started as a joke after he and some friends watched the Ben Stiller film *Mystery Men*.

By that point Delson and Shinoda had formed the band. But they didn't have a bass player, so they asked Phoenix to join them.

Rob Bourdon

Robert Bourdon was born in Los Angeles on January 20, 1979. Even as a

"There's a huge advantage to having played an instrument when I was younger," Phoenix admits, *"not only in terms of dexterity, but in having a basis in music theory and developing an ear for music. You can learn a ton about composition and structure from Mozart."*

toddler, he showed a passion for concentration and hard work: he once spent three hours learning to tie his own shoes. In third grade his parents took him to an Aerosmith concert—his mother was a former girlfriend of the band's drummer, Joey Kramer. The experience inspired him to start playing the drums himself.

Bourdon met Brad Delson at Agoura High School, and soon after that he started jamming with Brad and Mike. After graduation he worked as a waiter and in a bowling alley and even studied accounting at Santa Monica College. He ended up at the Art Center College of Design, where Mike Shinoda was a fellow illustration major. But Bourdon left after a year to try to make a living as a freelance illustrator. Among other things, he designed monsters and robots for the film industry. But he continued to jam with his high school friends whenever he could find the time.

Joe Hahn

Joseph Hahn was born in Los Angeles on March 15, 1977. His main interest when he was growing up was not so much music but the "sonic collages" that could be created by mixing sounds from different recordings, scratching records (see box on page 82), and adding keyboard loops and other bits of sound.

Hahn attended Art Center College of Design, where he met Mike Shinoda. But Hahn left college after his first year. He had already joined Xero as a DJ at this point, although he thought of it as a hobby rather than a possible career. The band now had five members — Delson, Shinoda, Phoenix, Bourdon, and Hahn — as well as a lead vocalist, Mark Wakefield.

Chester Bennington

Chester Bennington was born on March 20, 1976, in Phoenix, Arizona. His parents split up when he was 11 and he stayed with his father, who was a police officer. Bennington began singing before he was in kindergarten, but after that his musical tastes changed rapidly. "When I was in middle school, I was very into hip-hop," he recalls. "But when I went into high school I discovered punk rock, and that really changed my world."

"When I was in middle school, I was very into hip-hop," Bennington recalls. "But when I went into high school I discovered punk rock, and that really changed my world."

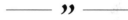

Bennington had a difficult childhood and adolescence. As a child, he suffered five years of sexual abuse. As a young teen, he became addicted to alcohol and drugs, including cocaine and methamphetamines. He dropped out of high school and worked at a number of minimum wage jobs. He was homeless for a period of time.

Soon he began turning his difficult experiences into music by writing songs for a hard rock band in Arizona called Grey Daze. He stayed with Grey Daze through most of the 1990s, but finally realized that he was not getting anywhere as an artist. "It was time for me to move on," he says.

FORMING LINKIN PARK

By 1995 Xero consisted of Delson, Shinoda, Bourdon, Phoenix, Hahn, and Mark Wakefield. But Wakefield never really fit in comfortably with the rest of the group, and by 1998 it became clear to the group that they would

What Is New Metal?

It's been called by many names, including rap-rock and rap-metal, but "new metal" music (also spelled "nu metal") commonly refers to a style that appeared in the late 1980s and early 1990s. New metal bands combine rap, metal, and punk styles, which is why they are also associated with the term "fusion." Many of their songs express anger, depression, and even violence, with the vocalists shouting, singing, and rapping. The lyrics are deeply personal and reflect the emotional turmoil of adolescence.

Distorted guitars and hip-hop rhythms are typical of new metal, as is an onstage DJ who "scratches" records and plays "samples." Scratching is when DJs stop the records from spinning with their hands and then move them back and forth to produce a rhythmic scratching sound. Samples are brief passages of music or sound from existing recordings that are reproduced digitally and then reused in a new song. Limp Bizkit, which uses a full-time DJ with lyrics delivered in rap style and often shouted or screamed, is consider a typical new metal band.

have to find a new vocalist. A mutual friend contacted Bennington in Phoenix and sent him Xero's demo tape. Bennington, who had always wanted to be a rock star, flew out to Los Angeles to audition two days later. When he heard the band play, he thought to himself, "This is the one. This [is] the golden ticket to get inside Willy Wonka's chocolate factory." He left his Phoenix-based band and quit his day-job at a digital services firm to join Xero.

What's in a Name?

One of the first things the band did when they started getting serious about their music in 1996 was to call themselves Hybrid Theory, a name that reflected their interest in combining existing musical styles. They began fusing hip-hop, rock, and electronic music in a way that had never been heard before. But before they could make a name for themselves, Limp Bizkit, Korn, and other "fusion" groups released albums that did the same thing. Rather than becoming discouraged, Hybrid Theory decided to continue doing what they were doing, but to do it better and differently than anyone else.

The group played showcases for more than 40 different record labels, but everyone turned them down. Then, after one of their first live performances at the Hollywood club known as Whiskey, they were offered a publishing (songwriting) contract by Zomba Music, where Brad had been an intern. This was great for their self-confidence, but it still wasn't a recording contract of their own. They continued to work hard on developing their own unique sound and started promoting their music over the Internet. They began visiting online chat rooms, uploading MP3s of their songs, and sending out free tapes and T-shirts via their web site. "We used the Internet as a tool to find people who were interested in the style of music we were playing, and to see if they wanted to help us by getting the word out," Phoenix explains. Group members would even pretend to be fans themselves, urging others to "check out this new band."

Finally, in 1999, they were offered a contract by Warner Brothers Records. There was only one problem: Warner Brothers had already signed another group called Hybrid, so they had to change their name again. This time they settled on Lincoln Park, the name of a park in Santa Monica near their rehearsal studio. But when they tried to register a domain name on the Internet, they discovered that the name "lincolnpark.com" was already taken, so they changed the spelling to "Linkin." This name seemed to reflect not only their own unique approach to making music but their effort to reach out to fans everywhere, since so many towns in America have their own "Lincoln Park."

> *"The first album* [Hybrid Theory] *has feelings of confusion and anger and paranoia,"* Shinoda explains. *"We were writing about those from the perspective of young 20-year-old guys."*

CAREER HIGHLIGHTS

Hybrid Theory

It took Linkin Park more than two years to write all the songs for their first album, *Hybrid Theory*. But their web-savvy approach to marketing their music paid off. When the album was released in October 2000, it climbed rapidly to the Top Ten on the *Billboard* Top 200 chart and stayed there. By March 2001 it had gone platinum.

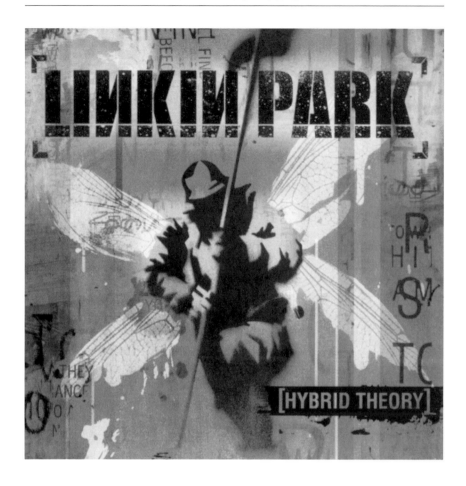

The songs on the album are mostly about difficult relationships. They combine punk and rap-metal styles, with the influence of hip-hop particularly strong in the lyrics and rhythms. Shinoda and Bennington, the group's principal songwriters, avoided the tendency to overuse obscenities in their lyrics and concentrated instead on finding the words that would express their anger and vulnerability. "We wanted something people could connect with, not just vulgarity and violence," Bennington explains. Swearing, he says, "seemed like a cheap way to say I'm angry." Shinoda adds, "The one thing we do that's different [from other rap-rock bands] is that we like to keep things a little more introverted, lyrically a little less aggressive."

Although *Hybrid Theory* followed the path established by Limp Bizkit, Papa Roach, Korn, and other "new metal" rap fusion groups (see box on page 82), it managed to create a sound that was unique. The *St. Louis Post-Dispatch* singled out the band's "emotionally charged" vocals, saying that it was not so much *what* they said as *how* they said it that gave the group its unique sound. Against DJ Joe Hahn's electronic backdrop, according to the *Chicago Daily Herald,* there are "menacing guitar riffs, and almost U2-esque underlying keyboard melody, and hip-hop vocals." The *Herald* concluded that Linkin Park is "an up-and-down band. When they get it right, they have an unstoppable power and intensity that recalls the early, more raw melodic metal sounds of the mid-90s, but at their worst they come off as just another Limp Bizkit clone."

Clone or not, the album went on to sell almost eight million copies in the U.S. and 14 million worldwide. It was the best-selling rock album in the country in 2001, crowding out established artists like Britney Spears, Destiny's Child, Alicia Keys, and 'N Sync. At the Billboard Music Awards that year, Linkin Park was named Modern Rock Artist of the Year, and the album was nominated for three Grammy Awards, eventually winning Best Hard Rock Vocal for "Crawling," a song that Delson describes as expressing "those feelings of insecurity and self-doubt that everyone goes through." Members of the band were stunned by their sudden success, which was unprecedented in Warner Brothers history.

"There's a misconception that angry music is going to make someone angry," Delson contends. *"I think it's cathartic, and I think that a lot of kids who do have problems . . . can relate to the lyrics and can go, 'Oh, it's OK to feel that way. I'm not uncool if I feel insecure.'"*

The success of *Hybrid Theory* was tarnished briefly by a tragic incident. Newspaper articles claimed that its music had inspired Andy Williams, a troubled California high school student, to open fire on his classmates in March 2001, killing two students and injuring 13 others. He was a fan of Linkin Park and claimed that songs from their album — especially "One Step Closer," "Papercut," and "In the End" — had given him the courage to carry out his tragic plan. Brad Delson responded to the negative publicity by saying, "There's a misconception that angry music is going to make someone angry. I think it's cathartic, and I think that a lot of kids who do have problems . . . can relate to the lyrics and can go, 'Oh, it's OK to feel that way. I'm not uncool if I feel insecure.'"

Linkin Park followed up their hit debut album by recording "Point of Authority" for the soundtrack for the film *Little Nicky* starring Adam

Sandler, Reese Witherspoon, and Harvey Keitel. The band also released a DVD based on digital video footage from the concert tour they made after the album's release.

Reanimation

The band's next release, *Reanimation* (2002), quickly became controversial. Instead of putting together a second album of new songs, they issued *Reanimation*, a remix version of *Hybrid Theory*. Their goal wasn't just to give their existing songs a new spin. Instead, they wanted to reinterpret the songs with the help of other, and not necessarily well-known, hip-hop artists, record producers, and dance music DJs. *Entertainment Weekly* described the album as "a hostile rap takeover of *Hybrid Theory* rather than a modest recasting of its songs. The drums, vocals, and bludgeoning air-blast guitars of the original recordings are thrown out and replaced by hip-hop minimalism — rumbling pianos, scratchy beats, air-raid-siren effects, and newly recorded raps by lesser-known rhymers." They also pointed out that the remixes "at times obliterate one of the band's most distinctive characteristics — the vocal interplay between singer Chester Bennington and MC Mike Shinoda." Shinoda said they did it for their fans, not for the increased record sales. "We want them to know they can look to us to mix different things together."

The critics' response to *Reanimation* was far from positive, but most agreed that it was an interesting effort. The reviewer for *USA Today* said, "The ambitious remix project succeeds in recasting the band's crunchy rockers with techno and hip-hop treatments but fails to improve on the originals, raising the question: Why bother?" But the reviewer went on to admit that "the resulting patchwork of radical tweaks by skilled understudies has a fresh allure." *Entertainment Weekly* suggested that despite the band's claim that they wanted to expand the limits of rap-rock, perhaps they just weren't ready for a whole new album and needed time to re-charge their creative batteries. *Rolling Stone* agreed that "It's not so much an album as it is a capital-P project, the kind of record that rock stars make when they get caught short of new material between albums."

―――― " ――――

"We definitely have one of the strongest, if not the strongest, fan bases around," Bennington boasts. *"We go from city to city, and we see the same faces over and over again. . . . A lot of bands neglect the fact that the reason they're able to tour and sell T-shirts is because of the kids. It amazes me to see the bands that take their fans for granted. They forget who got them there."*

―――― 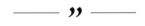 ――――

Meteora

Linkin Park's second album of original songs was released in March 2003. They called it *Meteora*, after a group of monasteries that are clustered on top of a huge rock formation in central Greece. Bennington says that he and Shinoda wanted to write songs that reflected the energy symbolized by the name, which means "hovering in air."

Many in the music industry believe that a jinx is often associated with a successful group's second album. To avoid that sophomore slump, Linkin Park took their time making *Meteora*. They wrote 80 songs before selecting the 12 that would appear on the album and labored for two years on "Somewhere I Belong," the album's first single. Shinoda believes that the result proves the band has grown up. "The first album has feelings of confusion and anger and paranoia," he explains. "We were writing about those from the perspective of young 20-year-old guys." The new album, he says, features songs that express more hope and optimism. It also experiments with different tempos. Songs like "Breaking the Habit" and "Faint" are much faster, while "Easier to Run" is much slower than their earlier songs.

Meteora entered the national pop chart at No. 1 a week after it first appeared in record stores and sold more than 800,000 copies its first week—twice as many as Celine Dion's new album, *One Heart*. But once again, praise was muted from critics who said that the band wasn't doing anything that was really new. The Fort Worth *Star Telegram* accused Linkin Park of "constantly rewriting the same basic song (loud intro, quiet verses, enormous choruses, Chester Bennington screaming his head off) over and over." *Rolling Stone* gave a more balanced appraisal when it said that "the band manages to squeeze the last remaining life out of this nearly extinct [rap-rock] formula with volatile performances and meticulous editing," pointing out that "the band's improved songwriting makes *Meteora* more than yet another remix of its predecessor." The band's fans agreed, and by October 2003 the album had sold more than three million copies.

Connecting with Fans

Perhaps one explanation for Linkin Park's unprecedented success is the importance they attach to spending time with their audience. It is routine for members of the band to walk into the crowd after performances and sign autographs for hours. "We definitely have one of the strongest, if not *the* strongest, fan bases around," Bennington says. "We go from city to city, and we see the same faces over and over again. . . . A lot of bands neglect the fact that the reason they're able to tour and sell T-shirts is because of the kids. It amazes me to see the bands that take their fans for granted. They forget who got them there."

The suddenness of their success has led to rumors that the band is "manufactured"—in other words, that they are the creation of marketing and publicity professionals rather than talented individuals in their own right. "That's the most deeply offensive thing that anyone can say about this band," Bennington comments. "I don't have to explain the way we work, how hard we've battled every step of the way to get heard, how much of the actual success of this band is down to what we've done with our fans and the relationship we've built up with people [who are] into our music."

—— *"* ——

"We like to talk about things we can relate to,"Bennington says. "When we write music, there has to be honesty in it. We're trying to say, 'I've gone through this, and we know other people are, too.'"

—— *"* ——

There is no disputing the fact that Linkin Park's lyrics and melodies set them apart from the angry lashing-out of other rap-metal groups. "We like to talk about things we can relate to," Bennington says. "When we write music, there has to be honesty in it. We're trying to say, 'I've gone through this, and we know other people are, too.'"

LIFE AT HOME

Now in their late 20s, the members of Linkin Park have settled down and lead relatively quiet lives when they aren't on tour. Hahn and Bourdon have steady girlfriends, while Bennington, Shinoda, and Farrell are married. Bennington and his wife Samantha had their first child, a son named Draven, in May 2002.

MAJOR INFLUENCES

Perhaps no group has had more influence on Linkin Park than The Deftones, with whom they have admitted a "hero-worship relationship." They have also been influenced by Depeche Mode, a group that managed

Linkn Park poses with their 2002 Grammy Award after winning for Best Hard Rock Performance for "Crawling."

to bridge the gap between the rock and pop worlds. "When I was a kid," Bennington says, "I used to have a recurring dream that Depeche Mode flew a jet into my schoolyard and asked me to be their fifth member. . . . So we performed a concert in front of my school mates and then we flew off on the jet and did a world tour together."

RECORDINGS

Hybrid Theory, 2000
Reanimation, 2002
Meteora, 2003
Live in Texas, 2003

HONORS AND AWARDS

Billboard Music Awards: 2001, Modern Rock Artist of the Year
MTV Music Video Award: 2002, Best Rock Video, for "In the End"
Grammy Award: 2002, Best Hard Rock Vocal, for "Crawling"

FURTHER READING

Periodicals

Billboard, Apr. 5, 2003, p.1
Current Biography Yearbook, 2002
Detroit Free Press, Feb. 3, 2002, p.E1
Guardian (London), Mar. 21, 2003, p.6
New York Post, Mar. 21, 2003, p.66
Philadelphia Inquirer, Mar. 30, 2003, p.H1
Rolling Stone, Mar. 14, 2002, p.42
Time, Jan. 28, 2002, p.52
USA Weekend, July 11-13, 2003, p.6

Online Articles

http://www.nyrock.com/interviews/2003/linkin_int.asp
    (*NY Rock,* "Interview with Mike Shinoda of Linkin Park," May 2003)

ADDRESS

Linkin Park
Warner Bros. Records
3300 Warner Boulevard
Burbank, CA 91505

WORLD WIDE WEB SITES

http://www.linkinpark.com
http://www.mtv.com

Lindsay Lohan 1986-

American Actress
Star of *The Parent Trap, Freaky Friday,* and *Mean Girls*

BIRTH

Lindsay Morgan Lohan (pronounced *LOW-han*) was born on July 2, 1986, in Cold Spring Harbor, Long Island, New York. Her father, Michael Lohan, started out as an actor in television soap operas and is now an investment banker for film projects. Her mother, Dina Lohan, was once a dancer with New York's famous Radio City Rockettes. She later became a Wall Street analyst and now manages her daughter's acting career. Lindsay has three younger siblings: her brother Michael, two years younger; sister Aliana (known as "Allie"), eight years younger; and brother Dakota, ten years younger.

YOUTH

Lindsay Lohan has been acting since the age of three. Her career started when she became the first redheaded child ever signed to a contract by Ford Models, one of the top modeling agencies in New York. She went on to appear in around 60 television commercials for such companies as The Gap, Pizza Hut, and Duncan-Hines. Lindsay gained her first real exposure acting alongside the veteran comedian and actor Bill Cosby in a commercial for Jell-O. In 1996, at the age of ten, she won the role of Alli Fowler on the television soap opera "Another World."

Lindsay always felt comfortable in front of the camera and found acting and modeling to be "a lot of fun." Although Dina Lohan supported her daughter's desire to act, she also tried to make sure that Lindsay kept things in perspective. "She's so not the stage mom type," Lindsay noted. "I was the one begging her to take me to auditions. My mom told me that the day I got a big head was the day I stopped. She wanted me to be a regular kid."

"She's so not the stage mom type," said Lohan of her mother. "I was the one begging her to take me to auditions. My mom told me that the day I got a big head was the day I stopped. She wanted me to be a regular kid."

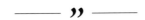

EDUCATION

Lindsay received her early education in the New York City public schools. When she was selected to star in *The Parent Trap* at the age of 11, however, she was forced to miss long stretches of school and received tutoring on the set. Once the filming was completed, Lindsay decided to take some time off from acting. "It was a lot all at once at that time," she acknowledged. "And after that, I kind of just wanted to be in school. I was just 12 years old, and I just wanted to be with my family and my friends."

Lindsay remained in public school until her junior year of high school. She was a straight-A student, and her favorite subjects were math and science. She was also quite popular among her classmates. "I made it a point to get along with everyone because if you're an actress, people assume that you think you're better than everyone else," she recalled. "I wanted to make sure that people had no reason to think that about me." Once Lindsay resumed her acting career, she decided to complete the last two years of her high school education through home schooling. She eventually hopes to enroll at New York University in Manhattan, where she is considering studying law.

CAREER HIGHLIGHTS

The Parent Trap

When Lohan was only 11, she landed the starring role in *The Parent Trap*, a remake of a hit Walt Disney comedy from 1961. *The Parent Trap* presented an unusually challenging acting assignment for her, because she was required to play two separate roles as a set of identical twins. The film's director, Nancy Meyer, spent a long time searching for a young actress who could duplicate the "DNA," or "Disarming Natural Ability," of Hayley Mills, the star of the original film.

More than 4,000 girls auditioned for the role, and only five were invited to Los Angeles for a screen test (a step in the audition process in which actors perform portions of their roles on film). "I had never done a screen test before," said Lohan. "In fact, I had never been to L.A. before." Meyer recalled that she and her husband, film producer Charles Shyer, were beginning to think that perhaps they would never find the right actress for the dual role. "Then I saw Lindsay's tape, and I heard the lines for the first time," Meyer said. "She did quirky things, made faces. She's animated. Brilliant, it turns out." After viewing Lohan's screen test, Meyer exclaimed, "I want that redhead!"

The Parent Trap tells the story of identical twins Hallie and Annie, whose parents divorced shortly after they were born. Their mother, a British wedding gown designer named Elizabeth (played by Natasha Richardson), then returned to her native London. Their father, an American vineyard owner named Nick (played by Dennis Quaid), returned to his home in Napa Valley, California. Since neither parent could bear to be separated from the girls—and they felt that sending young children back and forth across the ocean for visitation would be unfair—they ultimately decided that each parent would take custody of one of the twins. As a result, Annie grows up in London with their mother, while Hallie grows up in California with their father. Because of this unusual custody arrangement, neither twin is aware of the other's existence.

In The Parent Trap *Lohan played identical twin sisters Annie (left) and Hallie (right), who scheme to bring their divorced parents back together again.*

Years later, Hallie and Annie meet unexpectedly when their parents end up sending them to the same summer camp. The girls immediately notice their resemblance to each other. After comparing notes, they realize that they are not only sisters, but twins. Each girl longs to meet the parent she has never known, so they hatch a plan to switch identities. They decide that Annie will pretend to be Hallie and return to their father's home in California, while Hallie will pretend to be Annie and return to their mother's home in England.

The girls spend their remaining days at camp preparing themselves for the switch. Hallie must learn to speak with a British accent, for example, while Annie must drop her accent to sound more American. The girls must also master the basic facts about each other's lives. Once they leave camp, they successfully adopt each other's identities and fool their parents—though not without some awkward and comic moments. The girls finally reveal their true identities to their parents after Nick announces his engagement to a shallow and conniving younger woman. Hallie and Annie then work together on a new scheme to disrupt their father's wedding plans and rekindle the romance between their parents.

A Challenging Role

With the help of camera tricks and computerized images, Lohan played the roles of both twins in *The Parent Trap*. When the script called for Hallie and Annie to appear in the same scene, Lohan would play one of the parts, then change her outfit and her accent and repeat the scene playing the other part. A device called an "ear wink," which allowed Lohan to hear the other twin's lines so that she could respond with the proper timing, helped make it seem like there were two different people on screen.

> *As Lohan prepared for her dual role in* **The Parent Trap,** *she watched the original 1961 film. "Most of my friends had seen the Hayley Mills version on video," Lohan said. "But I didn't see it until after I got the role. I'm so amazed by her performance because they didn't have the technical stuff to do two of her that easily back then."*

Lohan acknowledged the challenges of playing two people in the same film. "I didn't really have any other acting experience," she said. "They just coached me before each scene." Although she admitted that it was scary, she also claimed that it was fun. As part of her preparation for the film, Lohan watched the original 1961 movie on video. "Most of my friends had seen the Hayley Mills version on video," she noted. "But I didn't see it until after I got the role. I'm so amazed by her performance because they didn't have the technical stuff to do two of her that easily back then."

In *Variety* magazine, film critic Joe Leydon gave Lohan high praise for her performance in the roles of both Hallie and Annie. "In the dual role originally played by 15-year-old Hayley Mills, newcomer Lohan makes a thoroughly winning impression," he wrote. "With a little help from the special-effects team, she artfully sustains the illusion of two physically similar but subtly different characters. She is particularly good at expressing each twin's efforts to hide the joy she feels when finally meeting the parent she's never known."

Lohan enjoyed making the film, even though most days included eight to ten hours of filming. She has said that she learned a lot from the other ac-

*Even as her show biz career began to soar, Lohan continued
to pursue her studies.*

tors, particularly Dennis Quaid. "He was so terrific, he really made me feel
comfortable," she recalled. Lohan also enjoyed working with her brother,
Michael, who had a cameo role in the film as a boy who is mistakenly sent
to an all-girls camp. The Lohan family spent a great deal of time on the set
during filming, and they even brought some of Lindsay's friends to Los
Angeles for a visit. They ended up going a little crazy in the hotel where
they were staying. "We put shaving cream all over my brother and made a
big mess in the hotel room," Lohan related. "In order to get us back, he
took whipped cream—it was one in the morning and my parents were
sleeping—coffee, and miles of sugar and threw it on me."

Other Projects

After she completed filming for *The Parent Trap*, Lohan took a break from
acting that lasted nearly three years. With her mother's support, she decided that she wanted to live a normal life and concentrate on school for
a while. But Lohan eventually found that she was ready to resume her
acting career. "After a while, I started to see other girls coming up, and I
was like, 'I wanna do this again,'" she recalled. Lohan's return to the
screen took place in the 2000 television movie *Life-Size*, in which she

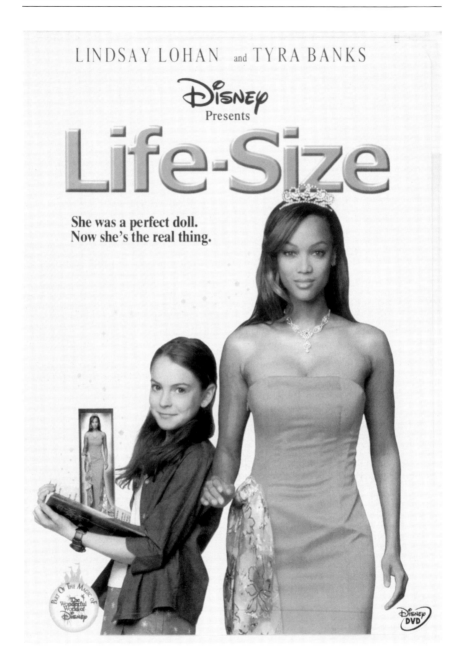

LINDSAY LOHAN and TYRA BANKS

Disney
Presents

Life-Size

She was a perfect doll.
Now she's the real thing.

played a young girl whose doll (Tyra Banks) unexpectedly comes to life. The movie was later released on home video, where it proved very popular. (For more information on Tyra Banks, see *Biography Today Performing Artists*, Vol. 2.)

Also in 2000, Lohan was cast as Bette Midler's daughter in the pilot episode of the TV sitcom "Bette." Lohan gave up her role when producers decided to move the location of filming from New York to Los Angeles, and the series was canceled a short time later. In 2002 Lohan appeared on TV once again in the Disney Channel movie *Get a Clue*.

Freaky Friday

Lohan's next big-screen opportunity came in the form of another remake of an earlier Walt Disney film, *Freaky Friday*, which was based on a 1972 novel by Mary Rodgers. The original film, released in 1976, starred a young Jodie Foster, who went on to have a successful career as an actress, director, and producer. In the remake, released in 2003, Lohan starred alongside the veteran actress Jamie Lee Curtis.

Freaky Friday tells the story of a widowed psychologist named Tess (played by Curtis) who is struggling to raise her rebellious 17-year-old daughter, Anna (played by Lohan). Although Anna is a nice girl and a good student, she manages to get on her mother's nerves by playing guitar in a garage rock band and wearing grungy clothes. At the same time, Anna feels frustrated by her mother's strict rules and conservative style. The differences between mother and daughter create a great deal of friction, particularly when Tess makes plans to remarry.

The story takes a wacky turn when Tess and Anna engage in a shouting match in a Chinese restaurant. The restaurant owner, an elderly Chinese woman with a gift for magic, decides that the mother and daughter need help to understand one another. She serves them enchanted fortune cookies that cause them to wake up the next morning—a Friday—in each other's bodies. Both are shocked and dismayed when they realize what has taken place. When Anna looks at herself in the mirror and instead sees Tess, for example, she shrieks, "I'm old! I'm like the Crypt Keeper!"

Unable to find a way to switch back, the mother and daughter have no choice but to try to impersonate each other for a day. Anna goes to Tess's office and counsels her patients, for instance, while Tess goes to Anna's school and attends her classes. Many comic scenes result as mother and daughter struggle to fit in to each other's world. In the end, they both gain increased understanding and respect for the other.

Another Acting Challenge

Freaky Friday once again offered Lohan the challenge of playing two roles. First she played the role of Anna, then—once the magical switch took

Scenes from Freaky Friday, the hit 2003 comedy starring Lohan and Jamie Lee Curtis.

place—she played the role of Tess inside of Anna's body. Although Curtis faced the same challenge, Lohan claimed that her counterpart had an advantage. "Jamie had it easier than I did because she was [once] a teenager," she noted, "but I've never been an adult so I didn't have the same kind of references." To help prepare for the challenge of filming Anna as Tess and Tess as Anna, the actresses videotaped themselves doing each other's lines and actions. "That way I watched how Jamie would have done and said things and then tried to imitate that," Lohan explained.

Lohan liked working with Curtis, whom she describes as "a lot of fun" and "really funny." "She is more energetic than I am," Lohan added. "She is very hyper and stuff." Curtis agreed with Lohan's assessment about which actress had the more difficult job. "It has to be believable that Lindsay's character becomes her mother," Curtis said. "I think she has the much harder job of the two of us. Lindsay has perfected the dual-role thing; she has a range that most teens never get to show."

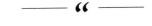

"Jodie [Foster] played the daughter more as a tomboy. I play her as a punk rocker. We both rebelled but in different ways."

Lohan chose not to see the original *Freaky Friday* until after she completed work on her own version. "I had never heard about this story but my mom had read the book and had seen the original movie," she noted. "She filled me in but I didn't rent the film until after we'd finished ours because that would have put too much pressure on me to be like Jodie, who is one of my acting role models." After she finally saw Foster's version, Lohan concluded that "Jodie played the daughter more as a tomboy. I play her as a punk rocker. We both rebelled but in different ways."

Lohan had to learn how to play guitar for her role in *Freaky Friday*. She was happy to have the opportunity to indulge her interest in music, including singing. "The band in the movie was made for the movie, but we had rehearsals like a real band. We would get together and go into these big rooms and play and practice our instruments together," she recalled. "I was kind of nervous, because I don't play guitar and I had to learn for the movie. Once I learned how to play it I had a lot of fun."

The fact that her first two starring roles came in remakes of Disney films does not bother Lohan. "It's great that Disney is bringing back films that our parents loved and modernizing them, especially ones that show how

In this scene from Mean Girls *set in the dreaded school cafeteria, Cady confronts the "Plastics": (from left) Amanda Seyfried, Rachel MacAdams, and Lacey Chabert.*

important strong parent and child relationships are," she stated. "It's clever marketing on Disney's behalf. Parents are the ones who buy movie tickets for their kids, and if they remember loving an old movie they're more likely to recommend it for their children." *Freaky Friday* turned out to be the surprise hit of the summer, earning more than $110 million at the box office.

Grabbing New Opportunities

The success of *Freaky Friday* brought Lohan a number of additional film opportunities. In 2004 she starred as Lola in *Confessions of a Teenage Drama Queen*, based on a popular novel of the same name by Dyan Sheldon. Lola is a sophisticated New York teenager who rebels against her divorced mother's decision to relocate to the boring New Jersey suburb of Dellwood. She struggles to fit in at her new school and ends up feuding with her rich and nasty classmate Carla. *Confessions* received mostly negative reviews upon its release and did not perform very well at the box office.

Lohan experienced greater success with her second film of 2004, *Mean Girls*. Lohan starred as Cady Heron, an American teenager who has spent most of her childhood being home-schooled in Africa by her parents, who were working there as researchers. Upon returning to the United States, Cady is suddenly plunged into the pettiness of a suburban Illinois high school. "What follows is an anthropological dissection of contemporary high school culture—its norms and traditions, its food chain and battle-grounds—with the villains [of the title] proving that the lions of the Serengeti have nothing on teenage girls," wrote Lynda Obst in *Interview*.

The screenplay for the movie had an interesting origin. It was written by Tina Fey, the head writer for the NBC skit comedy show "Saturday Night Live." Fey based the screenplay on the best-selling nonfiction book *Queen Bees and Wannabes: Helping Your Daughter Survive Cliques, Gossip, Boyfriends, and Other Realities of Adolescence* by Rosalind Wiseman. (For more information on Fey, see *Biography Today Authors*, Vol. 16.)

In *Mean Girls*, Cady sets out to fight the group of shallow girls known as the "Plastics" who rule the school, but she soon finds herself being drawn into their social circle instead. Fey appears in the movie as a math teacher who observes Cady's trans-

"I want to find something different from what I usually do [in future film roles]," said Lohan. "I don't want to give an image of doing only teen movies and just being this perfect teen. I just want to do something completely different and really rock at it."

formation from a thoughtful and caring friend into a social climber. In the end, she lectures Cady and the other female students about their tendency to be mean to one another. "Calling somebody else fat will not make you any thinner," she declares. "Calling somebody else stupid will not make you any smarter. And you've got to stop calling each other sluts and whores. It just makes it all right for guys to call you that." *Mean Girls* received generally positive reviews and opened in the No. 1 spot at the box office. Writing in *People*, Leah Rozen called the movie "a superior teen comedy with solid performances by its mostly young cast."

Lohan is scheduled to appear in several other films in late 2004 and 2005. In *Dramarama*, for example, she will play a promising drama student who is forced to transfer from her comfortable private school to a rundown public school. Since the new school has no drama program, she and a gang of misfits create their own drama club. They eventually face her old private school classmates in a drama competition. Lohan is also expected to star as

Blair Waldorf in *Gossip Girl*, based on the popular book series of the same name by Cecily von Ziegesar. Finally, she will appear in a remake of the classic Disney movie *Herbie the Love Bug*, called *Herbie: Fully Loaded*.

Spreading Her Wings

Lohan hopes that her successful movie career will lead to an additional career as a singer. "I started taking voice lessons when I was little," she explained. "I've always wanted to be an overall entertainer who sings, dances, and acts." Lohan has already contributed vocals to the soundtracks for two of her films—*Freaky Friday* and *Confessions of a Teenage Drama Queen*. In 2004 she signed a multi-album contract with Tommy Mottola's Casablanca Records.

In addition to her movies and her fledgling musical career, Lohan has appeared on the cover of numerous magazines and hosted several high-profile awards shows on television. She is seen in public so frequently that she has gained a reputation as a "party girl." Though she admits that she enjoys going to Hollywood clubs with her friends, she insists that she would never do anything to embarrass herself. "When we go out, we just get a table and observe what goes on. We're calm. We know our place. We don't have to get stupid and drunk—we can have fun without drinking," she stated. "I don't want to have a drink and have someone whip out a camera phone and [send the picture to] Disney. It's not worth it! I don't want to risk my career. . . . But it's hard being 17 years old and not being able to do the things that other 17-year-olds do, like going out, learning about yourself, finding out who you are."

> *Lohan hopes eventually to move beyond acting into different aspects of the film industry, including producing and directing. "Getting this sort of respect and all these opportunities at my age is incredible," she noted. "I've been talking to my friends at MTV about some ideas for shows. And I want to get into producing movies, too. If I have the skills to do something, I don't think my age should stop me."*

As she evaluates future film projects, Lohan is interested in moving away from her "teen queen" image and taking on roles that will show a different side of her abilities. "I want to act more. I want to really act in a film and commit to something and be a different person. I mean, the characters I've played so far are very similar to who I am, so it's hard to say that I'm actually fully acting. I want to find something different from what I usually do. I don't want to give an image of doing only teen movies and just being this perfect teen," she stated. "I just want to do something completely different and really rock at it. You can only do the same thing for so long."

Lohan also hopes eventually to move beyond acting into different aspects of the film industry, including producing and directing. "Getting this sort of respect and all these opportunities at my age is incredible," she noted. "I've been talking to my friends at MTV about some ideas for shows. And I want to get into producing movies, too. If I have the skills to do something, I don't think my age should stop me."

HOME AND FAMILY

Although Lohan recently moved into her own apartment in Los Angeles, she remains very close to her family. "I was raised by an amazing family, and I think that they've kept me grounded my whole life," she noted. "My mom and I are really close, which I think is cool. If I didn't confide in her it would be stupid because she knows what I do anyway." Her mother manages her career, while her brothers and sister often appear as extras in her movies.

Still, Lohan's family has been the subject of negative articles in the press. Rumors have surfaced numerous times about trouble in her parents' marriage. Her father was arrested for assault in the spring of 2004 following a brawl at the family home. This legal problem brought attention to his past record, which included serving a four-year prison term for securities fraud. Lohan refused to comment on her father's actions except to express continued support and admiration for him.

Lohan has been linked romantically to several famous young men, including singer Aaron Carter and actor Wilmer Valderrama, her current boyfriend, who is one of the stars on "That '70s Show."

HOBBIES AND OTHER INTERESTS

Lohan has a dog, a miniature bichon frise named Max, and enjoys listening to music by such artists as Avril Lavigne and Eminem. She has her driver's license and has just made her first big purchase—a pre-owned BMW 330 CI convertible. She said it took a lot to persuade her mother to let her buy the luxury car. In her spare time, she enjoys swimming, ice skating, in-line skating, gymnastics, singing, reading, writing, and shopping.

HONORS AND AWARDS

Young Artist Award: 1998, for *The Parent Trap*, for Best Leading Young
   Actress in a Feature Film
MTV Movie Award: 2004, for *Freaky Friday*, for Breakthrough Female

CREDITS
Films

The Parent Trap, 1998
Freaky Friday, 2003
Confessions of a Teenage Drama Queen, 2004
Mean Girls, 2004

Television

"Another World," 1996 (TV Series)
Life-Size, 2000 (TV Movie)
"Bette," 2000 (TV Series)
Get a Clue, 2002 (TV Movie)

FURTHER READING
Books

Contemporary Theatre, Film, and Television, Vol. 55, 2004

Periodicals

Entertainment Weekly, May 7, 2004, p.57
Interview, June 2004, p.88

Los Angeles Times, Apr. 18, 2004, p.E1
Newsday, Aug. 6, 1998, p.B3; Aug. 13, 2003, p.B12
People, May 10, 2004, p.31; May 24, 2004, p.79
Seventeen, June 2004, p.123
Variety, July 27, 1998, p.51; July 28, 2003, p.27; Feb. 23, 2004, p.34
YM, Aug. 2004, p.103

ADDRESS

Lindsay Lohan
Endeavor Agency
9701 Wilshire Boulevard
10th Floor
Beverly Hills, CA 90212

WORLD WIDE WEB SITES

http://llrocks.com
http://www.meangirlsmovie.com
http://disneyvideos.disney.go.com

Irene D. Long 1951-
American Aerospace Physician and Administrator
First Female Chief Medical Officer of NASA's
Kennedy Space Center

BIRTH

Irene D. Long was born Irene Duhart on November 16, 1951, in Cleveland, Ohio. Her father, Andrew Duhart, was a steelworker who was interested in planes and space travel. Her mother, Heloweise Davis Duhart, was a teacher of adult education. Long is the second of two children. Her older brother is a freelance artist.

YOUTH

Long was fascinated with medicine from a young age. She was just three years old when she saw an operation on television. She watched the open-heart surgery and decided it was something she wanted to do. She also had an interest in aviation and space. She was lucky to be growing up at the beginning of the era of space exploration.

When Long was young, in the 1950s and 1960s, the United States was in the middle of the "space race" with the Soviet Union (U.S.S.R.). After the end of World War II in 1945, the U.S. and the U.S.S.R. became rivals as the two countries emerged as the only world superpowers. These two nations became locked in the conflict known as the Cold War — a war defined not by open warfare, but by escalating hostilities between the two nations. The Cold War was also characterized by the division of the major world governments into pro-U.S. and pro-Soviet nations. With the Cold War raging, the two superpowers began what was known as the "arms race," in which the two nations were engaged in a potentially deadly competition to create ever more powerful weapons. The arms race led to the "space race," with the goal to be the first nation to land a man on the moon. Both the U.S.S.R. and the U.S. had the rocket technology necessary to place an orbiting vehicle into space — in fact they had developed that technology as part of weapons delivery systems used in World War II.

Long recalls the precise moment she discovered her dream. "I was watching a show on television called 'Man and the Challenge.' It was about getting ready for human spaceflight. There was a Lieutenant Colonel John Paul Stapp on the show, and it showed him working with sled tests and other research that they were doing at the time. I remember watching the credits, which showed that Lt. Col. Stapp was an Air Force physician specializing in aviation medicine, and I said to myself, 'Wow, that looks like fun.'"

The modern age of space exploration began in 1957 when the Soviet Union launched *Sputnik I*, the first satellite sent into space. The United States became determined to beat the Russians in developing its space program. In 1958, the United States founded the National Aeronautics and Space Administration (NASA). Three years later, President John F. Kennedy announced America's plans to send the first men to the moon. Astronauts and space exploration were in the news and on television.

Long recalls the precise moment she discovered her dream. "I was watching a show on television called 'Man and the Challenge.' It was about getting ready for human spaceflight. There was a Lieutenant Colonel John Paul Stapp on the show, and it showed him working with sled tests and other research that they were doing at the time. I remember watching the credits, which showed that Lt. Col. Stapp was an Air Force physician specializing in aviation medicine, and I said to myself, 'Wow, that looks like fun.'" Long was just nine years old when she told her parents that she wanted to be an aerospace physician when she grew up.

———— " ————

"My parents always gave me the impression that you could do whatever you set your mind to, and that the future depends upon how hard you work and how determined you are."

———— " ————

Long's upbringing inspired her in her dreams. She grew up in the Cleveland area, not far from NASA's Lewis Research Center (now called the John H. Glenn Research Center at Lewis Field). Her father was interested in flying and she sometimes tagged along on his flying lessons. Long's mother and father supported their daughter's plans. "My parents always gave me the impression that you could do whatever you set your mind to, and that the future depends upon how hard you work and how determined you are." Although some people believed that science wasn't a suitable field for an African-American woman, Long never let prejudice keep her from her goals.

EDUCATION

After graduating from East High School in Cleveland, Long tailored her education to her goals. She studied biology at Northwestern University in Chicago and received her bachelor's degree in 1973.

Becoming a doctor requires many years of training. After completing four years of college, students must then attend four years of medical school. At the end of medical school, new doctors decide what field of medicine they wish to practice. Then they complete a "residency" of at least three years in that field. Long entered the St. Louis School of Medicine and earned a medical degree (M.D.) in 1977. She followed this with residency training at the Cleveland Clinic and Mt. Sinai Hospital in Cleveland. She studied general surgery during this period of specialized training.

Long continued her education by accepting another residency at the Wright State University in Dayton, Ohio. This was a very specialized program in aerospace medicine that only accepted a few students each year. Long earned a master's degree in aerospace medicine through this residency. Her studies also included some time at NASA's Ames Research Center in California. There she continued researching the effects of space on the human body. She also got the chance to meet an inspiring figure, Colonel Charles Bolden, one of NASA's first African-American astronauts. "I went to hear him speak and I passed a note to the person who was in charge saying that I was working in an aerospace medicine residency program and I'd like to meet him. After his speech he came over and talked to me and listened to my goals and aspirations and said, 'You look like you'd be a nice person to work for NASA.'"

CAREER HIGHLIGHTS

Important Research into Sickle-Cell Anemia

Part of Long's special medical training included doing medical research. In 1982 she published an important research paper about the sickle-cell trait. Sickle-cell anemia is a genetic disease that affects red blood cells. Normal red blood cells are round, like doughnuts, and carry oxygen to the cells of the body. In people with sickle-cell anemia, the red blood cells can change into a crescent shape, like a sickle. This change happens when the cell gives up its oxygen. When many cells form the sickle shape, blood clots can form. This can lead to great pain or even a dangerous stroke, when a clot blocks an important blood vessel.

Sickle-cell anemia is genetic disease, meaning that you inherit it from your parents. If both parents pass you the sickle-cell gene, you have sickle-cell disease. If only one parent passes the sickle-cell gene to you, you have sickle-cell trait. The sickle-cell gene is particularly common among African-Americans, with 1 in 12 carrying the trait and 1 in 375 having sickle-cell disease, but people of any race or ethnic background can have the disease.

Long's research paper addressed the potential dangers of flying for people with the sickle-cell trait. Sickle-cells are formed when there is a shortage of oxygen in the blood. Situations that deprive the body of oxygen can cause painful attacks. These conditions include too much exercise, too much cold, and high-altitude flying. Long showed in her article that the reduced oxygen level in a plane will not affect people with the sickle-cell trait. This

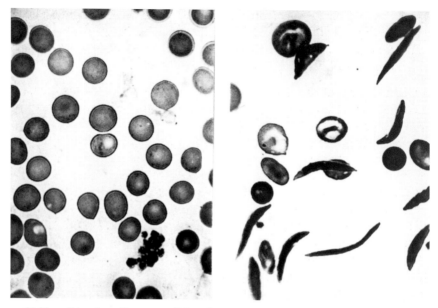

Sickle cell is a hereditary condition that involves the red blood cells that carry oxygen throughout the body. In these photos, the cells at left are in their normal round shape and the cells at right are deformed by sickle cell disease.

research helped reassure people with sickle-cell trait that flying posed no danger to them.

Achieving a Dream

Long spent many years preparing for a job as an aerospace physician. In 1982 she realized her dream when she joined the medical staff at NASA's Kennedy Space Center in Florida. One of her first duties was to help staff the biomedical consoles in the Launch Control Center. Her job was to monitor the heart rates and blood pressure of the astronauts to make sure they were safe to launch. She was on duty on January 28, 1986, the day the space shuttle *Challenger* exploded shortly after takeoff, killing everyone on board. On that day it was her job to make sure staff doctors, rescue teams, and local hospitals were ready for any possibility. "We had to be ready to provide emergency support in a situation where it was extremely difficult to know what was happening."

Shortly after joining the Kennedy Space Center staff, Long was chosen to head their Occupational Medicine and Environmental Health Office. She became the first African-American woman in this position. During her time as Chief of the Occupational Medicine and Environmental Health Office, Long oversaw a staff of more than 200 doctors, nurses, and environmental health specialists. Overall, she was responsible for the safety of the more than 18,000 people working at the Center.

Long and her staff had many responsibilities. They had to provide medical treatment in case of an emergency on the ground. All space launches, whether of rockets or the space shuttle, can be dangerous. There is the potential for fires, explosions, and exposure to toxic chemicals. All of these events could endanger many workers on the ground. There are also special dangers the astronauts face, such as decompression. This happens when there is a sudden change in air pressure in the cabin of the ship. Changes in air pressure can affect how blood works in the body, so people suffering from decompression need specialized medical treatment. Long's office had to be ready for these and other types of emergencies.

Another duty of Long and her staff was to make sure that all areas in the Kennedy Space Center were safe for the workers. In addition to the launch area, there are many other areas that needed to be inspected for safety issues. People working with rocket fuels needed to be protected from explosions. The Kennedy Space Center tests how tools work in space by using

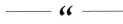

At NASA's Kennedy Space Center in Florida, Long helped staff the biomedical consoles in the Launch Control Center. She was on duty on January 28, 1986, when the space shuttle Challenger *exploded shortly after takeoff, killing everyone on board. "We had to be ready to provide emergency support in a situation where it was extremely difficult to know what was happening."*

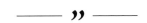

them underwater, and divers in these programs needed protection as well. People working with toxic chemicals needed a place safe from fumes. Long set up a Toxic Substance Registry System to keep track of these potential dangers. The workplace safety program Long directed was so thorough it has been a model for many companies and industries.

A final responsibility of Long and her staff was to give physicals to employees at the Space Center. Many jobs at NASA are physically demanding or potentially dangerous. Long's office made sure that the employees were both healthy and able to perform their duties. They also investigated how living in space affects an astronaut's body. Their research included experiments in the lab and careful observations of the astronauts' physical state, both before and after space flights.

Preparing for Life in Space

In 1994, Long became Director of the Kennedy Space Center's Biomedical Office. Her duties included program management of the center's programs in aerospace and occupational medicine, life sciences research, and environmental health. She was also responsible for the operations management of the life sciences support facilities. Part of her job became working on the development of the International Space Station (ISS).

The Kennedy Space Center does more than just send the space shuttle on missions. It also helps plan for America's involvement in the International Space Station, which is considered a scientific and engineering marvel. The International Space Station is in orbit in space, 220 miles above the earth, where there is very little gravity. It is a permanent human outpost in space that has been inhabited since November 2000 by crews from the United States, Russia, Canada, Japan, and several European countries. The ISS is gradually being built in space—modules are built on earth and then transported into space, where they are assembled by the astronauts. The astronauts do some of the assembly on spacewalks, and they also use a robotic arm and crane, which arrived on an early flight. A series of continuing space flights are delivering additional components, as well as food and other supplies for the crew members. When completed, the ISS will have room for up to seven astronauts and will house six separate research laboratories. Astronauts and cosmonauts are already living and working on the station in rotating crews, each staying up to six months. They perform scientific research that may one day allow humans to live in space permanently. Crew return vehicles will remain attached to the ISS, ready for use in the event of an emergency.

At this point, there is one crucial barrier to humans' ability to live permanently in space: humans will not be able to colonize space until they can supply their own food and water. But there is no room on a space station for agricultural fields. The moon and Mars have no healthy soil or sources of water. Under Long's direction, the space center's Controlled Ecological Life Support System (CELSS) project explored ways to grow food without soil. An important goal was for food production to be *bioregenerative*, meaning self-sustaining. This means that everything used to grow food, from the water to the air to the fertilizer, needs to be recycled. Even waste products on a space station would be used to grow food.

*The Controlled Environment Life Support System (CELSS), set up in a
self-contained bubble in an old hangar, has explored ways to produce food,
water, and oxygen and reduce carbon dioxide.*

Working in an old hangar, the CELSS team set up a self-contained, bubble-shaped station called the Biomass Production Chamber. Their experiments with bioregeneration have produced important crops, including wheat, soybeans, potatoes, tomatoes, and lettuce. They also helped generate purified water and air. People breathe in oxygen and breathe out carbon dioxide. Too much carbon dioxide is poisonous to humans. The crops in the CELSS experiment produced oxygen that people could breathe and reduced carbon dioxide levels before they became poisonous. Long is proud of the efforts of CELSS and her environmental and safety staffs. "I would like to think that we are pioneers in occupational medicine for the space program. What we're doing here now on the ground will someday be done in space, be it on a space station, the moon, or Mars."

Long is proud of the efforts of CELSS and her environmental and safety staffs. "I would like to think that we are pioneers in occupational medicine for the space program. What we're doing here now on the ground will someday be done in space, be it on a space station, the moon, or Mars."

Becoming NASA's First Female Chief Medical Officer

In 2000, Long became the first minority woman to achieve the civilian equivalent of a general's rank at Kennedy Space Center. That year she was named Chief Medical Officer and Associate Director of Spaceport Services. This also made her the Center's first female Chief Medical Officer. Her job in this position was to coordinate health and safety efforts throughout the entire Kennedy Space Center. This included planning for the Center's future needs and developing ways to prevent environmental and health problems before they happen.

As Associate Director of Spaceport Services, Long helps the Kennedy Space Center prepare for the future of space travel. Their goal is to make space travel safer, faster, and cheaper, so that space travel may some day be as common as air travel. They look at ways to make space launches and the delivery of space cargo more efficient. They try to improve procedures with new computer systems and new technologies. Long's efforts in this department are another way she works toward achieving the dream of a permanent human habitat in space.

Working in the Community

Throughout her career at NASA, Long has also been involved in outreach programs. In 1985 she helped start the Space Life Sciences Training

Program at Kennedy Space Center. This program encourages women and minority college students to explore careers in science. College students join the program and spend six weeks with the scientists at Kennedy Space Center. They learn about space physiology, or how the human body functions in space. They also study how space affects plants and animals. They learn to plan experiments and work as a team. A whole generation of students have now been inspired by this opportunity.

Long has also spread her knowledge through teaching and membership in professional organizations. She has taught about community health at the Wright State University School of Medicine. She is a member of the Society of NASA Flight Surgeons and served as that group's president in 1999. She also belongs to the Aerospace Medical Association and its Space Medicine Branch. These organizations and others have recognized her hard work. In 1986 she received the Kennedy Space Center's Federal Woman of the Year Award; in 1995 the Society of NASA Flight Surgeons gave Long their Presidential Award; in 1998 she earned an Outstanding Achievement Award from Women in Aerospace; and in 2001 she was named to the Ohio Women's Hall of Fame.

> **""**
>
> *Long knows that because of her success, she is now a role model for others. "I hope that I am someone that people can look at and say, 'I can do that too.'" She has made her dreams come true through hard work and persistence. "I made it happen," she said. "Every time someone told me I couldn't do something, I went out and did it."*
>
> **""**

Long knows that because of her success, she is now a role model for others. "I hope that I am someone that people can look at and say, 'I can do that too.'" She has made her dreams come true through hard work and persistence. "I *made* it happen," she said. "Every time someone told me I couldn't do something, I went out and did it." Her message to those who would follow her is to set goals and work hard to achieve them. "There's a saying that to know where you're going, you must know where you've been. I think it's just as important to say, to succeed and prosper in the present, you must know where you're headed."

HOME AND FAMILY

Long is single and lives in Merritt Island, Florida. She enjoys reading, cooking, and entertaining friends.

HOBBIES AND OTHER INTERESTS

Long has enjoyed creative craft projects since she was a little girl. She creates and sometimes sells her own flower wreaths. She also makes handmade lotions and soaps using homegrown herbs and plants. She collects antiques, including antique furniture and glassware. She also enjoys collecting dolls and doll house miniatures, and makes her own miniature furniture. She is involved in her community, serving on the board of directors of Crosswinds Youth Services. She is also a member of the National Association for the Advancement of Colored People (NAACP).

HONORS AND AWARDS

Federal Woman of the Year Award (Kennedy Space Center): 1986
Presidential Award (Society of NASA Flight Surgeons): 1995
Outstanding Achievement Award (Women in Aerospace): 1998
Named to Ohio Women's Hall of Fame: 2001

FURTHER READING

Books

Burns, Khephra, and William Miles. *Black Stars in Orbit: NASA's African American Astronauts,* 1995
Encyclopedia of World Biography, 1998
Notable Scientists: From 1900 to the Present, 2001
Notable Twentieth-Century Scientists, 1995
Webster, Raymond B. *African-American Firsts in Science and Technology,* 2000

Periodicals

Ebony, Sep. 1984, p.61
Florida Today, Aug. 23, 2000, p.1

Online Articles

http://www-pao.ksc.nasa.gov/release/1994/87-94.htm
   (*Kennedy Space Center,* "NASA News Release Online," Aug. 1, 1994)
http://www.scinfo.org/sicklept.htm
   (*The Sickle Cell Information Center,* "What Is Sickle Cell Anemia," Apr. 6, 2002)
http://medschool.slu.edu/oma/newsletter/march97.pdf
   (*The Supplemental Instructor, Saint Louis University School of Medicine,* "Physician of Color Highlight," Mar. 1997)

Online Databases

Biography Resource Center Online, 2003, articles from *Encyclopedia of World Biography,* 2001, and *Notable Scientists: From 1900 to the Present,* 2001

ADDRESS

Dr. Irene D. Long
NASA Kennedy Space Center
Chief Medical Officer
Kennedy Space Center, FL 32899

WORLD WIDE WEB SITES

http://www-pao.ksc.nasa.gov/bios/long.htm
http://www.ksc.nasa.gov
http://www.nasa.gov

John Mayer 1977-
American Singer and Songwriter
Creator of the Hit CDs *Room for Squares* and
Heavier Things

BIRTH

John Mayer was born on October 16, 1977, in Bridgeport,
Connecticut. His father, Richard Mayer, was a high school
principal. His mother, Margaret Mayer, was a middle school
English teacher. They have lived in the same house since 1984.
John has an older brother, Carl, and a younger brother, Ben.

YOUTH

Mayer grew up in Fairfield, Connecticut. According to his mother, Mayer was always "a peaceable kid. He would not demand a lot of attention. He would go off and do things by himself." Mayer participated in middle school and high school theater until he turned his attention to music.

Mayer has been exposed to music all his life. His father would often play jazz standards and show tunes on the piano at home. He also played the piano at the weekly Rotary Club meetings. "Growing up in Connecticut," Mayer recalled, "there was a piano in the house from the time I was born, and I just gravitated toward it." He would sit at the piano and create sounds out of nothing. He didn't really want to learn how to play the piano; he just wanted to play it.

> *"Growing up in Connecticut," Mayer recalled, "there was a piano in the house from the time I was born, and I just gravitated toward it." He would sit at the piano and create sounds out of nothing. He didn't really want to learn how to play the piano; he just wanted to play it.*

When he was 13 years old, Mayer got his first guitar. The first night he had the guitar, he tried to figure out how to play it by himself, and it didn't take long for him to figure out chords. He had the guitar for two weeks before he took lessons. After several months of guitar lessons, his parents stopped his lessons because he was not learning to read music.

In 1990, Mayer's neighbor gave him a tape of Stevie Ray Vaughan, a bluesy rock guitarist. When he listened to it, he thought, "What is this and where is the rest of it?" He became obsessed with Vaughan and such other rock guitarists as Jimi Hendrix, Buddy Guy, and Robert Cray. Soon, Mayer was spending all his free time playing guitar. Consequently, his grades suffered. Mayer asked his parents more than once to let him drop out of high school; he didn't think school was necessary since he was going to be a famous guitarist. His parents became concerned and sent him to two different therapists to try to convince him to stop playing guitar.

When Mayer was just 15 years old, he started playing guitar in clubs around the area. In the early 1990s, he and a high school friend, Joe Beleznay, played in a band called Villanova Junction. The band did not last long, but Mayer and Beleznay continued to work together on their music. The two went their separate ways when Mayer left for college.

When he was young, Mayer vowed that he would not drink alcohol or take drugs. "I really did say growing up that I won't drink and do drugs," he swears. "I wanted to shape my life toward making records." And he has kept that vow throughout his success.

EDUCATION

In 1995, Mayer graduated from Fairfield High School, home of the Fairfield Mustangs. He spent the next two years working at a gas station just a quarter of a mile from his parents' house. He continued to play his music at local clubs, determined to pursue a career in music. Eventually, however, he realized that he needed to do something more if he wanted to succeed in music. He remembers thinking, "OK. It's not going to happen here. It's not going to happen in Connecticut. It's not going to happen living at home." That's when he decided to enroll at the prestigious Berklee College of Music in Boston, Massachusetts. Such famous musical performers as Quincy Jones, Bruce Hornsby, and Natalie Maines of the Dixie Chicks had also studied at Berklee.

After less than one year at Berklee, Mayer decided that he had had enough. He felt that the school emphasized technical expertise rather than creativity. He soon started to skip classes and then eventually dropped out. "I went to Berklee by default," Mayer said. "I really had an interest in songwriting, and I eventually dropped out to write songs. . . . I have been an observationalist all my life, and I wanted to write songs in a way they hadn't been written before. I want to be the guy that people say hit the nail on the head with my lyrics, and I want to tell things from my perspective, not be a third-person storyteller. But I felt that I hadn't hit my mark yet."

CAREER HIGHLIGHTS

Starting Off Small

Mayer left Berklee with one of his classmates, Clay Cook, and headed to Atlanta, Georgia, to try to start a music career. (Cook later co-wrote three songs on Mayer's *Room for Squares* CD.) "The concept was to move to

someplace completely new and start from scratch," Mayer said. "I wanted the plane to touch down somewhere that I knew nothing of before going there. Atlanta was becoming a really cool place for singer-songwriters. So it became this mission for me to move down and just start playing."

When Mayer first arrived in Atlanta, he panicked. He had just dropped out of college with failing grades, and he had an outstanding bill from Berklee for supposedly drawing on his dormitory room wall. He found a day job at a videotape duplication factory. At night, he wrote songs and played his guitar at local coffee houses and clubs. He performed regularly at Eddie's Attic in Decatur, a popular hang-out for aspiring young musicians. Audiences loved him, and he soon developed a following. Mayer said, "People would go, 'You have a CD?' And I'd go, 'No,' and they'd put their $20 bill back in their pocket. That'll make you make a CD really fast."

Mayer took his music to several major record companies, hoping to secure a record contract. He was turned down time after time by these companies, however, because his musical style was so different from the music that was popular at the time. Mayer recalls, "I was so discouraged. It was so counterproductive that someone could sit in front of me and say, 'The direction's just going into like, really heavy metal and boy bands, and it's the flavor of the day right now.' I was very frustrated by that—that even the people who take risks, take calculated risks that are so calculated that they're not [risks]." Even though the record companies were not interested in his music, his popularity was growing among local fans. So in 1999, Mayer put his songs on a CD and released it himself. He titled the CD *Inside Wants Out* and spent the next two years touring the United States to promote it.

Defining Mayer's Music Appeal

Mayer is often compared to Dave Matthews of the Dave Matthews Band. He has also been compared to Sting, Ben Folds, and other artists. But Mayer has his own, individual style. When he first started to play the guitar, he played mostly blues. Over time, his musical style has changed. When asked to classify it, Mayer said, "It's definitely pop music with some jazz influence."

Record companies turned Mayer down repeatedly because his musical style was so different from the music that was popular at the time. "I was so discouraged," Mayer recalls. "It was so counterproductive that someone could sit in front of me and say, 'The direction's just going into like, really heavy metal and boy bands, and it's the flavor of the day right now.' I was very frustrated by that."

Music critic Doug Hamilton from the *Atlanta Journal-Constitution* described Mayer's music as a "sophisticated, accessible folk-rock sound dominated by striking acoustic guitar playing, video-ready looks, and a sizeable grass-roots following born in clubs across the South." And the reviewer from *Rolling Stone* described his sound as "curving, melodically rich tunes that weave folk, blues, rock, and wisps of jazz."

Mayer's music appeals to people of all ages with all different musical tastes. He said, "I've met 60-year-old people at my shows, and I've signed autographs for 6 year-old girls." His goal is to make music that appeals to as many people as possible. "If I'm making music that people come to, I don't

*Mayer poses for a photo backstage with just a small portion
of the equipment that's required on tour.*

care who comes," Mayer said. "I don't care if they're 15 years old; I don't
care if they're embryos. I'm not aiming it towards anybody; I'm aiming it towards everybody." That accessible and modest quality is part of his appeal.
"A big part of the singer-songwriter's charm," according to the *Boston Globe*,
"is the unassuming attitude that characterizes both him and his music."

Rising to Stardom

In March 2000, Mayer traveled to Austin, Texas, to perform at the annual
South by Southwest conference. This conference, known for discovering
alternative rock artists, is where he received his first big break. Many of the
major record companies were there and saw how the crowds reacted to his
music. By the end of the conference, representatives from several record
companies had given Mayer their business cards. He soon signed a contract with Aware Records, a subsidiary of Columbia Records.

In August 2000, Mayer traveled to the Atlantis Music Conference. The pur-
pose of the Conference is to focus the national and international music industry and related press on Atlanta's growing, talented, and diverse music
scene at a national level. As part of Atlantis, Mayer was presented an

award for Favorite Songwriter from ASCAP (American Society of Composers, Authors, and Publishers).

Mayer was still relatively unknown at the time, but he quickly gained exposure by word of mouth. According to the president of Aware Records, "If he plays for ten people, they'll all buy his CD and tell their friends." Mayer believes that allowing people to download music via the Internet also helped to boost his popularity. He has even called it his "saving grace." He believes that downloading music should be a right. He told the Internet site Yahoo! that "people don't have to be assaulted by this giant wheel of color and someone's image presentation; it's just a song and whether you like it or not. . . . And I think that people, in the beginning, were introduced to my music that way."

Room for Squares

With the support of his new record company, Mayer started work on his second CD, *Room for Squares*. The music on *Room for Squares* is much different from that on *Inside Wants Out*. There is far less blues influence on this second CD, and most of the songs were recorded with a full band.

When asked how he came up with the title for his CD, Mayer replied, "I'm a jazz fan and I was flipping through a Blue Note Records coffee

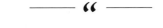

When asked how he came up with the title for his CD, Mayer replied, "I'm a jazz fan and I was flipping through a Blue Note Records coffee table book and saw [Hank] Mobley's album [No Room for Squares]. There was something about the words. I'm kind of a word guy, and it just looked great."

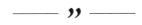

table book and saw [Hank] Mobley's album [*No Room for Squares*]. There was something about the words. I'm kind of a word guy, and it just looked great." It's not surprising that he's a word guy. Mayer said that he has been in love with words since he was a child. "My mother is an English teacher," he said. "I always wanted to impress her. I still travel with a dictionary and look up a word every day."

By the time Mayer released *Room for Squares* in September 2001, he was becoming better known. Radio stations of all types started to play songs from the CD, including "No Such Thing" and "Your Body Is a Wonderland." In fact, "No Such Thing" was one of the most played songs all over the country—in Chicago, Illinois; Boston, Massachusetts; Portland,

Oregon; Baltimore, Maryland; and Memphis, Tennessee. And his music was being played on stations with a variety of formats: modern adult contemporary, modern rock, and top 40 stations were all playing his song.

Soon, music critics were touting this new work. *Rolling Stone* gave *Room for Squares* four stars in its December 2001 review of the CD. In February 2002, Mayer was named one of the "10 Artists to Watch" on the *Rolling Stone* web site. As his music continued to receive more airplay, his record sales grew. By July 2002, *Room for Squares* was certified platinum (one million copies sold). At one point when Mayer was struggling at Berklee, his father had sent him a check for $250. He had attached a note that read, "John, remember me when you go platinum." Mayer kept that note. When he received his first platinum record plaque, he mounted his father's note inside the frame and gave it to his father. *Room for Squares* remained in the Top 100 after 80 straight weeks and reached triple platinum status by May 2003.

As Mayer's popularity continued to grow, he began to get more attention from the music industry. In August 2002, he was nominated for Best New Artist in the MTV Video Music Awards. In February 2003, he earned a nomination for Best New Artist at the Grammy Awards. Although he did not win that award, he did win the 2003 Grammy Award for Best Male Pop Vocal Performance for "Your Body is a Wonderland," beating Elton John, Sting, and James Taylor. In August 2003, "Your Body is a Wonderland" was nominated for Best Male Video at the MTV Video Music Awards. In October 2003, Mayer won the Artist of the Year — Adult Contemporary Radio at the Radio Music Awards. Also in October 2003, he was nominated for Favorite Pop/Rock Male Artist at the American Music Awards.

Any Given Thursday

In February 2003, Mayer released a live album titled *Any Given Thursday*. The two-disc set is a recording of a concert he performed on September 12, 2002, in Birmingham, Alabama. This was one of the last concerts on Mayer's summer 2002 tour. A DVD of the concert was released at the same time. Most of the songs performed during that concert are from the *Room for Squares* CD. By August 2003, *Any Given Thursday* was certified platinum.

At one point when Mayer was struggling at Berklee, his father had sent him a check for $250. He had attached a note that read, "John, remember me when you go platinum." Mayer kept that note. When he received his first platinum record plaque for Room for Squares, *he mounted his father's note inside the frame and gave it to his father.*

Perhaps the CD set achieved such quick success because fans wanted to see and hear more of Mayer's live music. Mayer had gained most of his early exposure through his relentless touring, and these stage performances were widely praised by music critics. As he continued to gain recognition, his shows started to sell out, sometimes to crowds as large as 10,000 people. He even allows his fans to record most of his live shows, as long as the recordings are for personal use or trading only. The recordings cannot be sold or commercialized in any way. Mayer clearly enjoys playing his music live, and he appreciates his audiences at his live shows. The *Richmond Times Dispatch* said that "only those who have seen him live would know the kid is a terrific guitarist, capable of noodling blues riffs that would make his idol, Stevie Ray Vaughan, proud."

Heavier Things

Soon Mayer went to work on *Heavier Things*, his third album on a major record label. Mayer felt that he was somewhat under pressure when he was making this CD. "There was pressure artistically for me to make another good record, a better record in some respects," he said at the time. "But I never looked at a platinum plaque on my wall and went, 'Oh, how do I get another one of these?'"

> ――― **"** ―――
>
> **"[Heavier Things]** *is superior to* **Squares.** *The songs are more focused, the musical backdrops are more varied and informed more by '60s soul and modern R&B, the production is lusher and thicker. And Mayer, in general, sounds more mature and comfortable within his music."* — **Fort Worth Star Telegram**
>
> ――― **"** ―――

The subjects of the songs on *Heavier Things* are more serious than those on *Room for Squares*. Mayer considered naming this album *Home Life*, the title of one song on the CD, because of his strong domestic leanings. Throughout his music, he expresses the desire to find stability, true love, and home. "Bigger Than My Body," the first single, is a song about "not being where you want to get in your life," Mayer said. "It's going to sound silly when people first hear it." He though that people would wonder why he was singing about making it someday when he had already made it. "Whether or not you win a Grammy, it doesn't really modify the plan," Mayer continued. "'Bigger Than My Body' is about the feeling you get when you want to be more and you can't." Mayer said that he loves *Room for Squares*, but *Heavier Things* has more emotional weight to it.

By the time Mayer released *Heavier Things*, his fans were eagerly waiting. In September 2003, MTV's web site gave fans the opportunity to preview *Heavier Things* when it made the album available for streaming (listening to it online). There were 1.3 million tracks requested, more than any other title featured. When the CD was finally released on September 9, 2003, it debuted at No. 1 on the music charts and sold over 315,000 copies in the U.S. during its first week. By October 2003, the album was certified platinum. Fans were buying the CD, and critics began to rave about it, too. For

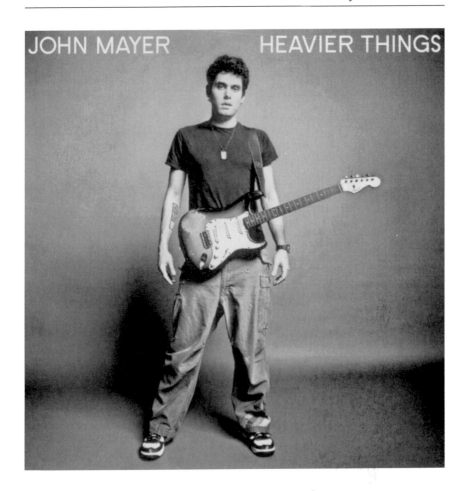

example, the *Fort Worth Star Telegram* said that *Heavier Things* is "superior to *Squares*. The songs are more focused, the musical backdrops are more varied and informed more by '60s soul and modern R&B, the production is lusher and thicker. And Mayer, in general, sounds more mature and comfortable within his music."

Living with Fame

Mayer's popularity led to appearances on several television shows, including "Late Night with Conan O'Brien," "The Tonight Show with Jay Leno," "Saturday Night Live," "Prime Time," "Last Call with Carson Daly," "The Late, Late Show with Craig Kilborn," and "Austin City Limits." In addition, his song "Not Myself," appears on the original motion picture soundtrack for the 2003 movie, *How to Deal*.

But for Mayer, all this attention was not important. "I don't want to be a fa-mous person, he told *Rolling Stone,* "I want to be a famous musician." Although he enjoys some of the benefits of being a celebrity, he also has had to face the challenges of being so widely recognized. Because he is young, attractive, and single, he is often asked about his love life. Many of the words to his songs are so sincere, leading Mayer to be labeled a "sensi-tive guy." When *Teen People* magazine compiled a list of the Hottest Entertainers Under 25 in 2003, Mayer was on the list as the "Hottest Sensitive Guy." *YM* magazine also named him one of the "20 Hottest Guys" in its August 2003 issue.

One of Mayer's biggest and most famous fans is singer Elton John. John has publicly praised Mayer's music and even interviewed him for the April 2002 issue of *Interview* magazine. Mayer is also a fan of Elton John. In January 2001, Mayer performed with several other musical artists in a benefit to pay tribute to him. The benefit raised money for music education. Mayer was the only performer to actually sing with John that night. The two sang John's first No. 1 single, "Sacrifice." Mayer and John are friends, and John will occasionally give Mayer advice.

Mayer credits singer Glenn Phillips, lead singer for Toad the Wet Sprocket, with teaching him how to handle fame and deal with fans. Mayer said, "I was able to see how he made himself available to people and fans. If I was left to my own devices, I probably would have imagined that I was going to be less accessible, because that's just the way it had to be." But Phillips gave him some valuable advice. According to Mayer, "Glenn was like, 'Here's how you are to people: you look them in the eye, you thank them, and it's OK to give them the same compassion and love that you would give to someone that you're meeting at a family get-together.'"

> *Mayer credits singer Glenn Phillips, lead singer for Toad the Wet Sprocket, for teaching him how to handle fame and deal with fans. Phillips gave him some valuable advice. According to Mayer, "Glenn was like, 'Here's how you are to people: you look them in the eye, you thank them, and it's OK to give them the same compassion and love that you would give to someone that you're meeting at a family get-together.'"*

HOME AND FAMILY

Mayer currently lives in a duplex in Manhattan in New York City. His duplex overlooks the Empire State Building and includes a recording studio on the second floor. This is where he recorded most of the songs for *Heavier Things*.

Mayer has never been married but would very much like to settle down some day. He says he has not yet found his soul mate, but he knows that he will someday. According to Mayer, "That is somebody who is confident enough to feel love at a moment when love is not being given. A lot of times, I feel like I'm on the road to support a family I don't even have yet. I don't have to tour as much as I do, but I want to for that future family."

When asked if it would be hard to have a serious relationship when he's on tour all the time, he said, "I would give this all up right now for a wife if it meant that if I didn't give it all up I'd never find one. Money? It's nothing until it means taking care of a wife and kids. I will gladly be former one-time successful rock musician John Mayer who pitches the first ball at Little League games."

MAJOR INFLUENCES

According to Mayer, "When I was a kid, I was influenced by whoever was on the radio—Michael Jackson and the Police and bands like that. Until I picked up a tape of Stevie Ray Vaughan's music. . . . My life was different once I heard that. I didn't know what that was, but I wanted to do it." Mayer said that the first moment he became interested in playing music was right after he heard Vaughan. "I got lost in the primal roots and the music spoke to me," he said. And even though his later music is more pop than blues, he still considers Vaughan his idol. Every time he holds a guitar, he still holds it like Vaughan. He said, "Anyone who has an idol is still going to reference themselves against the silhouette of their idol."

Mayer also lists Eric Clapton, Bonnie Raitt, Elton John, Ben Folds Five, Martin Sexton, and Freedy Johnston among his musical influences. Mayer said that he often watches an Eric Clapton concert DVD before his own performances so that he can remember how to "hold the stage without letting the stage crush him."

"When I was a kid, I was influenced by whoever was on the radio — Michael Jackson and the Police and bands like that. Until I picked up a tape of Stevie Ray Vaughan's music. . . . My life was different once I heard that. I didn't know what that was, but I wanted to do it."

HOBBIES AND OTHER INTERESTS

Mayer has said that he has no hobbies or interests outside of music. However, while on the road, he and his bandmates play video games on an XBox on the band's tour bus. In fact, they enjoy playing the sniper video game *Halo* so much that they wear fake Army dog tags with the names of their *Halo* aliases.

RECORDINGS

Inside Wants Out, 1999, re-released 2002
Room for Squares, 2001
Any Given Thursday, 2003
Heavier Things, 2003

HONORS AND AWARDS

Grammy Award (National Academy of Recording Arts and Sciences):
    2003, Best Male Pop Vocal Performance, for "Your Body is a Wonderland"
Radio Music Award: 2003, Artist of the Year — Adult Contemporary Radio

FURTHER READING

Periodicals

Atlanta Journal-Constitution, May 6, 2001, p.C6
Boston Globe, Feb. 22, 2002, p.D16
Cleveland Plain Dealer, July 24, 2002, p.E1; Aug. 8. 2003, p.4
Fort Worth Star-Telegram, Sep. 19, 2003, p.S25
Guitar Player, Feb. 2004, p.64
Guitar World Acoustic, Dec. 2003, p.28
Interview, Apr. 2002, p.114
Portland (Me.) Press Herald, Nov. 21, 2002, p.D3
Richmond (Va.) Times Dispatch, Feb. 20, 2003, p.D16
San Diego Union-Tribune, Aug. 15, 2002, Night & Day section, p.4
Tampa Tribune, Nov. 5, 2002, p.2
Teen People, June 1, 2002, p.99
YM, Aug. 2003, p.102

ADDRESS

John Mayer
Columbia Records
550 Madison Avenue
New York, NY 10022

WORLD WIDE WEB SITES

http://www.johnmayer.com
http://www.mtv.com/bands/az/mayer_john/artist.jhtml
http://www.vh1.com/artists/az/mayer_john/bio.jhtml

Mandy Moore 1984-
American Singer and Actress
Creator of the Hit Songs "Candy," "Crush," "In My
Pocket," and "Walk Me Home," and Star of the
Movies *A Walk to Remember* and *How to Deal*

BIRTH

Amanda Leigh Moore, who prefers to be called Mandy, was
born on April 10, 1984, in Nashua, New Hampshire. She is the
daughter of Don Moore, a commercial airline pilot for American Airlines, and Stacy Moore, a former journalist for the

Orlando Sentinel. Moore has two brothers: Scott, who is two years older, and Kyle, who is three years younger.

YOUTH

Mandy Moore was an entertainer in the making from the time she was a very young girl. Yet if her family had remained in New Hampshire, she might not have blossomed the way she did. But her parents moved the family to Orlando, Florida, when she was two months old. Orlando is the home of Disney World and many other tourist attractions, and by the early 1990s it was becoming a training ground for many of today's pop entertainers, including Britney Spears, Justin Timberlake, and Christina Aguilera. It was a much better place for a young entertainer to be discovered than the little city of Nashua.

However, it wasn't the pop scene that first attracted Moore; it was Broadway musicals. When she was just six years old, her parents took her to see a student performance of the Broadway hit *Oklahoma!* From that moment on, Moore knew what she wanted to do with her life: she wanted to become a singer, preferably in musical theater. She told her parents that she wanted to be a singer, but they thought it was just a phase. Nevertheless, they agreed to pay for some voice lessons; eventually, they became convinced she was serious. "When I was about nine my parents realized that I really wanted to perform, that it wasn't a phase. From then on all I did was appear in community theater shows. If anyone needed a little girl [in the cast], I was the one."

Moore also acted in school plays and with the Civic Kids troupe, which was part of the Civic Theatre of Central Florida. "I knew I wanted to have the lead in the sixth-grade play, and when I got to sixth grade, sure enough, I got the lead and was on stage performing, and that sealed the deal." Moore appeared in such shows as *South Pacific,* which was her first play, *Guys and Dolls, The Sound of Music, Bye Bye Birdie,* and *A Christmas Carol.*

FIRST JOBS

Moore's career took off very early. By the time she was just nine years old, her parents had arranged for her to perform the national anthem in front of more than 10,000 people at an Orlando Magic basketball game. Soon she was also performing at other sporting events and became known in Orlando as "The National Anthem Girl." When she was 11, her parents hired a professional talent agent, and she began finding small jobs on television, especially for Nickelodeon and Disney doing voice-overs for cartoons (providing voices for animated characters). Her first movie "role," in fact, was as the voice of Ducky in the dinosaur movie *The Land Before Time*.

It was while singing the title song for what she described as "a corny kids' cartoon show about sea turtles" that she was "discovered" at the age of 14. A Federal Express delivery man named Victor Cade, who worked as a part-time talent scout, heard her sing at a recording session and thought Moore had real talent. Without telling the young singer, he approached her parents and asked if they would give him a tape that he could mail to his friend at Sony Records, Dave McPherson. Figuring that it was worth a shot, they agreed. McPherson forwarded the demo tape to Epic/550 Records (part of Sony Records), and the executives there loved it. Moore was called in to audition, and within a week she had signed a recording contract.

"I had to leave school in December to start recording," Moore said about earning her first recording contract, "so I had to tell my teachers that I got a record deal. It was so unheard of, and they didn't take it seriously. They just said, 'Okay, Sweetie, see you next semester. Make sure you finish your homework. Have a Merry Christmas.' But I didn't go back. Since then, everything has fit together like a nice little puzzle."*

EDUCATION

The life of an up-and-coming singing star leaves little time for a traditional education. This was certainly true for Moore, who left Bishop Moore Catholic High School halfway through her freshman year, when she was working on her first record. "I had to leave school in December to start recording," she recalled, "so I had to tell my teachers that I got a record deal. It was so unheard of, and they didn't take it seriously. They just said, 'Okay, Sweetie, see you next semester. Make sure you finish your homework. Have a Merry Christmas.' But I didn't go back. Since then, everything has fit together like a nice little puzzle." Moore still stays close to two or three friends she made while in high school.

Although she doesn't have the opportunity to experience the social aspects of attending school, Moore is determined to get an education. She has been taking correspondence courses through Texas Tech University and the University of Nebraska. "I have a tutor back home," she explained. "When traveling I do it any time I can. I do my schoolwork on the Internet;

it's the most convenient. I want to go to college and study journalism. Even if I don't use it, I want to have it to fall back on. My mom was a journalist. I love to write. I guess it's in my blood." In addition to her regular schooling, Moore has also had some formal acting training; she attended the performing academy Stagedoor Manor for two summers.

———— " ————

"My music is pop but with an edge. Every song is different on the album. Some have an R&B edge, some have a rock edge, some have a dance edge. It's not just bubble-gum pop music. I think it's good to have a little variety and not just keep giving people the same thing over and over."

———— " ————

CAREER HIGHLIGHTS

Creating a Star

Moore got her start working for Epic/ 550 Records. From the beginning, executives knew that she had a lot of raw talent. But how to construct a career from that talent was the big question, one that Moore has been working on ever since she signed her first contract. To get the word out about the new singer, the music company created two Web sites on the Internet dedicated to her. The strategy worked, and soon young Web surfers were beginning to buzz about this new musical find. Next, Moore was set up as an opening act for the popular boy bands 'N Sync and The Backstreet Boys, and in the summer of 1999 she went on a tour with them. "I learned everything from being on tour with the Backstreet Boys," she said. "They're inspirational to me, because they're so down-to-earth and nothing has fazed them. All the success they've had hasn't changed them a bit. And 'N Sync was exactly the same."

Now that she was developing a fan base, it was time to get her first album out. Still only 15 years old, Moore herself couldn't believe she was actually going to record a CD. "It's really surreal. I thought a record company would sign an artist my age and wait until I was 17 or 18 before they started having me do stuff. But I just jumped right in." The songs for her first CD, *So Real*, were mostly written by Shaun Fisher and Tony Battaglia. Though Moore didn't have much say in the contents of her first CD, she liked the results. As she said in 1999, when *So Real* was released, "My music is pop but with an edge. Every song is different on the album. Some have an R&B edge, some have a rock edge, some have a dance edge. It's not just bubble-gum pop music. I think it's good to have a little variety and not just keep

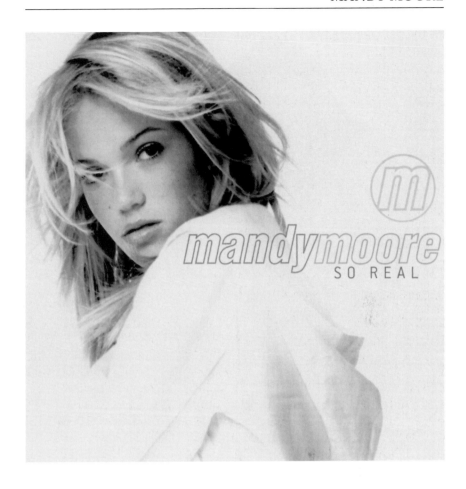

giving people the same thing over and over." The first single to be released was "Candy," and Moore got a big thrill when she heard it played on the radio. "It is the trippiest thing in the whole world just to [hear], 'And here's 'Candy' by Mandy Moore.' It's like, oh my gosh, it's a feeling you can never get used to. And it's a feeling that's so, so indescribable."

First CDs and MTV

So Real and "Candy" were released in 1999. Although they didn't skyrocket to the top of the charts, it wasn't long before *So Real* had sold over a million copies, making it a platinum record. By the next year, things were happening fast for Moore. She became a commercial spokesperson and model for the skin care line Neutrogena and the clothing designer Tommy Hilfiger, and she made several appearances on TV specials and on the

MTV show "Total Request Live" (TRL). Then, in 2000, she hosted her own program called "The Mandy Moore Show," in which she played videos and offered advice to teens. With her popularity soaring, she was voted one of "The Hottest Stars under 25" in *Teen People* magazine. With the success of *So Real,* her producers realized they had a new hot singer on their hands. To keep her in the spotlight, they quickly released a second album.

I Wanna Be with You (2000), Moore's follow-up release, includes remixes of songs from *So Real,* as well as several new songs. The second album went platinum, too; the title track became part of the soundtrack to the movie *Center Stage,* and sales of the album as a whole did even better than her debut CD. Even though only a year separates these first two albums, Moore and the managers at her record company felt the young singer had matured in that short time. "We had recorded a couple of these new tracks," she recalled about the time they were preparing the second CD, "thinking they would be for the next album, without even telling the label. My manager went in and played them for the record company. They were like, 'Who is this?' You can see there's a far cry between 'Candy' and 'I Wanna Be with You,' and there's more where that came from. I think it's a great transition." Some critics found the revamped record to be better than the original. "It doesn't stretch the teen pop formula much, just enough to give the record character. . . . Moore delivers the songs sturdily, never taking the forefront, but blending into the lush layered production, so the music just rolls forth as a whole," Thomas Erlewine wrote in *All Music Guide*. But many others were not as enthusiastic, including reviewer Cameron Adams. "Supplied with a bunch of love songs probably written by people twice her age, [Moore] sings them with all the conviction of a girl who is more likely to play with toys than boys. But the main problem here is that while Britney gets to work with the A-list of songwriters and producers, Mandy's songs really aren't all that good. . . . It's McMusic."

For Moore's third album, Mandy Moore, she said, "It's so cool to have more creative control on what songs are on it and who I work with. That makes everything a little bit more personal."

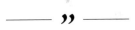

Moore's third album, the self-titled *Mandy Moore*, was released in 2001. With this CD, the singer had some clout with the studio, and she was able to write and perform a number of her own songs. For Moore, it marked a departure from her previous recordings. "I'm older, I'm not the same girl. That's why I wanted this album to be self-titled. For the first time, I really feel the music is a reflection of me. . . . I recorded the first album when I was just 14. I was excited just to be in the studio doing my own album, I wasn't concerned with the material." The first song Moore wrote for the album, the acoustic number "When I Talk to You," is not the usual love song. "It's not a song about romance, which is kind of cool," she commented. "It's so cool to have more creative control on what songs are on it and who I work with. That makes everything a little bit more personal."

Critics noted an improvement on this new CD. The album, overall, was called a bit more sophisticated than her previous efforts, with more advanced musical arrangements. According to the review on MTV.com, "Mandy Moore is stylistically confident enough to venture into sonic areas beyond the usual Aguilera/Spears axis. For one thing, there's more of a pronounced R&B flavor to Moore's songs than those of her contemporaries. The production takes more chances as well, as witnessed by the exotic textures that open the lush 'Saturate Me' and 'One Sided Love.'" And *Rolling Stone* reviewer Barry Walters went so far as to call *Mandy Moore* "the most startlingly liberated teen pop since [the] eighties." "With this album," said reviewer Nekesa Mumbi Moody, "Moore is slowly moving from a teen pop starlet into a credible adult pop singer."

——————  ——————

"The only thing I have in common with Britney or Jessica or Christina is the fact that we're all close in age. We all make fairly different-sounding records. As blessed as I feel to be working in this industry, it's frustrating to sometimes feel discounted or negatively judged because of superficial elements and not because of my actual work."

—————— 99 ——————

Creating Her Own Image

Moore has tried to create her own image as a singer. At first, she was often compared to other teen entertainers like Britney Spears, Christina Aguilera, and Jessica Simpson. Moore, however, sees significant differences between her and these other stars. Comparing herself to Spears, for example, she noted that her music is different and that she doesn't emphasize dancing as much in her performances: "I think as people pay attention, they can see we're pursuing different directions," she said in 2002. "I have a seven-piece band, and that's all. We don't use any recorded tracks, and I don't bring any dancers [to stage shows]. I don't dance. On my first video they had me dancing, and then they looked and said, 'Hmm, maybe Mandy shouldn't dance.'" In general, she doesn't like being categorized with the other singers who preceded her. "The only thing I have in common with Britney or Jessica or Christina is the fact that we're all close in age. We all make fairly different-sounding records. As blessed as I feel to be working in this industry, it's frustrating to sometimes feel discounted or negatively judged because of superficial elements and not because of my actual work."

Moore has also tried to create her own image as an actress. She turned down a role in the popular television series "Dawson's Creek" because, as she said, "the part was a little bit too old for me; it was a little too risqué." She has been equally careful when selecting parts for movies. Her first big role was in the 2001 G-rated Disney film *The Princess Diaries*, based on the

Heather Matarazzo, Anne Hathaway, and Mandy Moore (left to right) on the set of The Princess Diaries.

novel of the same name by Meg Cabot (for more information on Cabot, see *Biography Today Authors*, Vol. 12). The movie was directed by Garry Marshall and starred Julie Andrews, Anne Hathaway, and Heather Matarazzo. In the movie, Mia (played by Anne Hathaway), is a high school outcast who discovers she is actually the princess of a small country in Europe. Moore plays Mia's nemesis, Lana, who is a nasty socialite cheerleader. Although she auditioned for the part and won the role just as any professional actress might, Moore still felt a bit awkward at first. "I was intimidated, like, the first day going to the set," she admitted. "I mean, here I am, I'm like this singer, and I'm going to the set working with Garry Marshall and all these other professional actors—Julie Andrews—that really freaked me out!" *The Princess Diaries*, though not a blockbuster, generally did well in theaters and proved to be a big success with the teen audience, particularly the many fans of Cabot's novels.

A Walk to Remember

Next up for Moore was her biggest acting part yet: the starring role in *A Walk to Remember* (2002). Based on a novel by Nicholas Sparks, *A Walk to Remember* co-stars Shane West, Peter Coyote, and Daryl Hannah. Moore plays Jamie Sullivan, the dowdy daughter of a Baptist minister (Coyote).

Moore had her first starring role in
A Walk to Remember,
which also featured Shane West.

Quiet, studious, and oblivious to current fashions, Jamie is not a popular student among her high school peers. So the rebellious Landon Carter (West) is not very happy when she is made his tutor and acting partner in the school. Despite themselves, Jamie and Landon become attracted to each other, and both learn to grow in the process. The twist in the story comes when Landon learns a terrible secret about Jamie.

Some critics found *A Walk to Remember* to be touching and sweet — even a little too sweet and corny. Yet even those who didn't like the film still had good things to say about Moore's acting. For example, *Entertainment Weekly* writer Owen Gleiberman said bluntly that "It wasn't a good movie, yet some of the scenes between Moore and Shane West had a surprising tenderness." And Bob Strauss, the reviewer from the *Guardian*, felt that the movie "ladles even more syrup on the sappy Nicholas Sparks source novel." But he admired her for taking risks with her career in playing a conservative character and noted that *A Walk to Remember* did better at the box office than the Britney Spears movie *Crossroads*. "Moore does really bold stuff," Strauss concluded admiringly. "Moore, just 17, has screen appeal and poise as well," Richard Corliss wrote in *Time* magazine. "When pop-star status deserts her, she might become a movie star, or something more precious: a fine actress."

How to Deal

Moore's second starring role came in the 2003 film *How to Deal,* based on the novels *Someone Like You* and *That Summer* by Sarah Dessen. Moore played Halley Martin, who learns how to deal with a series of misfortunes in her life. Moore felt the character was completely unlike her. Whereas Halley is highly skeptical about the possibility of finding true love, Moore calls herself "a pretty romantic person. . . . I believe in love and falling in love at a young age." Halley, however, has good reasons for being cynical: her parents are breaking up, her sister constantly fights with the man in

Mandy Moore as Halley and Trent Ford as Macon in a scene from How to Deal.

her life, and her best friend is pregnant by her no-good boyfriend. But when Halley meets a similar skeptic named Macon (played by Trent Ford), finding a kindred spirit might lead to unexpected results. Moore has said that she chose the role of Halley because it would test her acting abilities. "I couldn't find two similarities between myself and the character," she commented. "But I think that's why I was so moved to take on a challenge like that. I wanted to get inside her head and figure out why someone who is obviously so loved felt unloved by those around her."

Critical reaction to *How to Deal,* like the reaction to *A Walk to Remember,* was mixed. Reviewers liked Moore's performance better than the movie itself. For example, a *USA Today* writer compared *How to Deal* to "a second-rate TV movie" but felt that "it's good for . . . showcasing the bona fide acting talents of pop singer Mandy Moore." Christian Toto was pleased to see that this "peppy pop singer can act," lamenting only that "Moore's efforts [are] squandered by a hollow script."

Recent Work

As a singer, Moore feels that she's just starting to mature and that her tastes in music are changing. "I've just grown up, and I think that's reflected in every aspect of my life, as an artist and as a person." It might not be surprising, then, that on her 2003 release, *Coverage,* she tries to challenge herself again. The songs on this album were all originally recorded during the 1970s and 1980s by such artists as Carly Simon, Joni Mitchell, Todd Rundgren, Elton John, Cat Stevens, and Joan Armatrading. But on her recordings, Moore rearranges them to fit her own personal style. "I guess I did the record for selfish reasons," she confessed, "because the music that's on the album isn't music I grew up listening to. Back then I was a huge musical-theater fan, and so this album is made up of music I've discovered only over the past two years. I feel like a lot of people my age are kind of missing out on it."

─────── **"** ───────

"[There] is no greater adrenaline rush than performing live at a concert. You can't duplicate that feeling doing a movie or hosting something on MTV. Live performance is the cream of the crop. It's a love affair, a wonderful cycle. The more an audience gives you, the more you give back."

─────── **"** ───────

For Moore to tackle songs that had become classics before she was born was a daring step for the young pop singer, according to some music critics. For example, Mim Udovitch of the *International Herald Tribune* wrote that "From one perspective, that kind of risk might be regarded as insane, but from another, it is an intelligent, slightly awkward, and sincere thing to do, the act of someone for whom contrivance has failed and whose strong attachment to music is that of a real 19-year-old young woman." Referring to the frequent comparisons between Moore and such pop singers as Britney Spears, Udovitch added, "If you're going to spend your life and career being compared to other people anyway, why not shoot for the moon?" Other critics were less enthusiastic, as in this comment from Chuck Arnold in *People* magazine: "*[Coverage]* feels like it was a rush job, a quick-and-easy way to get an album done for a girl who was too swamped to spend much time in the studio. . . . Maybe in another 10 to 20 years Moore might possess the interpretive powers to make *Coverage* work. For now, though, it sounds as if a girl was sent to do a woman's job."

As an actress, Moore next appears in the 2004 romantic comedy *Chasing Liberty* as Anna Foster, the 18-year-old daughter of the President of the United States. As the President's only child, Anna is constantly monitored by her parents, Secret Service agents, and the media. Foster just wants to be like any rebellious teenager, with the freedom to live her life without

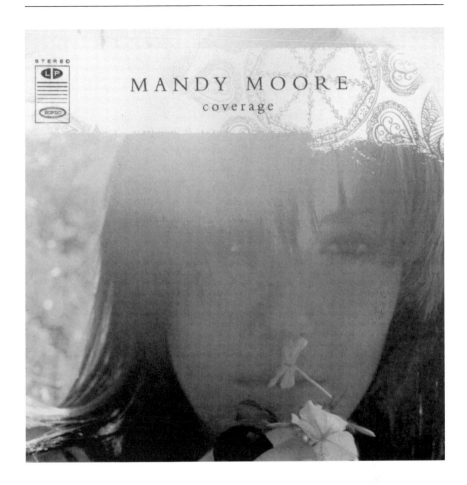

constant supervision. So while on a diplomatic trip to Europe she escapes and meets a boy (Matthew Goode), who doesn't know who she really is. They set out on a romantic road trip through Europe. But eventually she'll have to head back home — and Anna worries about what will happen when he discovers her real identity. Coincidentally, another movie about the President's daughter — titled *First Daughter* and starring Katie Holmes — will also be released in 2004.

Future Plans

Even though Moore has gained acceptance as an actress, she has said she still prefers singing. "Music is my first love. Acting is like a side career that just kind of took off," she commented. She also once said that "there is no greater adrenaline rush than performing live at a concert. You can't duplicate that feeling doing a movie or hosting something on MTV. Live performance is the cream of the crop. It's a love affair, a wonderful cycle. The more an audience gives you, the more you give back." Moore hopes to have the chance soon to go back on tour. "I want to get back on the road, especially with this music [from *Coverage*]. . . . I just want to be on stage, connecting with an audience, and continue to test my boundaries." Someday, this might take her back to the place where she started: live musical theater. As she once said, "My ultimate goal is to be on Broadway. . . . [Recording albums] has been a dream of mine, to sing my own music and get to perform everywhere. But Broadway is the ultimate thing for me." She added, "My sixth-grade play was *Guys and Dolls*. I got to play Miss Adelaide. That would be my dream role, to play Miss Adelaide on Broadway."

> ———— **"** ————
>
> *"I love my parents,"*
> *Moore proclaimed. "I have*
> *a great family. I have a great*
> *relationship [with them].*
> *They've been traveling with*
> *me since I was 14 and kind of*
> *started in all this madness.*
> *And they're great. They keep*
> *me sane. My family just*
> *keeps me grounded."*
>
> ———— **"** ————

MAJOR INFLUENCES

"I've been influenced by Madonna, Janet Jackson, Bette Middler, and Karen Carpenter," Moore has said, adding that "Karen Carpenter had one of the most beautiful voices in the entire world."

HOME AND FAMILY

Moore spent much of her life in Orlando, Florida, but more recently she purchased a home in Los Feliz, California. She brought her family with her to live in the spacious house because she likes being close to them. "I love my parents," she proclaimed. "I have a great family. I have a great relationship [with them]. They've been traveling with me since I was 14 and kind of started in all this madness. And they're great. They keep me sane. My family just keeps me grounded." Moore, who is single, is currently involved with American tennis star Andy Roddick.

FAVORITE MOVIES AND MUSIC

Moore is a fan of Bette Midler's music and movies. She claims to have seen the movie *Beaches* "at least 20 times," and she also remembers loving Midler's song "The Wind beneath My Wings," which she used to sing on her karaoke machine when she was about nine years old. Besides Midler, she is also a fan of actors Gwyneth Paltrow and Ryan Phillippe. As for music, she enjoys a wide variety of genres. Although she has said she doesn't have a favorite group, she once added: "I'm a huge fan of New Radicals. I'm constantly singing to them." Moore has also listed Norah Jones, Jeff Buckley, and Citizen Cope among her favorites.

HOBBIES AND OTHER INTERESTS

When she's not working, Moore likes to shop, especially on the Internet. "I am such a computer geek," she once confessed. "I couldn't live without the Internet."

RECORDINGS

So Real, 1999
I Wanna Be with You, 2000
Mandy Moore, 2001
Coverage, 2003

CREDITS

Movies

Dr. Dolittle 2, 2001
The Princess Diaries, 2001
A Walk to Remember, 2002
How to Deal, 2003

Other

"The Mandy Moore Show," 2000 (television series)

HONORS AND AWARDS

MTV Movie Award: 2002, for Best Breakthrough Female

FURTHER READING

Books

Bankston, John. *Mandy Moore,* 2002 (juvenile)
Contemporary Musicians, Vol. 35, 2002
Peters, Beth. *Pop Princesses: The Dish behind Today's Hottest Teen Divas,* 2000 (juvenile)

Periodicals

Billboard, June 10, 2000, p.94; Oct. 21, 2000, p.25
Entertainment Weekly, Aug. 11, 2000, p.85; Feb. 8, 2002, p.51; July 25, 2003, p.50
Girls' Life, June/July 2001, p.42 Feb./Mar. 2002, p.40
Interview, Aug. 2003, p.125
Los Angeles Times, Jan. 5, 2003, p.K1; July 18, 2003, p.E17
New York Times, May 5, 2003, p.C7; July 20, 2003, pp.AR11, E22
People, July 3, 2000, p.110; Dec. 24, 2001, p.27; Feb. 11, 2002, p.31; Mar. 4, 2002, p.59; Feb. 17, 2003, p.24; July 28, 2003, pp.22, 29
Rolling Stone, Mar. 16, 2000, p.23; Oct. 31, 2002, p.81
San Francisco Chronicle, Aug. 6, 2000, p.47; Jan. 20, 2002, p.37; July 28, 2002, p.36
Seventeen, Nov. 2000, p.123; May 2001, p.174; July 2001, p.122
Teen Magazine, Oct. 1999, p.52; Nov. 2000, p.6; Aug. 2001, p.154
Teen People, Feb. 1, 2002, p.110; Sep. 1, 2002, p.124; Aug. 2003, p.242
Time, Feb. 25, 2002, p.62
USA Today, Jan. 25, 2002, p.D11; Jan. 22, 2003, p.C2; July 16, 2003, p.D2; July 18, 2003, p.E4
Washington Post, Jan. 30, 2000, p.G1

Online Databases

Biography Resource Center Online, 2003, article from *Contemporary Musicians,* 2002

ADDRESS

Mandy Moore
Sony — Epic Records
2100 Colorado Avenue
Santa Monica, CA 90404

WORLD WIDE WEB SITES

http://www.mandymoore.com
http://www.mtv.com

Thich Nhat Hanh 1926-
Vietnamese Buddhist Monk
Leading Peace Activist, Respected Teacher of
Buddhism, and Author of Nearly 100 Books

BIRTH

Thich Nhat Hanh was born in October 1926 in central Vietnam, in Southeast Asia. Vietnam is south of China, on a pe-
ninsula near Thailand, Laos, and Cambodia. His father worked
for the Vietnamese government to resettle people from over-
crowded villages to new areas. Nhat Hanh was one of six chil-

dren. His name is pronounced "Tick-Naught-Han" or "Tick-Not-Han." "Thich" is an honorary title, similar to "Reverend," used by Vietnamese Buddhist monks. Nhat Hanh's followers call him "Thay" (pronounced "thai"), which means teacher.

YOUTH

The Buddhist religion has been a central part of Nhat Hanh's life. Buddhism does not center on a person's relationship with a god or gods. Instead, Buddhists focus on rising gradually to a higher spiritual level, by means of ethical, compassionate behavior. Buddhists believe that they can be reincarnated, or brought back to life, in a higher state of existence. The religion is named for its founder, Buddha Shakyamuni, who was born in northern India (now Nepal) in 624 B.C. About 360 million people worldwide practice Buddhism.

Nhat Hanh grew up in a family that was not particularly religious. "They belonged to the Buddhist tradition," he said of his parents. "They practiced not a lot." Yet Nhat Hahn discovered his spiritual calling very early in life.

> "In every one of us there is a baby monk or a baby nun. I was able to touch the baby monk in me when I was very little," Nhat Hanh said. "I was seven, and I saw a drawing of the Buddha sitting on the grass and looking very calm. Very, very calm. I said to myself, 'I want to be like that.' So the seed of the baby monk in me was watered."

"In every one of us there is a baby monk or a baby nun. I was able to touch the baby monk in me when I was very little," Nhat Hanh said. "I was seven, and I saw a drawing of the Buddha sitting on the grass and looking very calm. Very, very calm. I said to myself, 'I want to be like that.' So the seed of the baby monk in me was watered."

A little later, Nhat Hanh had an experience that convinced him of his destiny. He and his class went to the mountains for a picnic. "I was very excited because a hermit lived up there, and I had been told that a hermit is someone who practices to become a Buddha. But when we arrived on the mountain, very thirsty and very tired, I was very disappointed because the hermit wasn't there." Nhat Hanh guessed it was natural for a hermit to hide from a large group of people. So he set off to find the hermit on his own. "Suddenly, I heard the sound of water, like music." It was a natural well, where Nhat Hanh drank his fill, then slipped into a deep, restful sleep. "I had never had anything as delicious as that water, and it satisfied all my desires. I did not even want to see the hermit any more. In my little boy's brain I believed that the hermit had turned himself into the well so I could meet him privately."

As he grew up, Nhat Hanh witnessed the poverty and starvation of the Vietnamese people. The suffering around him reinforced his desire to enter religious life. "It was a dream of a little boy to go out and learn Buddhism, to practice Buddhism in order to relieve the suffering of other people in society," he said. "Later on, when I became a novice monk, I also learned and practiced by this kind of desire." Nhat Hanh said it took his parents a long time to accept their son's plans for a religious life. "My parents thought that monks have hard lives, " he said. "But in fact, as a monk I have had a lot of happiness."

Nhat Hanh said it took his parents a long time to accept their son's plans for a religious life. "My parents thought that monks have hard lives," he said. "But in fact, as a monk I have had a lot of happiness."

EDUCATION

When Nhat Hanh was a boy, Vietnamese education was guided by the French, who had colonized the country in 1884. "I attended elementary school, where French and Vietnamese were taught. We also learned a few hours of Chinese in elementary school," he said. "I had to learn history, geography, in French. And I also had to learn some Vietnamese history and geography in Vietnamese."

Nhat Hanh entered a Buddhist monastery at age 16 and completed his novitiate — or monk's training — at age 20. He studied literature and philosophy at Saigon University in Saigon, the major city in southern Vietnam. (It's now called Ho Chi Minh City.) Much later, in 1961, he traveled to the United States for graduate work in the philosophy of religion at Princeton University in New Jersey. During that period he also studied and taught Buddhism at Columbia University in New York City. Nhat Hanh is fluent in French and English as well as Vietnamese.

CAREER HIGHLIGHTS

Engaged Buddhism

During his early days as a monk, Nhat Hanh witnessed great suffering among the Vietnamese people. "There was a time when every morning when I got up I saw many dead bodies on the street because people did not have anything to eat," Nhat Hanh said. Students would go from house to house, begging for rice to give to the starving people. But they could not help everyone. "They were like God," he said of the students. "They had to decide who would live and who would die. I never can forget such an experience."

When Nhat Hanh was growing up in Vietnam, the country was a colony of France. After World War II ended in 1945, the country declared its independence. But France ruled over Vietnam until 1954, when Communist forces led by Ho Chi Minh took control of the north half of the country, which split the country into two separate nations: North Vietnam and South Vietnam. Communism is the name of a political and economic system based on the idea that all the people in a country should share equally in its property and resources. Communism eliminates most private property and gives it to the government to distribute as it sees fit. Under a Communist system, the central government exercises a great deal of control over the lives of citizens and places severe restrictions on individual rights. Throughout the 20th century, the United States was deeply opposed to the spread of Communism. The Soviet Union was a Communist country, as was China. A fierce rivalry developed between the U.S. and these nations, so when North Vietnam became Communist, it became an adversary of the United States. To prevent North Vietnam from conquering the South and to prevent the spread of Communism, the U.S. eventually gave military and economic aid to South Vietnam.

As the conflict between North and South Vietnam worsened, so did the suffering of the Vietnamese people. Nhat Hanh and his associates wanted to help the war's victims. They also wanted to promote non-violent resistance to the governments that started the war. But traditional Buddhism did not offer an outlet for these activities. So he and his colleagues founded what they called "engaged Buddhism." This practice combines traditional meditation with non-violent action to address social questions. Nhat Hanh says, "When I was in Vietnam, so many of our villages were being bombed. Along with my monastic brothers and sisters, I had to decide what to do. Should we continue to practice in our monasteries or should we leave the meditation halls in order to help the people who were suffering under the bombs? After careful reflection, we decided to do both—to go out and help people and to do so in mindfulness. We called it engaged Buddhism. Mindfulness must be engaged. Once there is seeing, there must be acting. Otherwise, what is the sense of seeing?" As he also said, "When bombs begin to fall on people, you cannot stay in the meditation hall all of the time."

In line with the teachings of engaged Buddhism, Nhat Hanh urged the Vietnamese people to demonstrate peacefully against the war. He suggested they protest by fasting, displaying religious altars in the streets to stop military tanks, refusing to cooperate with authorities, and shaving their heads. To help spread the message, Nhat Hanh established a publishing house and a weekly peace magazine. He founded Vietnam's first Buddhist high school and co-founded Van Hanh Buddhist University in Saigon.

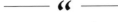

"When I was in Vietnam, so many of our villages were being bombed. Along with my monastic brothers and sisters, I had to decide what to do. Should we continue to practice in our monasteries or should we leave the meditation halls in order to help the people who were suffering under the bombs? After careful reflection, we decided to do both—to go out and help people and to do so in mindfulness. We called it engaged Buddhism. Mindfulness must be engaged. Once there is seeing, there must be acting. Otherwise, what is the sense of seeing?"

Another important aspect of engaged Buddhism was actively serving war's victims. Nhat Hanh helped to establish relief organizations for the injured and displaced. In 1963, he published *Engaged Buddhism*, an influential work that urged Buddhists to work for social change. In 1964, he founded the School of Youth Social Services. The SYSS, as it was called, drew about 10,000 student volunteers to its cause. The group rebuilt villages destroyed

Nhat Hanh's Way of Mindfulness

Nhat Hanh believes that people can become more conscious of society's needs by becoming "mindful"—that means living in intense awareness of each moment of life. He advocates slow, attentive breathing as the best way to be mindful. He explains: "You just become aware of the fact that you are breathing in—'right now, I am breathing in—right now I am breathing out—I know that I am breathing out, and I enjoy my in-breath and I enjoy my out-breath.' Suddenly I am truly alive, truly present."

According to Nhat Hanh, this sense of presence can nurture inner peace. Inner peace, in turn, extends to the external world. So, in Nhat Hanh's teaching, the first step to peace on Earth is what he calls "being peace." (This is the title of one of his best-known books.) The inner peace leads to feelings of joy and gratitude. Ultimately, these emotions lead the individual to think of others less fortunate and to perform charitable acts.

Nhat Hanh and his followers use a bell to remind people to stop and practice a few calm, mindful breaths. He suggests that individuals should stop for three meditative breaths whenever they hear a bell—a church bell or even a telephone ringing. The bell, he said, "is the voice of the Buddha calling me to my true home."

Nhat Hanh suggests that mindfulness can be applied to any small act, such as walking, eating, or even washing the dishes. He advises followers to eat slowly and silently, taking time to chew every mouthful of food up to 50 times. He suggests that the eater then can contemplate where the food came from, how it was grown and prepared, and how it links the eater to the Earth, to other people, and to his or her own needs. As for dishwashing, he said: "If you take time to enjoy dishwashing, then dishwashing can become meditation. If you think of the time of washing as time that you lose, then you lose yourself. It means that you continue to lose your life."

Nhat Hanh urges people to engage—not run away from—the problems of the world. He discourages people from focusing on themselves. "When you focus on yourself, you find many more problems," he said. "Not realizing the suffering around you in the world—I don't think that is a happiness. You feel loneliness and emptiness, and these are more unbearable than other kinds of suffering. The most effective medicine is an experience of the suffering around you. Then you heal."

in the war. They provided schooling and medical care. They also worked toward reconciliation by refusing to support either side in the ongoing conflict, claiming that the enemies were not people but ideology, hatred, and ignorance. All the while, the meditative practices of traditional Buddhism remained at the forefront, as Nhat Hanh emphasized "mindfulness" (see sidebar on page 126). "You have to learn how to help a wounded child while still practicing mindful breathing. You should not allow yourself to get lost in action," Nhat Hanh said. "Action should be meditation at the same time."

Nhat Hanh the Peacemaker

It was during the first half of the 1960s that the United States began to give military support to the South Vietnamese government in its struggle against Communist North Vietnam. As the war escalated, Nhat Hanh received worldwide attention for his peace-making efforts. In 1966, as the guest of American peace activists, he visited the United States. Speaking for his people, he brought the message that the U.S. troops and bombs were more damaging to the Vietnamese people than their purported enemy, the North Vietnamese.

On his visit, Nhat Hanh met with top U.S. government officials, including Robert McNamara, the U.S. Defense Secretary. McNamara was an early

> *In his letter to the Nobel Prize Committee to nominate Thich Nhat Hanh for the Nobel Peace Prize, Dr. Martin Luther King wrote this:*
>
> "I do not personally know anybody more worthy of the Nobel Peace Prize than this gentle Buddhist monk from Vietnam," King wrote in his nominating letter. "I know Thich Nhat Hanh, and am privileged to call him my friend. Let me share with you some things I know about him. You will find in this single human being an awesome range of abilities and interests. He is a holy man, for he is humble and devout. He is a scholar of immense intellectual capacity. . . . [He] is also a poet of superb clarity and human compassion. . . . His ideas for peace, if applied, would build a monument to ecumenism, to world brotherhood, to humanity."

proponent of U.S. involvement in the Vietnam War. Nhat Hanh also won the support of Martin Luther King, Jr., the influential leader of the civil rights movement. With Nhat Hanh at his side, King spoke out publicly for the first time against American intervention in Vietnam. Many believe that King's declaration helped turn the tide of public opinion against U.S. involvement in the war. In 1964, King had been awarded the Nobel Peace Prize, the world's highest recognition for promoting peace and justice. In 1967, he nominated Nhat Hanh for the same honor. No winner was selected for the Peace Prize that year.

During his time in the United States, Nhat Hanh also befriended Thomas Merton, a Roman-Catholic monk and well-known spiritual author. Merton wrote this of Nhat Hanh: "He represents the young, the defenseless, the new ranks of youth who find themselves with every hand turned against them except those of the peasants and the poor, with whom they are working. Nhat Hanh speaks truly for the people of Vietnam." After leaving the United States, Nhat Hanh met with Pope Paul VI, leader of the worldwide Roman Catholic church, and gained his support in seeking peace.

Exiled from Vietnam

While he was away spreading his message of peace, Nhat Hanh received word that the South Vietnamese government had barred his return home. South Vietnamese officials believed that the Buddhists were their enemies. Nhat Hanh went to live in France, where he continued his work as energetically as ever. In 1967 he published *Vietnam: Lotus in a Sea of Fire*, his account of the destructiveness of the war. The book was influential and sold well in eight languages.

In 1969, Nhat Hanh headed the Vietnamese Buddhist Peace Delegation at a high-level conference in Paris aimed at ending the war. As a result of the talks, the United States eventually pulled out of Vietnam. Nhat Hanh and his colleagues in the delegation went to work to help Vietnamese refugees and orphans. Around the same time Nhat Hanh established the Unified Buddhist Church, a non-profit organization to represent him and his associates. In 1975, while he was in Paris, the North Vietnamese Communist government took over South Vietnam, reuniting the North and the South as one country, Vietnam. Its leaders also mistrusted Nhat Hanh and forbade him from returning home. From his exile in France, Nhat Hanh organized a large network to aid the Vietnamese people, including those who fled the country. Among the refugees he assisted were the "boat people," desperate refugees who risked their lives to escape Vietnam by sea on rickety boats.

Travels and Teachings

For five years, beginning in 1977, Nhat Hanh retreated to a small Buddhist community about a hundred miles southwest of Paris. In the early 1980s, he returned to the public eye. Nhat

> **"**
>
> *According to editor Arnold Kotler, "A monk since 1942, [Nhat Hanh] had taught several generations of novices in Vietnam, developing the skill of expressing the deepest teachings of Buddhism in straightforward yet poetic language. Because of his experience of war and his willingness to face the realities of our time, his teachings were very much about suffering, reconciliation, and peace."*
>
> **"**

Hanh and his longtime associate, Sister Chan Khong, a Buddhist nun, co-founded Plum Village, a Buddhist community in southwest France. It is a retreat for spiritual pilgrims as well as a working plum orchard. All proceeds from the fruit go to needy children in Vietnam. About 100 nuns, monks, and lay people now live there. Thousands more come there each year to find spiritual guidance. Plum Village is part of a small network of monasteries and retreats now run by the Unified Buddhist Church, including sites in the United States, in Vermont and California.

Since his re-emergence, Nhat Hanh has traveled worldwide to lecture on engaged Buddhism and to lead retreats. In 1995, at a World Forum in San Francisco, he conducted a half-day session of walking meditation and mindful breathing for several world leaders, including the elder George Bush, former president of the United States; Margaret Thatcher, former prime minister of England; and Mikhail Gorbachev, former president of the Soviet Union. But more often, Nhat Hanh attracts ordinary people, often thousands at a time. He has held special retreats for such diverse groups as Vietnam veterans, psychotherapists, prison inmates, and ecologists. In the late 1990s, U.S. and other officials worked to persuade the Vietnamese government to lift Hanh's exile. But efforts failed when the Vietnamese officials insisted that only a government-sanctioned Buddhist organization could sponsor the visit. Nhat Hanh refused to accept the restriction.

———— *((* ————

According to Rev. Michael A. Fox, what Nhat Hanh does in his talks and writings "is to infuse the notion of inner peace with concrete meaning, bringing it down to earth in engaging, anecdotal, almost conversational language. By means of this endeavor, he clarifies the sense in which it can meaningfully be said that peace is already here, within us, or that peace begins with me. He delivers his message with skill, grace, and creative insight."

———— *))* ————

His Writings

Nhat Hanh has also spread his teachings through his writings. He has written several types of works: poetry, essays on the practice of meditation, meditation exercises, and teachings on Buddhism. These are published by Parallax Press in Berkeley, California, which the church established to distribute his writings and tapes of his talks. Nhat Hanh has proven especially adept at teaching his beliefs. According to editor Arnold Kotler, "A monk since 1942, he had taught several generations of novices in Vietnam, developing the skill of expressing the deepest teachings of Buddhism in straightforward yet poetic language. Because of his experience of war and his willingness to face the realities of our time, his teachings were very much about suffering, reconciliation, and peace."

What Nhat Hanh does in his talks and writings, according to Rev. Michael A. Fox, "is to infuse the notion of inner peace with concrete meaning, bring-

ing it down to earth in engaging, anecdotal, almost conversational language. By means of this endeavor, he clarifies the sense in which it can meaningfully be said that peace is already here, within us, or that peace begins with me. He delivers his message with skill, grace, and creative insight."

Among Nhat Hanh's most popular works are *The Miracle of Mindfulness* (1987) and *Being Peace* (1987). Originally written in 1974 as a long letter to a fellow monk at the School of Youth Social Services, *The Miracle of Mindfulness* is a clear and simple guide to meditation. It includes anecdotes and exercises that can be used by any reader in the quest for self-understanding and peacefulness. It shows how mindfulness can be applied to each moment of the day, from washing dishes to answering the phone. *Being Peace* is an introduction to mindful living and engaged Buddhism. Now considered a classic, it shows how the pressures and demands of daily life can be transformed into the opportunity for peace. Both have sold hundreds of thousands of copies around the world.

In other works, including *Living Buddha, Living Christ* (1995), Nhat Hanh has focused on the common ground shared by followers of Christ and Buddha, two of the most pivotal figures in history. Nhat Hanh doesn't suggest that followers of other religions change their beliefs. In fact, he ex-

NATIONAL BESTSELLER

THICH NHAT HANH
author of *Living Buddha, Living Christ*

ANGER

Wisdom for Cooling the Flames

presses deep respect for Christian and Jewish traditions. But he does encourage people to discover their own religious roots by practicing Buddhist mindfulness. "It's not my intention to convert Christians or Jews into Buddhists," he said. "It's my intention to make them better Christians and better Jews." He believes that there are not serious divisions between Christianity and Buddhism. "Most of the boundaries we have created between our two traditions are artificial. Truth has no boundaries." Nhat Hanh often notes that in his room in Plum Village, his private altar holds images of Christ as well as Buddha. He lights incense in tribute to both.

In 2001 Nhat Hanh published *Anger: Wisdom for Cooling the Flames* (2001), his teachings on the peaceful resolution of conflict. The book was published just one day before the September 11, 2001, terrorist attacks on New York City and Washington, D.C. After that dreadful day, as Americans struggled to cope with their rage and fear in the wake of the attacks, many turned to Nhat Hanh's book for guidance.

In *Anger*, Nhat Hanh shows how anger can ruin people's lives and then shows how to change. He describes two techniques to promote communication and foster peace. First, he encourages compassionate listening, listening with full attention and compassion, but without judgment or criticism. Second, he recommends gentle and loving speech, which he describes as "the kind of language that conveys what is in our hearts, without blaming or condemning." As he explains, "We live in a time of many sophisticated means of communication. . . . But it is exactly at this time that communication between people, father and son, husband and wife, mother and daughter, has become extremely difficult. If we cannot restore communication, happiness will never be possible. In the Buddhist teaching, the practice of compassionate listening, the practice of loving speech, the practice of taking care of our anger, are presented very clearly. We have to put into practice the teaching of the Buddha . . . in order to restore communication and bring happiness to our family, our school, and our community. Then we can help other people in the world." Nhat Hanh emphasizes that these techniques can work for individuals and also for governments. As a reviewer wrote for *Publishers Weekly*, "Nhat Hanh doesn't limit his task to discussing anger between families and friends; he also deals with anger between citizens and governments." He has shared his practices with small groups of Palestinians and Israelis, who come to Plum Village hoping to find common ground in their bitter political struggles. Forty years after the height of the Vietnam War, his anti-war message is still strong. "It's plain that bombs have not removed terrorism, but only created more hatred and violence," Nhat Hanh said. "America is capable of compassion, understanding, and deep listening to the suffering of her people. These are the practices all of us must take up right away."

According to many commentators, Nhat Hanh has become the second most prominent spokesman for Buddhism in the non-Asian world. (The first is the Dalai Lama, the exiled religious leader of Tibet. More information on the Dalai Lama is available in *Biography Today*, Sep. 1998). Nhat Hanh has expressed his surprise at his influential role. "It was not my intention to come here to the West and spread Buddhism. The intention was to come here and try to end the Vietnam War. But because of that and because of the need of the people, our friends, that is why we had to begin to share the [Buddhist] practice with our Western friends."

As Nhat Hanh approaches age 80, his commitment to peace and tolerance remains strong. This is clear in his most recent book, *Creating True Peace: Ending Violence in Yourself, Your Family, Your Community, and the World* (2003), a blueprint for both personal change and global change. It acknowledges the current crisis of violence and people's feelings of helplessness and fear—while showing unequivocally that we are not helpless and that we can make a difference. Relying on Nhat Hahn's stories of his own experiences practicing peace during wartime, *Creating True Peace* includes meditation instruction and peace practices to show people how to create nonviolent thoughts even in the midst of upheaval. And it shows how to create peace throughout all aspects of life—personal, family, community,

THICH NHAT HANH

Ending Violence in Yourself, Your Family, Your Community, and the World

CREATING TRUE PEACE

———— **"** ————

"True peace is always possible. Yet it requires strength and practice, particularly in times of great difficulty. To some, peace and nonviolence are synonymous with passivity and weakness. In truth, practicing peace and nonviolence is far from passive. To practice peace, to make peace alive in us, is to actively cultivate understanding, love, and compassion, even in the face of misperception and conflict. Practicing peace, especially in times of war, requires courage."

———— **"** ————

state, nation, and world. "True peace is always possible. Yet it requires strength and practice, particularly in times of great difficulty. To some, peace and nonviolence are synonymous with passivity and weakness. In truth, practicing peace and nonviolence is far from passive. To practice peace, to make peace alive in us, is to actively cultivate understanding, love, and compassion, even in the face of misperception and conflict. Practicing peace, especially in times of war, requires courage."

HOME AND FAMILY

When he is not traveling, Nhat Hanh lives in Plum Village, a retreat consisting of old stone farmhouses in rural southwest France. He has never married or had children. But that doesn't mean he was denied a family. As he told the *San Francisco Chronicle*: "When I became a novice monk, I lived in a temple where the atmosphere was quite like in a family. The abbot is like a father and the other monks are like your big brothers, your small, younger brothers. It is a kind of a family. So I don't think that the desire to set up a family, to live like everyone else, was so strong, because it is clear that I had a happy time of being a novice. I had a lot of joy, of happiness." Although Nhat Hanh has not set foot in his homeland in more than 35 years, he is at peace with his situation. "In the beginning, I missed my country very much. I used to dream of going back," he said. "But now I feel that I am home."

HOBBIES AND INTERESTS

Nhat Hanh enjoys gardening. He is involved with tending the plum orchards in the Plum Village retreat in France.

SELECTED WRITINGS

Vietnam: Lotus in a Sea of Fire, 1967
Vietnam Poems, 1972
A Rose for Your Pocket, 1987
The Miracle of Mindfulness: A Manual on Meditation, 1987
Being Peace, 1987
The Moon Bamboo, 1989
Our Appointment with Life: The Buddha's Teaching on Living in the Present,
    1990
Old Path, White Clouds: Walking in the Footsteps of the Buddha, 1990

A Taste of Earth, and Other Legends of Vietnam, 1991
Touching Peace: Practicing the Art of Mindful Living, 1992
The Blooming of a Lotus: Guided Meditation Exercises for Healing and Transformation, 1993
Call Me by My True Name: The Collected Poems of Thich Nhat Hanh, 1993
Living Buddha, Living Christ, 1995
Be Still and Know: Reflections from Living Buddha, Living Christ, 1996
The Heart of a Buddha's Teaching: An Introduction to Buddhism, 1996
Teachings on Love, 1997
Interbeing: Fourteen Teachings for Engaged Buddhism, 1998
Fragrant Palm Leaves: Journals 1962-66, 1998
Going Home: Jesus and Buddha as Brothers, 2000
Anger: Wisdom for Cooling the Flames, 2001
Essential Writings, 2001
Creating True Peace: Ending Violence in Yourself, Your Family, Your Community, and the World, 2003

FURTHER READING

Books

Button, John. *The Radicalism Handbook: Radical Activists, Groups, and Movements of the Twentieth Century*, 1995
Contemporary Authors, Vol. 167
Powers, Roger, and William B. Vogele. *Protest, Power, and Change: An Encyclopedia of Nonviolent Action from Act-Up to Women's Suffrage*, 1997
Willis, Jennifer Schwamm, ed. *A Lifetime of Peace: Essential Writings by and about Thich Nhat Hanh*, 2003

Periodicals

Boston Globe, May 18, 2001, p.B1
Christian Century, Oct. 16, 1996, p.964
Christian Science Monitor, Apr. 4, 2002, p.18
Denver Post, Sep. 1, 2002, p.L6
Los Angeles Times, Sep. 11, 1999, p.2
National Catholic Reporter, July 16, 1993, p.11
New Yorker, June 25, 1966, p.21
New York Times, Sep. 19, 1993, p.A30; Oct. 16, 1999, p.A8
Peace Research, Aug. 2000, p.40
San Francisco Chronicle, Oct. 12 1997, p.3/Z1
Washington Post, Sep. 28, 1993, p.C1

Online Databases

Biography Resource Center Online, 2003, articles from *Contemporary Authors Online*, 2003, and *Contemporary Heroes and Heroines, Book IV*, 2000

ADDRESS

Thich Nhat Hanh
Maple Forest Monastery
P.O. Box 354
South Woodstock, VT 05071

WORLD WIDE WEB SITE

http://www.plumvillage.org

OUTKAST
Antwan Patton (Big Boi) 1975-
André Benjamin (André 3000) 1975-

American Hip-Hop Duo

BIRTH

The music group OutKast includes two members: Antwan Patton (Big Boi) and André Benjamin (André 3000, or sometimes just Dré). Patton was born on February 1, 1975, in Savannah, Georgia. His parents were Tony Kearse, a Marine Corps sergeant, and Rowena Patton, a retail supervisor. Benjamin was born on May 27, 1975, in Atlanta, Georgia. His parents were Lawrence Walker, a collections agent, and Sharon Benjamin, a real estate agent.

YOUTH AND EDUCATION

Both Patton and Benjamin grew up in Georgia in families that were struggling. Patton, the oldest of five children, started out in Savannah. The family moved around a lot while he was growing up, and they relocated to Atlanta when he was a teenager. Some reports say that Patton spent some time living with various family members. Benjamin, an only child, grew up in a single-parent home. He was raised by his mother, and together they lived in a series of places around southwest Atlanta until Benjamin was 15, when he made the decision to move in with his father. Despite their different family arrangements, Patton and Benjamin would soon find out that their early environments gave them much in common. "We came from basically the same background. We grew up the same way, and were into a lot of the same things," Benjamin once recalled.

> **"**
>
> *Patton and Benjamin were both decent students, but until they met, neither gave serious consideration to a life in music. "I wanted to be a child psychologist or play football," Patton recalled. "I thought I'd be an architect, but I didn't like math," Benjamin added.*
>
> **"**

Patton and Benjamin each attended Tri-Cities High School in the Atlanta suburb of East Point. The school had an excellent reputation for producing talented musicians: the members of the popular R&B groups TLC and Xscape had also attended Tri-Cities High. Patton and Benjamin met in 1990 at a local mall and soon found that they had similar tastes in music, including Sly and the Family Stone, James Brown, Jimi Hendrix, Prince, Parliament/Funkadelic, and popular hip-hop artists. They also found that they had similar tastes in fashion, which would seem to be in direct contrast with the image they would later cultivate. "We were preps," Patton recalled. "We wore loafers, argyle socks, and V-neck sweaters with T-shirts. We were new to the school and we didn't know anybody." The pair became friends immediately. They worked on rhymes together and also developed their individual styles by having rhyming competitions in their school cafeteria.

Patton and Benjamin were both decent students, but until they met, neither gave serious consideration to a life in music. "I wanted to be a child psychologist or play football," Patton recalled. "I thought I'd be an architect, but I didn't like math," Benjamin added. But once the duo had legitimate careers in music ahead of them, they felt that their studies were less important. In his junior year, Benjamin dropped out a few credits short of his graduation requirements, but Patton was adamant about finishing high school and getting his diploma. "Right up until we got signed by LaFace Records, there were times when all we did was hang out," he once said. "I had been going to school for 11 years, had a 3.68 GPA and college plans, yet was on the verge of dropping out. I finally realized that school was something I needed just as much as music, and I didn't want not having a certain piece of paper to hold me back." Patton graduated on time from Tri-Cities in 1993, while Benjamin eventually went to night school to earn his diploma.

Patton later credited his high school years for being an important part of his career path. "Education is the foundation of my rhyme," he remarked. "All the things I say, all the words, came from English and science class. I like words. All I got come from words! The more words you learn the more rhymes you have!" The duo later wrote a song entitled "Git Up, Git Out," which urged their younger fans to stay in school and make the right choices.

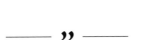

"Right up until we got signed by LaFace Records, there were times when all we did was hang out," Patton once said. "I had been going to school for 11 years, had a 3.68 GPA and college plans, yet was on the verge of dropping out. I finally realized that school was something I needed just as much as music, and I didn't want not having a certain piece of paper to hold me back."

CAREER HIGHLIGHTS

Getting Their Big Break

While they were still in high school, Patton and Benjamin met record producer Rico Wade through one of Patton's ex-girlfriends. Wade was a member of the Organized Noize production team, which worked with the artists TLC and En Vogue. Wade was also an accomplished musician with

expertise in the areas of keyboard samples and drum machines. The duo immediately impressed him with their rapping abilities, and he invited them to his studio. "I was in awe," Wade said. "I closed the store, we got in my Blazer and went straight to the [studio]." The three hit it off, as Benjamin later recalled. "From the first time Rico pressed 'play' on the tape, we knew we had our producer, because the beats were like nothing I had ever heard before."

Wade and Organized Noize had a studio called the Dungeon in the basement of an old house. The Dungeon attracted a lot of aspiring performers, and competition there was tough. "The basement wasn't finished," Patton recalled. "We have red clay in Georgia, so the beat machines had dust on 'em. There were old broke-up patio chairs. You had several people sitting on steps with their notebooks out. Guys sleeping upstairs on a hardwood floor. . . . We'd walk up to this deli inside a gas station and order the spaghetti special, because it came with five meatballs, so we could split it."

Organized Noize gave the duo their first break when they were invited to contribute a single to a Christmas album. At first, Patton and Benjamin were not very eager to record a Christmas song. "But we decided to do it Dungeon-style," Patton said, "a song where there's no tree, no gifts, barely a jug of eggnog." Their debut single "Player's Ball," about life on the streets, eventually went gold. They even got to record a video for the song—directed by the young up-and-comer Sean Puffy Combs.

By 1993, the duo had tried several different names for their act—including 2 Shades Deep and the Misfits—before deciding on OutKast. A pivotal moment in their careers occurred when they auditioned for record executive Antonio "LA" Reid, who at that time was president of LaFace Records. Reid wanted to sign OutKast to a contract. "Our parents wouldn't let us sign," Benjamin recalled. "We were 17. We had to wait a year. They didn't believe in rap." It was also around this time that Patton and Benjamin started using the names Big Boi and André 3000, respectively. Patton later recalled how their combination of good fortune and determination paid off. "We were lucky, no question," he admitted. "But we didn't sleep on the opportunity—every time we had a chance, we knew it, we stepped up and delivered."

Early Albums

In 1994, OutKast released its first album, *Southernplayalisticadillacmuzik*. While the CD contained two versions of "Player's Ball," Patton was quick to point out that the duo had more to say than just the themes addressed in their initial single. "A lot of people got the message of our first album mixed up," he remarked. "They just heard 'Player's Ball' and thought it was all about the pimps, the cars, and all that mess." Still, "Player's Ball" was eventually re-released as a single and went gold, selling over a half-million copies. In addition, it was Billboard's No. 1 song on the Rap Chart for six consecutive weeks. The album as a whole received praise for its casual funk, live instruments, and creative and raw grooves, all reminiscent of 1970s soul. With this commercial and critical success, OutKast set the stage for the group's later albums and gained more creative control on their next release.

By 1996, OutKast was putting the finishing touches on their second album, *ATLiens*. While the duo again worked with the Organized Noize production team, Patton and Benjamin also received producer credits on the album. The title of the record was a combination of the abbreviations for Atlanta and the word "aliens." Bubbling with originality, the album has been described as futuristic, haunting, and hypnotic.

ATLiens was considered a great leap forward for the duo, and it represented a departure in hip-hop. Unlike many of their hip-hop peers who sampled existing songs in their entirety for their own tunes, OutKast featured live instruments on many of the tracks. "While everyone else is content to steal an old hit song and add a new rap verse over it, we always start from scratch," Patton explained. "Picasso had plenty of influences, but you'd never catch him trying to remake another artist's work in the exact same way. We feel the same." Benjamin later recalled his feelings regarding the situation. "When we came up, everybody was playing straight beat machines and nobody was playing instruments like they did in my mama and them's generation. People are just starting to get back into that, and we have to research to find out about the blues, rock 'n' roll, progressive rock, calypso, reggae, jazz — anything we can learn from. If you listen to hip-hop all day long, all you're going to know is hip-hop. But if you listen more, you can mix things up to create another type of music." *ATLiens* proved to be another successful project for the duo, selling in excess of 1.5 million copies. The song "Elevators" was released as a single and became a No. 1 hit.

More Success Leads to Trouble with an American Icon

OutKast's third album, *Aquemini,* was released in 1998. The title was meant to convey a combination of the zodiac signs Aquarius (Patton) and Gemini (Benjamin). "It's simply that two people can come together as one and create," Benjamin explained. "Balance is the key. Balance in the music and balance with me and Dré," Patton added. While their partnership remained strong, the pair still maintained separate and original identities. Benjamin was starting to garner a lot of attention for his outlandish clothes, while Patton stayed true to his roots. "I'm more street, hard-core hip-hop, and Dre's more extraterrestrial," he explained. "Dré looks like the music and I look like the message." The pair even had lifestyles that were totally opposite. But *Aquemini* proved that their partnership was indeed intact, as the duo co-produced nine of the album's 14 tracks.

> *By 1998, Benjamin was starting to garner a lot of attention for his outlandish clothes, while Patton stayed true to his roots. "I'm more street, hard-core hip-hop, and Dre's more extraterrestrial," Patton explained. "Dré looks like the music and I look like the message."*

Aquemini proved to be OutKast's most diverse offering yet, complete with a star-studded lineup of guest stars including Erykah Badu, George Clinton, and members of the WuTang Clan and Goodie Mob. While the funk influence still predominated, the mix was expanded to include reggae, jazz, and world music. The album featured a number of strong tracks, including "Return of the G" and "Skew It on the Bar-B," but it was the song "Rosa Parks" that grabbed headlines. The tune, which aside from the title never mentions the famed civil rights activist by name, was OutKast's way of identifying with those who stand up for their beliefs. "When we were making the album, the music that was out at the time was not very creative. We refused to go with the flow. We wanted to be like Rosa Parks and do the opposite of what everybody else was doing. She refused to go to the back of the bus."

OutKast performing at the American Music Awards in January 2001.

While OutKast intended the song as a tribute to Parks, she was not flattered by the honor of having her name used as the title of their song. "You have her name associated with lyrics that contain vulgarity and profanity and she does not appreciate it," her attorney Gregory Reed explained. In 1999, Parks filed a lawsuit seeking $25,000 in damages for using her name without permission, claiming that the song violated her trademark rights and defamed her. In addition, she asked that her name be removed from all OutKast products. Patton and Benjamin were shocked at the actions of someone that they considered a role model. "Rosa Parks has inspired our music and our lives since we were children," they explained in a prepared statement released to the press.

OutKast won the first legal round when a federal court judge ruled that OutKast's right to use Rosa Parks's name was guaranteed by the right to free speech. At that point, the court decided that OutKast did not defame Parks. But her attorneys appealed the decision. "We won the first decision,

351

so they're appealing it," Patton later explained. "But everybody knows that there was never any disrespect meant at all. If you know anything about OutKast—if you listen to the song—it's not about Rosa Parks. When we sing 'everybody move to the back of the bus,' we're just using that as symbolism." In 2003, the case reached the United States Court of Appeals, where OutKast argued that the song wasn't false advertising, that it didn't violate her public name, and that Parks should not have the right to sue. But OutKast lost that round—Court of Appeals decided that Parks did have the right to sue, and the Supreme Court later upheld that decision. By mid-2004, a trial date had been set for early 2005; the lawsuit had been winding its way through the courts for five years and was still unresolved.

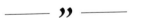

"In rap, there's nothing new under the sun," Benjamin explained. "But I think it's the way you say it and how you approach it. People are afraid to step out. There's a formula to making music now, and no one really has the courage to do their own thing."

When all was said and done, *Aquemini* was a solid success for OutKast, selling in excess of two million copies and earning several Grammy nominations in the process. The duo later went on a successful concert tour to promote the record, opening many dates for rap superstar Lauryn Hill.

Moving into New Territory

For their next release, *Stankonia* (2000), OutKast continued to push the boundaries in their music and their message. The album combined stories about life on the streets with funk, rock, and hip-hop, seasoned with heavy doses of rhythm. "In rap, there's nothing new under the sun," Benjamin explained. "But I think it's the way you say it and how you approach it. People are afraid to step out. There's a formula to making music now, and no one really has the courage to do their own thing." Patton went on to say "It's an experimental thing. I've met a lot of producers who know exactly what they're looking for. It's like etched in stone before they begin. But we start with one element and build on to it until we get to a point where we say, 'Yeah, that's it. That's jammin.'"

Indeed, the tracks contained on OutKast's fourth release backed up Benjamin's claims. "B.O.B. (Bombs Over Baghdad)" combined social criticism with the intense rhythm of drum-and-bass dance music. As the album's first single and one of its most exciting songs, "B.O.B. (Bombs Over Baghdad)" quickly grabbed listeners' attention. The moving "Ms. Jackson"

The cover of the CD Stankonia.

was an open letter to the grandmother of Benjamin's son proclaiming that he would always be a loving and responsible father. It later went on to become a No. 1 single on the pop music charts. "Toilet Tisha" was a dramatic track about a 14-year-old girl killing her newborn child. Benjamin later explained that the album's title was meant to convey a broad range of messages. "*Stankonia* is this place I imagined where you can open yourself up and be free to express anything," he said. Patton had his own interpretation of the album's mood. "*Stankonia* is where you can get butt-naked in your mind. It's the spiritual feeling where you can do whatever you want and not care what anybody else is going to say."

Stankonia was another smash hit for OutKast, selling in excess of five million copies. It impressed both fans and critics, appearing on many music critics' lists of the best albums of the year. It also won Grammy Awards for

Big Boi and André 3000 enjoy an exuberant performance at the 2004 Soul Train Music Awards.

Best Rap Performance by a Duo or Group (for "Ms. Jackson") and Best Rap Album. In addition, the record was nominated for Album of the Year and Record of the Year. But success was only part of the reward for the duo. "We decided early on that money couldn't be the motivation," Patton stated. "The motivation had to be in the love for music. We knew we wanted to be experimental, but at the same time, keep in touch with what's going on with the people. We wanted to take risks, and introduce people to something fresh."

The following year, the duo released a compilation album entitled *Big Boi and Dré Present . . . OutKast* (2001), which included the group's greatest hits as well as several rare, unreleased tracks. The collection served to document OutKast's growth over their first four albums. By this point, Patton and Benjamin had established their talent for smart, funny, and joyous funk mixed with jazz, blues, soul, R&B, rock, and world music. In many ways, their music seemed to defy musical conventions. With their continued experimentation on each new album, they had become known for their adventurous and inventive music that still claimed a retro feel. Over the years, they managed to make unconventional and ambitious music that was, at the same time, very popular. "It's this combination of eclecticism and accessibility that's made OutKast one of hip-hop's most unique forces," Lorraine Ali wrote in *Newsweek*. "The Atlanta duo mixes old and new musical styles—funk, R&B, hip-hop, rock—and ties them all together with organic jams, head-bopping rhythms, and improvisational rhymes. OutKast's cut-and-paste approach has garnered the respect of finicky underground musicians, while their chart-smart beats won over rap's mainstream crowd."

By this point, the two members of OutKast had also firmly established their separate identities. Some have called the two musicians the poet and the player. Benjamin was considered more cerebral, worried about social issues and the well-being of the community. He often brought a more futuristic and experimental flavor to the musical mix. Patton, on the other hand, was considered more of a gangster, concerned with more immediate issues like women and partying. His musical influences were more firmly based in the rap and hip-hop traditions. Yet despite their differences, both were firmly committed to the partnership.

"We decided early on that money couldn't be the motivation," Patton stated. "The motivation had to be in the love for music. We knew we wanted to be experimental, but at the same time, keep in touch with what's going on with the people. We wanted to take risks, and introduce people to something fresh."

Speakerboxxx/The Love Below

In 2003, OutKast released a double-disc set entitled *Speakerboxxx/The Love Below*. Like all of OutKast's work, this album was full of stylistic surprises. It was essentially two solo records in the form of one double album. *Speakerboxxx*, which contained Patton's material, was an eclectic hip-hop mix with intense and fluid tracks filled with bass, electronics, and fast-paced raps. The blend of hard-edged gangster beats and bouncy party cuts proved to many that Patton was one of the smoothest and funniest rappers around. *The Love Below*, which contained Benjamin's work, was a concept album about relationships that told a series of love stories using hip-hop, jazz, funk, and R&B influences. Called irreverent, incisive, exhilarating, and experimental, *The Love Below* was also proclaimed one of the most adventurous albums of the year. "Rather than an outright collaboration, it's a two-disc set," Allison Samuels wrote in *Newsweek*, "the first all by the more mainstream Big Boi, the second all by the more experimental André. If Big Boi is red beans and rice—you can hear the influence of gospel, funk, even Jimi Hendrix—André is a crazy

The hit album Speakerboxxx/The Love Below *includes separate disks from Big Boi and André 3000.*

organic salad. . . . André is all about emotional turmoil—he still seems to be hurting over his breakup with Badu—while Big Boi is the practical-minded hedonist. . . . Taken together, the discs complement each other. But they could just have easily been solo albums."

The news of two individual albums shocked the duo's longtime fans, who worried that the release signaled the beginning of the end for OutKast. But both Benjamin and Patton were quick to put a stop to those rumors. "There is some distance," Benjamin explained. "We may venture out and do other things, but we always give each other blessings. We will always be OutKast." Still, the rumors continued to persist, especially after Benjamin declared that he had no intention to tour in support of the record. Patton took that news in stride. "If he decides not to tour, it's all good," Patton remarked. "He knows I'm going to go on the road. Ain't nothing better than the crowd's reaction to new music. We've got six albums worth of material. That's plenty to work with."

The first single was the double-sided "The Way You Move/Hey Ya!" Together, the two songs dominated the pop charts for nine weeks. "The Way You Move,"from Patton's *Speakerboxxx*, was a bass-and-horn-driven track with an old-school R&B feel to it. Some have called it an instant R&B classic. The track "Hey Ya!" from Benjamin's *The Love Below*, had a more melodic feel; it proved to be the album's breakout hit.

Many said that "Hey Ya!" invoked memories of the Beatles, a connection that the singer didn't really understand. "People say 'Hey Ya!' sounds like the Beatles, or Ike Turner, or Cheap Trick, but I have no idea where that comes from," he remarked. "I've heard of those artists, but I'm not really hip to them. When you're in the studio, you're not really thinking about breaking barriers. You just think about writing the song." Of course, the video reinforced the connection to the Beatles, with a stage set that reminded many of the band's first appearances on "The Ed Sullivan Show." What many people did not know, however, was that the song "Hey Ya!" was nearly five years old—it was originally called "Thank God for Mom and Dad" and was slated for inclusion on *Stankonia*. Benjamin later recalled its evolution, stating that the song was influenced more by punk rock than by groups like the Beatles. "I started writing that song five or six years ago. That's when my friends started hipping me to the Ramones, the Buzzcocks, the Smiths, bands like that. I was getting to this music late," he explained. "The 'Hey Ya!' chords were the first guitar chords I ever learned."

"Rather than an outright collaboration, it's a two-disc set, the first all by the more mainstream Big Boi, the second all by the more experimental André," Allison Samuels wrote in **Newsweek**. *"If Big Boi is red beans and rice—you can hear the influence of gospel, funk, even Jimi Hendrix— André is a crazy organic salad. . . . André is all about emotional turmoil—he still seems to be hurting over his breakup with Badu— while Big Boi is the practical-minded hedonist. . . . Taken together, the discs complement each other. But they could just have easily been solo albums."*

"Hey Ya!" was that rare song that appealed to a wide range of music fans, including those who loved hip-hop, rock and roll, and Top 40. As the song became more and more popular, Benjamin became more and more surprised by its success. "People think it's a light song, but the lyrics are pretty serious," he said. "It's talking about the difficulty of relationships trying to stay together. But people just want to dance to it — even older people like it."

Recognition and Success

Speakerboxxx/The Love Below was another multi-million selling success for OutKast and was the No. 1 album for seven straight weeks. For over two months, "Hey Ya!" and "The Way You Move" were the top two singles on the pop chart, making OutKast the first group to achieve such a feat since the Bee Gees back in 1978. The set went on to sell over eight million copies.

Speakerboxxx/The Love Below also received six Grammy nominations. When the awards were announced on February 8, 2004, OutKast took home three trophies: Album of the Year, Best Rap Album, and Best Urban/Alternative Performance. About the only surprise of the evening came when "Hey Ya!" lost Record of the Year to Coldplay's "Clocks." Benjamin admitted that he was shocked about the way the whole evening turned out. "I thought we'd win that many awards, but not in those categories. I thought 'Hey Ya!' would get Record of the Year. When Coldplay won, I was like 'Oh really?'"

Benjamin later recalled the importance of the evening. "The best moment was when we won Album of the Year and Big Boi gave me a hug," he recalled. "The embrace lasted five — eight, nine — no maybe 15 seconds. *The Love Below* was originally supposed to be a solo album. At the last

> ──── **"** ────
>
> *"It's this combination of eclecticism and accessibility that's made OutKast one of hip-hop's most unique forces," Lorraine Ali wrote in* Newsweek. *"The Atlanta duo mixes old and new musical styles — funk, R&B, hip-hop, rock — and ties them all together with organic jams, head-bopping rhythms, and improvisational rhymes. OutKast's cut-and-paste approach has garnered the respect of finicky underground musicians, while their chart-smart beats won over rap's mainstream crowd."*
>
> ──── **"** ────

minute, management and the record company said it wasn't a good time to do that so Big Boi did *Speaker-boxxx*. But I was taking so long to finish *The Love Below* that he wanted to release that as a solo album. A lot of people don't know the album almost wasn't made. So there were a lot of emotions in those seconds."

Despite the happiness surrounding their success, OutKast still managed to generate controversy on their big night. During a performance of "Hey Ya!" Benjamin and several dancers pranced around a tepee dressed in feathers, fringe, and war paint. The San Francisco-based Native American Cultural Center called the performance racist and urged a boycott of CBS (the network that broadcast the event); OutKast; their record company, Arista; and the National Academy of Recording Arts and Sciences, which sponsors the Grammy Awards. The Native American Cultural Center also filed a complaint with the Federal Communications Commission (FCC). While OutKast had no comment about the situation, CBS was quick to apologize. "We are very sorry if anyone was offended," said CBS spokeswoman Nancy Carr.

Big Boi and André 3000 pose with their three Grammy Awards, February 2004.

Their successful double album might lead to other projects as well. OutKast plans to make a film together for Home Box Office (HBO), using cuts from *Speakerboxxx/The Love Below* and OutKast's next album as the movie's soundtrack. Patton was quick to point out that the project was not going to be autobiographical. "It's set in the Thirties, during Prohibition," he explained.

Sticking Together or Growing Apart?

Despite the success of *Speakerboxxx/The Love Below*, Patton and Benjamin have continually emphasized that they have no plans to split up and pursue solo careers. "We're not breaking up," Benjamin proclaimed around the time of the Grammy Awards, "but we're most definitely growing up." Patton reinforced that the duo's partnership was stronger than music. "He's just like my brother. I'm his kids' godfather — he's my kids' godfather. Our mamas hang out together."

Still, each has gotten involved in individual projects, leading to questions about their long-term plans. Patton likes to breed rare dogs like blue pit bull terriers, English bulldogs, Yorkshire terriers, and Neapolitan mastiffs. He owns Pitfall Kennels and has sold dogs to celebrities like tennis player Serena Williams and pop star Usher. He also runs the duo's OutKast Clothing Company and their Aquemini record label. In addition, he recently released a documentary about the band called *Big Boi's Boom Boom Room*.

> ——— **"** ———
>
> *"We're not breaking up,"*
> *Benjamin proclaimed*
> *around the time of the*
> *2004 Grammy Awards,*
> *"but we're most definitely*
> *growing up." Patton*
> *reinforced that the duo's*
> *partnership was stronger*
> *than music. "He's just like*
> *my brother. I'm his kids'*
> *godfather—he's my kids'*
> *godfather. Our mamas*
> *hang out together."*
>
> ——— **"** ———

Benjamin enjoys painting pictures and selling them through the group's website. He also enjoys yoga and plans to start up his own line of retail clothing accessories, including ties, gloves, scarves, ascots, and bracelets. He has dabbled in acting, auditioning for the lead role in a proposed movie about Jimi Hendrix and appearing in a small role in *Hollywood Homicide* with Josh Hartnett and Harrison Ford. Benjamin has recently been filming *Be Cool*, the sequel to the hit film *Get Shorty*. In *Be Cool*, he plays a thug in a rap group called the Dub MDs. John Travolta, Uma Thurman, Cedric the Entertainer, Harvey Keitel, Danny DeVito, The Rock, and James Gandolfini are also appearing in the film. The costumes have become part of the fun for Benjamin. "I get to dress stupid over-the-top," he said. "Platinum jewelry, pants half-down my waist."

As the members of OutKast pursue their separate interests, they also seem to be diverging in their musical tastes as well, with Patton emphasizing rap and Benjamin moving toward a more eclectic mix. With so many individual projects and such different styles, many music critics and fans have wondered if OutKast will remain a group or if Patton and Benjamin will decide to go their separate ways.

MARRIAGE AND FAMILY

Benjamin is single, but in 1998 he and singer Erykah Badu had a son named Seven Sirius. The couple never married. Benjamin and Badu maintain an amicable relationship and share responsibility for Seven's upbringing, but he admits that he was initially hurt by their breakup. "When you've given love to someone and then take it away, that's terrible," he said. "I don't wanna do nobody else like that. When I was with Erykah, I wrote some terrible wraps." Benjamin also remains close to his mother, Sharon.

Patton is also unmarried, but he and his long-time girlfriend, Sherilita, have two sons: Bamboo, born in 2000, and Cross, born in 2001; he also has a daughter, Jordan, born in 1995, from an earlier relationship. Patton is a devoted father, but still insists that music will always be the most important thing in his life. "My work pays for their schools and everything else they need, so I gotta do it," he explained. "And I love performing. So why would I stop? My first love is music, then my kids. I ain't worried about much else."

SELECTED WORKS

Southernplayalisticadillacmuzik, 1994
ATLiens, 1996
Aquemini, 1998
Stankonia, 2000
Big Boi and Dré Present . . . OutKast, 2001
Speakerboxxx/The Love Below, 2003

HONORS AND AWARDS

Grammy Awards (National Academy of Recording Arts and Sciences): 2000 (two awards), Best Rap Album for *Stankonia*, Best Rap Performance by a Duo or Group for "Ms. Jackson"; 2002 (one award), Best Rap Performance by a Duo or Group for "The Whole World" featuring Killer Mike; 2003 (three awards), Album of the Year for *Speakerboxxx/The Love Below*, Best Rap Album for *Speakerboxxx/The Love Below*, Best Urban/Alternative Performance for "Hey Ya!"
Video Music Awards (MTV): 2001, Best Hip-Hop Video for "Ms. Jackson"
Image Awards (NAACP): 2004, Outstanding Duo or Group

FURTHER READING

Periodicals

Atlanta Journal-Constitution, Oct. 30, 2000, p.D1
Ebony, Jan. 2004, p.74
Jet, Feb. 2, 2004, p.58

Life, Nov. 3, 2000, p.E13
Los Angeles Sentinel, Nov. 11, 1998, p.8
Los Angeles Times, Dec. 22, 1996, p.78; Sep. 21, 2003, p.35
Newsweek, Oct. 30, 2000, p.88; Sep. 22, 2003, p.86
People, Feb. 16, 2004, p.87
Rolling Stone, Nov. 23, 2000, p.62; Nov. 13, 2003, p.62; Mar. 18, 2004, p.58
Time, Sep. 29, 2003, p.71; Feb. 16, 2004, p.87; Apr. 26, 2004, p.95

Online Articles

http://www.cbsnews.com/stories/2004/02/04/entertainment/main598016
.shtml
(*CBS News,* "OutKast Fans in for 'Weirdo' Ride," Feb. 4, 2004)
http://www.usatoday.com/life/music/news/2003-09-21-OutKast-main
_x.htm
(*USA Today,* "OutKast Has a Funky Formula," Sep. 21, 2003)
http://www.usatoday.com/life/music/news/2003-09-21-OutKast-albums
_x.htm
(*USA Today,* "Through the Years with OutKast," Sep. 22, 2003)

ADDRESS

OutKast
Arista Records/Zomba
137-139 West 25th Street
New York, NY 10001

WORLD WIDE WEB SITES

http://www.outkast.com
http://www.stankonia.com
http://www.aristarec.com/aristaweb/Outkast

Raven 1985-

American Actress and Singer
Star of "That's So Raven" and *The Cheetah Girls*

BIRTH

Raven-Symone Christina Pearman, known as Raven to her
many fans, was born on December 10, 1985, in Atlanta, Georgia. Her parents are Lydia Gaulden Pearman and Christopher
Barnard Pearman. According to her parents, Raven was named
for the first bird that Noah released from the Ark. "When the
rain had subsided, Noah released the raven first, not the dove,"
her father says. "The raven is very, very intelligent. And to us,
she was this beautiful black bird . . . her spirit was high and
free."

When Raven was born, Lydia was a computer systems analyst and Christopher was a musician. Now, they're both involved in managing Raven's career, with Christopher writing music and producing for his talented daughter. Raven also has a younger brother named Blaize.

CAREER HIGHLIGHTS

Raven got started in show business as a baby. When she was just 16 months old, she became a baby model for an Atlanta department store and was soon appearing in television commercials for nationally known products like Ritz Crackers, Cheerios, and Cool Whip.

Raven credits Cosby with teaching her some important things about show business. "Stay professional and always stay sweet," he told her. "I haven't been the kid on the set that throws tantrums, even today," she says now. "That advice still works. Thanks, Mr. Cosby."

"The Cosby Show"

According to her parents, Raven was a very bright young toddler. "She was saying her ABCs and the Pledge of Allegiance when she was two," says her dad. One day, while watching "The Cosby Show," she announced, "I can do what Rudy can do." She was talking about the actress Keshia Knight Pullman, who played Bill Cosby's youngest daughter on "The Cosby Show," one of the most popular comedies ever on television. The Pearmans decided to give Raven a chance. They took her to New York, where the Cosby show was filmed, and her parents signed her with the prestigious Ford modeling agency. That led to other contacts, which led to an audition for a TV movie, "Ghost Dad." She didn't get the part, but the show's producers were impressed with her and they thought Cosby would be, too. (For more information on Cosby, see *Biography Today*, Jan. 1992.)

Raven met and talked to Bill Cosby, and he loved her. He added a part to the show for her, and she was on her way. From 1989 to 1992, she played the role of Olivia, the stepdaughter of Denise, played by Lisa Bonet. (At this point, while working on "The Cosby Show," she used the name Raven-Symone as her professional name.) Raven soon became a favorite with viewers all over the country. Her family moved to New York, where her dad took her to work and spent every day on the set.

Raven with Bill Cosby on the set of the TV series "The Cosby Show."

Her father also worked with Raven on her lines. He remembers that he would read the scripts to her as if they were a story. Raven was always a quick learner, and she loved it. Cosby was amazed. "She is professional in every way," he said in an interview in 1990. "Raven comes to the studio on time, knows her lines, and is ready to work." She doesn't remember too much about the show, but does recall that she loved the cast, and Cosby especially. She credits him with teaching her some important things about show business. "Stay professional and always stay sweet," he told her. "I haven't been the kid on the set that throws tantrums, even today," she says now. "That advice still works. Thanks, Mr. Cosby."

Early Projects

Raven's first acting job after "Cosby" was in the made for TV movie *Queen*, which broadcast in 1993. It was based on the last work of the African-American author Alex Haley, who wrote *Roots*. (For more information on Haley, see *Biography Today*, April 1992.) *Queen* was Haley's tribute to his own grandmother, who had been born a slave in the South in the 19th century. Raven played Queen as a five year old.

> ──── **❝** ────
>
> *Raven has some funny memories about making* **Dr. Doolittle** *with Eddie Murphy. "He does things to see how well you can not laugh," she says. "When the camera's rolling and the scene is supposed to be over, he keeps going and ad-libbing, and it's really hard to keep a straight face."*
>
> ──── **❞** ────

Raven next moved on to the world of music. Her parents knew she loved to sing, and they arranged a contract for her with MCA Records. Her first album, titled *Here's to New Dreams*, was recorded when she was five and released three years later, in 1993. She was the youngest star ever to sign a contract with MCA. Her dad co-wrote three of the songs, including the title track, "Here's to New Dreams." Raven made other musical appearances at the time, including a Broadway debut singing with the Boys' Choir of Harlem in 1993.

The same year her first record came out, Raven joined the cast of another TV hit, "Hangin' with Mr. Cooper." The show, which starred Mark Curry, featured Raven as Cooper's niece Nicole, a sassy, smart little girl who steals her uncle's heart. She was delighted with the role. "I love this show," she said in 1993. "It's great working with Mark. He's real, real tall and real, real funny." For Raven, the character of Nicole was very different from Olivia. "For one, I'm a lot older here. Olivia was a lot younger. Olivia has grown into Nicole. I'm in a new city and trying to learn new things." Raven played the role for four years, from 1993 to 1997, and when the show ended, she went back to music.

Raven's second album, *Undeniable*, featured a new single, "With a Child's Heart," that was written by Stevie Wonder. Wonder wrote another song for

Raven and Eddie Murphy in a scene from Dr. Doolittle 2.

the album, and Raven also got to spend time with the great musician in the studio. "He was wonderful!" she claimed. "I got to work with him for three days." *Undeniable* also featured a song she had written, "Best Friend," and several written by her father and the record's producer. To promote the record and her singing career, Raven toured with 'N Sync, one of the most popular boy bands of the era. She loved performing and touring, but always kept her hand in acting, too.

Raven made a brief appearance in *The Little Rascals*, a 1994 film version of the beloved TV classic. She enjoyed it very much, and her parents looked for other good roles. Raven made several guest appearances on TV, performing in shows like "A Different World," "The Fresh Prince of Bel-Air," and "Sesame Street."

More Recent Projects

In 1998, Raven appeared in *Dr. Doolittle*, which starred Eddie Murphy (see *Biography Today Performing Artists*, Vol. 2). The movie followed the misadventures of Murphy as Dr. Doolittle, a famous vet who can talk to animals—and they talk back. Raven played Murphy's oldest daughter, Charisse, and has some funny memories about making the movie. "He does things to see how well you can not laugh," she says. "When the camera's rolling and the scene is supposed to be over, he keeps going and ad-libbing, and it's really hard to keep a straight face."

Raven's next film was a made-for-TV movie titled *Zenon: Girl of the 21st Century*, which first aired on the Disney Channel in 1999. Raven played Nebula, the best friend of Zenon, played by Kirsten Storms. The movie is based on the children's book by Marilyn Salder and Roger Bollen, which also became a comic strip. The movie is set in the year 2049 and features the exploits of Zenon as she spends some time on Earth unraveling the clues to a mystery involving the space station she calls home.

In 2001, Raven returned to the big screen again in *Dr. Doolittle 2*, a sequel to the earlier movie. Once again, she played Eddie Murphy's daughter, and once again the set was filled with all kinds of rambunctious animals. "I love the monkey, Crystal, who I held on my shoulders," Raven recalled. "Crystal's really sweet, very friendly, and doesn't bite." Not all the animals were so easy to get along with. "Once, when I was holding the chameleon, he wouldn't let go of my hand. I was wearing lace and he kept sticking to it—they had to pull him off."

> "I thought she looked just like me!" Raven said about her animated character Monique on "Kim Possible." "The animators watch you while you're talking to see your facial expressions and the way you move your hands while you talk, and they try to copy that for the cartoon characters."

"Kim Possible"

In 2002, Raven appeared as the voice of Monique on the hit cartoon "Kim Possible," which appears on the Disney Channel. The show features the exploits of teenager Kim, who seems like a normal kid, but who really possesses secret powers. Raven says it's fun to play her friend Monique "because I just get to go crazy on her voice. I can do all types of ups and downs and not have to worry about how my face is coming off on screen." When she first saw her animated character on the show, she was amazed. "I thought she looked just like me!" she recalls. "The animators watch you while you're talking to see your facial expressions and the way you move your hands while you talk, and they try to copy that for the cartoon characters."

A scene from "Kim Possible."

Big Breakout: "That's So Raven"

Raven's big breakout role came in 2003, when she starred in a new Disney Channel hit, "That's So Raven." The show debuted in January 2003, and soon it was one of the most popular on the network. She plays Raven Baxter, a teenager who's psychic—but with a twist. She can see into the future, but she doesn't see everything in quite the right way. "It's all about a girl who has psychic visions," Raven explains. "However, as the visions are always incomplete, she has to figure out exactly what they mean. This often lands her and her friends in hot water." The show is hilarious, with Raven and her two best friends, Eddie (Orlando Brown) and Chelsea (Anneliese van der Pol), trying to avoid the disaster that always seems to come their way as they try to figure out the future. Raven has been praised for her slapstick, physical humor, which came easily. "In real life, I just be fallin' all over the place unintentionally, so I just told them to put my clumsiness on the screen," she says.

"We have such a laugh on the set," she says. "There's a lot of physical comedy in the show, especially dressing up in strange and weird costumes. It's a real blast." Some commentators have compared her comedic talents to those of TV icon Lucille Ball. Raven graciously accepts the compliment, saying that she's loved watching "I Love Lucy" reruns for years. Disney's delighted with her success, too. In fact, the original title for the show was

369

Raven with the cast from her hit Disney show "That's So Raven."

"Absolutely Psychic," and she had a supporting role. But Raven was so great and so captivating that they rewrote the show with her in the lead. "Raven sparkled and overshadowed everybody. She was the show," says director Sean McNamara. "She learned some things from Cosby. Her comedic timing is perfect. She totally gets it. She reads a script once and knows where to go and when to pause and when to nail the joke." She actually helps out the writers with teen slang, offering what she calls a "hip-hop-ictionary."

Raven looks forward to doing the series for several years. She says that in the second season her character gets a boyfriend "and gets into a lot more crazy things—but it's hilarious!" Is she like the character she plays? "I'm not as vibrant as she is," says the real Raven. "Her hyperness takes a lot out of me. I don't make my own clothes, but we both love to shop. Our love for friends and family are the same. I also have a best girlfriend and a best guy friend."

With the success of "That's So Raven," some observers have suggested that Disney seems to be grooming Raven as its next It Girl, in line with Hilary Duff and Lizzie McGuire. "Lizzie was on for a year and a half before it exploded," said Disney Channel entertainment president Rich Ross. "Raven was on for six months. We expect her to be a big star for this company." As industry analyst Lily Oei remarked, "Her quick rise may herald a new era at the network, one with a curvy, sassy black girl as its poster child."

The Cheetah Girls

In the summer of 2003, Raven appeared in the made-for-TV movie *The Cheetah Girls*, based on the popular series of books by Deborah Gregory. Raven played Galleria Garibaldi, a fashion queen who's trying to get her girl group to win the high school talent show. The other three characters in this urban fairy tale are Chanel (played by Adrienne Bailon), Aqua (played by Kiely Williams), and Dorinda (played by Sabrina Bryan); both Adrienne and Kiely are actually in the teen pop/hip-hop group 3LW.

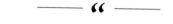

"Raven sparkled and overshadowed everybody. She was the show," says director Sean McNamara. "She learned some things from Cosby. Her comedic timing is perfect. She totally gets it. She reads a script once and knows where to go and when to pause and when to nail the joke."

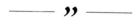

Raven loved appearing in *The Cheetah Girls*. "The first thing that attracted me to the role is that I got to act, sing, and dance," she says. She also loved the clothes, the hair, and the fancy makeup. But it was her charm and comedic skills that caught many viewers' attention. "She reminds me of Bea [Arthur], Gilda [Radner], and Carol [Burnett]," says Disney president Rich Ross. "Raven's in their league. She's fearless." Raven just shrugs off such compliments: "I'm very comfortable with what I do. I like entertaining people and making them laugh."

The Cheetah Girls debuted on Disney in August 2003; the studio also released a soundtrack CD with music from the film. The movie received

Raven with the Cheetah Girls.

mixed reviews from critics. Many praised Raven's performance while criticizing the film overall, as in this remark from *Daily Variety*: "Ironically, *Cheetah Girls* supposedly denounces manufactured pop music and marketing over artistry, yet it plays like a two-hour fashion commercial and culminates in a ridiculous lip-synching extravaganza." But viewers seemed to love it, and the movie earned great ratings. It was a top-ranked show when it was first broadcast, prompting Disney to replay it later that month with an alternate ending and 12 extra minutes of footage.

EDUCATION

Throughout her performing career, Raven has mixed being tutored on the set with attending a regular public school in Atlanta. From the late 1990s until she started work on "That's So Raven," she was able to have several years of a normal teenage life, going to class at North Springs High School, shopping, and having sleepovers with her friends. But when "That's So Raven" started, it was back to the challenges of working and learning on the set. She says that kids in her position should be appreciated for all their hard work. "Hey, you know, adults need to give the kids in this business more credit, because we have to be on the set, plus three hours of school, so we have to know the whole script, plus the War of 1812 and take a test on it."

Raven graduated from North Springs in Atlanta in the fall of 2003, and she plans to go to college in a few years. She's now based in California, and she hopes to attend either UCLA or USC in the future. "Hopefully, I will stay in the business," she says, "but it's very flaky and you never know if you're going to get a job. So when I go to college, what I major in is going to be something different than acting, just in case it doesn't work out." Raven also loves to cook, and she'd like to go to culinary school, too, and maybe open her own restaurant someday.

FUTURE PLANS

Right now, Raven is working on several new movies and new records. She's slated to appear in the film *All-American Girl*, based on the book by Meg Cabot; she plays a girl who saves the president's life. She'll also appear in *Sparkle*, a movie about a girl group similar to the Supremes. She's working on her third album and on a soundtrack for the "That's So Raven" show. She says she's open to all kinds of new roles. "I want to do everything," she says. "I want to do a 'dramedy' and mix the comedy and drama all up."

Even though she's been in show business for 15 years, Raven will always be Olivia to some fans. "People are funny," she laughs. "They'll come up to me and they're like, 'You look like the girl in 'The Cosby Show,' but you're not her because she's three.' And I'm like, 'That was 14 years ago!'"

Even though she's been in show business for 15 years, Raven will always be Olivia to some fans. "People are funny," she laughs. "They'll come up to me and they're like, 'You look like the girl in 'The Cosby Show,' but you're not her because she's three.' And I'm like, 'That was 14 years ago!'"

HOME AND FAMILY

Raven still lives with her family, and they split their time between a home in Atlanta and one in California, near the studios. She's very close to her family, and says they help her stay grounded. "I mean, I have to clean my room," she says. In her spare time, she likes to hang out with friends, shop, and listen to all kinds of music. She also likes to paint.

Raven is active in many charities, including Colin Powell's Children First program, the Paralympics, the March of Dimes, DARE, Juvenile Diabetes, Pediatric AIDS, and the Ronald McDonald Houses. She's also a spokeswoman for Disney's Adventure All-Star volunteer program, and she encourages kids to help out in their own communities. "Kids especially need to try to make a difference, because we're going to have to run this world one day," she says. "We don't want to live in a world where everyone's mad at each other or where there's dirt everywhere. We want to make it better."

Raven is also something of a role model for girls who have curves. She doesn't have a thin, model-like body. "I have a little tummy-tummy," she says. "I do my crunches. I'm muscular. My girls know I like to eat." At one point, she thought her shape might prevent her from getting good roles, because most TV and movie actresses are very thin. But it didn't stop her from getting starring roles in "That's So Raven" and *The Cheetah Girls*, and now she's proud to look the way she does. "The other teenage stars out there today, are, like, puny," she says. "Don't get me wrong, they look great. But I can't get that small. I'm telling my girls it's okay." She says she might like to have her own line of clothes someday, too. "If I was to do my own clothing line, I would do it for girls who are built like me. When I shop for myself it's very hard to find clothes. I'm curvy and there should be more clothes for curvy girls."

CREDITS

Television

"The Cosby Show," 1989-92 (TV series)
Queen, 1993 (TV movie)
"Hangin' with Mr. Cooper," 1993-97 (TV series)
Zenon: Girl of the 21st Century, 1999 (TV movie)
"Kim Possible," 2002- (TV series)
"That's So Raven," 2003- (TV series)
The Cheetah Girls, 2003 (TV movie)

Movies

The Little Rascals, 1994
Dr. Doolittle, 1998
Dr. Doolittle 2, 2001

Recordings

Here's to New Dreams, 1993
Undeniable, 1999
The Cheetah Girls, 2003

FURTHER READING

Books

Who's Who Among African Americans, 2003

Periodicals

Atlanta Journal-Constitution, Apr. 29, 1996, p.B3; May 31, 1999, p.C6
Bergen County (NJ) Record, June 22, 2001, p.5
Boston Globe, Jan. 16, 2003, p.D5

Boston Herald, Jan. 16, 2003, Arts and Life section, p.41
Chicago Tribune, Dec. 13, 1994, Kidnews, p.1
Daily News, Aug. 11, 2003, Television section, p.85
Detroit Free Press, Sep. 11, 2003, Yak's Corner, p.4
Ebony, May 1990, p.106
Entertainment Weekly, Oct. 17, 2003, p.42
Essence, Oct. 3, 2003, p.148
Houston Chronicle, June 25, 1998, p.5
Jet, Apr. 2, 1990, p.22; May 20, 1991, p.54; Nov. 8, 1993, p.58; Sep. 8, 2003, p.60
Los Angeles Times, Jan. 17, 2003, Part 5, p.2
Newsday, June 9, 1991, Part II, p.4; May 30, 1993, Part II, p.1; Oct. 19, 2003, Kidsday, p.1
New York Post, June 23, 2001, p.21
New York Times, Jan. 12, 2003, p.59
Philadelphia Tribune, Mar. 30, 1999, p.B4
People, June 26, 2000, p.68; May 20, 2002, p.140
Teen People, Feb. 1, 2004, p.93
Toronto Sun, Nov. 26, 2002, Entertainment, p.60
USA Today, Oct. 26, 1989, p.D3
USA Weekend, Aug. 8-10, 2003, p.6

Online Articles

http://www.timeforkids.com
(*Time for Kids,* "Who's News," Aug. 20, 2003)

Online Database

Biography Resource Center Online, article from *Who's Who Among African Americans,* 2003

ADDRESS

Raven
Disney Channel
3800 West Almeda Avenue
Burbank, CA 91505

WORLD WIDE WEB SITE

http://psc.disney.go.com/disneychannel/thassoraven

Ronald Reagan 1911-2004

American Politician and Former Actor
40th President of the United States

BIRTH

Ronald Wilson Reagan was born on February 6, 1911, in Tampico, Illinois, to John Edward and Nelle Wilson Reagan. John was a shoe salesman and Nelle was a homemaker who also worked as a dressmaker. Ronald was the youngest of two boys in the family, with an older brother named Neil. When Ronald was born, his father said he looked like "a little bit of a fat Dutchman"; from then on, his nickname was "Dutch."

YOUTH

John Reagan was outgoing, ambitious—and an alcoholic. He often lost jobs, and the family moved from town to town in Illinois as he moved from job to job. Ronald Reagan remembered that the family didn't have a lot of money. "We were poor, but we didn't know we were poor," he recalled. Yet he didn't feel deprived and remembered his early life as "a rare Huck Finn idyll." He developed the sunny, optimistic disposition that he had throughout his life, first as an actor and later as a politician.

> *Reagan grew up at a time when alcoholism brought shame on the families of addicts. Yet his mother had an enlightened and compassionate approach to the disease, and she taught her boys to love and forgive their alcoholic father. "My mother told us—my brother and I when we were both just kids and she knew that we would be exposed to this and see it—that we must not turn against our father . . . that this was a sickness he could not help."*

Still, his father's alcoholism affected the family deeply. Reagan recalled that once, when he was 11, he came home and found his father passed out on the front porch. He felt like just leaving his dad on the porch, stepping over him, and trying to forget the whole thing. But he thought better of that decision. "I bent over him, smelling the sharp odor of whiskey from the speakeasy. I got a fistful of his overcoat. Opening the door, I managed to drag him inside and get him to bed." He recalled in his autobiography that the incident proved to be "the first moment of accepting responsibility."

Reagan's mother, Nelle, was a hardworking, devout Christian, and she had a tremendous influence on Ronald. She shared her strong faith with her sons, who were raised in the Protestant faith in the Disciples of Christ Church. Ronald Reagan grew up at a time when alcoholism brought shame on the families of addicts. Yet Nelle Reagan had an enlightened and compassionate approach to the disease, and she taught her boys to love and forgive their father. "My mother told us—my brother and I when we were both just kids and she knew that we would be exposed to this and see it— that we must not turn against our father . . . that this was a sickness he could not help."

LEFT: The Reagan family Christmas card, 1916 or 1917.

BELOW: Reagan in the 1920s.

LEFT: Reagan as a lifeguard in Lowell Park, Illinois, 1927.

Nelle Reagan also loved the theater. With her encouragement, Ronald became involved in drama from a very young age, appearing in church pageants and later in high school theater. She also taught him to read when he was five, and Reagan spent many hours reading adventure stories by Edgar Rice Burroughs and other action writers. In addition, Nelle Reagan encouraged his optimistic, trusting nature and the belief that there was good to be found in every human being.

—— *"* ——

Reagan was among a group of students at his college who organized a strike to oppose plans to cut back faculty. Speaking to the group, "I discovered that an audience had a feel to it, and that the audience and I were together. When I came to actually presenting the motion . . . there was no need for parliamentary procedure. They came to their feet with a roar. It was heady wine."

—— *"* ——

EDUCATION

Reagan went to school at the local public schools wherever his family lived. He had trouble reading as a young child and remembered that the blackboard was often a blur. Later, it was discovered that he was severely nearsighted, and after he got his first pair of glasses, he was able to see the board with ease. When Reagan was nine, the family settled in the Illinois town of Dixon. There, Ronald attended elementary and high school. At Northside High, he was a good student and an outstanding athlete, especially on the football field; he also appeared in school plays. After graduating from Northside in 1928, Reagan went on to Eureka College, a small, Christian school in Peoria, Illinois. He paid for his tuition partly through a scholarship and also by washing dishes and working as a lifeguard over the summers. He was an outstanding lifeguard and saved some 77 swimmers during his summers working at Dixon's Lowell Park.

Reagan studied economics at Eureka, but was more devoted to football and drama than to his studies. An average student in college, he was well-liked by his teachers and fellow students. His nearly photographic memory helped, too, whether he was reading a book just before a test or memorizing lines for a play. He had a chance to see live theater at Eureka and was especially moved by an antiwar play that came to town called *Journey's*

End. He identified with the idealistic young hero, and he yearned to act. "Nature was trying to tell me something," he said later, "namely that my heart is a ham loaf."

It was at Eureka that he got his first taste of politics, too. When the college president announced plans to cut back faculty, Reagan was among a group of students who organized a strike. Speaking to the group, "I discovered that an audience had a feel to it, and that the audience and I were together. When I came to actually presenting the motion . . . there was no need for parliamentary procedure. They came to their feet with a roar. It was heady wine." Reagan graduated from Eureka College in 1932.

FIRST JOBS

When Reagan left college in 1932, the country was in the grips of the Great Depression. During this era, which lasted for much of the 1930s, America and many other countries suffered a severe economic downturn. Millions of people had trouble finding jobs and providing food and shelter for their families. In fact, up to 25% of the population was out of work.

Yet despite the difficult economic times, within six weeks Reagan found a job he loved: he became a sports broadcaster with radio station WOC in Davenport, Iowa, covering the University of Iowa football games. Reagan was able to combine two things he knew and loved—football and acting. And acting came in handy in broadcasting in those days. When WOC was acquired by a larger station, WHO in Des Moines, Iowa, Reagan was hired by them to cover several sports on the radio, including the baseball games of the Chicago Cubs. In those pre-television times, the broadcaster relied on the information coming over the telegraph wire, then "created" the play-by-play. Reagan never saw the games he broadcast. Instead, he'd take the information from the tape off the wire, which just included the name of the batter and whether or not he'd made a hit. Reagan would review it quickly, then recreate the games for his audience, describing balls, strikes, hits, and outs, adding commentary, and embellishing whenever necessary.

Reagan recounted one memorable day when the telegraph transmission failed and he was on his own: "I had a ball on the way to the plate and there was no way to call it back. At the same time, I was convinced that a ball game tied up in the ninth inning was no time to tell my audience we had lost contact with the game." He went on to describe a series of foul balls that went on for quite some time, until the transmission was repaired and he could continue with what was going on in the "real" game. The audience never knew the difference. The anecdote became one of Reagan's favorite stories to tell about his radio days.

ABOVE: Reagan as an announcer for WHO radio in Des Moines, Iowa, 1934-1937.

ABOVE: A still of Reagan from the film Knute Rockne — All American, *1940.*

RIGHT: Reagan in the U.S. Army Air Force, 1940s.

CAREER IN HOLLYWOOD

What Reagan wanted most in those days was to be an actor, so on a 1937 trip to California to cover the Cubs for WHO he took a screen test in Hollywood. Much to his delight, he was hired by Warner Brothers at $200 a week, a great salary in those tough times. Reagan embarked on a film career that included 53 movies, including his first, *Love Is in the Air*, in which he played a radio announcer. He was never an A-list actor, but his handsome, athletic, and friendly presence made him a popular one.

In 1940, while filming *Brother Rat*, he met Jane Wyman, who became his first wife. That same year he lobbied for, and won, the role that made him famous. He played football player George Gipp in a film about Knute Rockne, Notre Dame's legendary football coach. In *Knute Rockne—All American*, Reagan appeared in the film's most famous scene, where Gipp, on his deathbed, pleads with Rockne to "win one for the Gipper." Years later, Reagan said that he still "got a lump in my throat . . . just thinking about it." The role became identified with him throughout his career, and, like "Dutch," "Gipper" became a nickname.

In 1942 Reagan appeared in *King's Row*, which is considered his best film. He plays a womanizer named Drake McHugh, who seduces the daughter of a surgeon in a small town. In revenge, the sadistic doctor amputates Drake's legs. Waking up, Reagan's character screams, "Where's the rest of me?" The line became as closely associated with Reagan as his famous Gipper phrase, and also provided him with the title of his autobiography, which was published in 1965.

King's Row was well-received, and Reagan's performance was widely praised, but it was his last Hollywood film for a few years. It appeared just as the U.S. entered World War II, and Reagan tried to enlist. His eyesight was so poor that he wasn't considered fit for combat, so he spent the war stateside, making training films for the U.S. armed services. After the war, Reagan continued to act in many films, most of them forgettable. He starred in a series as Brass Bancroft, Secret Service Agent, and also co-starred with a chimp named Bonzo in several films.

Screen Actors Guild

But by then, Reagan's interests had changed. In 1941, he had been appointed to the board of the Screen Actors Guild (SAG), the union representing movie actors. He became more and more involved in his work with the Guild, and was elected president of SAG five times. In 1946 Reagan was asked to mediate a dispute that brought him into contact with some union leaders who were allegedly Communists. This happened in the era after World War II, when the American political landscape was transformed by changes in world politics. During the Depression of the 1930s, some Americans, including actors, had been drawn to Communism as a possible way out of the financial and social misery of the times. After World War II, the U.S. and the Communist Soviet Union emerged as the two superpowers in the world. These two nations became locked in the conflict known as the Cold War—a war defined not by open warfare, but by escalating hostilities between the two nations, one democratic and one Communist, and the division of the major world governments into pro-U.S. and pro-Soviet nations. The era was also defined by mutual distrust, suspicion, hostility, and the constant underlying fear of a third world war that might destroy humanity.

Reagan met the actress Nancy Davis in Hollywood; they married in 1952. He called Nancy the most important thing in his life. "Put simply, my life really began when I met her and has been rich and full ever since," he said.

The tensions created by the Cold War had a tremendous influence on the political climate in the U.S. In the U.S. House of Representatives, the House Un-American Activities Committee, or HUAC, was searching to root out and expose Communists in every industry, including the movie industry. In doing so, they sometimes ruined the lives and careers of innocent people. Simply to be accused, or "named," before the committee was often enough to get an individual "blacklisted"—which took away their ability to make a living and ruined their reputations. As a labor leader, Reagan was called to testify before HUAC in 1947. When asked to "name names" of Communists in the film industry, Reagan refused. Years later, historian Garry Wills uncovered evidence, including some in released FBI files, that Reagan had indeed given the government names, in secret.

Reagan's growing interest in politics had a damaging effect on his marriage to Jane Wyman. She filed for divorce in 1948, alleging "mental cruelty." Reagan was devastated by the divorce and considered it the darkest time of his life. A few years later, he met the actress Nancy Davis in Hollywood; they married in 1952. They were a devoted couple, and Reagan called Nancy the most important thing in his life. "Put simply, my life really began when I met her and has been rich and full ever since," he said.

A Change of Political Philosophy

Around this time, Reagan began to have a change of heart politically. He had been a lifelong Democrat, believing in the New Deal concepts developed during the presidency of Franklin Delano Roosevelt (1933-1945). As president during much of the Depression, Roosevelt had created the New Deal, which promoted a strong federal government and domestic programs designed to help struggling Americans financially. Reagan described himself at the time as a "near-hopeless hemophiliac liberal." But while continuing to support Democratic candidates, he also began to be drawn to the Republican Party. He even headed a movement called Democrats for Dwight Eisenhower when Ike ran for President in 1952 and 1956.

Reagan and "General Electric Theater," 1954-1962.

Reagan's philosophy was changing at the same time his career took a turn, from film to television. Soon he was hired by General Electric for a new series, "General Electric Theater," one of the first theatrical series on TV. Every week, Reagan appeared in millions of homes all over the country as host and sometimes as star of the television drama series. As part of his contract, he also appeared at GE plants throughout the country, giving speeches to the employees. Thus, he had a forum to introduce himself to Americans throughout the nation and to speak with them one-on-one. What he learned there changed him forever.

Between 1954 and 1962, Reagan visited 139 GE plants, meeting some 250,000 employees, and, he recalled, "enjoying every whizzing minute of it." In his countless speeches, he honed his delivery and listened to the concerns of the American public. "That did much to shape my ideas," he said. "These employees I was meeting were a cross section of Americans, and damn it, too many of our political leaders, our labor leaders, and certainly a lot of geniuses on Madison Avenue, have underestimated them. They want the truth, they are friendly and helpful, intelligent and alert. They are concerned with their very firm personal liberties. And they are moral." What he heard made Reagan reconsider his politics and his career.

In 1960, Reagan campaigned for Republican presidential candidate Richard Nixon as a "Democrat for Nixon," and in 1962 he officially switched his political affiliation from Democrat to Republican. That same year, the political rhetoric of his speeches had grown so conservative that GE let him go. He used key phrases like "Government is not the solution to our problem. Government is the problem," and attacked large government subsidized programs, like Social Security and the Tennessee Valley Authority (TVA). The TVA is a federally funded program created in the 1930s to prevent flooding and to develop the energy resources of the Tennessee River Valley. By the 1960s, GE had millions of dollars in contracts with the TVA to provide electricity to the area, so Reagan's criticisms directly conflicted with the company's business.

_____ " _____

In 1964, Reagan gave a speech that mesmerized conservative Republicans and set his course in politics. "You and I have a rendezvous with destiny," he said. "We will preserve for our children this, the last best hope of man on earth, or we will sentence them to take the first step into a thousand years of darkness."

_____ " _____

A Major Speech

In 1964, Reagan gave a speech, "A Time for Choosing," that mesmerized conservative Republicans and set his course in politics. Reagan spoke as part of a nationally televised broadcast in support of Barry Goldwater, the arch-conservative Republican presidential candidate that year. He attacked the "Great Society" programs of then-President Lyndon Johnson, claiming they were the type of "big government" that, according to Reagan, compromised the future of the nation. "You and I have a rendezvous with destiny," he told them. "We will preserve for our children this, the last best hope of man on earth, or we will sentence them to take the first step into a thousand years of darkness."

Goldwater went down to defeat in one of the biggest landslides in history, but Ronald Reagan had made a name for himself in politics.

CAREER IN POLITICS

In a political career that spanned more than 30 years, Ronald Reagan symbolized the conservative movement in American politics. From his surprise election as governor of California to his election as President of the United States, he confounded critics and pundits alike. He appealed directly to voters with his positive, optimistic message of America as a place of endless possibilities, combined with his promise to "get government off the backs" of the American people.

That potential was first seen by a group of California businessman, who contacted Reagan soon after the 1964 presidential election. This wealthy group of conservative Republicans would promote and finance Reagan throughout his political career. In 1964, they wanted Reagan to run for governor of California, and they proceeded to form

Campaigning as candidate for governor of California, November 1966.

his campaign. Reagan announced his candidacy in January 1966, taking on a popular Democratic governor, Pat Brown. Like many of Reagan's political opponents, Brown didn't take Reagan seriously, making light of his Hollywood career. But Reagan was serious and ran on a platform that promised to reduce the size of government and "clean up the mess at Berkeley," referring to the student protests that had begun to foment at the University of California at Berkeley and at college campuses all around the nation.

Governor of California

Reagan surprised many when he beat Brown by over one million votes to win the race for governor in 1966. He then served two terms as governor, from 1966 to 1974. As governor, he gained a reputation as a pragmatic, effective leader who could forge compromises between parties and run a state with one of the largest economies in the world. According to Lou Cannon, a journalist who followed Reagan from California to Washington and wrote an acclaimed biography of him, the secret to Reagan's success wasn't easy to explain. "On one level, he seemed the 'citizen-politician' he claimed to be, almost completely ignorant of even civics-books information about how bills were passed or how an administration functioned. But on another level, he seemed the most consummate and effective

Governor-elect Reagan and Governor Edmund G. Brown meet after Reagan's landslide victory over Brown, November 1966.

politician I had ever met." It was that political savvy that took him to the top of American politics.

Although Reagan had campaigned on a platform that included cutting taxes and spending, as governor he inherited a large budget deficit and a Democratic state legislature. As would happen throughout his political career, he agreed to increase taxes; by the time his second term was over, the state's budget had doubled. Reagan also signed legislation in welfare, education, and tax reform. But by the end of his years of governor in 1974, he had his eyes on a bigger prize: the presidency.

Running for President

Reagan had actually made his interest in the office known in 1968, when Richard Nixon was the presumptive candidate for the Republicans. The movement to draft Reagan as the Republican candidate in 1968 was begun by political adviser Lyn Nofziger and backed by the wealthy California businessmen who had encouraged Reagan to run for governor. He ran in the early primaries and stayed in the race until the Republican convention, when he gave his support to Nixon. Nixon beat Democrat Hubert Humphrey to win the election in 1968 and was reelected in 1972, but resigned from office in the wake of the Watergate scandal.

The term Watergate refers to a political scandal that occurred from 1972-1974 during Nixon's presidency. A group of people linked to his re-election campaign were arrested while committing a burglary at the offices of the Democratic Party headquarters at the Watergate Hotel in Washington, D.C. After their arrests, Nixon and his aides created a massive cover-up to conceal any links between the burglars and the White House. But their efforts were unsuccessful, as journalists and other investigators soon revealed the involvement of the President and his aides. Americans became angry and disillusioned as they learned about Watergate, and Nixon became the first president in U.S. history to resign from office. (For more information on Richard Nixon, see *Biography Today*, Sept. 1994.)

Reagan had been a great supporter of Nixon throughout the turmoil of Watergate, and he was deeply disappointed to learn that Nixon had lied to the American people. By the time of Nixon's resignation, Reagan was once again a private citizen. He began to write a newspaper column, and he also broadcast a weekly commentary on 200 radio stations nationwide. He went back to the "mashed potato circuit" — his term for the type of speaking engagements he'd done for GE — which brought him in touch with many potential voters. Even out of elected office, Reagan reached out to millions of Americans every week, promoting his message of conservative, Republican government. In doing this, he solidified his voting base in a way that confounded the general wisdom among politicians. He used the appeal he'd enjoyed as an actor to continue to attract interest as a potential political candidate. As Lou Cannon writes in his biography, "the earnest, affable Reagan was rapidly forming a relationship with potential voters that was an extension of the bond he had forged with movie and television audiences during his long career. . . .He was the wholesome citizen-hero who inhabits our democratic imaginations, an Everyman who was slow to anger but willing to fight for the right."

"The earnest, affable Reagan was rapidly forming a relationship with potential voters that was an extension of the bond he had forged with movie and television audiences during his long career. . . . He was the wholesome citizen-hero who inhabits our democratic imaginations, an Everyman who was slow to anger but willing to fight for the right."
— *Lou Cannon, Reagan biographer*

389

In 1976, Reagan again made a run for the Republican nomination for president, going head-to-head with President Gerald Ford in the Republican primaries. He almost beat Ford, an incumbent president, missing the nomination at that year's convention by a vote of 1,187 to 1,070. That fall, Ford ran against Democrat Jimmy Carter, who narrowly won the presidency. Reagan regrouped, planning to launch his challenge to Carter in 1980.

——— **"** ———

In accepting the Republican nomination at the 1980 convention, Reagan outlined the political philosophy that would prove a winning one: "They say that the United States has had its day in the sun, that our nation has passed its zenith. They expect you to tell your children that the American people no longer have the will to cope with their problems, that the future will be one of sacrifice and few opportunities. My fellow citizens, I utterly reject that view."

——— **"** ———

The Election of 1980

Reagan announced his candidacy for the Republican nomination in 1980 and ran well in the primaries. His principal opposition was George H.W. Bush, whom he chose as his vice presidential running mate. In accepting the Republican nomination at the convention that year, Reagan outlined the political philosophy that would prove a winning one: "They say that the United States has had its day in the sun, that our nation has passed its zenith. They expect you to tell your children that the American people no longer have the will to cope with their problems, that the future will be one of sacrifice and few opportunities. My fellow citizens, I utterly reject that view."

Jimmy Carter's term as president had been troubled. Domestically, high inflation, high interest rates, and high unemployment made the economy stagnant. On the international front, the U.S. was facing down the Soviet Union, which had invaded Afghanistan. More urgently, the government of the Shah of Iran had been toppled by an Islamic fundamentalist movement; in November 1979, Iranian militants stormed the U.S. embassy in Tehran and took 52 Americans hostage. Throughout their long ordeal, their fate became an obsession with the American public and the media; the ABC-TV show "Nightline" was begun in 1979 specifically to monitor the situation.

Reagan campaigning for president in November 1980 in Peoria, Illinois, with former President Gerald Ford and Reagan's running mate George H. W. Bush.

Despite all his troubles, Carter underestimated his Republican opponent's appeal to American voters. He called Reagan "dangerous," but that didn't affect Reagan's standing in the polls. When the Democrats made an issue of Reagan's age—he was 69 years old when he was running—he showed, through his vigor on the campaign trail and his robust good health, that he was equal to the task. In televised debates, Carter tried to attack Reagan's record on issues like Medicare, but Reagan countered with lines like, "There you go again," diminishing Carter's effectiveness. One line in particular resonated with voters: Reagan asked the American public, "Are you better off today than you were four years ago?" He ran on a platform that promised a 30% tax cut, reductions in government spending, and a balanced budget. He questioned Carter's defense policy against the Soviet Union and the threat of Communism around the world. And he told the American people that its best days were ahead, offering his optimistic vision of the country in difficult times.

President of the United States

On November 4, 1980, Reagan was elected President of the United States in an overwhelming victory. He won 50.7% of the vote to Carter's 41% (an additional 6.6% of voters cast their ballots for independent candidate John Anderson). Reagan was later reelected in a landslide to a second term in office, serving as president from 1981 until 1989.

The Reagans celebrating in the limousine in the inaugural parade, January 1981.

Reagan's first term in office got off to a good start: on the day of his inauguration, January 20, 1981, the government of Iran released the 52 American hostages, who had been held for 444 days. As President, Reagan set out his policies immediately. He called for tax cuts and cuts in government spending, especially in welfare programs, but argued for large defense budgets. At the same time, he brought a very different approach to the position of President. Reagan believed in balancing work and free time. He delegated responsibility to staff, worked a regular eight-hour day, and enjoyed taking naps. He spent a good deal of time away from Washington, at his beloved California ranch.

As President, Reagan again showed the same lack of interest in and knowledge of the everyday responsibilities of governing that he had exhibited as governor of California. In his biography, Lou Cannon relates how Reagan's staff prepared a daily list of meetings and appointments for him, along with 3 x 5 cards outlining his positions on political issues. Once, in a meeting with then-Speaker of the House Tip O'Neill, the congressman became furious with the President, who refused to talk to the Speaker directly, referring instead to the points on the 3 x 5 cards. But Reagan was able to talk about some issues in detail and with a great deal of authority. And he never lost his ability to talk directly to the American people and to move them. For this, he gained the title he was known for in the presidency, "The Great Communicator."

Shortly after taking office, Reagan endured a terrible ordeal: an assassination attempt. On March 30, 1981, Reagan and three others were shot by John Hinckley, Jr., outside a Washington hotel. The President was wounded in the lung; his press secretary, James Brady, was struck in the head by a bullet. When Reagan was rushed to the hospital, his sense of humor remained intact. While being wheeled into surgery, he said to the doctors, "Please tell me you're Republicans." When he first spoke with Nancy Reagan, he told her, "Honey, I forgot to duck." In recovery he joked, "If I had had this much attention in Hollywood, I would have stayed." After the shooting, James Brady suffered permanent brain damage and was partially paralyzed for life. He and his wife, Sarah Brady, became active supporters of gun control. Their work resulted in the Brady Bill, legislation that mandated a waiting period before people could buy handguns and created a system for national criminal background checks for prospective gun buyers.

Domestic Issues

Back at work, Reagan and his aides lobbied hard for his tax cut package, and he got most of what he wanted: a 25% reduction in taxes and $35 billion trimmed from the federal budget, but with additional spending for defense. The Federal Reserve Board raised interest rates (the rate that banks charge customers to lend them money) to try to stem inflation, and the immediate result was a recession, with unemployment rising to over 10%, and the poverty rate growing at a rapid clip. Many of the tax cuts targeted social services programs that were designed to help poor people, including health care, food assistance, welfare, and school lunch programs, which further contributed to the difficulties faced by the poor.

> ―――― **"** ――――
>
> *"Ronald Reagan's domestic policies . . . were almost uniformly appalling. He shifted the tax burden downward, exacerbated economic inequality, created gigantic deficits, undermined environmental, civil-rights, and labor protections, neglected the AIDS epidemic, and packed the courts with reactionary mediocrities. . . . Reagan was a pretty poor President in a lot of way."*
> *— Edmund Morris, Reagan biographer*
>
> ―――― **"** ――――

393

Reagan at work in the Oval Office.

Reagan's economic policy, called "Reaganomics," was based on an economic theory known as "supply-side economics," which argues that tax cuts promote economic growth. This premise, which is also known as "trickle-down economics," says that if wealthy individuals and businesses get a tax break, they would put money back into the economy in the form of consumer spending and investment in businesses. Stimulating savings and investments, therefore, would create higher productivity, jobs, and profits.

Reagan firmly believed that things would get better, and gradually, they did. In the eight years of his presidency, the prime interest rate fell from 15.3% to 9.3%; inflation fell from 12.5% to 4.4%; and unemployment fell from 10.8% to 5.5%. Whether or not the positive economic news was due to Reagan's policies—or other factors—is still debated by economists. Some experts note that the rise in poverty levels during his administration demonstrated his lack of concern for the poor and his insistence on high spending for defense led to a huge national deficit. Still, the turnaround in the economy is considered one of the highlights of the Reagan presidency.

International Issues

Reagan had been a fervent anti-Communist since his days in Hollywood. As President, he saw it as his mission to try to destroy Communism and its grip on millions the world over. In a speech early in his presidency, he referred to the Soviet Union as "the Evil Empire," and he vowed to do all he could to end Communism. He made speeches outlining the U.S. defensive strategy against the Soviet Union and proposed a controversial defense system called the Space Defense Initiative (SDI). The SDI would create a "shield" in space to protect the U.S. from a Soviet nuclear attack; it was also called "Star Wars" since it would destroy missiles from space. Many believed the plan was not tenable, but it had an immediate effect. It forced the Soviet Union to retaliate by spending furiously on its military, escalating the arms race between the nations and weakening an already fragile Soviet economy.

At the same time, a new leader came to head the Soviet Union, Premier Mikhail Gorbachev. Gorbachev was not a typical hard-liner. Instead, he was a reformer, offering new options, called *glasnost* (openness) and *perestroika* (reform), Russian terms for an opening up of ideas and encouraging change from within the Soviet Union. He and Reagan had a series of historic meetings that were first hostile, then gradually more cordial, as the conservative Republican and the Communist leader became friends. In the course of their relationship, Reagan went from a famous speech before the Berlin Wall in which he charged the Soviet leader, "Mr. Gorbachev, tear down this wall," to signing historic treaties to destroy the nuclear arsenals of both nations. And just one year after Reagan left office, in 1989, the Berlin Wall—the symbol of Soviet domination throughout the world—did

———— **"** ————

"Clare Booth Luce famously said that each President is remembered for a sentence: 'He freed the slaves'; 'He made the Louisiana Purchase.'... Ronald Reagan knew going in the sentence he wanted, and he got it. He guided the American victory in the Cold War. Under his leadership, a conflict that had absorbed a half-century of Western blood and treasure was ended—and the good guys finally won."
—Peggy Noonan, former speechwriter for President Reagan

———— **"** ————

Reagan with Vice President George H. W. Bush and Soviet President Mikhail Gorbachev on Governor's Island, New York.

come tumbling down, as Communist nations throughout Eastern Europe broke free from Soviet control and established democracies. Then, in December 1991, the Soviet Union itself collapsed, ending more than 70 years of Communist rule. In the opinion of many, it was Reagan's determination to force the Soviet Union to spend so much on defense that caused the demise of Communism and the end of the Cold War. Many consider Reagan's fight against Communism to be the greatest achievement of his presidency.

During his presidency, Reagan also dealt with terrorist threats from abroad. In 1983, a suicide bomber destroyed the barracks housing a U.S. Marines peacekeeping force in Lebanon, killing 241 American troops. Reagan took personal responsibility for the incident and removed all U.S. troops from the area within months. In 1986, there was a terrorist bombing at a nightclub in Berlin, which killed a U.S. serviceman. In retaliation, Reagan sent bombers to Libya, home of Muammar Qaddafi, a known sponsor of terrorists.

The Iran-Contra Affair

Perhaps the most controversial episode in Reagan's presidency was the Iran-Contra affair. In the mid-1980s terrorists were holding seven American hostages in Lebanon, and Reagan's efforts to free them led to the greatest crisis in his administration. It began in 1985. Iran and Iraq were at war, and Iran made a secret request to buy weapons from the U.S. Several members of the administration, notably National Security Adviser Robert McFarlane, John Poindexter, and Lt. Colonel Oliver North, together conspired to sell arms to Iran. At that time, Iran was an enemy of the U.S. and was also an ally of the Shiite terrorists who were holding the American hostages. In exchange for the weapons, Iran was to negotiate the return of the hostages. Selling arms to Iran violated two of Reagan's stated principles: he opposed negotiating for hostages and he opposed aiding Iran.

Further, McFarlane, Poindexter, and North had taken the money from the sales of arms to Iran and sent the money to Nicaragua to fund the group known as the Contras. The anti-Communist Contras were fighting the pro-Communist Sandinistas for control of the country. Reagan had made clear his support for the Contras; but what was less clear was whether he ever gave Poindexter, North, and McFarlane the authorization for what was clearly an illegal activity. It was a violation of the Boland Amendment, a congressional act that forbid any U.S. military aid to the Contras.

The allegations first came to light in a Lebanese newspaper. Initially Reagan vehemently denied it, then a week later he went on television and retracted his earlier denial. The U.S. Congress held an investigation, after which North was fired and Poindexter resigned. McFarlane pled guilty to withholding information from Congress. But most damaging to Reagan was that when he testified, it was clear that he was not in control of his administration. When asked whether he gave his approval to the initial idea of arms-for-hostages, Reagan said he couldn't remember. It was unclear exactly what had happened. Was Reagan aware of the illegal activities, had he approved them, and was he now lying to the American public? Or was he simply unaware of what was going on in his own administration? Either way, it was disturbing to Americans and damaging to Reagan's reputation.

Yet despite Iran-Contra, Reagan did not seem to suffer in the eyes of the public for long. When he left office, his approval ratings remained high. He was, as Congresswoman Patricia Schroeder had so aptly called him, the "Teflon President." It was hard to make anything negative stick to him.

Leaving the White House

Reagan left the White House in January 1989 and headed home to California and his beloved ranch. He had loved being President, but he was ready to retire and enjoy life as a private citizen again. He spent time on the ranch riding his horse and clearing brush. At the end of 1989, he had a

———— " ————

In 1994, Ronald Reagan wrote a letter to the American people revealing that he had been diagnosed with Alzheimer's disease. "Let me thank you, the American people, for giving me the great honor of allowing me to serve as your President. When the Lord calls me home, whenever that may be, I will leave with the greatest love for this country of ours and eternal optimism for its future. I now begin the journey that will lead me into the sunset of my life. I know that for America there will always be a bright dawn ahead."

———— " ————

serious fall while riding that injured his head and required surgery. After that, he had to give up riding. He continued to travel and give speeches, but by the early 1990s, he began to show signs of mental deterioration. At the Republican Convention in 1992, he seemed tired and confused, unlike the "Great Communicator" and leader of the past. At other public events he seemed disoriented and unsure of himself.

In 1994, Ronald Reagan wrote a letter to the American people revealing that he had been diagnosed with Alzheimer's disease. The disease causes irreversible damage to the brain, ending in dementia and death. There is no cure. With characteristic humility and warmth, Reagan wrote: "Let me thank you, the American people, for giving me the great honor of allowing me to serve as your President. When the Lord calls me home, whenever that may be, I will leave with the greatest love for this country of ours and eternal optimism for its future. I now begin the journey that will lead me into the sunset of my life. I know that for America there will always be a bright dawn ahead."

The Reagans had decided to make the diagnosis public to help raise awareness of the disease and also to shed light on its effects on family members. In the past decade, much has been learned about Alzheimer's, including some of its genetic components; it is now believed to be a hereditary disease. In Reagan's case, both his mother and brother suffered from the disease. After his announcement, Reagan continued to go to his office for a while and to play golf. But in later years he was not able to leave the house in Bel-Air, California, where he and Nancy Reagan lived.

On June 5, 2004, Ronald Reagan died at the age of 93. There was an immediate outpouring of grief from the nation, and Reagan was given a full

The President and First Lady about to enter the helicopter as they leave Washington on his last day in office, January 1989.

state funeral in Washington, D.C. There, thousands of Americans came to view his casket and to pay their last respects. His funeral service was broadcast around the world and attended by current President George W. Bush, as well as all the living past Presidents—Gerald Ford, Jimmy Carter, George H.W. Bush, and Bill Clinton. In addition, hundreds of world leaders attended the funeral, past and present, including his good friend and former British Prime Minister Margaret Thatcher and former Soviet leader Mikhail Gorbachev. Now weakened by a series of strokes, Thatcher gave a warm video tribute to her former colleague and Cold Warrior. Reagan was buried at his presidential library in Simi Valley, California.

LEGACY

Reagan's legacy lies in his achievements in both domestic and foreign policy. And yet that legacy is mixed. His economic policies turned around a financial crisis fueled by inflation, high interest rates, and high unemployment, yet the deficit also increased enormously. While he imagined America as "a shining city on a hill," there were some who saw it differently. As Mario Cuomo said in his address to the Democratic Convention in 1984, "The hard truth is that not everyone is sharing in this city's splendor and glory. . . . There's another part to the shining city; the part where some people can't pay their mortgages and most young people can't afford one, where students can't afford the education they need and middle-class parents watch the dreams they hold for their children evaporate."

In foreign policy, Reagan's legacy, despite Iran-Contra, rests on the part he played in ending the Cold War and on his stance against the Soviet Union and Communism. According to presidential historian Michael Beschloss, he was indispensable. "His first-term efforts to escalate the competition with the Soviet Union and his revival of American willpower may well have helped to usher in the reformist Gorbachev. . . . Reagan's defense of SDI, so ridiculed at the time, pressed Gorbachev, while his economy was collapsing, to make arms deals and improve relations with the West, which contributed to the unraveling of his empire. After FDR's death in 1945, the *New York Times* predicted that 'men will thank God on their knees 100 years from now' that FDR had been the president to fight Hitler and Tojo. It is not too much to suggest that, with Ronald Reagan's death, Americans might now give similar thanks that they twice elected a president who saw the chance to end the Cold War in his own time."

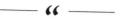

In the words of historian Kenneth Lynn, "Reagan fulfilled a restorative function we desperately needed. His belief that we can come out of our travail with a renewed strength, his ebullience, his optimism, and his lack of guilt in his personal life and in America in general were a breath of fresh air. To have someone speak in terms of possibility, of limitlessness rather than of limits, was an elixir."

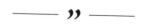

But perhaps Reagan is best remembered for his confidence, hopefulness, and optimism, an optimism "so radiant that it seemed almost a force of

A Reagan family photo: (standing, from left to right) Geoffrey Davis,
Dennis Revell, Michael Reagan, Cameron Reagan, President Reagan, Neil Reagan,
Dr. Richard Davis, Ron Reagan; (sitting, from left to right) Anne Davis,
Maureen Reagan, Colleen Reagan, Nancy Reagan, Bess Reagan,
Patricia Davis, Patti Davis, Doria Reagan.

nature," according to the *New York Times*. He came to the presidency at a time when many Americans needed to be reassured that the nation was still proud and strong. In the words of historian Kenneth Lynn, "Reagan fulfilled a restorative function we desperately needed. His belief that we can come out of our travail with a renewed strength, his ebullience, his optimism, and his lack of guilt in his personal life and in America in general were a breath of fresh air. To have someone speak in terms of possibility, of limitlessness rather than of limits, was an elixir."

MARRIAGE AND FAMILY

Reagan was married twice. He married actress Jane Wyman in 1940, and they had two children: Maureen, born in 1941, and Michael, whom they adopted in 1945. Wyman filed for divorce in 1948. Neither Reagan nor Wyman ever publicly discussed the divorce. In 1952, he married Nancy Davis, who was also an actress when they met. They had two children: Patricia, born in 1952, and Ronald, born in 1958. Ronald and Nancy Reagan spent many of their happiest times at their California ranch, Rancho del Cielo.

WRITINGS

Where's the Rest of Me? 1965
An American Life, 1990

FURTHER READING

Books

Buckley, William F. *Ronald Reagan: An American Hero,* 2001
Cannon, Lou. *President Reagan: The Role of a Lifetime,* 1991; rev. ed., 2000
Encyclopedia Britannica, 2004
Morris, Edmund. *Dutch: A Memoir of Ronald Reagan,* 1999
Reagan, Ronald. *Where's the Rest of Me?* 1965
Reagan, Ronald. *An American Life,* 1990
World Book Encyclopedia, 2004

Periodicals

Current Biography Yearbook, 1949, 1967, 1982
Los Angeles Times, June 6, 2004, p.A1, A31, A34, A42; June 7, p.A1, A9, A11, E1, E2, E3
New York Times, June 6, 2004, p.A1; June 7, 2004, p.A28 and A29; June 8, 2004, p.A23; June 11, 2004, p.A1; June 12, 2004, p.A1; June 15, 2004, p.D5
New Yorker, June 28, 2004, p.69
Newsweek, Special Commemorative Edition, June 14, 2004
Time, Special Commemorative Issue, June 14, 2004
Times (London), June 7, 2004, Features, p.28
Wall Street Journal, June 7, 2004, p.A1; June 8, 2004, p.A16 and A17
Washington Post, June 6, 2004, p.A1, p.A8

WORLD WIDE WEB SITES

http://www.ipl.org/POTUS
http://www.reaganlibrary.com
http://www.pbs.org/wgbh/amex/reagan/timeline/index.html
http://www.whitehouse.gov

Keanu Reeves 1964-

Canadian Actor
Star of *Bill and Ted's Excellent Adventure, Speed,* and
The Matrix Trilogy

BIRTH

Keanu Charles Reeves was born on September 2, 1964, in
Beirut, Lebanon. Beirut is the capital of Lebanon, a country located on the Mediterranean Sea in the region known as the
Middle East. Keanu is the son of Samuel Nowlin Reeves, Jr., a
geologist, and Patricia Reeves, a stage performer from England
who later became a costume designer. His father, who is half-

Chinese and half-Hawaiian, gave him the name Keanu (pronounced key-AH-new), which is a Hawaiian word that means "cool breeze over the mountains." Keanu has a sister, Kim, who is two years younger, and a half-sister, Karina, who is 12 years younger, from his mother's later marriage to rock promoter Robert Miller.

YOUTH

Reeves's parents met in Beirut in the early 1960s, when he was working for an oil company and she was performing as a nightclub showgirl. Back then, the city was known as the "Paris of the Middle East." It was full of expensive hotels and casinos that served as popular vacation spots for wealthy Europeans. As their relationship deepened, both of his parents became heavily involved in the use of illegal drugs. His mother gave up drugs when they started a family, but his father refused to do so. As a result, Keanu's parents divorced when he was two years old.

By this time, the entire Middle East was engulfed in political turmoil and tensions between the Jewish state of Israel and the region's many Arab nations. In 1967 Patricia Reeves decided to leave Lebanon, believing that the escalating tensions between Israel and the region's Arab countries were building toward war. She took Keanu and his younger sister Kim to Australia,

> *Thanks to his mother's career as a costume designer, Reeves met a number of movie stars and musicians during his childhood. "I remember [rock star Alice Cooper] brought fake vomit and dog poo to terrorize the housekeeper,"* he recalled. *"He'd hang out, a regular dude. . . . I wrestled with him once."*

where they lived for a year, and then to New York City. In 1970 Patricia Reeves married a film and stage director named Paul Aaron. The family then relocated to Toronto, Canada, where Keanu spent the remainder of his childhood. Keanu grew close to his stepfather, who first sparked his interest in show business. His mother and Aaron divorced after a few years, but Keanu stayed in touch with his stepfather afterward and sometimes visited him during school breaks. During these visits Reeves often accompanied Aaron to work. He saw him direct such films as *A Force of One* and the television drama *The Miracle Worker*. This early exposure to filmmaking had an enormous impact on Reeves, who became a serious film buff. Before long, he was watching all sorts of movies, and he almost never missed the premiere of a new film at Toronto University's Repertory Cinema.

In the meantime, Patricia Reeves used her background in theatrical design to build a successful career as a costume designer. Over time, she created costumes for such stars as Dolly Parton and David Bowie. Thanks to his mother's career, Keanu met a number of movie stars and musicians during his childhood. "I remember [rock star Alice Cooper] brought fake vomit and dog poo to terrorize the housekeeper," he recalled. "He'd hang out, a regular dude. . . . I wrestled with him once." Meeting famous entertainers further increased Reeves's fascination with show business.

> "You won't find any stories of poverty or ghettos in this dude's closet," Reeves once said. "When I see stuff in Los Angeles now, I realize how safe and sheltered my upbringing was. [Toronto] was a great place, no graffiti, cool people. The roughest it got was when we slung chestnuts at each other and built go-karts. I was a middle-class white boy with an absent father, a strong-willed mother, and two beautiful younger sisters."

In the mid-1970s Patricia Reeves married her third husband, rock promoter Robert Miller. This marriage lasted five years before ending in divorce. Keanu, meanwhile, continued to pay occasional visits to his biological father, who had settled in Hawaii. But Samuel Reeves abruptly disappeared when Keanu was 13 years old. Family members spent the next several years looking for him, but his whereabouts remained a mystery. Finally, in 1994—the same year he starred in the blockbuster movie *Speed*—Keanu learned that his father had been arrested for dealing drugs. This news infuriated Reeves, who felt that it marked another instance in which his father had abandoned his family.

Although Reeves lived in four countries and had three different father figures during his childhood, he considered himself a normal kid. Growing up in Toronto, he had a paper route and a pet dog named Jupiter. He loved to eat peanut butter and crackers. He played ice hockey, and his skills as goalie earned him the nickname "The Wall." In addition, the success of his mother's business meant that the family was financially comfortable. "You won't find any stories of poverty or ghettos in this dude's closet," Reeves once said. "When I see stuff in Los Angeles now, I realize how safe and sheltered my upbringing was. [Toronto] was a great place, no graffiti, cool people. The roughest it got was when we slung chestnuts at each other and built go-karts. I was a middle-class white boy with an absent father, a strong-willed mother, and two beautiful younger sisters."

Still, Reeves did carry some emotional scars from his childhood. His father's disappearance left him feeling abandoned and empty. During his adolescence, he became something of a loner who had trouble forming close relationships with other people. "I think a lot of who I am is a reaction against [my father's] actions," he once said.

EDUCATION

Reeves was a poor student throughout his school years. His teachers at Jesse Ketchum Grade School in Toronto remember him as a kid who was always late for class and usually forgot his homework. Some of his problems in school stemmed from the fact that he suffered from dyslexia. Dyslexia is a condition in which the brain mixes up letters and numbers, making it very difficult to read. Reeves underwent special training that helped him overcome his dyslexia, but he still struggled with his schoolwork.

Reeves attended several different high schools in Toronto. He completed the ninth and tenth grades at North Toronto Collegiate School. He played on the basketball team and even joined the chess club. But he disliked the school's emphasis on structured learning, so he transferred to De La Salle College, a private Catholic high school. This move turned out to be a disaster for Reeves. He failed all of his courses except for Latin, which was the one subject that interested him. He even failed gym, even though he was an excellent athlete.

After one year at De La Salle, Reeves transferred to the Toronto School for the Performing Arts. Given his growing interest in acting, this should have been the perfect place for him. However, he was kicked out of the school in 1983 following an argument with his acting coach. At this point, Reeves dropped out of high school without earning a diploma. Instead, he enrolled in acting classes at the Leah Posluns Theatre School, which was located at a theater in a Toronto suburb. He studied formal acting techniques at the school, including proper breathing and how to "project" himself into a character.

FIRST JOBS

Reeves took his first tentative steps into the world of acting at age 14, when he began appearing in high school theatrical productions. "I started doing some acting and I got hooked—it allowed me to be somebody different," he explained. "I did a lot of pretending as a child. It was my way of coping." Nevertheless, he claimed that he did not decide to become an actor until he turned 18 and entered the Leah Posluns Theatre School. "I started taking classes at night, mostly out of respect for acting," he recalled. "I was taking classes and playing hockey a lot, and I started crashing some auditions with friends from the Performing Arts High School. I got some jobs, then I got an agent, and it all sort of fell together. I started doing community theater and commercials. I did a Coke commercial and this killer Kellogg's commercial."

"I started doing some acting and I got hooked—it allowed me to be somebody different," Reeves explained. "I did a lot of pretending as a child. It was my way of coping."

Reeves built on this foundation to claim larger acting roles in Canadian television and theater. He was awarded a small part on the Canadian television show "Hangin' In," and he earned a starring role in the play *Wolfboy* at Toronto's Passe Muraille Theater. In *Wolfboy*, Reeves's character is placed in a mental hospital, where he meets a man who believes he is a werewolf. The play aroused some controversy for its homosexual themes, and Reeves's performance was panned by some critics. Even the director of the play, John Palmer, recognized that the young actor had problems. "He would skip words and say lines like he was trying to figure out what they meant," Palmer remembered. Like other actors, Reeves disliked hearing negative remarks about his performances. But he did not let the comments distract him from his goal of building a successful acting career.

As a young adult, Reeves also developed a passion for the plays of William Shakespeare. He read all of the great playwright's works and memorized many of the lines. His knowledge of Shakespeare helped him win the role of Mercutio in *Romeo and Juliet* at the Hedgerow Theater in Pennsylvania. Armed with this experience, Reeves auditioned for the prestigious Shakespeare Festival in Stratford, Ontario. When he failed to win any roles, he decided to move to Los Angeles and try to break into American movies.

CAREER HIGHLIGHTS

Keanu Reeves is a hard-working, prolific actor who has appeared in over 40 films. He has worked in a wide range of genres, from comedy to horror

Reeves and Ione Skye Leitch (Clarissa) co-starred in the controversial film River's Edge.

and from romance to action films. He has appeared in small, independent films as well as big-budget blockbusters. Throughout his career, Reeves has been criticized by reviewers who claim that he has a bland, emotionless style of acting. In fact, some critics have dubbed him the worst actor in Hollywood. But Reeves has overcome this label to become one of the world's most popular and highest-paid movie stars. He has starred in some of the most successful movies of the past two decades, including *Bill and Ted's Excellent Adventure, Speed, The Matrix, The Matrix Reloaded*, and *The Matrix Revolutions.*

Getting Started

In 1986, at the age of 21, Reeves drove his 1969 Volvo to Los Angeles. He moved in with his former stepfather, director Paul Aaron, who helped him find an agent. Within a few weeks, Reeves landed a supporting role as a hockey goalie in the 1986 movie *Youngblood,* which also featured Rob Lowe and Patrick Swayze. Other parts quickly followed. For example, in 1986 he also worked with Charles Bronson in the movie *Act of Vengeance,* appeared in a film about alcoholism called *Under the Influence,* and sang in the television musical *Babes in Toyland.*

Reeves's big break came that same year, when he won a supporting role in the disturbing and thought-provoking teen drama *River's Edge* (1986). The plot is based on a true story about a teenager who kills his girlfriend and leaves her body next to a river. The movie traces what happens when the boy tells his rebellious group of friends about his crime. All of the teens come from poor homes and lack parental supervision and moral guidance. Their feelings of alienation and hopelessness allow them to disregard the murder, and they all agree not to tell their parents or the police. But a few days later, one of the killer's friends, Matt (played by Reeves), breaks down under feelings of guilt and reports the crime. *River's Edge* received positive reviews from critics, although it did not fare particularly well at the box office. Several critics praised Reeves's performance. In a review for *Time* magazine, for example, Richard Schickel said he played the part of Matt with "exemplary restraint," and *People* magazine reviewer Peter Tranvis called his performance "sharply characterized."

Although Reeves was not yet a star, he worked consistently over the next few years. His work included a couple of successful films as well as a number of stinkers. One of his films that earned good reviews was *Dangerous Liaisons* (1988), a period drama set in 18th-century France. His co-stars included Glenn Close, Michelle Pfeiffer, John Malkovich, and Uma Thurman. The following year Reeves appeared alongside Steve Martin, Mary Steenburgen, and Dianne Wiest in *Parenthood* (1989), a popular comedy about the struggles involved in family life, shown through multiple generations in a large extended family. He played the weird but good-hearted boyfriend of one of the family members in the film.

Bill and Ted's Excellent Adventure

Reeves gained his first taste of fame with the 1989 release of the teen comedy *Bill and Ted's Excellent Adventure*. This silly time-travel adventure starred Reeves as the dim-witted Ted Logan and Alex Winter as the equally dense Bill Preston. Bill and Ted are terrible musicians who form a band called the Wyld Stallyns. They dream of becoming rock stars, but their dream is threatened by their poor grades in high school. If Ted fails history, his father will send him away to military school and break up the band.

As the boys agonize over this possibility, a telephone booth falls out of the sky. Inside is a man named Rufus (played by George Carlin) who says he is from the future. Rufus has traveled through time to help the boys in the present, because it turns out that the Wyld Stallyns eventually become famous and influence the world of the future. Rufus claims that the peaceful world of the future may not exist if the boys fail their history final exam.

The success of Bill and Ted's Excellent Adventure *brought Reeves movie stardom.*

Bill and Ted use the phone booth as a time machine to travel to various eras in history and meet famous figures of the past. They learn about history firsthand through a series of crazy adventures. In the end, the teens

411

transport Abraham Lincoln, Socrates, Beethoven, Joan of Arc, Genghis Khan, and other historical figures back to their school to stage a wild show for their oral history exam. *Bill and Ted's Excellent Adventure* won the approval of young audiences and became a surprise box-office hit. The low-budget picture, which was filmed for about $10 million, ended up grossing over $45 million in theaters.

Reeves enjoyed his role in the film. "I got to play a guy who's like a child of nature," he said of Ted. "He's almost an idiot savant, except he's not that smart. But he's pure and good. He's a good soul." Reeves returned to the role in the 1991 sequel *Bill and Ted's Bogus Journey*, in which the boys travel to heaven and hell. Upon meeting God, Ted says in his typical goofy fashion, "Congratulations on a most excellent planet. Bill and I enjoy it on a daily basis." The boys later play the devil in a game of Battleship in order to save their souls.

———— **"** ————

"I got to play a guy who's like a child of nature,"Reeves said of the character Ted. "He's almost an idiot savant, except he's not that smart. But he's pure and good. He's a good soul."

———— **"** ————

While the success of the *Bill and Ted* movies brought Reeves stardom, it also contributed to a lasting image of him as a limited and rather vapid actor who could only play teen roles. Reeves admitted that he sometimes fostered this image by using Ted's "Valleyspeak" language in interviews. "Ted hung a label on me," he confessed, "and I hung a label on myself, to a certain extent."

Expanding His Range as an Actor

After the *Bill and Ted* films, Reeves took on a variety of challenging roles in an effort to avoid being typecast. For example, he returned to his love of Shakespeare by doing a summer workshop production of *The Tempest* in Massachusetts. He also co-starred with Patrick Swayze in the 1991 action-thriller *Point Break*. In this film, which was a box office success despite mediocre reviews, Reeves plays an undercover FBI agent who takes up surfing in order to infiltrate a group of criminals.

Also in 1991, Reeves starred in the controversial movie *My Own Private Idaho* with River Phoenix, a long-time friend (for more information, see *Biography Today*, Apr. 1994). Both actors appeared in the film in hopes of escaping their teen-idol images and branching out into more challenging material. In this film, Reeves plays Scott Favor, a lazy, Shakespeare-quoting

Reeves as Jonathan Harker is confronted with Dracula (Gary Oldman).

rich kid who is waiting to turn 21 so he can inherit his father's fortune. In the meantime, he becomes involved in the underground world of homosexual street hustlers. He makes friends with Mike Waters (Phoenix), a fellow hustler who suffers from narcolepsy (a condition in which people fall asleep without warning). Scott helps Mike search for his missing mother, but all the while he plans to return to his rich family once he receives his inheritance.

My Own Private Idaho was controversial because of its homosexual themes, violence, and gritty depiction of the life of male prostitutes. In order to prepare for their roles, Reeves and Phoenix hung out with real-life street hustlers and experimented with drugs. Reeves was able to put the drug use behind him, but Phoenix developed an addiction. In 1993, Phoenix died of a drug overdose outside a Los Angeles nightclub. Reeves was devastated by the death of his friend.

In 1992 Reeves appeared in *Bram Stoker's Dracula,* a retelling of the famous vampire legend. In a cast that included Anthony Hopkins, Winona Ryder, and Gary Oldman, he played London lawyer Jonathan Hacker. Hacker goes to Dracula's castle to discuss a real estate matter, but he finds much more than he bargained for when he meets the vampire and his bloodsucking brides.

Although *Bram Stoker's Dracula* did fairly well in theaters, Reeves's perfor-mance generated some of the harshest criticism of his career. One critic quipped, "[Reeves] is so limited and stamped with his *Bill and Ted* roles you can practically hear him saying, 'Most excellent fangs, Drac dude.'" The actor himself admitted he was not very good in the movie, partly because he found it difficult to master an English accent. "I got killed in *Dracula*—I got slaughtered," he acknowledged. "The other actors' performances were so operatic, and I didn't hold up my end of the bargain. My performance was too introverted, closed in, and safe. Since *Dracula* came out I've always felt that I could have played it much more aggressive. . . . I didn't act very well. I'll leave it at that."

_____ **"** _____

Speed *was a huge hit at the box office and established Reeves as a new breed of sensitive action hero.* "At last an action picture out of Hollywood that satisfies," wrote John Simon in National Review.

_____ **"** _____

Reeves chose yet another unusual role in 1993, when he played Prince Siddhartha in the film *Little Buddha*. The main story concerns a young American boy who is believed to be the reincarnation of an important lama, or Buddhist holy man. Buddhist monks from the Asian country of Tibet come to Seattle to meet the boy and convince his parents to let him visit their monastery in the Himalayas. A series of flashbacks to ancient India shows the transformation of Siddhar-tha from a spoiled young prince into the serene spiritual leader known as Buddha. *Little Buddha* received mixed reviews, as did Reeves's performance. Some critics felt that he was miscast, but others claimed that his low-key acting style worked well in the role. Stanley Kauffmann of the *New Republic*, for example, said Reeves played Siddhartha with "surprising grace and focus."

Becoming an Action Hero in *Speed*

Reeves's popularity soared to new heights when he starred in the 1994 ac-tion-blockbuster *Speed*. He played Jack Traven, a heroic police officer who matches wits with a deranged ex-cop looking for revenge (played by Den-nis Hopper). The main action of the film takes place on a speeding bus that contains a bomb set to explode if the bus slows down below 50 miles per hour. With the help of Annie (played by Sandra Bullock), an attractive young woman who takes the wheel when the bus driver is injured, Traven saves the passengers and confronts the madman. *Speed* was a huge hit at the box office and established Reeves as a new breed of sensitive action hero. "At last an action picture out of Hollywood that satisfies," wrote John Simon in *National Review*.

Thanks to the success of *Speed*, Reeves's asking price per picture increased to $7 million. Yet he turned down an amazing $11 million to reprise his role as Jack Traven in the sequel *Speed 2*. Reeves did not like the script and was not eager to be pigeon-holed as an action hero. Instead, he chose to play the title role in *Hamlet* for $2,000 per week at a small theater in Winnipeg, Canada. "To perform Shakespeare you get to say very profound words and in the body it feels more thrilling," he explained. "Your spirit, your intellect, your heart, and your voice all have to, at a very high degree, melt into

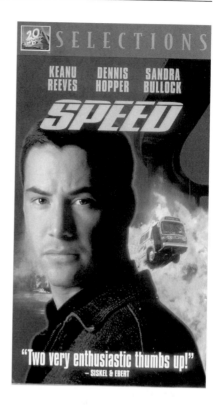

the speaking of words and behavior. For me all of these things are missing in action pictures. In Shakespeare, it's pure." For the first few performances, Reeves was noticeably nervous playing the challenging character of Hamlet. But he eventually grew into the role. In fact, Roger Lewis of *Vanity Fair* called him "one of the top three Hamlets I have seen."

Reeves's next starring role came in the 1995 futuristic action movie *Johnny Mnemonic*. He plays the title character, who has the ability to store computer data inside his brain. He works as a high-tech courier, delivering sensitive information in person to prevent it from being intercepted by computer hackers. But he is forced to run for his life when a group of criminals seeks to capture him and seize the data he is carrying. Unfortunately, *Johnny Mnemonic* was a box office disappointment, and critics lined up to deliver scathing reviews of the film. In *Entertainment Weekly*, for example, reviewer Owen Gleiberman wrote that "*Johnny Mnemonic*, a slack and derivative future-shock thriller, offers the embarrassing spectacle of Keanu Reeves working overtime to convince you that he has too much on his mind."

In 1997 Reeves starred opposite Al Pacino in the supernatural thriller *The Devil's Advocate*. Reeves plays Kevin Lomax, a successful Florida criminal-

defense attorney who joins a powerful, glitzy New York law firm. Eager to please his new boss, John Milton (Pacino), Kevin grows increasingly immoral and ruthless. But his relationship with his wife, Mary Ann (Charlize Theron), begins to fall apart. Eventually, however, Kevin begins to understand his boss's intentions, triggering a dramatic showdown. Although the film received generally poor reviews, some critics admitted that it kept their interest. "*The Devil's Advocate* is a fairly entertaining supernatural potboiler that finally bubbles over with a nearly operatic sense of absurdity and excess," Todd McCarthy wrote in *Variety.* "Reeves does a serious and pleasing job in believably conveying Kevin's legal skill, personal allure, and willingness to be distracted from domestic life by the heady experience of big-city success."

The Matrix

For five years following the release of *Speed,* none of Reeves's films achieved more than mild success. But this situation changed dramatically in 1999, when Reeves starred in an action-packed science-fiction film called *The Matrix.* In this film, Reeves plays Thomas Anderson, a 21st-century computer programmer who secretly acts as a hacker under the nickname Neo. Late one night, Neo is awakened from his ordinary life to discover that the world is not as it seems.

─── **"** ───

"I'd be a liar if I told you I understood everything that was going on when I first read the script,"Reeves said about **The Matrix.** *"But I knew immediately that I had never read anything like it and that I wanted to be part of it. I had no idea it would become what it has become. . . . I was just happy to be part of something that was so original and challenging."*

─── **"** ───

Under the guidance of the mysterious Morpheus (Lawrence Fishburne), Neo learns that a race of intelligent machines has taken over Earth. The machines control human beings and use their bodies as a source of energy. In order to keep the human race dormant, the machines use a sophisticated computer simulation to convince people that they remain free and are living a normal life. What millions of people perceive as reality is in fact an elaborate, computer-generated hallucination—a type of virtual reality. Only a few people have escaped the control of the machines. Led by Morpheus, they have formed bands of underground freedom fighters to try to regain control of the planet.

As Neo struggles to understand and accept this awful truth, he receives another shock. Morpheus believes that Neo is "the One," a great hero who is destined to help the humans overcome the oppressive machines. With the help of Morpheus, another freedom fighter named Trinity (Carrie-Anne Moss), and others, Neo works hard to develop his intellectual powers and fighting abilities in order to fulfill his destiny.

Reeves was determined to win the role of Neo from the first time he read the movie script. The scripts for *The Matrix* and its sequels were written by Andy and Larry Wachowski, who also directed the films. Reeves was intrigued by the complex, yet highly original story and characters. "I'd be a liar if I told you I understood everything that was going on when I first read the script," he noted. "But I knew immediately that I had never read anything like it and that I wanted to be part of it. I had no idea it would become what it has become. . . . I was just happy to be part of something that was so original and challenging."

> "**The Matrix** *changed not only the way we look at movies, but movies themselves,*" *David Edelstein* wrote in the **New York Times**. "**The Matrix** *cut us loose from the laws of physics in ways that no live-action film had ever done, exploding our ideas of time and space on screen.*"

Reeves underwent months of preparation before filming began. He jumped into a strenuous training routine to achieve top conditioning for the physically demanding role. He also studied martial arts so that he could perform most of his own stunts in the film's long fight sequences. "We knew it would take a maniacal commitment," director Larry Wachowski stated. "Keanu was our maniac." "Keanu was amazing," added producer Joel Silver. "He put his life and career on hold to learn to do the fights. Even after intense training and with all the precautions, the actors would hurt their wrists and ribs on a daily basis. Keanu never once complained or played the prima donna." (For more information on the film's martial arts choreography, see the entry on Yuen Wo-Ping in *Biography Today Performing Artists,* Vol. 3.)

The Matrix became a huge, unexpected hit within a few weeks of its release. It enjoyed tremendous word-of-mouth among moviegoers because it was so different from anything they had ever seen before. Writer-directors Andy and Larry Wachowski, known simply as "the brothers," ac-

A scene from The Matrix.

knowledged such influences as American comic books, Chinese kung fu pictures, Japanese anime, and world philosophy and spiritual texts. They used state-of-the art, computer-generated images and spectacular special effects to bring the story to life. Shot in Australia for $63 million, *The Matrix* grossed an incredible $460 million in worldwide box office receipts.

The popularity of *The Matrix* changed the look of action movies from that time forward. In fact, *Entertainment Weekly* called it "the most influential action movie of its generation." Since its release, countless other movies have featured 360-degree camera sweeps, bullets rippling through the air in slow motion, and heroes wearing black trench coats and trendy sunglasses. "*The Matrix* changed not only the way we look at movies, but movies themselves," David Edelstein wrote in the *New York Times*. "*The Matrix* cut us loose from the laws of physics in ways that no live-action film had ever done, exploding our ideas of time and space on screen." The phenomenal success of *The Matrix* soon spawned two sequels, *The Matrix Reloaded* and *The Matrix Revolutions*. But first, Reeves appeared in several very different films.

Looking for Variety in Recent Projects

After starring in *The Matrix*, Reeves looked for roles that were as different as possible from Neo. In 2000 he starred in *The Replacements*, a feel-good sports story about a group of misfit athletes who fill in when professional football players hold a labor strike against the National Football League (NFL). Reeves plays Shane Falco, a star college quarterback whose disastrous play in his last college bowl game cost him a chance at NFL stardom. He is making a living by scraping barnacles off the bottoms of rich people's

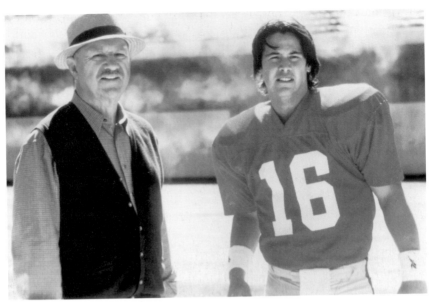

Reeves, shown here with Gene Hackman, gave a noteworthy performance in The Replacements.

yachts when he is recruited to help the fictional Washington Sentinels finish the season. Though most critics claimed that the movie followed a familiar formula, some praised Reeves's performance. "When it matters most, *The Replacements* really does engage you emotionally and make you root for this ragtag, madcap, zany pack of wackies," reviewer Tom Shales said on National Public Radio's *Morning Edition*. "A team depends on its quarterback, and so does this film. . . . He's winningly played by Keanu Reeves."

Reeves received glowing reviews for his supporting role in the 2000 thriller *The Gift*. This film follows the story of a psychic (Cate Blanchett) whose visions lead her to the heart of a murder mystery in a small Southern town. Reeves plays Donnie Barksdale, a mean-tempered redneck who beats his wife, Valerie (Hilary Swank), and stalks the psychic. Reeves spent several weeks hanging out with rough characters in the South to prepare for the role. His preparation seemed to pay off. The film received only fair reviews, but Reeves received a great deal of notice for his menacing performance. "Keanu Reeves is bad, very bad in *The Gift*. But intentionally, and quite effectively," wrote Bob Strauss in the *Guardian*.

In 2001 Reeves took a romantic leading role opposite Charlize Theron in *Sweet November*. Theron plays a free-spirited San Francisco woman who finds a new boyfriend every month. When she meets advertising executive Nelson Moss, played by Reeves, they become romantically involved for the month of November. The couple ends up falling in love, but it turns out that she is hiding a tragic secret. *Sweet November* received poor reviews and achieved only moderate success at the box office. "The movie is a very low-grade romantic drama indeed, a love story with all the life-and-death intensity of a heat rash," wrote Lisa Schwarzbaum in *Entertainment Weekly*.

Also in 2001, Reeves appeared in the family-oriented movie *Hardball*. He plays Conor O'Neill, a hard-drinking Irish gambler who repays a favor by taking over the coaching responsibilities for a hard-luck Little League baseball team. He experiences conflict with the members of the team, a group of underprivileged African-American kids from a local housing pro-

Reeves took a romantic leading role opposite Charlize Theron in the love story Sweet November.

ject. But the coach and the players ultimately bond together to make an exciting championship run. "*Hardball* works where it counts, on the emotional level," wrote Bob Graham in the *San Francisco Chronicle*. "Some of the movie's heart-tugging effects stack the deck — one is a whopper — but Reeves, as a borderline alcoholic and compulsive gambler, makes up for it with a very sympathetic performance."

Returning as Neo in Two Highly Anticipated Sequels

"I've been working out for up to three hours a day and I reckon I'm in the greatest physical condition I've ever been in my life. I've been training with a mix of aerobics, weights, kick-boxing, and karate," Reeves noted. "This is more physically demanding than the original movie. Trust me, you would not want to be my knees in the morning before I start limbering up."

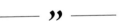

By the time those movies were out in theaters, Reeves was already back at work on the sequels to *The Matrix*: *The Matrix Reloaded* and *The Matrix Revolutions*. The two sequels were filmed back-to-back, first in California for several months in mid-2000 and then in Australia from September 2001 through August 2002; they were released in May and November of 2003. Reeves received a record paycheck of $30 million for appearing in the two movies. He also received 15 percent of the gross box-office receipts, which was expected to increase the total to between $90 and $200 million. He thus became the best-paid actor in Hollywood in 2003.

In *The Matrix Reloaded*, Neo continues to battle against the non-human forces of the matrix. He is beginning to learn how to control his powers, as he remains locked in a massive struggle with Agent Smith. He is also beginning to understand the mysteries of the matrix. The machine world is out to destroy the underground city of Zion, where the few remaining free humans live. Neo and his friends must fight to protect Zion from the machines that control the rest of humanity, and time is running out. "The film picks up six months after the first movie ended with Neo having 72 hours to stop 250,000 probes from discovering mankind's last stronghold," Reeves explained. The film ended in a cliffhanger, leaving the audience wondering what would happen next.

The Wachowski brothers ramped up the action in the sequel and included a number of special effects never before seen on screen. "There are more

Scenes from The Matrix Reloaded.

action sequences than the last film, and instead of fighting one-to-one I fight one-against-many, although the writers have made the movie more sophisticated and demanding," Reeves stated. The best-known example of the film's unique effects is the Burly Brawl—an extended fight sequence between Neo and his main rival, Agent Smith (Hugo Weaving), in which Smith continually duplicates himself. Neo eventually ends up facing dozens of agents in the battle. The Burly Brawl features lots of computer-generated characters blended with footage of the actors performing their own stunts. Reeves trained for nine weeks to perfect the 500 moves he performs in the scene.

> ───── *"* ─────
>
> *Reeves claimed that he enjoyed the physical demands of* **The Matrix** *series. "I've always been a bit reckless," he admitted. "The more physical acting gets, the more comfortable I feel. I love the danger in doing stunts and physical stuff in films."*
>
> ───── *"* ─────

In *The Matrix Revolutions*, the concluding chapter of the series, the story focuses on the war between humans and machines. The story takes place inside the matrix, in Zion, and in Machine City. The movie opens with Neo trapped in limbo between the world of the matrix and the real world. He eventually escapes and meets Smith in battle once again. Meanwhile, the humans of Zion engage in a spectacular battle against the machines that want to destroy them. In addition, several pivotal scenes take place in Machine City, where Neo continues his quest to save humanity.

As he did in the first movie, Reeves trained hard in order to perform nearly all of his own stunts in *The Matrix Reloaded* and *The Matrix Revolutions*. "I've been working out for up to three hours a day and I reckon I'm in the greatest physical condition I've ever been in my life. I've been training with a mix of aerobics, weights, kick-boxing, and karate," he noted. "This is more physically demanding than the original movie. Trust me, you would not want to be my knees in the morning before I start limbering up." But Reeves claimed that he enjoyed the physical demands of *The Matrix* series. "I've always been a bit reckless," he admitted. "The more physical acting gets, the more comfortable I feel. I love the danger in doing stunts and physical stuff in films." Indeed, the action sequences were widely considered the most impressive parts of the new films.

Unfortunately, the final two installments of *The Matrix* series did not earn the acclaim enjoyed by the opening film. "The original *Matrix* was full of

Scenes from The Matrix Revolutions.

—— **"** ——

"I love Neo. I find Neo to be a beautiful man. I love his dignity, his love for Trinity, his search. Playing him is like playing the best parts of us. I like that he's a man who, in **The Matrix,** *has this superhuman ability but also has this incredible responsibility,"Reeves said. "I love* **The Matrix** — *love it through and through. And so the sacrifices — what it demands, what it hopes for — had me body and soul. And to feel that is one of the more remarkable things in my life."*

—— **"** ——

dizzying surprises," wrote *Newsweek* critic David Ansen. "But it's turned out that the Wachowskis didn't have many more tricks up their sleeves. . . . Though they're full of undeniably spectacular moments, great production values, and unusual ambition, a simple thing has gotten lost in these sequels: they're not much fun."

Many critics and fans expressed some disappointment with the final two films of *The Matrix* series, saying that they didn't live up to the incredible promise of the first film. But the movies did earn Reeves legions of new fans. "*The Matrix* series has seen [Reeves] reborn as the last word in cool machismo — and it's a role for which his lack of animation is ideally suited," wrote Christopher Tookey in the *Daily Telegraph*. "He is having the last laugh on all his critics." "The success or failure of a Reeves performance depends greatly on how well he's chosen — on whether the role flatters his uneven gifts," added Lucy Kaylin in *GQ* magazine. "No actor dead or alive has ever been better matched with a role than Reeves is with Neo, the computer hacker who comes to learn that humans are living in a sinister dreamscape generated by machines that are actually, systematically, turning them into batteries. . . . Apart from being a slick and credible action hero, he owned the movie because he committed so totally, fusing himself to its arcane internal logic. And his ramrod seriousness underscored the notion of profound questions lurking beneath the elaborate cinematic armature."

For his part, Reeves enjoyed playing the role of Neo, and he felt a twinge of sadness when filming of *The Matrix* series concluded. "I love Neo. I find Neo to be a beautiful man. I love his dignity, his love for Trinity, his search. Playing him is like playing the best parts of us. I like that he's a man who, in *The Matrix,* has this superhuman ability but also has this incredible re-

Reeves as Neo in a scene from The Matrix Revolutions.

sponsibility," he said. "I love *The Matrix*—love it through and through. And so the sacrifices—what it demands, what it hopes for—had me body and soul. And to feel that is one of the more remarkable things in my life."

Recent Projects

After wrapping up the *Matrix* series, Reeves turned his attention to a role totally different from his Neo character. He played a doctor in *Something's Gotta Give* (2003), a romantic comedy with Jack Nicholson and Diane Keaton. When asked about his flair for playing wildly different personalities from film to film, he explained that "My goal remains the same [throughout my career]: to play different types of characters and do different kinds of films in style and scope. I guess it's just me wanting to act and not be just one thing."

HOME AND FAMILY

Although Reeves has been romantically linked to a number of women, he has never been married. "I'm a coward, frightened of falling in love. Isn't everybody?" he noted. "It would be great to marry because it would be very important to me to have a home and a family, but work means I'm on the road a lot and when I'm working I think only about work." Reeves's most serious relationship was with actress Jennifer Syme, who became pregnant with his child in 1999. Sadly, the baby girl was stillborn and the couple broke up a short time later. In 2001 the couple tried to reconcile, but Syme was killed in a tragic automobile accident.

When asked about his flair for playing wildly different personalities from film to film, Reeves explained that "My goal remains the same [throughout my career]: to play different types of characters and do different kinds of films in style and scope. I guess it's just me wanting to act and not be just one thing."

Reeves remains close to his mother and his two younger sisters. He took time off from acting in the late 1990s to help his sister Kim battle leukemia (a type of cancer that affects the blood). "The last few years have been tough for me," he admitted.

Because his busy filming schedule kept him on the road for long periods of time, Reeves resisted buying a home of his own for many years. Instead, he lived in hotels or with friends. "I don't need a house," he said at the time. "I prefer to be free, unfettered. I like being in the desert or high in a tree. I'm not a homebody type of guy." But Reeves recently changed his mind. He bought a three-bedroom, 5,600-square-foot contemporary home in the Hollywood Hills, with glass walls that overlook the ocean and the Los Angeles skyline. Reeves has not lived in Canada for many years, but he maintains his Canadian citizenship, which dates back to his childhood in Toronto.

HOBBIES AND OTHER INTERESTS

In addition to acting, Reeves has two great passions: riding motorcycles and playing bass guitar. As a guitarist, he plays in the band Dogstar, which also includes singer Bret Domrose and drummer Rob Mailhouse. "I'm committed to it as long as we're interested in writing together and playing," he said of the band. "For me, it's a great experience when I'm not working, because there's kind of a carefree aspect to it that I cherish. It's a different kind of good time. I hope that my band brothers will keep enjoying it and get along. It's hard to keep a band together, but we're working on it." Some of Reeves's quieter hobbies include playing chess and reading.

Reeves with his band, Dogstar, *in 2000.*

SELECTED CREDITS

Films

Youngblood, 1986
River's Edge, 1986
Dangerous Liaisons, 1988
Parenthood, 1989
Bill and Ted's Excellent Adventure, 1989
Point Break, 1991
Bill and Ted's Bogus Journey, 1991
My Own Private Idaho, 1991
Bram Stoker's Dracula, 1992
Much Ado about Nothing, 1993
Little Buddha, 1993
Speed, 1994
Johnny Mnemonic, 1995
A Walk in the Clouds, 1995
Feeling Minnesota, 1996
The Devil's Advocate, 1997
The Matrix, 1999
The Replacements, 2000
The Gift, 2000
Sweet November, 2001

Hardball, 2001
The Matrix Reloaded, 2003
The Matrix Revolutions, 2003
Something's Gotta Give, 2003

Recordings

Happy Ending, 2000 (with Dogstar)

HONORS AND AWARDS

MTV Movie Award as Most Desirable Male: 1991, for *Point Break*
MTV Movie Award as Best On-Screen Duo: 1994, for *Speed* (with Sandra
Bullock)

FURTHER READING

Books

Bystedt, Karen Hardy. *Before They Were Famous: In Their Own Words,* 1996
Goodrich, J.J. *The Keanu Matrix: Unraveling the Puzzle of Hollywood's
Reluctant Superstar,* 2003
Membery, York. *Superstars of Film: Keanu Reeves,* 1998
Nickson, Chris. *Keanu Reeves,* 1996
Robb, Brian J. *Keanu Reeves,* 1997

Periodicals

Biography, Sep. 2000, p.52
Current Biography Yearbook, 1995
Entertainment Weekly, Oct. 29, 1993, p.12; June 10, 1994, p.20; July 21, 1995,
p.61; June 14, 1996, p.7; Sep. 6, 1996, p.75; Apr. 9, 1999, p.26; Feb. 16,
2001, p.81; May 16, 2003, p.24; Nov. 7, 2003, p.24
GQ, May 2003, p.147
Maclean's, Jan. 23, 1995, p.52
New Republic, Dec. 14, 1992, p.28; July 4, 1994, p.26
New York Times, Dec. 19, 1986, p.C38; June 6, 1987, p.9; July 29, 1995, p.11;
May 11, 2003, p.AR1; Nov. 5, 2003, p.E1
Newsweek, May 5, 2003, p.56; Nov. 10, 2003, p.63
People, Mar. 13, 1989, p.16; July 22, 1991, p.10; Sep. 30, 1991, p.18; Nov. 16,
1992, p.25; June 20, 1994, p.18; July 11, 1994, p.49; May 8, 1995, p.82;
June 5, 1995, p.70; June 5, 2000, p.18; Aug. 28, 2000, p.17; June 2, 2003,
p.63

Time, June 1, 1987, p.73; Oct. 28, 1991, p.101; Feb. 6, 1995, p.79; Apr. 5, 1999, p.68; Apr. 19, 1999, p.75; May 12, 2003, p.64
USA Today, June 9, 1994, p.D1; May 24, 1995, p.D2; Aug. 4, 2000, p.E1; Aug. 9, 2000, p.D6; Nov. 5, 2003, p.D5
Vanity Fair, Feb. 2001, p.108
Variety, Nov. 3, 2003, p.30
Washington Post, Jan. 19, 2001, p.T42

Online Databases

Biography Resource Center Online, 2003, article from *International Dictionary of Films and Filmmakers, Vol. 3: Actors and Actresses,* 1996

ADDRESS

Keanu Reeves
Creative Artists Agency
9830 Wilshire Blvd.
Beverly Hills, CA 90212

WORLD WIDE WEB SITES

http://whatisthematrix.warnerbrothers.com
http://www.biography.com
http://entertainment.msn.com/celebs
http://www.eonline.com

Ricardo Sanchez 1951-

American Lieutenant General, United States Army
Former Commanding General of U.S. and Coalition
Forces in Iraq

BIRTH

Ricardo Sanchez was born in 1951 in Rio Grande City, Texas.
His father, Domingo Sanchez, was a welder for a gravel company. His mother, Maria Elena Sauceda, worked at a variety of
jobs. Ricardo was the second child born to his parents: he has
three brothers and two sisters, as well as two half brothers.

YOUTH

Rio Grande City is in the far southern part of Texas and takes its name from the river that flows past the town and forms the border between the United States and Mexico. As he grew up, Ricardo was able to look across the Rio Grande and see the country where his ancestors had lived. His father and mother had spent their lives on the Texas side of the border, but both of their families originally hailed from Mexico.

In a lot of ways, southern Texas is not much different from Mexico. The weather is hot and dry, and many of the residents speak Spanish more than English. It's also a poor area where lots of people struggle to get by. Starr County, where Rio Grande City is located, was named the poorest county in the United States in the 2000 Census, and it didn't fare much better in the years when Ricardo was growing up.

Sanchez has described his background as "dirt poor." For several years the family lived in a one-room house on the outskirts of Rio Grande City. There was no indoor plumbing, so they had to use an outdoor bathroom (an outhouse) and get their water from a faucet in the yard. At that point the family included Ricardo, his parents, and two siblings, who all shared the

"[We] really looked forward to Thursdays, every other week as I recall, because that was when Mom would go to the VA relief center to draw our rations. . . . That meant we would have some meat, cheese, and butter in the house for at least a couple of days. With a family of six, that didn't last long, and there were many days when we had only beans and rice."

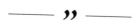

tiny home. Because there were no bedrooms, they used a metal table to separate the area where they slept from the area where they ate their meals. Later, the family moved to a better house with two bedrooms, a kitchen, and a living room, but they still didn't have an indoor toilet.

Learning from His Mom

To make matters worse, Sanchez's parents divorced when he was nine years old. The children stayed with their mother, who faced the tough job of supporting her large family. Maria Elena worked a full-time job, and she also got some help from welfare programs. Sanchez said that "we really looked forward to Thursdays, every other week as I recall, because that was when

Mom would go to the VA [Veteran's Administration] relief center to draw our rations. . . . That meant we would have some meat, cheese, and butter in the house for at least a couple of days. With a family of six, that didn't last long, and there were many days when we had only beans and rice."

Even though times were tough, Sanchez recalls many good things about his childhood. "We weren't suffering," he once said. "We never went hungry that I could remember. It was very basic living, a good environment for family values. It taught you a lot of discipline." A lot of the lessons came directly from his mother, and the biggest one was the importance of education. Maria Elena had dropped out of school at a young age. As an adult, she wanted a second chance at completing her studies, so she managed to attend night classes even though she was busy with work and raising her family. Eventually she earned her general equivalency degree (GED). Sanchez has said that it was his mother's "unbelievable desire to succeed in getting her GED, in spite of all obstacles, that taught me perseverance, dedication, focus and, of course, the will to succeed."

> ─── " ───
>
> *"We weren't suffering,"
> Sanchez once said. "We never
> went hungry that I could
> remember. It was very basic
> living, a good environment
> for family values. It taught
> you a lot of discipline."*
>
> ─── " ───

While still very young, Sanchez showed that he was ready to imitate his mom's hard work. He had his first job at age six. Over the years he worked in his uncle's tailor shop, swept the floor at a drug store, and delivered clothes for a dry cleaner. But, like his mom, he would put his biggest effort into his studies.

"At the time, you don't look at it as being tough," Sanchez recalled about those early days. "It's just the condition that you exist in. In reality, when you look back, there were some pretty tough times. But our mother was very focused on making sure we got our education, and she was a pretty good disciplinarian, too, making sure that we were not messing around and getting into trouble and making sure that we were at school. When we thought otherwise, she had her means of getting us back in line."

EDUCATION

Maria Elena put a lot of emphasis on her children's schooling. "I told them that I wanted them to have the education that my parents didn't give me," she recalled. Sanchez got along okay in his first years of schooling, but when he was in the sixth grade, he faced a new challenge. When he had difficulty solving a math problem in class, his teacher called him a "dummy." It could have been a discouraging incident, but Sanchez turned it to his advantage. "I was going to show her that I was better than that," he recalled, and he applied himself to his math studies like never before. Soon, math was his favorite subject, and he would later major in the subject in college. "That negative event had a tremendous impact on my life," Sanchez said of the teacher's comment. "It really made me who I am today. . . . It was the first instance where I remember being challenged and reacting in a way that was very focused in order to prove people wrong."

Still, like many other kids Sanchez grew tired of classes. When he was 13, he and his older brother announced that they didn't want to go to school anymore. Rather than argue with them, their mother told them that they could give up school only if they went to work picking cotton. The boys agreed, and the next morning they went to work in the fields at five a.m. "They came home and they were very tired," Maria Elena told the *Corpus Christi Caller-Times*, "but I just gave them some dinner and told them, 'Go to bed because tomorrow you have to wake up early. You have to get up at 5 a.m. and pick cotton for the rest of your life.'" Sanchez and his brother decided that school was easier than the fields, and they went back to hitting the books.

"At the time, you don't look at it as being tough," Sanchez recalled about his early days. *"It's just the condition that you exist in. In reality, when you look back, there were some pretty tough times. But our mother was very focused on making sure we got our education, and she was a pretty good disciplinarian, too, making sure that we were not messing around and getting into trouble and making sure that we were at school. When we thought otherwise, she had her means of getting us back in line."*

Admiring the Uniform

Sanchez found his way to the military because other members of his family had followed the same path. His father had learned to be a welder while in the service, and his half brothers Ramon and Domingo were in the armed forces as Sanchez grew up. Domingo, who served as an Air Force paratrooper in Vietnam, became an especially big influence in the boy's life. Sanchez began to think seriously about a military career while in junior high school. In high school he joined the Reserve Officer Training Corps (ROTC), in which students train for a future in the armed forces.

Meanwhile, Sanchez didn't ignore his other studies. His good grades made him a member of the National Honor Society, and he graduated eighth in his class at Rio Grande City High School in 1969. His high marks and ROTC studies earned him an Army-Air Force scholarship for college.

The Vietnam Era

> During the Vietnam War, anti-war protesters directed a lot of anger at Sanchez and other ROTC cadets. "I remember being in altercations with protestors who were trying to take down the flag and burn it," Sanchez said. "We wouldn't allow them to. Sometimes they'd come around during formations and throw tomatoes at us or spit on us."

His future looked set except for one thing: the Vietnam War. By 1969, when Sanchez graduated from high school, large numbers of U.S. troops had been fighting in Vietnam for four years, and America had become bitterly divided over the conflict. Following Domingo's example, Sanchez wanted to aid in the fight, but to do so, he would have had to give up his scholarship and enlist immediately as a soldier. In the end, Sanchez opted for college, mostly because of advice he received from Domingo. His older half brother told him to get his education while he had the chance and that "the war would be waiting" for him after he graduated.

Sanchez enrolled at the University of Texas in Austin in the fall of 1969, but his experiences at the state's largest university weren't pleasant. While he was a student there, heated antiwar protests took place on campus. The Vietnam War had a polarizing effect on American society, creating deep divisions between those who supported and those who opposed the war. Sentiment against the war was very intense, especially on college campuses. And some of that anger was directed at Sanchez and other ROTC cadets. "I remember being in altercations with protestors who were trying to take down the flag and burn it," Sanchez said. "We wouldn't allow them to. Sometimes they'd come around during formations and throw tomatoes at us or spit on us."

At the end of his first year, Sanchez transferred to Texas A&M University in Kingsville, which he found much more to his liking. Sanchez described

Sanchez greets soldiers of the 4th Infantry Division, 1-66th Armored Regiment, during an August 2003 visit to their base in Samarra, Iraq.

A&M as "a conservative area, with encouraging, mentoring professors." It was also a smaller school that had fewer antiwar protests. While in Kingsville, Sanchez met Maria Elena Garza (who coincidentally had the same first names as his mother); the two were married shortly after Sanchez received his bachelor's degree in mathematics and history in 1973. Later, after several years of military service, he attended the Naval Postgraduate School in Monterey, California. There, he received a master's degree in operations research and systems analysis engineering. He has also completed courses at the Command and General Staff College and the U.S. Army War College.

CAREER HIGHLIGHTS

As it turned out, Sanchez never got the chance to fight in Vietnam. By the time he graduated from college, U.S. involvement in the conflict was coming to an end. He was still intent on a military career, however. He was commissioned as a second lieutenant in the 82nd Airborne Division of the U.S. Army in 1973 and began his long climb up the ladder of military command.

Between the mid 1970s and the early 1990s, Sanchez was stationed in many different spots in the United States and in foreign countries, including assignments in Korea, Germany, and Panama. In the course of his career, his family has moved 16 different times. As he advanced through the ranks, Sanchez was one of relatively few Hispanics to become a senior Army officer. He hasn't complained very much about encountering discrimination in the service, but he believes his ethnic background did create some obstacles for him. "You just knew you had to work a little harder if you wanted to succeed," he said of being a Mexican American. "Just performing well wasn't good enough."

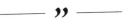

> *Sanchez was one of relatively few Hispanics to become a senior Army officer. He hasn't complained very much about encountering discrimination in the service, but he believes his ethnic background did create some obstacles for him. "You just knew you had to work a little harder if you wanted to succeed," he said of being a Mexican American. "Just performing well wasn't good enough."*

Sanchez specialized in commanding tank battalions, which required him to lead several hundred soldiers at a time. Because the United States wasn't involved in any large wars in the late 1970s and 1980s, most of his assignments didn't involve actual combat missions. Instead, his troops maintained a presence in important areas such as Korea, and they trained hard so that they would be ready to fight when they were called upon. In 1990, they received that call.

The Persian Gulf War

In August 1990, the Iraqi army, commanded by President Saddam Hussein, invaded nearby Kuwait and threatened Saudi Arabia. Hussein was widely considered a brutal, cruel, and ruthless dictator who executed or imprisoned those who challenged his authority. Under his abusive regime, the Iraqi people had few rights and suffered greatly. The Iraqi invasion of Kuwait was considered an act of aggression against a sovereign nation, and the United Nations and the international community were determined to stop it. The UN set a series of deadlines for Iraq to withdraw from Kuwait. At the same time, U.S. President George Bush put together an international coalition to oppose the Iraqi forces, and troops from the U.S. and other countries took up positions in Saudi Arabia. Sanchez and his tank battalion were among them. (For more information on Hussein, see *Biography Today*, July 1992, and Updates in the Annual Cumulations for 1996, 2001, and 2002.)

In January 1991, the U.S. launched Desert Storm, a UN offensive that included more than half a million U.S. troops. The first part of the war was an air offensive that included attacks on Iraqi forces in Kuwait and Iraq, targeting command and control operations. The air offensive lasted five weeks, followed by a ground war. Iraqi troops suffered heavy losses during that part of the war, and in their retreat they set fire to many oil wells, creating massive environmental damage. The Iraqis were forced to surrender after six weeks of war. The war had been swift and devastating, leaving approximately 200,000 dead (mostly Iraqis) and many more displaced from their homes. By the end of the war, UN forces had defeated the Iraqis, but Saddam Hussein was allowed to remain in power. At the time, many questioned whether fighting should have continued until UN forces ousted Hussein from power.

Sanchez and his troops played a part in two important engagements. They came to the aid of an infantry battalion that had run out of fuel in the Iraqi desert, arriving on the scene in the middle of the night to help fight off the enemy. His battalion also attacked Tallil Air Field in southern Iraq. Sanchez's tanks made a daring assault through the main gates of the airfield, braving enemy artillery fire. They captured the airfield and destroyed Iraqi planes and anti-aircraft batteries.

"Your adrenaline is just pumping," Sanchez said of his Gulf War experience. "You don't think about it. You focus on leading your soldiers through the mission and getting them out of there." For his exploits in the war, Sanchez was awarded the Bronze Star with the "V Device" that indicates valor. Following the war, he was promoted to the rank of brigadier general.

Serving in Eastern Europe

Later in the 1990s, Sanchez was involved in another world hotspot — in Kosovo in the Balkan region of Eastern Europe. In the 1990s, the country of Yugoslavia was torn apart by ethnic conflicts among the different peoples living there, including Albanians, Bulgarians, Romanians, Serbs, Croats, Slovenes, Bosnians, Macedonians, Montenegrans, Greeks, and Turks. The wars in the region began in 1991 when the republic of Slovenia declared its independence from Yugoslavia. Other conflicts followed, as other republics within Yugoslavia tried to gain their independence, and Yugoslav forces led by President Slobodan Milosevic fought to stop them. Milosevic and the Serbian troops were widely accused of crimes against humanity, genocide, and ethnic cleansing — the systematic torture and murder to eliminate their enemies, whom they hated solely because of their ethnic group. (For more information on Milosevic, see *Biography*

Sanchez speaks to Albanian soldiers at the Mosul airfield during a visit to the 101st Airborne Division.

Today, Sep. 1999, and Updates in the Annual Cumulations for 2000, 2001, and 2002.)

Fighting in Kosovo, a province of Serbia, started in the summer of 1998, as an armed group of ethnic Albanians fought to win independence from Serbia. The Serbian soldiers attacked civilians, as they had in earlier conflicts in other parts of Yugoslavia. To protect the ethnic Albanians of Kosovo, troops were sent there by the United States and some of its allies from NATO, a military alliance made up of the U.S. and many European countries. Sanchez commanded NATO peacekeeping forces that helped restore order after the Yugoslav army was forced out of Kosovo.

Regardless of where he was stationed, Sanchez earned a reputation for looking out for the soldiers he commanded. One example comes from the Gulf War. In the weeks before the fighting started Sanchez was given the option of making a brief visit home to attend to a family emergency. His commander, Retired General Barry McCaffrey, remembers that he told Sanchez, "we're not going to war in the next 14 days for sure. Go home, get involved in the situation . . . and come back. . . . You're not going to miss the fighting." Sanchez refused to leave. "I'm not going home until I can take my soldiers home," he told McCaffrey. Another of his former commanders, Retired Lieutenant General Randy House, said that "[Sanchez] had a feeling for soldiers that all officers do not have. . . . He could accomplish any mission while always looking out for the benefit of his troops."

In the United States Army, there are several different ranks of generals. When Sanchez first became a general, he was at the lowest rank—a one-star or brigadier general. He later received his second star, becoming a major general. In 2001, while still a two-star general, he was given command of the 1st Armored Division of V Corps, the oldest armored division in the U.S. forces. This put Sanchez in command of more than 10,000 soldiers.

The division soon had to prepare for a new engagement against an old enemy. In 2002 a coalition led by the U.S. and the United Kingdom confronted Iraqi leader Saddam Hussein once again. Alarmed by the possibility that the Iraqi leader was developing nuclear and biological weapons, the coalition demanded that Iraq comply with UN disarmament resolutions. Hussein refused. The U.S. argued that under Hussein, Iraq had developed weapons of mass destruction. Some also questioned whether he had been involved in terrorist activities, including the terrorist attacks of September 11, 2001. Soon, the coalition began massing forces near Iraq. Negotiations and weapons inspections failed to end the standoff, and in March 2003 the Iraq War began. Coalition forces quickly routed the Iraqi Army and took control of the country.

Return to Iraq

In June 2003, just six weeks after major combat operations ended in Iraq, Sanchez received a new promotion. He became a three-star or lieutenant general and was placed in command of the army's V Corps, which included more than 20,000 troops. He was also given a very large responsibility: he was put in charge of all military operations in Iraq.

> *Retired Lieutenant General Randy House said that "[Sanchez] had a feeling for soldiers that all officers do not have. . . . He could accomplish any mission while always looking out for the benefit of his troops."*

In some ways, Sanchez's task was just as difficult as that faced by the commanders who had overseen the actual combat operations in Iraq. First of all, the fighting wasn't over. Insurgents opposed to the coalition forces staged attacks on both civilian and military targets. In some cases bombs were planted next to roads, then detonated when military vehicles passed by. The insurgents also used rocket-propelled grenades and car bombs with deadly effect. In August 2003, the number of coalition forces killed by these types of attacks surpassed the number that had been killed in combat operations. The death toll continued to rise in ensuing months.

The situation was made more difficult because Sanchez's troops had to assist in rebuilding the war-torn country. The electrical system had been badly damaged, and the machinery and pipelines used to pump and process oil—Iraq's biggest trade commodity—desperately needed repair. The general also faced a tough political situation. Iraq is made up of several different ethnic groups and religious factions, and there was a danger they

Sanchez walks with Secretary of Defense Donald H. Rumsfeld after his arrival in Baghdad, where he planned to meet with coalition forces.

might begin fighting with one another as they tried to establish their positions in the new nation. Sanchez was honest about the challenges. "We did expect instability before we arrived here," he said, but he also admitted that "we did not expect . . . the political and economic structures to shut down. That was clearly a surprise — at least for me it was." In spite of the difficulties, he remained confident that the coalition forces could not be beaten in battle by the insurgents. "The stark reality is that they cannot defeat us, and they know it. I am supremely confident of this reality."

The Search for Weapons

In addition to their other duties, the coalition forces searched the country for the weapons of mass destruction that the Iraqis were believed to possess. After months of hunting for evidence of chemical and nuclear weapons, the coalition forces found no weapons of mass destruction. This led some people in the U.S. and other countries to criticize the invasion of Iraq: the weapons of mass destruction had been the main reason for going to war, and now they couldn't be found. In fact, it wasn't clear that Iraq had possessed any such weapons. When Sanchez was asked whether he believed that Saddam had such weapons, he replied "That's a question I can't answer."

Even after the war ended, fighting continued in Iraq and U.S. troops continued to die. Some people began to compare the engagement to the Vietnam War, where U.S. forces had become involved in a prolonged conflict that they had difficulty winning or ending. Sanchez felt such comparisons were totally wrong. "It's not Vietnam," he said, "and there's no way you can make the comparison to the quagmire of Vietnam, when you look at the progress that's being made." The general went out of his way to point out the positive things that were happening in Iraq. "The progress is unbelievable. We just have to make sure that the American public realizes that and understands that their sons and daughters are making a tremendous contribution to the peace and stability and the democratic future of Iraq."

Where's Hussein?

When coalition forces took over Iraq in April 2003, they toppled Saddam Hussein's government, but Hussein himself had escaped capture. So had his sons and some other key figures in the government. In the months that followed, Sanchez directed his troops to hunt these people down. In July 2003, U.S. troops killed Saddam's two sons, Uday and Qusay Hussein, in the town of Mosul. Still, Saddam Hussein remained on the loose.

Sanchez believed that finding the former dictator was crucial because it would show Iraqis that Hussein could never return to power. Also, it might

—— *"* ——

Sanchez was honest about the challenges in Iraq. "We did expect instability before we arrived here, . . . [but we did not expect] the political and economic structures to shut down. That was clearly a surprise—at least for me it was." Yet he remained confident that the coalition forces could not be beaten in battle by the insurgents. "The stark reality is that they cannot defeat us, and they know it. I am supremely confident of this reality."

—— *"* ——

discourage the insurgents who were attacking coalition forces. In the fall of 2003, the hunt was still on. When Sanchez was asked how close he had come to capturing Saddam, he replied "not close enough. I don't know how close I've got to him, but by God I've got to get closer."

Soon he did. On December 13, U.S. forces searched an area around a mud hut near the town of Tikrit. In a hidden underground room that the soldiers called a "spider hole" they found Hussein. He was captured without a fight and transferred to a detention facility. There, Sanchez had his first face-to-face meeting with the former dictator. Hussein was now a bearded and bedraggled figure who looked as if he had suffered during his months on the run. "It was sobering to be able to stand in the presence of a man that was such a brutal dictator," Sanchez said of the meeting, "and to ensure that he's no longer going to abuse his people." Sanchez didn't feel that Hussein's capture was going to end the armed opposition in Iraq, but he did see it as a step in the right direction. "I think what we've accomplished clearly by arresting Saddam is that we've eliminated the source of fear that has pervaded across Iraq for at least 35 years, and that still continued to hinder our progress toward safety and stability."

> "I think what we've accomplished clearly by arresting Saddam is that we've eliminated the source of fear that has pervaded across Iraq for at least 35 years, and that still continued to hinder our progress toward safety and stability."

New Challenges

As Sanchez predicted, the dangers faced by coalition forces continued. Insurgent attacks continued through the early months of 2004, and the situation got worse in April. That month, 139 soldiers from the U.S. and its allies were killed. Many of them died in terrorist-style attacks, but there was also a pitched battle in the town of Fallujah. After laying siege to the town, coalition troops withdrew without ousting the insurgents based there. Sanchez had his hands full with the ongoing attacks and the many problems involved in managing affairs in Iraq. But then in May 2004, he faced a challenge of a different kind. It proved to be the most serious of his command.

A series of news stories revealed that U.S. troops had been involved in the mistreatment of Iraqi prisoners. The news stories were accompanied by very disturbing photos of U.S. troops abusing the prisoners. The incidents had taken place at Abu Ghraib (*a-boo GRAAYB*) prison near Baghdad between October and December of 2003. Prisoners had been beaten, deprived of clothing, forced to pose in humiliating positions, and threatened and attacked by guard dogs. One prisoner was killed while in custody. These actions were violations of the Geneva Conventions, a series of specific guidelines created by the international community that govern the way prisoners of war should be treated. Some of the U.S. soldiers involved said they had treated the prisoners badly so the Iraqis would give information to military intelligence interrogators.

Sanchez reviewing Iraqi troops on parade.

The photos created an uproar in the United States and all around the world. President Bush and many other U.S. officials had repeatedly said that the war in Iraq would help the Iraqi people. The stories of abuse cast doubt on those claims and made the U.S. presence in Iraq less popular among Americans. Seven soldiers faced criminal charges for their role in the mistreatment, but the story didn't end with them. There were suspicions that those charged were following orders from superior officers.

Facing Questions

Because he was the senior commander in Iraq, Sanchez faced tough questions about what had happened at Abu Ghraib. He was called to Washington, D.C., to testify before the Senate Armed Services Committee. He reported that he had first learned of the abuse in January 2004 and had launched an investigation soon afterward. (That investigation became the basis of the news stories that appeared several months later.) While few people believed that Sanchez had a direct role in the prisoner mistreatment, he had issued an order in mid November 2003 that placed Abu Ghraib under the command of military intelligence personnel. Some people believed that this change had set the stage for the abuse.

In July 2004, Sanchez stepped down as the senior commander in Iraq and was replaced by General George Casey Jr. When the change was announced in late May, senior U.S. officials claimed that the change had nothing to do with the Abu Ghraib incident. Secretary of State Colin Powell said that replacing Sanchez was part of "the normal scheme of things," and President Bush stated that Sanchez had "done a fabulous job" in Iraq. Other observers, however, felt that the reassignment had been partly caused by the prison controversy. After turning over command to Casey, Sanchez admitted that "Abu Ghraib was a great defeat for the coalition here in this country." Sanchez has made few other comments to the press, but his wife, Maria Elena, said that the general isn't shaken by the controversy. "He's not worried, " she said, "because he has nothing to be ashamed of and nothing to regret." She also reported that Sanchez had told her, "don't worry, they will find out. The truth will come out." The general's next assignment has yet to be decided.

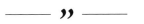

Sanchez feels that U.S. forces have a very good chance of succeeding, as long as people in the United States remain committed to the mission. "I really believe that the only way we are going to lose here is if we walk away from it like we did in Vietnam. . . . If the political will fails and the support of the American public fails, that's the only way we can lose."

Whatever the ultimate outcome of events, Sanchez has expressed a strong commitment to the U.S. mission in Iraq. This is partly due to similarities he noticed between the tough conditions in Iraq and those he experienced as a boy. "At times I fly around and see situations that remind me of the tough times that I went through, some of the poverty. . . . I sometimes see myself in the kids that are out there." He believes that the intervention of the coalition forces will do a lot to help those young people and that the U.S. has done "absolutely the right thing for this country by having gotten rid of Saddam." He also feels that U.S. forces have a very good chance of succeeding, as long as people in the United States remain committed to the mission. "I really believe that the only way we are going to lose here is if we walk away from it like we did in Vietnam. . . . If the political will fails and the support of the American public fails, that's the only way we can lose."

A change of command ceremony at Al-Faw Palace in Baghdad, July 1, 2004: Lt. General Ricardo Sanchez (left), outgoing Commanding General of Coalition Forces in Iraq; General John P. Abizaid (center), Commanding General of U.S. Central Command; and General George W. Casey (right), incoming Commanding General of Coalition Forces in Iraq.

Being a Role Model

As the highest-ranking Hispanic in the U.S. Army and only the ninth Hispanic general in the army's history, Sanchez has become an important role model for many young Hispanic soldiers. When asked about his willingness to be a role model, Sanchez answered without hesitation: "Absolutely. Whether you like it or not, once you are honored with these kinds of responsibilities, and more importantly blessed by all those great people over the years who allowed you to succeed, it's inevitable that you will be looked at as a role model. There's a tremendous responsibility that goes along with it. Primarily, it's making sure that at every opportunity you can engage with young people and share with them some of the difficulties and successes and maybe even some of the breaks that allowed you to succeed." The accusations about the scandal at Abu Ghraib prison have made his status as a role model more problematic. Still, many are glad to see a Hispanic leader attain a position of such authority.

MAJOR INFLUENCES

Sanchez has made it clear that his mother was the greatest influence on his life and his values. "She was very disciplined and focused and taught

———— **"** ————

"She was very disciplined and focused and taught us about perseverance and dedication and definitely about family," Sanchez said about his mother. "Those are the values the Hispanic community embraces. It's patriotism, service to country, and being very loyal to your family. When I became a soldier, the ethics and the value system of the military profession fit almost perfectly with that ethic. It made it very easy for me to adapt to the military value system."

———— **"** ————

us about perseverance and dedication and definitely about family," he recalls of her firm approach. "Those are the values the Hispanic community embraces. It's patriotism, service to country, and being very loyal to your family. When I became a soldier, the ethics and the value system of the military profession fit almost perfectly with that ethic. It made it very easy for me to adapt to the military value system."

MARRIAGE AND FAMILY

Sanchez met his wife, Maria Elena Garza (she has the same first name as Sanchez's mother), while attending college in Kingsville, Texas, and they were married in December 1973. Sanchez has said that his wife is "my best friend and my greatest supporter. . . . She's just made so many sacrifices for me and my family. She's the reason I am a general today." The Sanchezes have four children, two boys and two girls; a fifth child died in a car accident.

HOBBIES AND OTHER INTERESTS

In his spare time, Sanchez likes to jog and play racquetball and tennis. He also enjoys studying military history.

HONORS AND AWARDS

Distinguished Alumni Award (Texas A&M University): 2003
Hispanic of the Year (*Hispanic* magazine): 2003
Army Commendation Medal
Army Achievement Medal with Oak Leaf Cluster
Bronze Star with "V" Device and Oak Leaf Cluster
Defense Superior Service Medal
Joint Service Commendation Medal

Legion of Merit
Liberation of Kuwait Medals (Saudi Arabia and Kuwait)
Master Parachutist Badge
Meritorious Service Medal with Four Oak Leaf Clusters
Southwest Asia Campaign Medal

FURTHER READING

Periodicals

Chicago Tribune, Oct. 20, 2003, p.CN1
Corpus Christi (Tex.) Caller-Times, Dec. 21, 2003, p.A1; May 26, 2004, p.A1
Hispanic, Dec. 2003, pp.8 and 44
International Herald Tribune (Paris), Jan. 12, 2004, p.2
Los Angeles Times, Sept. 14, 2003, p.A10
New York Times, Nov. 12, 2003, p.A8; Dec. 15, 2003, p.A18; May 9, 2004, section 1, p.1
San Antonio Express-News, June 23, 2003, p.A1; Dec. 28, 2003, p.A1
USA Today, May 26, 2004, p.A5

Online Articles

http://www.cnn.com/SPECIALS/2003/iraq
(CNN.com "War in Iraq," undated)

ADDRESS

Lt. General Ricardo Sanchez
V Corps, U.S. Army
Römerstrasse 168
Geb. # D-69126
Heidelberg, Germany

WORLD WIDE WEB SITE

http://www.vcorps.army.mil/Leaders/LTGS.htm

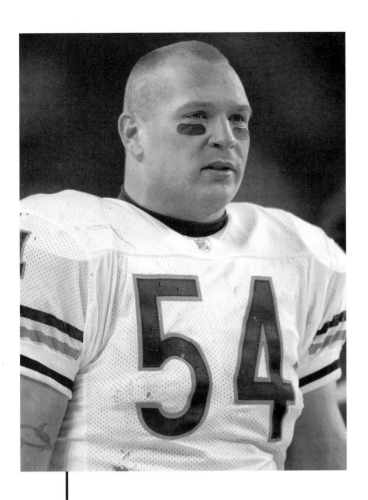

Brian Urlacher 1978-

American Professional Football Player with the
Chicago Bears
NFL Defensive Player of the Year for 2001

BIRTH

Brian Keith Urlacher (pronounced *UR-LACK-ER*) was born on
May 25, 1978, in Pasco, Washington. He weighed a whopping
11 pounds, 8 ounces at birth—an early clue that he was going
to be big. Brian is the son of Brad Urlacher and Lavoyda (Bee-
man) Urlacher. His parents divorced when he was in elementary school, and Brian saw little of his biological father after

that. He was raised by his mother and his stepfather, Troy Lenard. Brian has an older sister, Sheri, and a younger brother, Casey.

YOUTH

Brian spent his early years in Washington State. When his parents divorced in the mid-1980s, the children remained with their mother. In 1986 Lavoyda Urlacher decided to move the family to Lovington, New Mexico, where her parents lived. Brian spent the rest of his youth in Lovington, a small town of about 9,000 people in the southeastern part of the state, near the Texas-New Mexico border. His father remained in Washington and had little contact with his children after they moved to New Mexico.

The family did not have much money. Lavoyda was sometimes forced to work several jobs in order to make ends meet. In fact, she once held three different jobs at the same time—at a grocery store, a convenience store, and a laundry. "We ate a lot of macaroni and cheese during that time," Lavoyda recalled, "but the kids never went without. I had energy and desire, and I swore we were going to make it one way or another." Busy as she was, Lavoyda still found time to enroll her children in sporting activities and attended as many of their games as she could. Brian and Casey, who are just a year apart in age, became obsessed with sports, competing in everything from basketball to baseball to football to swimming.

> *Urlacher's family did not have much money, and his mother worked several jobs in order to make ends meet. "We ate a lot of macaroni and cheese during that time," she recalled, "but the kids never went without. I had energy and desire, and I swore we were going to make it one way or another."*

A New Dad

For several years the Urlacher children missed having a father in their lives. Then, in 1992, Lavoyda married a man named Troy Lenard. Lenard had a son of his own and worked in the oilfields that surround Lovington. The Urlacher children had no trouble accepting their new stepfather's presence in their lives. "Troy stood right in for our biological father," Brian recalled. "To this day we consider him our real dad. . . . Just like my mom, he took care of us."

Though Troy and Lavoyda later divorced, Lenard was there at a key time for Brian. He provided a sense of discipline for a boy who was just entering his teenage years. Though he was not overly strict, Troy let the children know that if they got out of line, they risked a meeting with "Uncle Henry"—a board that Troy threatened to use as a paddle. The mere threat was usually enough to make the boys behave. In fact, Troy recalled that he only paddled the boys once: "I made them grab their ankles, they got one swat, and that was it."

In most cases, though, Brian did not require any kind of punishment. His mother had laid down the law very clearly even before Troy was around. If Brian seriously misbehaved—by cutting classes or drinking alcohol, for instance—he would not be allowed to play sports. This was a threat far more terrifying than Uncle Henry, so Brian followed the rules. In fact, the only heavy drinking that Brian did in high school was downing lots and lots of chocolate milk.

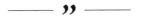

> "*Casey could always stay right with me in everything,*" *Urlacher remembered.* "*It felt more like we were competitors sharing the same house than like we were brothers.*"

Like many brothers, Brian and Casey became strong rivals, always trying to outdo one another. This was true when they were competing on the field, and even when they went fishing or lifted weights. Their competition became so intense that it sometimes seemed as if the boys really disliked one another. Their mother started signing Brian and Casey up for separate teams to help create a little breathing room between them. "Casey could always stay right with me in everything," Brian remembered. "It felt more like we were competitors sharing the same house than like we were brothers."

EDUCATION

Urlacher attended public schools in Lovington, where he earned mostly As and Bs. Not surprisingly, playing on the school athletic teams was very important to him. By the time he got to high school, his favorite sports were football and basketball. He played both of these sports for the Lovington Wildcats, as well as being a member of the track team.

Though he was very large as a baby and eventually became a big, imposing football player, Urlacher was a rather normal-sized teenager during his first years in high school. As a freshman, he stood about 5 feet, 10 inches tall and weighed around 160 pounds. Fortunately, he was not done growing. In his final two years he shot up to 6 feet, 3 inches and packed on an additional 50 pounds. Most of the new weight was muscle, as Urlacher launched an intensive weight-training program at the suggestion of one of the Wildcat football coaches. He had always been a fast runner, and he lost none of his quickness as he got larger, posting an impressive time of 4.57 seconds in the 40-yard dash. This combination of strength and speed has been the key to Urlacher's success.

Hometown Star

Urlacher started his high school football career as a wide receiver. But as his size and skills increased, he played a lot of different roles for the Wildcats, including safety on defense, receiver and running back on offense, and kick returner on special teams. With his help, Lovington became one of the best teams in the state of New Mexico. The Wildcats made it to the division AAA state championship in his junior year, but lost.

In Urlacher's senior year, the team went undefeated in the regular season and once again reached the championship game. The Wildcats took a 14-7 lead late in the game. Then, in a moment that became legendary in Lovington, Urlacher made a leaping interception to seal the game and claim the state title for the Wildcats. He finished his senior year with 61 catches for 15 touchdowns, and he added a total of eight more touchdowns through rushing, punt returns, and kickoff returns. Urlacher received all-state honors as both a wide receiver and a safety.

Even though he was the star of his high school football team, Urlacher did not receive much attention from college recruiters — partly because Lovington High was a small school. He dreamed of attending Texas Tech, which was located just 100 miles from Lovington, but the university did not offer him a scholarship. As it turned out, the University of New Mexico (UNM) in Albuquerque was the only major college to offer him an athletic scholarship, and he was not even considered one of their hottest prospects. In fact, the university sent an assistant coach to meet with Urlacher because, as he recalled, "I wasn't a big enough recruit for the head coach to visit."

Still, Urlacher was grateful for the opportunity to attend college and continue to play football. "I'm just glad someone found me," he said. "The chance I got from New Mexico was a blessing." After graduating from high school in 1996, Urlacher packed his bags and moved to Albuquerque. He majored in criminology at UNM, but he did not complete his degree. He

*Urlacher was a star defensive back during his colllege days playing for the
University of New Mexico Lobos.*

stopped attending classes following his final season of college football, as he was preparing to begin his NFL career.

CAREER HIGHLIGHTS

College — The University of New Mexico Lobos

Urlacher's college football career with the UNM Lobos got off to a rather slow start. During his freshman season in 1996, he failed to make the starting defensive squad and played mostly on the kicking teams. Although he was not yet making a big splash on the field, Urlacher continued to work hard. "I just feel like I always have something to prove," he explained. "If you have that attitude throughout your career, I think you're always going to do well because you're going to work harder than everybody else." Urlacher spent many hours in the weight room, bulking up to 235 pounds. He also grew another inch to reach his current height of 6 feet, 4 inches. His growth caused a sensation when he returned to Lovington following his first year of college. "I didn't recognize him," recalled a friend of the Urlacher family. "I couldn't find his neck."

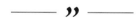

"I just feel like I always have something to prove," Urlacher explained. "If you have that attitude throughout your career, I think you're always going to do well because you're going to work harder than everybody else."

Like most new college students, Urlacher had to adjust to being away from his home and family. He found it most difficult to be separated from his brother Casey, even though their sibling rivalry had led to numerous fights over the years. "Until Casey wasn't around anymore, I didn't realize how much I could miss someone and how much they could mean to me," Urlacher said.

During his sophomore season in 1997, Urlacher still did not make the starting lineup. But he did see a lot of action at linebacker (a defensive position in which the player lines up behind the line of scrimmage and is responsible for both pass and run defense). Ranking second on the team in tackles by season's end, he was beginning to show his skills. The Lobos had a good season that year, winning nine games and going to the Insight.com Bowl, where they lost to Arizona.

Prior to Urlacher's junior year UNM got a new head coach, Rocky Long, who decided to reorganize the team's defense. In fact, Long decided to make Urlacher the centerpiece of the new design. Instead of playing as a standard linebacker, Urlacher was moved to the "Lobo back" position—a combination of free safety and linebacker. From his position about ten yards behind the line of scrimmage, he could defend against passes and also pursue rushers carrying the ball. As Coach Long explained it, the new defense "allowed Brian a chance to be in on every play."

The new position was perfectly matched to Urlacher's skills, and he wasted no time in making his mark. He racked up 178 tackles for the 1998 season, the highest total in the nation. His outstanding defensive production continued in his senior season, when he tallied 154 tackles to rank fourth in the nation. Over the course of these two seasons, Urlacher went from a mostly unknown second stringer to one of the best defensive players in the country. He also continued to demonstrate his versatility on the field. He returned punts and kickoffs for the Lobos and, in his senior year, occasionally played as an offensive receiver, scoring six touchdowns. Unfortunately, UNM posted losing seasons in both Urlacher's junior and senior years.

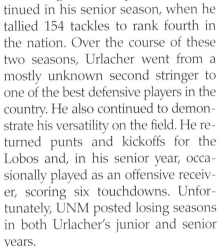

"This kind of thing had never happened to me before," Urlacher said of his early struggles as an NFL rookie. "I was so disappointed. I was down on myself, and I wasn't sure what I could do to get myself playing again."

At the close of his last college season, Urlacher was named to several All-America teams and was one of three finalists for the Jim Thorpe Award, which is presented each year to the best defensive back in the country. He even finished 12th in the voting for the prestigious Heisman Trophy, which honors the best college football player of the year.

NFL—The Chicago Bears

Urlacher's performance impressed many professional football scouts. When the 2000 NFL draft took place in April, he was selected ninth overall by the Chicago Bears. He soon signed a five-year contract that paid him $13 million. Urlacher knew that he might have received a larger contract if he would have extended the negotiations, but he was eager to start playing football. "I want to be with my teammates from the beginning," he said, meaning that he did not want to miss training camp by holding off on signing his contract. "And I don't want to disappoint the fans."

Urlacher tackles New York Giants wide receiver Ike Hilliard in action from his rookie season.

At first Urlacher had trouble adjusting to the fact that he was suddenly a millionaire. Shortly before the draft he had admitted, "I think a hundred dollars is a lot of money." That attitude did not change quickly after his big payday. In fact, the first meal he ate after signing his contract was not at a fancy restaurant, but at McDonald's.

Unfortunately, the transition to the NFL did not go smoothly for Urlacher. Unlike UNM, the Bears did not design a special defense around him. Instead, Urlacher had to play as a true linebacker—up close to the line of scrimmage. He started out as the team's strong-side linebacker, meaning that it was usually his responsibility to match up against the offensive tight end. It was a position he had no experience with, and he had difficulty adjusting. "Most of what I'm learning now, it's all new," he admitted in an early training camp. "I screw up every play just about."

Urlacher also found that the speed of the professional game was much different from what he had experienced in college. "Here everything is much faster, especially being close to the line of scrimmage," he explained. "You don't have as much time to react because the linemen are on you so quick." On top of everything else, Urlacher faced the pressure of trying to fill the shoes of some of the great linebackers who had played for the Chicago Bears in the past, including Dick Butkus and Mike Singletary.

Even before preseason, the Bears had announced that Urlacher would start on defense. But the coaches grew discouraged by the troubles he was having. Just before the regular season got underway, Urlacher was demoted and another player took over his starting spot. "This kind of thing had never happened to me before," he said. "I was so disappointed. I was down on myself, and I wasn't sure what I could do to get myself playing again." As it turned out, all he could do was wait for another chance. Fortunately, the wait was short.

Before the third game of the season, the Bears' starting middle linebacker, Barry Minter, was injured. Urlacher took over the position, and suddenly everything clicked. In his first game in this new position, he racked up 13 tackles and one quarterback sack. He had found his place, and he was not about to give it up. Minter never got his starting job back. "I needed more space to roam," Urlacher said of playing in the middle. "I was too confined at outside linebacker." By the close of the 2000 season he had notched 165 tackles, eight sacks, and two interceptions. He was voted the NFL Defensive Rookie of the Year and played in the Pro Bowl. In just 14 games, Urlacher had proven himself one of the best linebackers in the business.

In the Spotlight

During the off-season following his stellar rookie year, Urlacher made a brief visit to Lovington for a special occasion: his high school football and basketball jerseys were retired in a half-time ceremony at a Wildcats basketball game. He also became the first inductee into the Lovington Hall of Fame. To his hometown, Urlacher had already become a legend. Josh Faith, the son of the high school football coach, said that Urlacher's success "lifts the whole town up because he's a Lovington product. It makes us all feel good. It shows us that dreams really do come true, and if you set your mind to it, you can do anything." The visit brought back fond memories for Urlacher. "It's the same way as when I left it," he said of Lovington. "That's why I like it. It will always be the way I left it." In appreciation of the help he got from his high school, Urlacher donated warm-up suits and other equipment for the sports teams.

The honors he received in Lovington were an early sign that Urlacher was becoming famous—and not just in his hometown. The city of Chicago needed just one season to go crazy over Urlacher, and the attention he received there and all around the country grew more intense over the next few years. At one point in 2002, replicas of his jersey outsold those of all other players in the NFL. Urlacher has never been the type to bask in the spotlight, and he sometimes had difficulty dealing with his fame. "Man, I'll

Urlacher scored the winning touchdown on a fake field goal in this 2001 game against the Washington Redskins.

never get used to it," he said of the endless interviews with reporters. "They always ask the same questions over and over again."

Fame also made it more difficult for him to do simple things like go out to a restaurant for dinner. He found that he had to choose the places he appeared in public carefully, and he often wore a hat to avoid being recognized. On the other hand, Urlacher willingly devoted a lot of time to sign-

459

In 2001 Urlacher earned NFL Defensive Player of the Year honors.

ing autographs. He realized that without sports fans, he would not get paid to play football. "The people are coming out here . . . to see you," he said. "They expect you to give something back to them, which I don't mind doing." He was especially happy to give his autograph to young fans. "I'll sign for kids all day long," he stated. But he found some grown-up autograph hounds less to his liking. "When you see the adults pushing the kids out of the way, it kind of makes you mad," he acknowledged.

Winning and Losing with the Bears

Urlacher's emergence as one of the league's best linebackers was one of the few bright spots for the Bears in 2000. The team finished with just five wins that year, and they were not expected to fare much better the following season. But the 2001 season turned out to be a pleasant surprise for Chicago. With an explosive offense and a tough defense anchored by Urlacher, the team posted a 13-3 record and won the NFC Central Division. They faced the Philadelphia Eagles in the playoffs, but were beaten 33-13. Urlacher posted 148 tackles, 6 sacks, and 3 interceptions for the year. He even scored two touchdowns: one by running back a fumble he recovered, and the other by catching a pass on a fake field-goal play. Urlacher led all defensive players in fan voting for the Pro Bowl, and he was named the NFL Defensive Player of the Year by *Football Digest*.

> ——— **"** ———
>
> *"It makes things easier for me and my family, I know that much,"Urlacher said about his many endorsement deals."And that's really what it comes down to in life, I think, is how well you take care of yourself and your family. But we don't flaunt it or anything like that."*
>
> ——— **"** ———

The Bears entered the 2002 season with high hopes. But many key players went down with injuries, and Chicago finished with just four wins for the year. Though he was disappointed with his team's record, Urlacher posted the best numbers of his career. He tallied 17 tackles in the opening game against the Minnesota Vikings, and his season total of 214 set a new record for the Bears, breaking the mark held by Dick Butkus for 30 years.

Given Urlacher's performance and popularity, it was clear that his next contract was going to make him very wealthy. Many wondered if he would become a free agent when his contract expired, so he would be able to field offers from other NFL teams. But Urlacher claimed that he wanted to stay in Chicago. "I can't imagine playing anywhere else," he said. "Never." Although his initial contract extended through the 2005 season, the Bears were so eager to hang onto their star that they began negotiating with Urlacher early. Before the 2003 season began, he signed a new deal worth $56 million over nine years.

Thanks to his popularity, Urlacher was able to supplement his income by signing endorsement deals with a number of companies, including Nike, Sega, Campbell's Soup, and Cadillac. "It makes things easier for me and my family, I know that much," he admitted. "And that's really what it comes down to in life, I think, is how well you take care of yourself and your family. But we don't flaunt it or anything like that." Urlacher had long been known as a humble and down-to-earth person, and he was determined to stay that way. "I like to think of myself as a regular guy, except I play football for a living," he explained. "I try not to be an arrogant turd out there."

Unfortunately, the Bears had another disappointing season in 2003, finishing 7-9. Head coach Dick Jauron—the only NFL coach Urlacher had known—was fired at the end of the season and replaced by Lovie Smith. Although Urlacher had a good year by most linebackers' standards, racking up 153 tackles, his production declined from the previous year. He also failed to cause a fumble or make an interception all season long.

If his past accomplishments are any indication, Urlacher will certainly be working as hard as he can to put Chicago back on the winning track. "The reason I'm here is because of my work ethic," he stated. "I've always had it instilled in me that you have to work hard if you want something." This attitude has contributed to his reputation as one of the top linebackers in the league. Mike Brown, who has played beside Urlacher in the Bears defense, has witnessed the linebacker's talents at close range: "I've seen him take on linemen and drive them into the backfield," Brown noted. "I've seen him hit fullbacks and stop them cold. I've seen him run down running backs from behind. I've seen him cover wide receivers. Who else can do all those things?"

MARRIAGE AND FAMILY

Urlacher married Laurie Faulhaber in 2000. They have a daughter named Pamela, who was born in December of that year. The family lives in Lake Bluff, Illinois, a suburb north of Chicago. Their home features a first-class game room and big-screen television in the basement.

Laurie has described Urlacher as "an amazing father," and there are many accounts of his devotion to his family. As a result, many fans were shocked when he filed for divorce in the spring of 2003. That September, he was spotted at a Las Vegas nightclub with model and celebrity Paris Hilton. A short time later, Hilton sat in Urlacher's skybox during a Bears home game. But Urlacher insisted that reports of a romance between them were exaggerated. "You're seen with someone and all of a sudden you're getting mar-

Urlacher pressures Green Bay quarterback Brett Favre in 2003 action.

ried to them," he said. "It's unbelievable. Things get blown out of proportion so bad." While Urlacher and his wife subsequently tried to reconcile, they ultimately decided to divorce.

Urlacher remains close to his parents and his brother and sister. Once he signed his first NFL contract, he used some of the money to show them his appreciation. He bought every member of his family a new car, for example, and purchased a ranch in Texas for Troy Lenard. He also brought his brother Casey to Illinois and helped him enroll at Lake Forest College. Casey lived with his older brother and played football for Lake Forest until his graduation in 2002.

HOBBIES AND OTHER INTERESTS

Urlacher had been an enthusiastic ping-pong player since he was young, and also enjoys playing air hockey. He likes to relax while listening to music, especially by pop groups like N'Sync and the Backstreet Boys.

HONORS AND AWARDS

First Team Collegiate Football All-American (Football Writers Association of America): 1999
First Team Collegiate Football All-American (Associated Press): 1999

Brian Piccolo Award (Chicago Bears): 2000
NFL Defensive Rookie of the Year (Associated Press): 2000
NFL Rookie of the Year (*Sporting News*): 2000
NFL Pro Bowl: 2000-2003
Unsung Hero Award (NFL Players Association): 2000
All-Pro Team (Associated Press): 2001-2002
NFL Defensive Player of the Year (*Football Digest*): 2001

FURTHER READING

Books

Urlacher: Windy City Warrior, 2002

Periodicals

Albuquerque Journal, Jan. 13, 2002, p.D1
Chicago, Aug. 2002, p.78
Chicago Tribune, Apr. 24, 2000; Feb. 12, 2001, p.N1; Aug. 1, 2001, p.N1; Dec.
    9, 2001; Aug. 8, 2002, p.N10
Dallas Morning News, Apr. 13, 2000, p.B13
Denver Post, Aug. 9, 2002, p.D1
New York Times, Jan. 15, 2002, p.D5
Sporting News, Mar. 27, 2000, p.18; Aug. 6, 2001, p.10; Nov. 5, 2001, p.42
Sports Illustrated, May 8, 2000; Oct. 29, 2001, p.50; Sep. 23, 2002, p.52

ADDRESS

Brian Urlacher
The Chicago Bears
Halas Hall
1000 Football Drive
Lake Forest, IL 60045

WORLD WIDE WEB SITES

http://www.brianurlacher.com
http://www.nfl.com/players
http://www.nflplayers.com
http://www.chicagobears.com/team

Alexa Vega 1988-
American Actress
Stars as Carmen Cortez in the Popular *Spy Kids*
Movie Trilogy

BIRTH

Alexa Vega was born on August 27, 1988, in Miami, Florida.
She is of Colombian and Italian ancestry and is fluent in Spanish. She has three younger sisters, Krizia, Makenzie (who also
acts), and Greylin, plus an older half-sister, Margaux. Her
mother, Gina Rue, was a model and actress who now serves as
Vega's manager. No information is available about her father.

—— " ——

Despite her success as an actress, Vega still faces the same types of experiences at school that all kids face. She had this to say about ninth grade: "To a certain extent it's wonderful but you still have all these gossipy girls, the cheerleaders. It's so cliquey." Still, she says she enjoys attending a regular school: "I love it cause it's the best of both worlds. I can go back and be a normal kid, play sports, and have fun."

—— " ——

Vega doesn't really talk about him, except that he isn't part of the family anymore: "I have four sisters and since my dad's not here anymore, we're all girls."

YOUTH AND EDUCATION

Vega was just four years old when her family moved from Florida to southern California. Her mother hoped to break into acting, and Alexa had an offer to audition for the sitcom "Full House." The move to Hollywood took so long that Alexa missed the audition. Instead, her mother found a job with a talent agency, a business that helps artists and performers find acting jobs. She soon realized that her precocious daughter had the talent to be an actress. Vega's first audition was successful, and she soon won a part on the TV series "Evening Shade" starring Burt Reynolds.

Because she spends a lot of time filming, Vega often gets tutored on the movie set. But when she's not making a movie, she attends a regular school. In 2003, Vega began tenth grade at Notre Dame Girls Catholic High School in Sherman Oaks, California. Despite her success as an actress, she still faces the same types of experiences at school that all kids face, some great and some not so great. She had this to say about her experiences in ninth grade: "To a certain extent it's wonderful but you still have all these gossipy girls, the cheerleaders. It's so cliquey." Still, she says she enjoys attending a regular school: "I love it cause it's the best of both worlds. I can go back and be a normal kid, play sports, and have fun." Her favorite subject is math, and she plans to attend college after she graduates from high school.

CAREER HIGHLIGHTS

Developing a Career in Television

Vega has been working in the entertainment business her whole life. She began her career at age five, when she landed the role of Emily Newton on the CBS series "Evening Shade." This series focused on Wood Newton, a football coach in small-town Arkansas, and his family and friends. Vega joined the cast as the Newtons' youngest daughter during the show's last season, from 1993 to 1994. During this first acting experience Vega was surrounded with well-known performers: Burt Reynolds and Marilu Henner played her parents, and Ossie Davis, Hal Holbrook, and Charles Durning were also regular cast members. After the series concluded, Vega made guest appearances on the hit medical dramas "ER" and "Chicago Hope." She also won small parts in two television movies, *It Was Him or Us* (1995) and *A Promise to Caroline* (1996). In both of these melodramas she appeared in flashbacks as a younger version of the main character.

In 1996 Vega returned to series television with a role in the ABC sitcom "Life's Work." This series followed the work and home lives of Lisa Hunter, a busy lawyer married to a basketball coach. Vega played Tess, the oldest of Lisa's two kids. The series didn't find a big audience and lasted only a single season. Vega had better luck with her next sitcom role, in the CBS series "Ladies Man." The show starred Alfred Molina as a furniture maker in a household full of women, including Vega as one of his daughters. This series lasted two full seasons, from 1999 to 2001, but wasn't a big hit.

As she grew older, however, Vega began finding bigger parts in television movies. In 2000 she appeared in *Run the Wild Fields*, a historical drama aired by the cable network Showtime. Vega played Pug, the tomboy daughter of a soldier missing in action during World War II. The film shows Pug and her mother struggling to run their farm alone until a young drifter lends them a hand. Vega had a large role in this film, in which she received third billing. In 2001 she had another significant role in the Hallmark Hall of Fame drama *Follow the Stars Home*. She played Amy, a girl who helps a neighbor woman with her disabled child. While Amy is a good-natured girl, she comes from an unstable home: her widowed mother drinks too much, and her mother's boyfriend is abusive. While the movie itself didn't get terrific reviews, one critic singled out Vega's excellent performance and noted that the young actress "is so winning that she makes a good case for building the movie around Amy."

Making a Mark in Hollywood

Vega's early career wasn't limited to just television. She had small parts in several movies, including *Little Giants* (1994) and *Nine Months* (1995). In both of these comedies she had a bit role as someone's daughter or little sister. In the 1996 film *Twister* she had a brief but memorable part as the

Vega appeared with Joanne Whalley and Sean Patrick Flanery in the Showtime historical drama Run the Wild Fields.

young version of Helen Hunt's tornado-chasing scientist, JoAnne. In the opening scene of the film we see young JoAnne, played by Vega, as she and her family hide from a deadly tornado. The scene required Vega to look terrified as her father is snatched away by fierce winds — a special effect that was added after she filmed her scene.

Vega continued her Hollywood career with a series of film roles where she played the daughter to some of Hollywood's biggest stars. In *The Glimmer Man* (1996), for instance, she played the daughter of action star Steven Seagal. That same year she played Alec Baldwin's daughter in the drama *Ghosts of Mississippi*, which was based on a true story. Baldwin stars as prosecutor Bobby DeLaughter, who re-opened a 25-year-old murder case against white supremacist Byron De La Beckwith. Beckwith shot black civil-rights activist Medgar Evers to death in 1963, but went free after two all-white juries failed to convict him. The film tells the story from the point-of-view of the prosecutor, including how his discoveries affect his relationships with his family. Many critics felt these family scenes detracted from the drama of the story, but they gave Vega valuable experience nonetheless.

In 1999, Vega co-starred as Michelle Pfeiffer's daughter in the film *The Deep End of the Ocean*. This family drama shows the devastating effects of a kidnaping on a Midwestern family, especially when the missing son is rediscovered after an absence of seven years. Vega played Kerry, the daughter who was only a baby when her brother went missing. She is confused when this complete stranger moves into her house and changes her family. The film received mixed reviews overall, but was praised for the believable family dynamics portrayed by Vega and her co-stars.

Despite working on big Hollywood films, Vega has tried to stay a normal, down-to-earth girl. Working on film sets meant that she was surrounded by adults—and adult language. So she developed a method of getting people to watch their language by charging cast and crew for each swear word said in her presence. "I collect a dollar for each dirty word I hear, five dollars for each use of one particularly dirty four-letter word," she explained. "During the filming of one movie . . . I collected a total of $700. I gave it to charity."

> **"**
>
> *Working on film sets meant that Vega was surrounded by adults— and adult language. "I collect a dollar for each dirty word I hear, five dollars for each use of one particularly dirty four-letter word," she explained. "During the filming of one movie . . . I collected a total of $700. I gave it to charity."*
>
> **"**

Starring as a Spy Kid

Vega spent half a year auditioning and then training for her first starring role, as Carmen Cortez in *Spy Kids* (2001). Robert Rodriguez, the writer and director of the movie, originally thought Carmen's character should be younger than a preteen, but he decided to change the part after seeing Vega audition. "From the first time I saw her, I thought she was amazing," Rodriguez remarked. "You buy that she's strong, take-charge, and confident, that she can strap on a jet pack and rescue her brother." To prepare for her role, Vega dyed her blond hair dark brown and spent over a month in gymnastics training. She ended up performing most of her own stunts,

Vega admits that she and Daryl Sabara fought while making Spy Kids, *"but it was play-fighting, normal brother-sister stuff."*

including her favorite, a spectacular chase scene wearing a jet pack. "Every kid dreams of flying, and I got to do that." She also contributed one of the funniest one-liners in the film: Carmen's "Oh, shiitake mushrooms!" came from Vega's own experience — a phrase a crew member used to avoid paying one of her "cursing fines."

Vega plays Carmen Cortez, a normal 12-year-old girl with an irritating little brother (played by Daryl Sabara) and boring parents (played by Antonio Banderas and Carla Gugino). When her parents are kidnaped, Carmen discovers they had a secret life as OSS spies before they retired to raise their family. In fact, not only were they spies, they were among the greatest spies in history. Carmen and her brother, Juni, must spring into action to locate and rescue their mom and dad. Along the way they find a lost uncle, amazing gadgets, robotic children, a sinister television show host, and an evil lair that is more fun house than madhouse. Although there is plenty of action, in the end the film emphasizes the importance of families and sticking together.

Spy Kids was a surprise number one hit at the box office and earned over $112 million dollars in U.S. ticket sales. Critics and audiences alike were charmed by the film's mix of family togetherness, action adventure, and spy gadgets. Vega and Sabara's performance as bickering siblings was also praised for its realism. The two child actors first worked together in 1996 on the set of the series "Life's Work" and got along very well. Vega admitted that she and Sabara fought off the set, "but it was play-fighting, normal brother-sister stuff." Director Rodriguez became a father figure to her, and the family atmosphere on the set translated to the screen. The strong, loving, talented Latino family of *Spy Kids* is one of the things that Vega, who is half-Hispanic and fluent in Spanish, loves best about the movie.

Becoming a Full-Fledged Spy

No sooner had the first *Spy Kids* movie made its debut than Vega began working on its sequel, *Spy Kids 2: The Island of Lost Dreams* (2002). Having proven their abilities as spies, Carmen and Juni are now full-fledged members of the OSS spy organization. They attend a specialized spy school, use even cooler spy gadgets, and go out on assignments. The one thing that spoils their new life is competition from the irritating Gary and Gerti Giggles, who try to steal the spotlight from Carmen and Juni. The Cortez siblings' father, Gregorio, is also competing against Gary and Gerti's father, Donnagon Giggles, to become the new director of the OSS. But when the Giggles siblings manage to get Juni thrown out of the OSS, and Donnagon takes over the agency, Carmen and Juni strike back. They get the Giggles sent to the middle of the desert while they take on the prime assignment of recovering a stolen piece of technology. The "transmooker" device prevents electronic tools from working and has the potential to destroy the world in the wrong hands.

— **"** —

Robert Rodriguez, the writer and director of Spy Kids, *originally thought Carmen's character should be younger than a preteen, but he decided to change the part after seeing Vega audition. "From the first time I saw her, I thought she was amazing," he remarked. "You buy that she's strong, take-charge, and confident, that she can strap on a jet pack and rescue her brother."*

— **"** —

Carmen and Juni's mission takes them to a mysterious island inhabited by strange, mutant creatures. These are strange cross-breed animals, from a spider monkey to horse flies and bull frogs. Carmen and Juni find their gadgets are useless on the island and they must use their intelligence to

Vega's standout performance in Spy Kids 2 *led a* New York Times *critic to write: "Forget Vin Diesel. For my money the multicultural action-movie star of the moment is Alexa Vega."*

succeed. Eventually they gain the help of the island's strange scientist to destroy the transmooker device and save the day. Not only do their parents give them an assist, but their retired spy grandparents, played by Ricardo Montalban and Holland Taylor, join in as well. Again, the film emphasizes the importance of family. Vega and Sabara continued to be believable as a brother and sister who bicker back and forth but are there for each other when trouble strikes.

In *Spy Kids 2* Vega showed new talents. The ending shows Carmen Cortez disguised as a singer, and Vega provided her own vocals for the scene. Her song also appeared on the *Spy Kids 2* soundtrack. Vega was able to expand the character of Carmen, showing her growing up a bit: she has a crush on the handsome Gary Giggles, even though she knows he's a sneak. The actress also had to use her imagination when filming scenes with the island's animals, including a fight scene against an army of skeletons. All these creatures were created using special effects after Vega shot the scenes. So she often acted in an empty space in front of a blank screen, so filmmakers could go back later and add the backgrounds and the rest of the scenery through special effects. But Vega didn't mind the challenge. "We get to imagine these crazy, scary creatures. It makes it more fun and exciting to see the finished product and say, 'Ooh cool, that's what it looks like.'" Her standout performance in *Spy Kids 2* led a *New York Times* critic to write: "Forget Vin Diesel. For my money the multicultural action-movie star of the moment is Alexa Vega."

> **—— " ——**
>
> *Vega often acted in an empty space in front of a blank screen, so filmmakers could go back later and add the special effects. But she didn't mind the challenge. "We get to imagine these crazy, scary creatures. It makes it more fun and exciting to see the finished product and say, 'Ooh cool, that's what it looks like.'"*
>
> **—— " ——**

Finishing the Game

In 2003 Vega again appeared as Carmen Cortez in *Spy Kids 3-D: Game Over.* This film has Carmen working for the OSS and investigating a sinister video game designed to trap children's minds. As the film opens, Carmen has been lost inside the game; only her brother Juni, who has retired from the spy business, can save her. He enters the game, a computer-generated virtual world that the movie audience sees in three dimensions (3-D) by using special glasses. After facing many challenges Juni catches up to Carmen on Level 4 of the game. The two of them then pursue the creator of the game, the evil Toymaker (played by Sylvester Stallone). They need to shut down the game and keep him from escaping. When he does escape, it is only with the help of all their family and friends that Carmen and Juni triumph.

Because much of the action in *Spy Kids 3-D* takes place in a video game, there were many more special effects shots than in the first two films. So Vega spent a lot of time in front of a blank screen pretending that she could see the scenery or creature that would be added later through special effects. Vega did her own stunts again in this film — her favorite was the scene where she surfs through a river of lava. "There was this contraption shaped like a really wide U; it looked like we were either on a skateboard or snowboard, and we had all these stunt guys pulling us back and forth. I thought it was going to be really weird going up there, and it was, but it was really cool because you really felt like you were up there surfing with all the wind blowing and hearing Robert [Rodriguez, the director] shout: 'there's a monster behind you!'"

> Vega admits to crying during the last day of filming Spy Kids 3. "It's sad because we've worked with everyone for four years, they've become like my family and they've seen me grow into a teenager. But it's been a wonderful experience, because Robert's given us a real boost and hopefully we can go far in our careers."

Vega sang again for the third *Spy Kids* soundtrack, and also got the chance to perform live before the *Spy Kids 3* premiere. She enjoyed it so much she is now thinking of including music in her career. "We were trying to practice everything on stage and it was kind of chaotic. But when it happened it was fun. When I finished I told my mom I wanted to be a rock star, because the rush you get on stage is so great."

Spy Kids 3: Game Over, as the title suggests, was the last of the series. Vega admits to crying during the last day of filming. "It's sad because we've worked with everyone for four years, they've become like my family and they've seen me grow into a teenager. But it's been a wonderful experience, because Robert's given us a real boost and hopefully we can go far in our careers." Vega is also looking forward to trying something new. After *Spy Kids 3* she noted that "I want to be able to move on and be good and be able to do different things."

Future Plans and Projects

Although the *Spy Kids* series is over, Vega has many plans for the future. In fall 2003 she began working on the movie *Sleepover*. In this comedy Vega plays a girl whose best friend is moving away the summer before they enter high school. She throws a slumber party for her friends on the same night that a group of popular girls are having their own get-to-gether. The two groups of girls end up competing in a scavenger hunt, with the prize being the rights to the best lunch table at the high school. Vega also has a role in the upcoming drama *State's Evidence,* and she has considered making another television series as well.

Outside of acting, Vega is looking forward to continuing her education. After high school, she hopes to attend college some day. She would like to study film, and perhaps add writing and directing to her Hollywood résumé. She has already written film scripts and

Vega enjoys attending movie premieres, like this one for Freaky Friday.

made her own home movies. "I have a lot of ideas, but the writing takes so long," she commented. "I'm serious about it, though." She is also thinking about turning her contributions to the *Spy Kids* soundtracks into a singing career. "When I grow up, I want to be an actress if not a director, or a writer or a singer. I can't decide. But I do want to go to college for other choices."

In the meantime, Vega doesn't mind being recognized by her fans. "It's kind of weird but I like it; I like making little kids happy." She hopes to live up to her fans' expectations, adding that it's "exciting that someone looks up to you so much. That's why you have to set a good example, make sure you're always being humble and grounded." Luckily for Vega, that's something she gets from her family. Her mother and little sisters remind her she's just a normal kid. "My mom says if I let this all go to my head and misbehave she's going to flush my action figure down the toilet," Vega jokes. She and her *Spy Kids* co-stars are just like anyone else, she says: "We're not really movie stars; we're just in a movie."

FAVORITE MOVIES

Vega enjoys watching action movies like *Austin Powers* and *Mission Impossible.* Her favorite actress is Natalie Portman, who played Padme in *Star Wars 1: The Phantom Menace* and *Star Wars 2: Attack of the Clones.* Vega also admires Jodie Foster, a former child actor who grew up to become an Oscar-winning actress and director.

HOBBIES AND OTHER INTERESTS

Vega calls herself a tomboy. She enjoys fishing, gymnastics, and playing football and basketball (she once played point guard on a boys' basketball team). She also enjoys her family pets, which include a dog, cat, chickens, and hairless rats. Like many teenagers, she likes spending time with friends and hanging out at the mall. She also enjoys listening to music and dancing to hip-hop.

SELECTED CREDITS

Movie Roles

Little Giants, 1994
Nine Months, 1995
Twister, 1996
The Glimmer Man, 1996
Ghosts of Mississippi, 1996 (also released as *Ghosts from the Past*)
Dennis the Menace Strikes Again, 1998
The Deep End of the Ocean, 1999
NetForce, 1999
Spy Kids, 2001
Spy Kids 2: The Island of Lost Dreams, 2002
Spy Kids 3: Game Over, 2003

Television Movies and Series

"Evening Shade," 1993-94 (series)
It Was Him or Us, 1995 (movie)
"Life's Work," 1996 (series)
A Promise to Caroline, 1996 (movie),
Shattered Mind, 1996 (movie; also known as *The Terror Inside*)
"Ladies Man," 1999 (series)
Run the Wild Fields, 2000 (movie)
Follow the Stars Home, 2001 (movie)

FURTHER READING

Books

Contemporary Theatre, Film, and Television, Vol. 40, 2002

Periodicals

Boston Herald, Aug. 5, 2002, p.29
Dallas Morning News, Aug. 7, 2002, p.C1

Detroit News, Aug. 10, 2002, p.1
Houston Chronicle, Apr. 5, 2001, p.6
New York Times, Aug. 7, 2002, p.E6
Ottawa (Ontario) Sun, Mar. 30, 2001, p.33
People, Apr. 16, 2001, p.145
Tennessean, Apr. 4, 2001, p.D3
Vanity Fair, July, 2003, p.96
Washington Post, Mar. 30, 2001, p.C11

Online Articles

http://actionadventure.about.com/library/weekly/2001/aa033001a.htm
   (*About.com,* "What You Need to Know About Action-Adventure Movies:
   Kids . . . *Spy Kids*—Alexa Vega and Daryl Sabara," 2001)
http://actionadventure.about.com/library/weekly/2002/aa032002.htm
   (*About.com,* "What You Need to Know About Action-Adventure Movies:
   Exclusive Alexa Vega Interview," 2002)
http://www.bbc.co.uk/films/
   (*BBC,* "Films—Interviews: Alexa Vega," July 30, 2003)
http://www.tribute.ca/?newsletter=95
   (*Tribute Moviemail,* "Star Chat: An Interview with Alexa Vega," July 18,
   2003)

Online Databases

Biography Resource Center Online, 2003, article from *Contemporary Theatre,
Film, and Television,* 2002

ADDRESS

Alexa Vega
SDB Partners, Inc.
1801 Avenue of the Stars, Suite 902
Los Angeles, CA 90067

WORLD WIDE WEB SITES

http://www.spykids.com

Michelle Wie 1989-
American Golf Prodigy

BIRTH

Michelle Sung Wie (pronounced *wee*) was born on October 11, 1989, in Honolulu, Hawaii. Her parents, Hyun Kyong (Bo) Wie and Byung-Wook (B.J.) Wie, immigrated to the United States from Korea in the 1980s. Her mother, Bo Wie, is a real estate agent in Honolulu and a Korean amateur golf champion. Her father, B.J. Wie, is a professor at the University of Honolulu and also an accomplished golfer, a skill he learned from his wife. They also help manage their daughter's career. Michelle is their only child.

YOUTH

Wie began hitting a golf ball at age four with a set of junior clubs, smacking her first shot more than 100 yards. She fell in love with the game, playing for hours on end. She played her first round of golf—the complete 18 holes—at age seven, finishing 14 strokes over par. Soon Wie could beat her parents. "I think I started beating them when I was seven or eight," she once said. "Well, they say I . . . started beating them when I was nine, but I refuse to believe that."

In golf scoring, "par" refers to the standard number of strokes it should take a player to complete each hole. For example, most golf courses include short holes, which are usually designated as "par 3," as well as longer holes, which are designated "par 5." On a regulation, 18-hole golf course, par for all holes will add up to 72. In golf terminology, a player makes a "birdie" by completing a hole in one shot under par, or a "bogey" by completing a hole in one shot over par.

By age nine, Wie played her first sub-par round, meaning she was able to complete the 18 holes with fewer shots than expected—in fact, fewer shots than most adults would require for that course. Since then, she has never shot more than 100 for 18 holes of golf. At the same time, Wie began competing in tournaments, winning five out of the seven Oahu Junior Golf Association tournaments at age nine. Through all this time, Wie combined her childhood activities with her dedication to golf.

EARLY CAREER

By this point, Wie was already on the way to become a professional golfer. Professional golfers typically compete in a series of events over the course of the year. The winners of the events can earn big monetary prizes. These events, or tournaments, are offered by golf associations. There are several associations around the world, but in the U.S. the most prestigious for professional golfers are the LPGA (Ladies Professional Golf Association) for women and the PGA (Professional Golf Association) for men.

Most golf tournaments take place over a series of days. Each day, the players shoot one "round" of 18 holes. Players have to make the cut in order to continue in a tournament, or else they are eliminated. The "cut" is the score, set by tournament officials, that players must beat after two rounds to continue. After several rounds, the scores are totaled and the player with the lowest score wins the tournament. There are many individual tournaments on the women's professional golf tour, but the most prestigious are the four major or "Grand Slam" events: the Kraft Nabisco Championship, the U.S. Women's Open, the McDonald's LPGA Championship, and the Weetabix Women's British Open.

In addition to the events for professional golfers, there are tournaments offered for amateur golfers, who do not earn prize money. There are also junior golfer programs, designed to introduce kids to golf. At all these levels, players can qualify for golf events based on their scores and their performance in other tournaments.

Most golfers spend years developing their skills in the amateur ranks, and very few ever learn to play at such advanced levels. What's amazing about Wie is that she has become so accomplished at such a young age.

———— **"** ————

"I think I started beating [my parents] when I was seven or eight," Wie once said. "Well, they say I . . . started beating them when I was nine, but I refuse to believe that."

———— **"** ————

Getting Started

In 2000, at age 10, Wie became the youngest girl to qualify for a USGA amateur championship event. (The United States Golf Association, or USGA, is the national governing body of golf.) At the USGA Women's Amateur Public Links Championship, Wie attained the impressive score of 64. At age 10, she had already developed her game enough to compete in this championship against some of the best women amateurs. Her game so impressed Bev Kim and Lily Yao, two of the top women's amateurs, that they began mentoring her. In 2002, at age 12, Wie became the youngest player ever to qualify for an LPGA event, shooting an 83 to qualify for the LPGA Takefuji Classic. That same year, she became the youngest semi-finalist at the U.S. Women's Amateur Public Links Championship.

The year 2003 brought continued success, as she played in both women's and men's events. She started the year by trying to qualify for the PGA Sony Open, a men's event that was being held in Hawaii. In this and several other events she was granted an exemption—a tournament sponsor's invitation to try to make the cut into the tournament without completing all of the qualifying rounds. She shot a 73 and finished 47 out of 97 in the event—at the age of 13. It was considered a remarkable achievement, and people in the golf world started to take notice. She next played in the Hawaii Pearl Open, a professional men's tournament with players from the Japan Tour. The only female in the tournament, she placed 43rd. She

Despite her youth, Wie's golf game is incredibly well-rounded and complete.

followed that event with an appearance in her first LPGA major tournament, the Kraft Nabisco Championship. Playing against such accomplished golfers as Patricia Meunier-Lebouc and Annika Sorenstam, Wie ended up in ninth place. Her play included a round of 66, which tied the lowest score by an amateur in an LPGA major. In addition, she was the youngest player ever to make the cut at an LPGA event.

Her next event in 2003 was another appearance at the U.S. Women's Amateur Public Links Championship. At just 13 years old, Wie won the tournament, taking her first national title. In the process, she also became the youngest champion of the event and the youngest player ever to win an adult national event.

Wie next appeared at the Canadian Tour's Bay Mills Open Players' Championships, held in Michigan. In her first professional men's event in the mainland United States, she shot 74-79, missing the cut by five strokes. Another men's event followed: the Albertsons Boise Open on the Nationwide Tour, a development tour (like the minor leagues) for the PGA. She shot 78-76 in that event and missed the cut. Her final major event for 2003 was the LPGA Safeway Classic. She shot 69-72-73, or two under par, tying for 28th place. Overall for 2003, she qualified for five out of the six LPGA

Wie follows the flight of her ball after a towering tee shot.

events she entered. And while she had not made the cut in the professional men's tournaments she entered, she had gained experience and
exposure.

Playing in the 2004 Sony Open

In early 2004, Wie got an opportunity to play against some of the world's
best male professional golfers at the Sony Open on the PGA Tour when the
sponsor granted her an exemption. "It's like a dream come true," she said.
For two months before the tournament, she practiced diligently in an effort
to improve enough to make the cut at the Open. The event was being held
on the tournament course near her home in Honolulu, so from November

until the January tournament Wie played nearly 100 hours there. She spent her Thanksgiving school break at the David Leadbetter Academy in Orlando, Florida, learning to perfect her swing.

At the Sony Open in January 2004, Wie became the youngest player (and the fourth woman) to compete at a PGA event, giving her a chance to play with one of her heroes, Ernie Els, in a practice round. During the four-hour practice, Els taught Wie a new way to hit a long-range putt. Els advised her not to swing hard and smack the ball, but rather swing at the same pace through the entire stroke. After her practice round with Els, Wie said in a press conference that she was "very nervous" to play with him because "I didn't want to embarrass myself or anything. . . . I was more excited about this than the tournament." Praising Wie as a "phenomenal player," Els also said, "Michelle is 14. Give her a couple of years to get stronger. I mean, she can play on this tour. If she keeps working, keeps doing the right things, there's no reason why she shouldn't be out here."

Wie's performance at the tournament impressed many golf fans. She hit the ball an average of 270 yards off the tee, five yards less than the average of all the players but 20 yards farther than her partner, professional Craig Bowden. She even impressed her caddy, Bobby Verwey, who said "That golf swing of hers, it's the best golf swing I've ever seen in my life." Wie's practice with Els showed in her putting; 13 of her holes were made with one putt. She made a total of eight putts longer than 40 feet, including one 60-footer and another 50-footer. In her second round, Wie became the first woman in history to shoot under-par at a men's PGA event, shooting a 68, or two under par. Although she made the course par of 140, the cut was 139. She missed it by one stroke. In the end, she had tied 16 other players for 80th place, including the British Open winner Ben Curtis and U.S. Open winner Jim Furyk, and finished ahead of 47 other professional male golfers. It was an outstanding performance for such a young teenager at a professional men's event.

> **"**
>
> *Praising Wie as a "phenomenal player," Ernie Els once said, "Michelle is 14. Give her a couple of years to get stronger. I mean, she can play on this tour. If she keeps working, keeps doing the right things, there's no reason why she shouldn't be out here."*
>
> **"**

Wie (left) and teammate Erica Blasberg celebrate their team's victory at the 2004 Curtis Cup Matches in Formby, England.

Recent Events

After her near-qualifying play at the Sony Open, invitations to other tournaments came pouring in. In March she finished in the Top 25 at her first LPGA event of the year, the Safeway International; she then finished fourth in the Kraft Nabisco Championship, her first LPGA major tournament of 2004.

In June 2004, Wie was the youngest player ever to be selected to represent the United States at the Curtis Cup Match in England. The Curtis Cup, which pits a team from the U.S. against a team from Great Britain and Ireland, has been played every other year since 1932. According to Wie, it was like being chosen to be in the Olympics. She and the seven other American players retained the U.S. dominance of the Curtis Cup for the fourth match in a row. Wie won both her singles matches to help the U.S. defeat Great Britain and Ireland 10-8. As an added reward, she accepted the 2004 World Newcomer of the Year Award at the Laureus World Sports Awards in Lisbon, Spain.

Wie continued her excellent play in the qualifier for the 2004 U.S. Amateur Public Links Championship, a men's event. She shot 71-71 and finished two strokes behind the winners. Although she failed to make the cut and earn a bid to the finals, she earned status by becoming one of the four alternates to the event. Soon after, she received an exemption from the sectional qualifying rounds of the U.S. Women's Open. The U.S. Golf Association executive director David Fay explained that based solely on her performance, Wie was offered the U.S. Women's Open second-ever exemption. The Open invites the top 35 professional players each year. Although she wasn't even a professional, Wie would have been ranked 28th if she had been a pro in 2004. The exemption was certainly an honor, but not undeserved. At the July 2004 event, she shot 71-70-71-73, tying for 13th place. At the age of 14, Wie had already made six holes-in-one—which is pretty impressive considering that some professionals have never made even one.

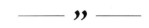

According to PGA veteran player Fred Couples, "When you see her hit a golf ball . . . there's nothing that prepares you for it. It's just the scariest thing you've ever seen."

Wie's Gifts as a Golfer

Wie has what many call "the gift," a kind of talent and charisma that can't be taught. Vice president of the PGA Tour Duke Butler said, "I honestly feel she's going to be one of the top 10 athletes of our lifetime." Many have said that Wie's powerful drive sets her apart from other female golfers. Her ability to send 300-yard drives with accuracy puts her in the same league as some of the top professional male golfers; her drives outdistance those by most female professional golfers by more than 50 yards. Her swing and strike have been described as "a dream," "perfect," and "unfathomable." According to PGA veteran player Fred Couples, "When you see her hit a golf ball . . . there's nothing that prepares you for it. It's just the scariest thing you've ever seen." Another player, fellow golfer Davis Love III, would agree. "She probably has one of the best golf swings I've ever seen, period," Love said. "She has a lot going for her. Plus, she's tall and strong. No telling what she's going to do when she gets a little older."

Wie has more than physical talent going for her. According to her father, "There is something unique, especially in her mind. . . . She can handle the pressure. She has something different." Her coach, Gary Gilchrist, echoes that idea. "She's got the touch, the feel, and the power," Gilchrist said. "All she needs is time. And she's got plenty of that." Wie has a kind of composure that few adults maintain in the heat of competition. Whether she's playing as the youngest among professional female golfers or as the only woman in a field of the game's best men, Wie remains cool and calm—even with thousands of fans crowding the course to catch a glimpse of her. "You kind of expect a 14-year-old to crack at this level," pro-golfer Kevin Hayashi said about playing with Wie on the PGA Tour.

———— " ————

Fellow golfer Davis Love III said that "She probably has one of the best golf swings I've ever seen, period. She has a lot going for her. Plus, she's tall and strong. No telling what she's going to do when she gets a little older."

———— " ————

But Wie doesn't choke. She concentrates and tries her best. "Her poise is unbelievable," said *Golf Digest* writer Tom Lehman. "Either you've got it or you don't." Coach Gilchrist once admitted that "I'm expecting her, by the time she is 16, to have the mental capacity to play at any level. On any tour."

With all her natural talent comes a great deal of media attention. Her record-breaking firsts, her powerful shots, and, in her own words, her "freakishly tall" stature (she stands six-feet, one-inch tall), all draw journalists and cameras. Wie doesn't shy away from all the attention; in fact she thrives on it. "I always want to look at the tournaments where no one has gone in before, and I want to be the first one in everything," she said. Her father said that "Michelle really likes the media attention, she really likes the fans. She signs autographs with a smile."

Is Wie's Youth Being Stolen?

Wie's penchant for playing against professionals—rather than other amateurs closer to her age—has inspired some concerns in the golf world. Some observers wonder if she is being pushed too hard by her parents and if she is trying to do too much, too soon. But her supporters disagree. "It's her ambition," her mentor Yao said. "All [her parents are] doing is encouraging and supporting it." Her coach Gary Gilchrist said that Wie and her family do a good job of balancing her life. "[When] I first met them, I could tell Michelle loves school in Hawaii. She has great friends in Hawaii, and her mom and dad had done a great job with her game. I could tell there

Wie tees off at the 2004 U.S. Women's Open, where she posted the best score of all amateur players, nine shots behind winner Meg Mallon.

was a great balance." Many believe that her parents are not pushing her to turn pro or to make money; instead, they have said that she will remain an amateur for several more years, until she is an adult.

Wie does well in school, enjoys her friends, relaxes in front of the Disney Channel, and plays golf. Her schedule includes a 30-minute workout of her core muscles each day, three hours of golf after each school day, and eight hours every weekend. But Wie doesn't think of the time as drudgery; she's having fun. "I just like everything about golf, really," Wie admitted.

Other observers trying to assess her emotional and social development have called her intelligent, charming, well-adjusted, happy, and very mature. They claim that she seems to socialize easily with peers and with adults, and also seems to get along well with her parents.

Future Path

Wie's performance on the golf course at such a young age makes some analysts worry about her future. Will she be exploited by sponsors hoping to entice the public and to draw attention to the sport? Confronting that issue will be tough for the Wies. The family has few role models to follow, since few young people have demonstrated such great talent so early in life.

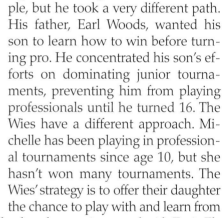

According to her father, "There is something unique, especially in her mind. . . . She can handle the pressure. She has something different."

Tiger Woods might be the best example, but he took a very different path. His father, Earl Woods, wanted his son to learn how to win before turning pro. He concentrated his son's efforts on dominating junior tournaments, preventing him from playing professionals until he turned 16. The Wies have a different approach. Michelle has been playing in professional tournaments since age 10, but she hasn't won many tournaments. The Wies' strategy is to offer their daughter the chance to play with and learn from the world's best golfers. After Michelle played a practice round with Ernie Els at the Sony Open, her father said that "Michelle is a visual learner, and that's the beauty of her entering PGA Tour events. Because you can learn so much from a player like that."

Wie's schedule for the coming years will most likely be a mix of junior and professional tournaments. Eventually, she plans to split her time between women's and men's tournaments, hoping at some point to beat Tiger Woods in competition. "It's like my hobby, playing in men's tournaments, because they're really exciting and give me something new to try. I want to go to the next level. I don't want to restrict myself to one level," Wie once said. Her ultimate dream is to play the Masters at Augusta National some day, which no woman has ever done. "I'm not looking to prove a point," Wie explained. "I just want to play the best there is." As an amateur Wie can qualify to play at the Masters if she wins the U.S. Amateur, the U.S. Mid-Amateur, or the U.S. Public Links men's tournaments. Talking about women playing against men in the future, Wie said that "I don't think it will be such a big deal later on. Women will want to go farther. More women will be brave enough to play against the men."

Golf fans are watching Wie with great anticipation, eager to see what the future will bring. As Bob Williams of Burns Sports Celebrity Service explained, "she has the ability to forever change the attitudes and opinions of people in sport." When asked how she sees the future, Wie confided that "I guess I'm not normal first of all, so I can't have a normal life. I guess if you grow up normal, you'll always be normal, and I don't want to be normal. I want to be something else."

EDUCATION

Wie attends Punahour High School near her home in Hawaii. She stays focused by separating her life into neat compartments: "When I'm in school, I don't even want to think about golf. It's just school and my friends," she once said. "When I'm on the golf course, I don't really feel like a ninth-grad-

Wie with her father, B.J. Wie, who has often served as her caddy.

er." Wie is so attached to her home and friends that she turned down a full scholarship to one of the country's top golf schools, the David Leadbetter Academy.

Wie, a mostly A-student, is already thinking about college. She is looking at Stanford—the alma mater of her uncle as well as her hero Tiger Woods, and the school where her grandfather taught as a visiting professor from Korea. "I want to be an educated person," Wie has said. When asked whether she's tempted to become a professional golfer soon so that she can start winning lots of money, she replied that first, "I'd like to go through the basic steps of life, like go to high school and then go to college and be in a dorm and stuff like that. I think I just want to go through the basic steps of life, and then I think I'd be fine from then."

Certainly Wie's attitudes about her life have been influenced by her parents. Both tour with her regularly, and until recently her father served as her caddy. Her parents, with whom she speaks Korean, are very careful to balance their daughter's golfing life with good doses of friends and school. "There's a very fine line between challenging and pushing," 19-year-old golf prodigy Christina Kim said, adding "She's not being pushed at all."

FAVORITE FOOD

Wie's favorite food is a Korean stew called Kimchee Chigae and rice.

MAJOR INFLUENCES

Wie often lists Ernie Els and Tiger Woods as her golf heroes. Wie has said that she tried to copy their golf swings, first imitating Woods and then Els. She is a good study; her smooth, effortless swing has earned her the nickname "The Big Wiesy," a takeoff on Els's nickname "The Big Easy."

HOBBIES AND OTHER INTERESTS

Wie has said that she ranks shopping as one of her favorite things to do. She likes to go to the mall with her friends, and she also likes to read, draw, watch television, use the computer, and listen to Coldplay and Good Charlotte.

HONORS AND AWARDS

Hawaii State Women's Stroke Play Championship: 2001
Jennie K. Wilson Invitational, Hawaii: 2001
Hawaii State Open: 2002, Women's Division Winner
U.S. Women's Amateur Public Links Championship: 2003

FURTHER READING

Periodicals

Detroit News, Aug. 13, 2003, p.E1
Golf World, June 27, 2003, p.18; Jan. 23, 2004, p.14
Honolulu Advertiser, Mar. 20, 2003, p.D6; June 8, 2003, p.C1; Sep. 16, 2003, p.D1; Nov. 9, 2003, p.C1
Houston Chronicle, July 2, 2003, p.1
Los Angeles Times, Jan. 13, 2004, p.D1; Jan.14, 2004, p.D1; Mar. 25, 2004, p.D3; Mar. 27, 2004, p.D6
New York Times, Jan. 13, 2004, p.D1; Mar. 29, 2004, p.D3
Orlando Sentinel, June 25, 2003, p.D8
Palm Beach Post, June 29, 2003, p.B1

Sports Illustrated, July 7, 2003, p.32; July 14, 2003, p.G6; Jan. 26, 2004, p.17; May 3, 2004
Sports Illustrated for Kids, Aug. 1, 2003, p.47
USA Today, June 27, 2003, p.C1; Mar. 24, 2004, Sports section

Online Articles

http://sports.espn.go.com/golf/news/story?id=1832101
   (*ESPN,* "Girl on the Verge," June 19, 3004)
http://www.golfdigest.com/gfw/gfwinstruction/index.ssf?/gfw
   /gfwinstruction/gfw200310wie.html
   (*Golf Digest,* "Michelle Wie Steps Up," Sep.-Oct. 2003)
http://www.golfdigest.com/features/index.ssf?/features/gd200408myshot
   .html
   (*Golf Digest,* "My Shot: Michelle Wie," Aug. 2004)
http://www.kidzworld.com/site/p1848.htm
   (*KidzWorld,* "Michelle Wie: Pro Golfer," no date)
http://www.lpga.com/entertainment_content.aspx?pid=2483&mid=3
   (*LPGA,* "Quick 18 with Amateur Michelle Wie," no date)

Other

"60 Minutes" TV transcript, CBS News, Apr. 11, 2004

ADDRESS

Michelle Wie
LPGA
100 International Golf Drive
Daytona Beach, FL 32124

WORLD WIDE WEB SITE

http://sports.espn.go.com/golf/players

Will Wright 1960-
American Game Designer
Creator of the Best-Selling Computer Games
"SimCity," "The Sims," and "The Sims Online"

BIRTH

William R. Wright was born on January 20, 1960, in Atlanta, Georgia, to William (Bill) Wright, a chemical engineer and owner of Wright Plastics Company, and Beverly Edwards, a community theater actress. Will had one sister. When he was nine years old, his father died. Seeking the support of her family, Will's mother moved with her children to her hometown of Baton Rouge, Louisiana, where Will lived until he was 18.

YOUTH

Wright was a bright and motivated child. He read widely from an early age and once described his appetite for knowledge as "obsessive." "I would usually get very obsessed with some subject or area of interest for six months or a year, and just totally learn everything I (could) about it."

For fun, Wright loved to play board games, especially chess, a Chinese game named "Go," and complex military strategy and historical war games. Wright ranked "Go" as his favorite game because its two simple rules "give rise to incredible strategy."

Wright "always associated fun with making something." He spent hours building toy models of airplanes, ships, and tanks. "I was always building things," he remembered. From toy models, he moved on to robots. His first, built when he was 13, was a hydraulic arm created out of injection syringes.

Wright read widely from an early age and once described his appetite for knowledge as "obsessive." "I would usually get very obsessed with some subject or area of interest for six months or a year, and just totally learn everything I (could) about it."

EDUCATION

Although Wright was smart, he didn't fit well within the confines of regular school. He sped through high school in three years, graduating at age 16. He began his university studies at Louisiana State University, but soon transferred to Louisiana Tech, and then to the New School University in New York. Five years of college work — during which he studied architecture, mechanical engineering, aviation, brain physiology, and psychology — left him with no degree and no interest in continuing school. He dropped out in 1981. He had fallen in love with an artist named Joell Jones and moved to live with her in California.

Dropping out of college didn't stop Wright's active mind — he had never needed school to motivate him to learn. His interest in his own projects continued unabated; he earned his pilot's license and became a minister. But his greatest obsession became the computer. At age 20, the

―――― "" ――――

The computers that appeared on the market beginning in the late 1970s allowed programmers to type code directly into a personal computer and to test their programs instantly. Wright was delighted. "Once I got my hands on my first PC, I became totally enamored with it," he recalled.

―――― "" ――――

year before leaving his college studies, Wright played a flight simulator game produced by Bruce Artwick Productions. The life-like experience portrayed on the computer screen fascinated Wright.

Although the game captured his interest, Wright didn't immediately get hooked on computer programming. When he took computer programming courses in college, programming was done by creating hundreds or even thousands of punched cardboard cards (called keypunch cards), which were fed into a large mainframe computer. Keypunch cards made programming a very slow, laborious process, and Wright hated it. But advances in computer technology soon helped foster his interest in programming.

The computers that appeared on the market beginning in the late 1970s allowed programmers to type code directly into a personal computer and to test their programs instantly. Wright was delighted. "Once I got my hands on my first PC, I became totally enamored with it," he recalled. With his Apple II computer, Wright could write a program and immediately test the results. He first used it to animate the robots that he continued to build as a hobby. "I was very interested in the idea of animating inanimate objects," he remembered. One of his first computer-controlled robots, Mr. Rogers, was a three-wheeled creation that mapped the rooms in his house with ultrasonic sensors that radioed data back to his computer.

By age 22, Wright discovered the Commodore 64 personal computer and perfected his computer programming skills enough to develop his first game, "Raid on Bungeling Bay." The game was simple: a player pilots a helicopter over islands and blows things up. In Wright's opinion, however, it was "a very stupid game."

FIRST JOBS

Despite Wright's opinion, "Raid on Bungeling Bay" became his first success. In 1982, Wright presented his game to a software distribution company, which immediately agreed to distribute it. "I walked in the door and they said 'Oh great, we'll take it.' I didn't have to talk them into it," Wright remembered. "Raid on Bungeling Bay" became one of the first computer games exported from America to Japan. Although not very popular in the United States, it sold 800,000 copies in Japan alone. The market response stunned Wright. "I was amazed I could make a living at this," he recalled. "It was something I was willing to do for free."

But Wright discovered a glitch in his plan to become a game developer while making "Raid on Bungeling Bay." He'd had more fun building the city that was destroyed — the landscape, roads, and buildings — than he did flying the helicopter around bombing targets. Instead of creating another destruction oriented game, the kind of game that dominated the market in the mid-1980s, Wright dove into an intensive research project that would ultimately result in the creation of "SimCity," the game that set him apart from all other game developers.

CAREER HIGHLIGHTS

To flesh out the details for his new game about building a city, Wright read about 20 books on urban planning theory, especially the work of MIT electrical engineering professor Jay W. Forrester, author of *Urban Dynamics*. Wright also researched computer simulation techniques. He created a game based on land use, traffic, power distribution systems, and other urban development structure research conducted in the late 1960s and 1970s. He called his game prototype "Metropolis."

Wright's research resulted in a game that offered players a job as mayor of a virtual city. Players took responsibility for building houses and roads, attracting businesses, raising taxes, and keeping the citizens happy. Depending on the player's skill, Simulated Citizens (or Sims) either moved into the city to build homes, businesses, hospitals, schools, and churches, or moved out to search for a better place to live. The player decided how to define success in the game. For one player, success might mean a prosperous city with good schools, low crime, and no traffic, while another player might define

—— **"** ——

"Raid on Bungeling Bay" became one of the first computer games exported from America to Japan. Although not very popular in the United States, it sold 800,000 copies in Japan alone. The market response stunned Wright. "I was amazed I could make a living at this," he recalled. "It was something I was willing to do for free."

495

success in the game as a decaying city that Sims tried to escape. The game could be played differently each time.

Unlike other games on the market at the time, "Metropolis" had no winner, no loser, no hero, no enemies, no bloody attacks, and no end. And no game publisher wanted to market it, either. Discouraged, Wright shelved "Metropolis" until Jeff Braun enticed him to unpack it in 1987.

———— *"* ————

"SimCity" piqued the interest of both domestic and foreign governmental agencies, including the Central Intelligence Agency and the Defense Department. Large businesses wondered how the idea of simulation might aid their training programs and other goals. In addition, "SimCity" gained attention as an educational tool and made its way into more than 10,000 classrooms.

———— *"* ————

"SimCity"

Jeff Braun would soon become integral to the development of Wright's game. At the time, Braun was working for a video-game distributor in California. But he'd grown tired of working for someone else and was looking for a way to enter the video gaming industry himself. Braun invited Wright and some other game developers to a pizza party at his home near San Francisco in 1987. At the party, Wright described his shelved game to Braun. Intrigued, Braun asked to see it. Once Braun looked at Wright's game, he "went ballistic," as he told *Time.* "I knew immediately," he recalled. Convinced that Wright's game would be a success, Braun persuaded Wright to stop his worrying that "no one likes it."

Braun and Wright soon formed Maxis Studios in Walnut Creek, California. For the next two years Braun, Wright, and a handful of developers worked out of Braun's apartment. They used the living room for programming, the kitchen as a mail room, and one bedroom as an administrative office. Maxis struck a deal with Broderbund, one of the largest game companies in America, to distribute the game. "SimCity" debuted in stores in 1989, and it became an instant success. *Newsweek* featured it in a full-page review, which gave the game national publicity and helped sales soar. By the end of the year sales had reached $3 million.

As the popularity of "SimCity" grew, Wright's creation piqued the interest of both domestic and foreign governmental agencies, including the Central

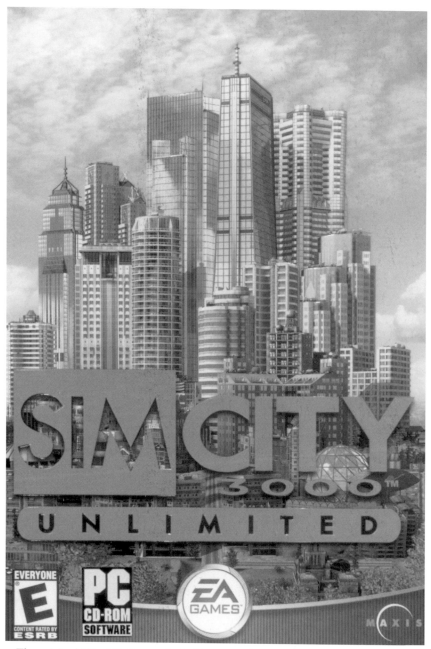

The original "SimCity" game in 1989 eventually led to a very successful line of related games, including "SimCity 3000," the top-selling game of 1999.

Intelligence Agency and the Defense Department. Large businesses wondered how the idea of simulation might aid their training programs and other goals. In addition, "SimCity" gained attention as an educational tool and made its way into more than 10,000 classrooms. By 1995 Maxis had grown to a company of almost 300 employees with sales of $38.1 million.

As interest in the game continued, Wright did more research to improve the game experience. He interviewed city planners, police administrators, public works officials, and others to create new editions and expansion packs to enhance the original game. While the enhancements did not change the structure of the game, they enabled players to customize the look of their cities with terrain from samples from the 48 contiguous United States, ward off disasters based on both reality and fantasy, and customize the architectural styles of their buildings, among other things. "SimCity 3000" became the top-selling game of 1999, adding tornadoes and UFO attacks to the game. By 2003 the various versions of "SimCity" had won more than 24 awards.

─────── **"** ───────

"Some subject that I'm reading about . . . will pique my interest and then I'll slowly become obsessed with it," Wright explained about his design process. "I've always liked studying different things. That's one reason why I really like doing game design. It gives me an excuse to go out and research these wildly different things for a year or two and then move onto the next thing later."

─────── **"** ───────

Creating Games in the "Sim" Series

Keen to repeat the success of "SimCity," Maxis supported the development of other games in the "Sim" series. In 1990 "SimEarth—The Living Planet" debuted, becoming a bestseller by 1991; "SimAnt—The Electronic Ant Colony" came out in 1991; "SimFarm" hit the stores in 1993; and "SimCopter" and "SimPark," among others, debuted in 1996.

Each new game was sparked by Wright's love of reading. "Some subject that I'm reading about . . . will pique my interest and then I'll slowly become obsessed with it," he explained about his design process. "I've always liked studying different things. That's one reason why I really like doing game design. It gives me an excuse to go out and research these wildly different things for a year or two and then move onto the next thing later."

Indeed, the "Sim" series of games did have vastly different sources of inspiration. "SimEarth" developed from Wright's interest in James Lovelock's Gaia theory, which emphasizes the interconnectedness of all Earth's living matter and their planet's atmosphere. Players create a whole planet by setting the planet's evolutionary timescale, geological features, and environmental conditions. From these set points, life forms develop. Players can manage their planet to create intelligent life forms and civilizations, which give rise to the development of technology. Some of the dangers to the players' creations are such natural disasters as earthquakes or volcanic explosions or competitive problems that lead to the outbreak of wars. "SimAnt" was inspired by the work of Edward O. Wilson, a Harvard entomologist. (For more information on Wilson, see *Biography Today Scientists & Inventors*, Vol. 8.) With co-author Bert Hölldobler, Wilson detailed the history, evolution, social structures, and communication of ants in *The Ants*,

"The Sims" games include scenes like these from "The Sims Superstar Expansion Pack."

for which they won the Pulitzer Prize for non-fiction in 1991. Wright used their research to develop a game in which players control the life of an ant colony.

The diverse subjects of these games indicate, as Jeff Braun told *Wired*, that Wright is "a perpetual student." His friend Bruce Joffe, a geographic information systems consultant, once said that "Everything about life interests Will; he has a childlike fascination. . . . [He] drinks information in, synthesizes it, and then creates something useful out of it." Wright recognizes his own intensity, saying that "I typically go overboard when I research new projects." But his ability to translate the vast knowledge he gathers into games enjoyed by both children and adults has transformed the computer game market.

The "Sim" series of games offered players an experience unlike any other games. "With most games, the game itself is the constraint on what you can do," Wright explained. "In 'Doom,' you can't go up to the monsters and ask them why they're trying to kill you, and if there's a wall, you can't climb over it. Behaviors are very regular and predictable." Instead, Wright's games contrasted with these shoot, chase, and kill games by offering players the chance to explore and be creative. The *Los Angeles Times* pinned the success of his games on his ability to create "realistic simulations, which previously had been available only to scientists and the military, to home computers." As Wright explained, his games offer players "something less like a slide—where you can do one fun thing over and over—and more like a sandbox."

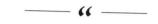

"With most games, the game itself is the constraint on what you can do," Wright explained. "In 'Doom,' you can't go up to the monsters and ask them why they're trying to kill you, and if there's a wall, you can't climb over it. Behaviors are very regular and predictable."

Struggles to Repeat Success

"SimCity" was a huge market success with correspondingly high profit levels. The desire to maintain these profit levels put pressure on Maxis. The company had grown very quickly to support "SimCity." But when its sales began to level off, Maxis found it difficult to reach its earlier profit levels. The company had so many employees that just paying salaries left the company with few resources for game research. Instead of original games, Maxis employees rushed to create "SimCity" spin-offs in order to keep a steady flow of income. But the games that Maxis hastily sent to market were less and less appealing to customers. By 1996 Maxis posted a loss of $1.7 million. Instead of trying to churn out more games, Maxis began accepting acquisition offers. One of the largest American game publishers, Electronic Arts (EA) of Redwood City, California, bought Maxis in 1996 for $125 million. EA immediately laid off 40 percent of the Maxis employees in order to refocus the company for success. But it also offered Maxis the financial support it needed to take the time to create best-selling games.

When EA took over Maxis, it soon realized that Wright's design ideas had been abandoned by Maxis. Wright was working on his own ideas with almost no help or money from Maxis. "We saw a hall-of-fame designer who wanted to do crazy stuff everyone knew couldn't be done," said the executive vice president and chief creative officer from Electronic Arts. "We thought, 'Let's help him.'" EA assembled a team to brainstorm with Wright.

Wright had been working on a game he called "doll house." "Kids build a story around what they are doing. The doll house becomes the scaffolding to hold up their story. It's a place for them to think about or play roles of the person they would like to be," Wright said. His game provided players with the "props and sets and actors, and the idea is to build a story."

"The Sims"

Wright had been working on a game he called "dollhouse" since 1994. As he described it, instead of dealing with a larger world, this new idea took "'SimCity' to the level of the individual." Instead of a whole city, the game would focus on the minute details of the home. One book in particular influenced his thinking about the game: *A Pattern Language* by Christopher Alexander, who laid out an architectural theory based on function rather than form. Alexander described a way for people to "score" building plans that Wright incorporated into his game design.

Wright wanted his game to allow people to design their perfect home with feedback on the success of their design from game characters who inhabited the house. While creating the perfect home began as the object of the game, Wright quickly realized that the characters, or Sims, were more interesting than the architecture, and he shifted the game's focus to the time management and activities involved in normal daily life.

The perfect home became the stage for people to play with everyday life. "Kids build a story around what they are doing. The doll house becomes the scaffolding to hold up their story. It's a place for them to think about or play roles of the person they would like to be," Wright said. His game provided players with the "props and sets and actors, and the idea is to build a story." The game developed so that Sim characters have emotional and biological needs, just like real people. The Sim characters have personality

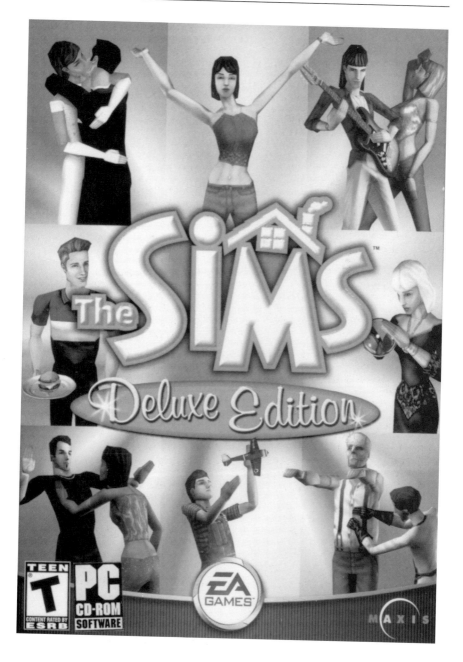

traits, including Neat, Outgoing, Active, Playful, and Nice. Players set Sims' characteristics then manage their virtual lives, helping them build homes, find jobs, and make friends. Players must also make sure the Sims eat, get plenty of rest, wash, and take regular restroom breaks. Players can struc-

ture the lives of Sim characters any way they like. If players attend to their characters' needs, Sims go to work, keep their house in order, make friends or fall in love, and even have babies. If players neglect their Sims' needs, the characters fall ill, get depressed, lose their jobs, get divorced, or have their babies taken away by social services. Wright enjoyed the open-ended nature of the game, saying "I think that letting the players choose their goals and pursue them gives the game so much re-playability and also allows the players to be so much more creative with what they do in the game."

Released in 2000, "The Sims" became the top-grossing computer game the same year. Expansion packs quickly followed that enabled Sims to go on dates, own pets, vacation on tropical beaches or at fancy resorts, host costume parties, and dance at nightclubs, among other things. By 2001 "The Sims" and four of its expansion packs were among the top 10 best-selling computer games in the United States. In 2002, "The Sims" became the best-selling computer game of all time. *Entertainment Weekly* named "The Sims" one of the 100 greatest computer games of all time in 2003, by which time eight million copies of the game and almost 16 million expansion packs had been sold. "Reaction to 'The Sims' by both customers and critics have exceeded our most ambitious expectations," said EA president John Riccitiello. "'The Sims' has become a cultural phenomenon. Its worldwide appeal spans hard-core gamers, casual computer users, and even gaming's most elusive group of consumers, women. Over 50 percent of new 'Sims' players are female."

As Lev Grossman wrote in Time *magazine, "Experiencing 'The Sims Online' is less like playing a game than taking part in an open-ended community theater production, where the dialogue is improvised, the theme is modern life, and the star is you."*

"The Sims" Move Online

With such success, Wright imagined "The Sims" on yet another level: online. Instead of interacting with preset programs, players would interact with each other over the Internet. "The Sims Online" launched in 2002 after more than a year of feedback from 38,000 online test players. Wright and his team created the game so that each Sim character represents a real individual. The characters have the power to create their own communities together, marry each other, share houses, and even build businesses and political systems. As Lev Grossman wrote in *Time* magazine, "Experiencing 'The Sims Online' is less like playing a game than taking part in an open-ended community theater production, where the dialogue is improvised, the theme is modern life, and the star is you." By 2004, "The Sims Online" had attracted several thousand players.

Game players create and control characters like these from "The Sims Superstar Expansion Pack."

What makes this game different from other online multi-player games is that players' successes are measured by the happiness of other people. One of the designers of "The Sims Online," Gordon Watson, said that the game will allow people to interact "on a pure intellectual and emotional level." But Wright admitted that the idea scared him, saying "we're building something that could potentially be a very powerful experience for a lot of people. So it's an opportunity as well as a danger. Realistically, I think this game is going to be a tremendous help for a lot of people and tremendously bad for a lot of people. I just wonder what the net is going to be."

When asked by the *Los Angeles Times* if he thought he might push the boundaries of interactive entertainment too far, Wright replied: "I'm not sure what too far would be. Interactive entertainment's a relatively new medium. . . . This industry resembles the Wild West. Nobody know the rules; we're trying to figure things out by doing them. I'd be more worried about not going far enough."

Beyond "The Sims"

When Wright isn't working on his computer games, he concentrates on having fun in other ways. He founded the Stupid Fun Club, a think tank for fun ideas. Housed in a 3,800 square-foot warehouse in Berkeley, California, the Stupid Fun Club has two full-time workers and several part-time employees helping Wright come up with ideas for films and television. In 2003, he contracted with the Fox Network to develop new, innovative ideas for television. With his partners Michael Winter and Marc Thorpe, who work with him at the Stupid Fun Club studio, Wright developed an animated show called "M.Y. Robot" and a reality-based show in which people would be filmed reacting to a life-size, remote-controlled robot. About the new projects, Mike Darnell, head of alternative programming for Fox, told the *Hollywood Reporter* that "Clearly, Will's a genius . . .

so we decided to give him a basic development deal and see what he comes up with." Indeed, with Wright's diverse interests, it will be interesting to see what he develops.

Advice for Future Game Designers

When asked for advice for those who would like to follow in his footsteps as a game designer, Wright offered these words of wisdom: "Be patient. Hit games can take years. It's easy to get frustrated. Maintain your passion. It's the biggest indicator of eventual success."

MARRIAGE AND FAMILY

Wright met his wife, Joell Jones, in Louisiana while spending one summer between college courses at home. Jones remembered that summer, saying "We'd fallen madly in love. I'm 12 years older . . . so there was that age difference, but we couldn't drop it." Within a year, Wright dropped out of college and moved to California, where Jones worked as an artist. The couple remains happily married in California; their daughter, Cassidy, was born in 1986.

Wright says his wife is "probably the most computer illiterate person" he knows. "She's never played any of my games. That's probably why we get along so well." But Cassidy shares her father's interest in technology. Wright has implemented Cassidy's suggestions for his games since she was five, when she requested an option for frogs to rule the planet in "SimEarth." One of her most sweeping suggestions was to base "Sims" characters in their homes, not their workplaces. After trying a prototype of the game, Cassidy realized that "What was interesting was the people, not what they did for a living," she told *Teen People*. She also suggested that "The Sims" game include more opportunities for shopping, since teenagers enjoy hanging out at the mall.

HOBBIES AND OTHER INTERESTS

Wright's interest in the hobby he began as a 13 year old has lasted. He continues to create robots in his spare time and has nurtured his daughter's interest in the same hobby. Cassidy has designed robots with her father since 1994. The two have competed in BattleBots robotic competitions (which were shown on the cable network Comedy Central). Father and daughter share a sense of humor as well, giving their creations such names as "Kitty Puff Puff," "Misty the WonderBot," and "ChiaBot," instead of the menacing names of their competitors, "Battle Scar" and "Dawn of Destruction."

SELECTED HONORS AND AWARDS

The Time Digital 50 (Time.com): 1999
Invisionary Award (NewMedia Invision Festival): 2000
GDC Game of the Year Award: 2001, for "The Sims"
Lifetime Achievement Award (Gama Network and the International Game Developers Association): 2001
Inducted into the Academy of Interactive Arts and Sciences Hall of Fame: 2002
Champion Award (Interactive Digital Software Association): 2002

FURTHER READING

Periodicals

Computer Gaming World, May 2000, p.64
Contra Costa (Calif.) Times, Feb. 18, 2001, p.C1
Current Biography, Feb. 2004
Entertainment Weekly, Dec. 6, 2002, p.38
Esquire, Dec. 2002, p.146
Forbes, May 28, 2001, p.12
Los Angeles Times, Oct. 19, 2000, p.T12; May 17, 2001, p.T2
New York Times Magazine, Oct. 31, 1999, p.24
Newsweek, Oct. 24, 1994, p.48; Nov. 25, 2002, p.53
PC Magazine, May 14, 2002
San Francisco Examiner, May 8, 1994, p.C1
Time, Feb. 19, 1996; Nov. 25, 2002, p.78
Washington Post, Apr. 14, 2002, magazine section, p.W8
Wired, Nov. 2002, p.176

Online Articles

http://www.cnn.com/COMMUNITY/transcripts/2000/12/1/wright.chat/
(*CNN.com*, "Will Wright on Creating 'The Sims' and 'SimCity,'" Nov. 30, 2000)

http://www.firstmonday.dk/issues/issue4_4/friedman/
(*First Monday*, "Semiotics of SimCity," 1999)
http://www.gamespot.com/features/maxis/index.html
(*Gamespot.com*, "SIMply Divine," undated)
http://www.gamespot.com/gamespot/features/pc/simsonline/index.html
(*Gamespot.com*, "The Endless Hours of The Sims Online," undated)
http://www.gamespot.com/gamespot/features/pc/simsonline/1.html
(*Gamespot.com*, "The Back-Burner Blockbuster,"undated)
http://www.prospect.org/print-friendly/print/V5/17/starr-p.html
(*American Prospect*, "Seductions of Sim," Mar. 21, 1994)

Online Databases

Biography Resource Center Online, 2003, article from *Newsmakers*, 2003

ADDRESS

Will Wright
Electronic Arts/Maxis
2121 North California Boulevard
Walnut Creek, CA 94596

WORLD WIDE WEB SITES

http://www.maxis.com

Photo and Illustration Credits

Natalie Babbitt/Photo: Farrar, Straus and Giroux; copyright © Disney Enterprises, Inc. (p. 20). Covers: THE SEARCH FOR DELICIOUS copyright © 1969 by Natalie Babbitt; KNEEKNOCK RISE copyright © 1970 by Natalie Babbitt; TUCK EVERLASTING copyright © 1975 by Natalie Babbitt. Cover art copyright © 1975 by Natalie Babbitt; THE EYES OF AMARYLLIS copyright © 1977 by Natalie Babbitt, all Sunburst Books/Farrar, Straus and Giroux; PEACOCK AND OTHER POEMS (Farrar, Straus and Giroux) text copyright © 2002 by George Bahlke. Illustrations copyright © 2002 by Natalie Babbitt.

David Beckham/Photos: Steve Finn/Getty Images; Shaun Botterill/Getty Images (pp. 32, 35); Ross Kinnaird/Getty Images; AP/Wide World Photos; Stuart Franklin/Getty Images; AP/Wide World Photos.

Francie Berger/Photos: copyright © Nancy Rica Schiff from her book, *Odd Jobs: Portraits of Unusual Occupations* (pp. 47, 54); AP/Wide World Photos (pp. 50, 53).

Tony Blair/Photos: Patrick Kovarik/AFP/Getty Images; copyright © CORBIS Sygma; copyright © Royalty-Free/CORBIS; copyright © Polak Matthew/CORBIS Sygma (pp. 67, 69); AP/Wide World Photos; Mike Theiler/Getty Images; AP/Wide World Photos.

Orlando Bloom/Photos: Kevin Winter/Getty Images; copyright © 2001 New Line Productions, Inc. (p. 84); copyright © 2002 New Line Productions, Inc. (p. 87); Elliott Marks, SMPSP/copyright © Disney Enterprises, Inc. and Jerry Bruckheimer, Inc. All rights reserved (p. 89); Sidney Baldwin/copyright © 2001 Revolution Studios (bottom, p. 89); Alex Bailey/copyright © 2004 Warner Bros. Entertainment Inc. (p.91); Matt Dunham/Reuters (p.93).

Kim Clijsters/Photos: AP/Wide World Photos; Ian Waldie/Reuters; Al Bello/Getty Images; Jeff Gross/Getty Images (p. 105); AP/Wide World Photos; Greg Wood/AFP/Getty Images.

Celia Cruz/Photos: AP/Wide World Photos; Reuters/Landov; Deborah Feingold/Getty Images; copyright © Emerson Sam/CORBIS; AP/Wide World Photos. Album/CD covers: CANCIONES PREMIADAS copyright © & (p) 1989. Palladium-Latin Jazz and Dance Records. Licensed by Met Richmond Records Inc. for West Side Latino; LA INCOMPARABLE CELIA copyright © & (p) 1989. Palladium-Latin Jazz and Dance Records. Licensed by Met Richmond Records Inc. for West Side Latino; REGALO DEL ALMA (p) 2003, 2000 Sony Music Entertainment Inc. Copyright © 2003 Sony Music Entertainment Inc.

Matel Dawson, Jr./Photos: AP/Wide World Photos (p. 131); Wayne State University; Ric Bielaczyc/Wayne State University.

The Donnas/Photos: copyright © Chapman Baehler/Retna; copyright © Jay Blakesberg/Retna; AP/Wide World Photos. CD covers: AMERICAN TEENAGE ROCK 'N' ROLL MACHINE copyright © & (p) 1998 Lookout!; THE DONNAS copyright © & (p) 1998 Lookout! Records LLC; THE DONNAS TURN 21 copyright © & (p) 2001 Lookout! Records LLC; GET SKINTIGHT copyright © 1999 Lookout! Records LLC; SPEND THE NIGHT copyright © 2002 Atlantic Recording Corporation for the United States and WEA International Inc. for the world outside the United States.

Tim Duncan/Photos: Andrew D. Bernstein/NBAE/Getty Images; Rick Stewart/Getty Images; Doug Pensinger/Getty Images; AP/Wide World Photos; Todd Warshaw/Getty Images; AP/Wide World Photos.

Shirin Ebadi/Photos: Jack Guez/AFP/Getty Images; copyright © Attar Maher/CORBIS Sygma; AP/Wide World Photos; Atta Kenare/AFP/Getty Images; Odd Andersen/AFP/Getty Images (pp. 193, 194); copyright © France Keyser/In Visu/CORBIS. Front cover: Abedin Taherkenareh/EPA/ Landov.

Carla Hayden/Photos: ALA; Enoch Pratt Free Library (pp. 202, 204); AP/Wide World Photos; Hilary Schwab.

Ashton Kutcher/Photos: Larsen & Talbert/FOX; G. Lange/FOX; Michael Lavine/FOX; Tracy Bennett; Chris Large/Dimension Films; TM and copyright © 2002 Twentieth Century Fox; CTV; copyright © New Line Productions, Inc.

Lisa Leslie/Photos: Andrew D. Bernstein/WNBAE/Getty Images; AP/Wide World Photos; Ken Levine/Getty Images; Doug Pensinger/Getty Images; Garrett Ellwood/WNBAE/Getty Images; Mike Blake/Reuters; AP/Wide World Photos; Jed Jacobsohn/Getty Images.

Linkin Park/Photos: copyright © Joe Giron/CORBIS; copyright © Clay Patrick McBride/Retna; copyright © Jason Messer/Retna; Mike Blake/ Reuters. CD covers: HYBRID THEORY copyright © 2000 Zomba Songs Inc.; METEORA © (P) 2003 Warner Bros. Records Inc.

Raven/Photos: copyright © Disney (pp. 363, 369, 370, 372, 374); Time Life Pictures/Getty Images (p.365); Bruce McBroom (p.367).

Ronald Reagan/Photos: courtesy Ronald Reagan Library (pp. 377, 379, 382, 385, 392, 394, 396, 399, 400, 402); AP/Wide World Photos (pp. 387, 388, 391).

Keanu Reeves/Photos: Kimimasa Mayama/Reuters/Landov; Jane O'Neal; copyright © 1992 Columbia Pictures Industries, Inc.; Reuters/TIMEPIX; Ron Phillips; copyright © 2001 Warner Bros.; Jasin Boland, Melinda Sue Gordon (close-up)/copyright © 2003 Warner Bros.; Jasin Boland/copyright © 2003 Warner Bros.; copyright © Mitchell Gerber/CORBIS. VHS/ DVD covers: BILL AND TED'S EXCELLENT ADVENTURE copyright © 1988 Orion Pictures Corporation. Package Design copyright © 2001 MGM Home Entertainment Inc.; SPEED copyright © 2000 Twentieth Century Fox Home Entertainment, Inc.; THE MATRIX copyright © 1999 Warner Bros. Front cover: Jasin Boland/copyright © 2003 Warner Bros.

Ricardo Sanchez/Photos: Mike Theller/EPA/Landov; Scott Nelson/Getty Images; PFC Joshua Hutcheson/photo courtesy of U.S. Army; USDOD; Jamal A. Wilson/EPA/ Landov; Chris Hondros/Getty Images.

Brian Urlacher/Photos: Brian Bahr/Getty Images; Marc Piscotty/Getty Images; Frank Polich/UPI/Landov; Gary Cameron/Reuters/Landov; Sue Ogrocki/Reuters; AP/Wide World Photos.

Alexa Vega/Photos: copyright © Paul Smith/Featureflash/Retna; Newscom. com; Dimension Films; AP/Wide World Photos; copyright © Ernie Stewart/Retna

Michelle Wie/Photos: Stuart Franklin/Getty Images; Jonathan Ferrey/Getty Images; Kim Kyung-Hoon/Reuters/Landov; Stuart Franklin/Getty Images; Andy Lyons/Getty Images; AP/Wide World Photos.

Will Wright/Photos: courtesy of Maxis/Electronic Arts. Covers: SIM ANT copyright © 1995, 1997, 1999 Electronic Arts Inc.; SIM CITY 3000 copyright © 2001 Electronic Arts Inc.; THE SIMS copyright © 2003 Electronic Arts Inc.; THE SIMS ONLINE copyright © 2002, 2003 Electronic Arts Inc. All Maxis/Electronic Arts.

How to Use the Cumulative Index

Our indexes have a new look. In an effort to make our indexes easier to use, we've combined the Name and General Index into a new, Cumulative Index. This single ready-reference resource covers all the volumes in *Biography Today*, both the general series and the special subject series. The new Cumulative Index contains complete listings of all individuals who have appeared in *Biography Today* since the series began. Their names appear in bold-faced type, followed by the issue in which they appear. The Cumulative Index also includes references for the occupations, nationalities, and ethnic and minority origins of individuals profiled in *Biography Today*.

We have also made some changes to our specialty indexes, the Places of Birth Index and the Birthday Index. To consolidate and to save space, the Places of Birth Index and the Birthday Index will no longer appear in the January and April issues of the softbound subscription series. But these indexes can still be found in the September issue of the softbound subscription series, in the hardbound Annual Cumulation at the end of each year, and in each volume of the special subject series.

General Series

The General Series of *Biography Today* is denoted in the index with the month and year of the issue in which the individual appeared. Each individual also appears in the Annual Cumulation for that year.

Special Subject Series

The Special Subject Series of *Biography Today* are each denoted in the index with an abbreviated form of the series name, plus the number of the volume in which the individual appears. They are listed as follows.

Adams, Ansel .... Artist V.1	(Artists)
Collins, Billy .... Author V.16	(Authors)
Dell, Michael .... Business V.1	(Business Leaders)
Diaz, Cameron .... PerfArt V.3	(Performing Artists)
Fay, Michael .... Science V.9	(Scientists & Inventors)
Patterson, Carly .... Sport V.12	(Sports)
Peterson, Roger Tory .... WorLdr V.1	(World Leaders: Environmental Leaders)
Sadat, Anwar .... WorLdr V.2	(World Leaders: Modern African Leaders)
Wolf, Hazel................. WorLdr V.3	(World Leaders: Environmental Leaders 2)

Updates

Updated information on selected individuals appears in the Appendix at the end of some issues of the *Biography Today* Annual Cumulation. In the index, the original entry is listed first, followed by any updates.

Arafat, Yasir .... Sep 94; Update 94;
Update 95; Update 96; Update 97; Update 98;
Update 00; Update 01; Update 02
Gates, Bill .... Apr 93; Update 98;
Update 00; Science V.5; Update 01
Griffith Joyner, Florence........ Sport V.1;
Update 98
Sanders, Barry .... Sep 95; Update 99
Spock, Dr. Benjamin .... Sep 95; Update 98
Yeltsin, Boris........... Apr 92; Update 93;
Update 95; Update 96; Update 98; Update 00

Cumulative Index

This cumulative index includes names, occupations, nationalities, and ethnic and minority origins that pertain to all individuals profiled in *Biography Today* since the debut of the series in 1992.

Places of Birth Index

The following index lists the places of birth for the individuals profiled in *Biography Today*. Places of birth are entered under state, province, and/or country.

New Zealand

Nigeria

North Carolina

Birthday Index

Biography Today

General Series

Biography Today **General Series** includes a unique combination of current biographical profiles that teachers and librarians — and the readers themselves — tell us are most appealing. The **General Series** is available as a 3-issue subscription; hardcover annual cumulation; or subscription plus cumulation.

Within the **General Series**, your readers will find a variety of sketches about:

- Authors
- Musicians
- Political leaders
- Sports figures
- Movie actresses & actors
- Cartoonists
- Scientists
- Astronauts
- TV personalities
- and the movers & shakers in many other fields!

"Biography Today will be useful in elementary and middle school libraries and in public library children's collections where there is a need for biographies of current personalities. High schools serving reluctant readers may also want to consider a subscription."
— *Booklist,* American Library Association

"Highly recommended for the young adult audience. Readers will delight in the accessible, energetic, tell-all style; teachers, librarians, and parents will welcome the clever format, intelligent and informative text. It should prove especially useful in motivating 'reluctant' readers or literate nonreaders."
— *MultiCultural Review*

"Written in a friendly, almost chatty tone, the profiles offer quick, objective information. While coverage of current figures makes *Biography Today* a useful reference tool, an appealing format and wide scope make it a fun resource to browse." — *School Library Journal*

"The best source for current information at a level kids can understand."
— Kelly Bryant, School Librarian, Carlton, OR

"Easy for kids to read. We love it! Don't want to be without it."
— Lynn McWhirter, School Librarian, Rockford, IL

ONE-YEAR SUBSCRIPTION
- 3 softcover issues, 6" x 9"
- Published in January, April, and September
- 1-year subscription, $60
- 150 pages per issue
- 10 profiles per issue
- Contact sources for additional information
- Cumulative General, Places of Birth, and Birthday Indexes

HARDBOUND ANNUAL CUMULATION
- Sturdy 6" x 9" hardbound volume
- Published in December
- $62 per volume
- 450 pages per volume
- 25-30 profiles — includes all profiles found in softcover issues for that calendar year
- Cumulative General, Places of Birth, and Birthday Indexes
- Special appendix features current updates of previous profiles

SUBSCRIPTION AND CUMULATION COMBINATION
- $99 for 3 softcover issues plus the hardbound volume

1992

Paula Abdul
Andre Agassi
Kirstie Alley
Terry Anderson
Roseanne Arnold
Isaac Asimov
James Baker
Charles Barkley
Larry Bird
Judy Blume
Berke Breathed
Garth Brooks
Barbara Bush
George Bush
Fidel Castro
Bill Clinton
Bill Cosby
Diana, Princess of Wales
Shannen Doherty
Elizabeth Dole
David Duke
Gloria Estefan
Mikhail Gorbachev
Steffi Graf
Wayne Gretzky
Matt Groening
Alex Haley
Hammer
Martin Handford
Stephen Hawking
Hulk Hogan
Saddam Hussein
Lee Iacocca
Bo Jackson
Mae Jemison
Peter Jennings
Steven Jobs
Pope John Paul II
Magic Johnson
Michael Jordon
Jackie Joyner-Kersee
Spike Lee
Mario Lemieux
Madeleine L'Engle
Jay Leno
Yo-Yo Ma
Nelson Mandela
Wynton Marsalis
Thurgood Marshall
Ann Martin
Barbara McClintock
Emily Arnold McCully
Antonia Novello

Sandra Day O'Connor
Rosa Parks
Jane Pauley
H. Ross Perot
Luke Perry
Scottie Pippen
Colin Powell
Jason Priestley
Queen Latifah
Yitzhak Rabin
Sally Ride
Pete Rose
Nolan Ryan
H. Norman
    Schwarzkopf
Jerry Seinfeld
Dr. Seuss
Gloria Steinem
Clarence Thomas
Chris Van Allsburg
Cynthia Voigt
Bill Watterson
Robin Williams
Oprah Winfrey
Kristi Yamaguchi
Boris Yeltsin

1993

Maya Angelou
Arthur Ashe
Avi
Kathleen Battle
Candice Bergen
Boutros Boutros-Ghali
Chris Burke
Dana Carvey
Cesar Chavez
Henry Cisneros
Hillary Rodham Clinton
Jacques Cousteau
Cindy Crawford
Macaulay Culkin
Lois Duncan
Marian Wright Edelman
Cecil Fielder
Bill Gates
Sara Gilbert
Dizzy Gillespie
Al Gore
Cathy Guisewite
Jasmine Guy
Anita Hill
Ice-T
Darci Kistler

k.d. lang
Dan Marino
Rigoberta Menchu
Walter Dean Myers
Martina Navratilova
Phyllis Reynolds Naylor
Rudolf Nureyev
Shaquille O'Neal
Janet Reno
Jerry Rice
Mary Robinson
Winona Ryder
Jerry Spinelli
Denzel Washington
Keenen Ivory Wayans
Dave Winfield

1994

Tim Allen
Marian Anderson
Mario Andretti
Ned Andrews
Yasir Arafat
Bruce Babbitt
Mayim Bialik
Bonnie Blair
Ed Bradley
John Candy
Mary Chapin Carpenter
Benjamin Chavis
Connie Chung
Beverly Cleary
Kurt Cobain
F.W. de Klerk
Rita Dove
Linda Ellerbee
Sergei Fedorov
Zlata Filipovic
Daisy Fuentes
Ruth Bader Ginsburg
Whoopi Goldberg
Tonya Harding
Melissa Joan Hart
Geoff Hooper
Whitney Houston
Dan Jansen
Nancy Kerrigan
Alexi Lalas
Charlotte Lopez
Wilma Mankiller
Shannon Miller
Toni Morrison
Richard Nixon
Greg Norman
Severo Ochoa

River Phoenix
Elizabeth Pine
Jonas Salk
Richard Scarry
Emmitt Smith
Will Smith
Steven Spielberg
Patrick Stewart
R.L. Stine
Lewis Thomas
Barbara Walters
Charlie Ward
Steve Young
Kim Zmeskal

1995

Troy Aikman
Jean-Bertrand Aristide
Oksana Baiul
Halle Berry
Benazir Bhutto
Jonathan Brandis
Warren E. Burger
Ken Burns
Candace Cameron
Jimmy Carter
Agnes de Mille
Placido Domingo
Janet Evans
Patrick Ewing
Newt Gingrich
John Goodman
Amy Grant
Jesse Jackson
James Earl Jones
Julie Krone
David Letterman
Rush Limbaugh
Heather Locklear
Reba McEntire
Joe Montana
Cosmas Ndeti
Hakeem Olajuwon
Ashley Olsen
Mary-Kate Olsen
Jennifer Parkinson
Linus Pauling
Itzhak Perlman
Cokie Roberts
Wilma Rudolph
Salt 'N' Pepa
Barry Sanders
William Shatner
Elizabeth George
    Speare

Dr. Benjamin Spock
Jonathan Taylor
  Thomas
Vicki Van Meter
Heather Whitestone
Pedro Zamora

1996

Aung San Suu Kyi
Boyz II Men
Brandy
Ron Brown
Mariah Carey
Jim Carrey
Larry Champagne III
Christo
Chelsea Clinton
Coolio
Bob Dole
David Duchovny
Debbi Fields
Chris Galeczka
Jerry Garcia
Jennie Garth
Wendy Guey
Tom Hanks
Alison Hargreaves
Sir Edmund Hillary
Judith Jamison
Barbara Jordan
Annie Leibovitz
Carl Lewis
Jim Lovell
Mickey Mantle
Lynn Margulis
Iqbal Masih
Mark Messier
Larisa Oleynik
Christopher Pike
David Robinson
Dennis Rodman
Selena
Monica Seles
Don Shula
Kerri Strug
Tiffani-Amber Thiessen
Dave Thomas
Jaleel White

1997

Madeleine Albright
Marcus Allen
Gillian Anderson
Rachel Blanchard
Zachery Ty Bryan
Adam Ezra Cohen
Claire Danes
Celine Dion
Jean Driscoll
Louis Farrakhan
Ella Fitzgerald
Harrison Ford
Bryant Gumbel
John Johnson
Michael Johnson
Maya Lin
George Lucas
John Madden
Bill Monroe
Alanis Morissette
Sam Morrison
Rosie O'Donnell
Muammar el-Qaddafi
Christopher Reeve
Pete Sampras
Pat Schroeder
Rebecca Sealfon
Tupac Shakur
Tabitha Soren
Herbert Tarvin
Merlin Tuttle
Mara Wilson

1998

Bella Abzug
Kofi Annan
Neve Campbell
Sean Combs (Puff
  Daddy)
Dalai Lama (Tenzin
  Gyatso)
Diana, Princess of Wales
Leonardo DiCaprio
Walter E. Diemer
Ruth Handler
Hanson
Livan Hernandez
Jewel
Jimmy Johnson
Tara Lipinski
Jody-Anne Maxwell
Dominique Moceanu
Alexandra Nechita

Brad Pitt
LeAnn Rimes
Emily Rosa
David Satcher
Betty Shabazz
Kordell Stewart
Shinichi Suzuki
Mother Teresa
Mike Vernon
Reggie White
Kate Winslet

1999

Ben Affleck
Jennifer Aniston
Maurice Ashley
Kobe Bryant
Bessie Delany
Sadie Delany
Sharon Draper
Sarah Michelle Gellar
John Glenn
Savion Glover
Jeff Gordon
David Hampton
Lauryn Hill
King Hussein
Lynn Johnston
Shari Lewis
Oseola McCarty
Mark McGwire
Slobodan Milosevic
Natalie Portman
J. K. Rowling
Frank Sinatra
Gene Siskel
Sammy Sosa
John Stanford
Natalia Toro
Shania Twain
Mitsuko Uchida
Jesse Ventura
Venus Williams

2000

Christina Aguilera
K.A. Applegate
Lance Armstrong
Backstreet Boys
Daisy Bates
Harry Blackmun
George W. Bush
Carson Daly
Ron Dayne
Henry Louis Gates, Jr.
Doris Haddock
  (Granny D)
Jennifer Love Hewitt
Chamique Holdsclaw
Katie Holmes
Charlayne Hunter-Gault
Johanna Johnson
Craig Kielburger
John Lasseter
Peyton Manning
Ricky Martin
John McCain
Walter Payton
Freddie Prinze, Jr.
Viviana Risca
Briana Scurry
George Thampy
CeCe Winans

2001

Jessica Alba
Christiane Amanpour
Drew Barrymore
Jeff Bezos
Destiny's Child
Dale Earnhardt
Carly Fiorina
Aretha Franklin
Cathy Freeman
Tony Hawk
Faith Hill
Kim Dae-jung
Madeleine L'Engle
Mariangela Lisanti
Frankie Muniz
*N Sync
Ellen Ochoa
Jeff Probst
Julia Roberts
Carl T. Rowan
Britney Spears
Chris Tucker
Lloyd D. Ward
Alan Webb
Chris Weinke

2002

Aaliyah
Osama bin Laden
Mary J. Blige
Aubyn Burnside
Aaron Carter
Julz Chavez
Dick Cheney
Hilary Duff
Billy Gilman
Rudolph Giuliani
Brian Griese
Jennifer Lopez
Dave Mirra
Dineh Mohajer
Leanne Nakamura
Daniel Radcliffe
Condoleezza Rice
Marla Runyan
Ruth Simmons
Mattie Stepanek
J.R.R. Tolkien
Barry Watson
Tyrone Willingham
Elijah Wood

2003

Yolanda Adams
Olivia Bennett
Mildred Benson
Alexis Bledel
Barry Bonds
Vincent Brooks
Laura Bush
Amanda Bynes
Kelly Clarkson
Vin Diesel
Eminem
Michele Forman
Vicente Fox
Millard Fuller
Josh Hartnett
Dolores Huerta

Sarah Hughes
Enrique Iglesias
Jeanette Lee
John Lewis
Nicklas Lidstrom
Clint Mathis
Donovan McNabb
Nelly
Andy Roddick
Gwen Stefani
Emma Watson
Meg Whitman
Reese Witherspoon
Yao Ming

2004

Natalie Babbitt
David Beckham
Francie Berger
Tony Blair
Orlando Bloom
Kim Clijsters
Celia Cruz
Matel Dawson, Jr.
The Donnas
Tim Duncan
Shirin Ebadi
Carla Hayden
Ashton Kutcher
Lisa Leslie
Linkin Park
Lindsay Lohan
Irene D. Long
John Mayer
Mandy Moore
Thich Nhat Hanh
OutKast
Raven
Ronald Reagan
Keanu Reeves
Ricardo Sanchez
Brian Urlacher
Alexa Vega
Michelle Wie
Will Wright

Biography Today

Subject Series

Expands and complements the General Series and targets specific subject areas . . .

Our readers asked for it! They wanted more biographies, and the *Biography Today* Subject Series is our response to that demand. Now your readers can choose their special areas of interest and go on to read about their favorites in those fields. Priced at just $39 per volume, the following specific volumes are included in the *Biography Today* Subject Series:

- **Authors**
- **Business Leaders**
- **Performing Artists**
- **Scientists & Inventors**
- **Sports**

FEATURES AND FORMAT

- Sturdy 6" x 9" hardbound volumes
- Individual volumes, $39 each
- 200 pages per volume
- 10 profiles per volume — targets individuals within a specific subject area
- Contact sources for additional information
- Cumulative General, Places of Birth, and Birthday Indexes

NOTE: There is *no duplication of entries* between the **General Series** of *Biography Today* and the **Subject Series**.

AUTHORS

"A useful tool for children's assignment needs." — *School Library Journal*

"The prose is workmanlike: report writers will find enough detail to begin sound investigations, and browsers are likely to find someone of interest." — *School Library Journal*

SCIENTISTS & INVENTORS

"The articles are readable, attractively laid out, and touch on important points that will suit assignment needs. Browsers will note the clear writing and interesting details." — *School Library Journal*

"The book is excellent for demonstrating that scientists are real people with widely diverse backgrounds and personal interests. The biographies are fascinating to read." — *The Science Teacher*

SPORTS

"This series should become a standard resource in libraries that serve intermediate students." — *School Library Journal*

Authors

VOLUME 1

Eric Carle
Alice Childress
Robert Cormier
Roald Dahl
Jim Davis
John Grisham
Virginia Hamilton
James Herriot
S.E. Hinton
M.E. Kerr
Stephen King
Gary Larson
Joan Lowery Nixon
Gary Paulsen
Cynthia Rylant
Mildred D. Taylor
Kurt Vonnegut, Jr.
E.B. White
Paul Zindel

VOLUME 2

James Baldwin
Stan and Jan Berenstain
David Macaulay
Patricia MacLachlan
Scott O'Dell
Jerry Pinkney
Jack Prelutsky
Lynn Reid Banks
Faith Ringgold
J.D. Salinger
Charles Schulz
Maurice Sendak
P.L. Travers
Garth Williams

VOLUME 3

Candy Dawson Boyd
Ray Bradbury
Gwendolyn Brooks
Ralph W. Ellison
Louise Fitzhugh
Jean Craighead George
E.L. Konigsburg
C.S. Lewis
Fredrick L. McKissack
Patricia C. McKissack
Katherine Paterson
Anne Rice
Shel Silverstein
Laura Ingalls Wilder

VOLUME 4

Betsy Byars
Chris Carter
Caroline B. Cooney
Christopher Paul Curtis
Anne Frank
Robert Heinlein
Marguerite Henry
Lois Lowry
Melissa Mathison
Bill Peet
August Wilson

VOLUME 5

Sharon Creech
Michael Crichton
Karen Cushman
Tomie dePaola
Lorraine Hansberry
Karen Hesse
Brian Jacques
Gary Soto
Richard Wright
Laurence Yep

VOLUME 6

Lloyd Alexander
Paula Danziger
Nancy Farmer
Zora Neale Hurston
Shirley Jackson
Angela Johnson
Jon Krakauer
Leo Lionni
Francine Pascal
Louis Sachar
Kevin Williamson

VOLUME 7

William H. Armstrong
Patricia Reilly Giff
Langston Hughes
Stan Lee
Julius Lester
Robert Pinsky
Todd Strasser
Jacqueline Woodson
Patricia C. Wrede
Jane Yolen

VOLUME 8

Amelia Atwater-Rhodes
Barbara Cooney
Paul Laurence Dunbar
Ursula K. Le Guin

Farley Mowat
Naomi Shihab Nye
Daniel Pinkwater
Beatrix Potter
Ann Rinaldi

VOLUME 9

Robb Armstrong
Cherie Bennett
Bruce Coville
Rosa Guy
Harper Lee
Irene Gut Opdyke
Philip Pullman
Jon Scieszka
Amy Tan
Joss Whedon

VOLUME 10

David Almond
Joan Bauer
Kate DiCamillo
Jack Gantos
Aaron McGruder
Richard Peck
Andrea Davis Pinkney
Louise Rennison
David Small
Katie Tarbox

VOLUME 11

Laurie Halse Anderson
Bryan Collier
Margaret Peterson
    Haddix
Milton Meltzer
William Sleator
Sonya Sones
Genndy Tartakovsky
Wendelin Van Draanen
Ruth White

VOLUME 12

An Na
Claude Brown
Meg Cabot
Virginia Hamilton
Chuck Jones
Robert Lipsyte
Lillian Morrison
Linda Sue Park
Pam Muñoz Ryan
Lemony Snicket
    (Daniel Handler)

VOLUME 13

Andrew Clements
Eoin Colfer
Sharon Flake
Edward Gorey
Francisco Jiménez
Astrid Lindgren
Chris Lynch
Marilyn Nelson
Tamora Pierce
Virginia Euwer Wolff

VOLUME 14

Orson Scott Card
Russell Freedman
Mary GrandPré
Dan Greenburg
Nikki Grimes
Laura Hillenbrand
Stephen Hillenburg
Norton Juster
Lurlene McDaniel
Stephanie S. Tolan

VOLUME 15

Liv Arnesen
Edward Bloor
Ann Brashares
Veronica Chambers
Mark Crilley
Paula Fox
Diana Wynne Jones
Victor Martinez
Robert McCloskey
Jerry Scott and Jim
    Borgman

VOLUME 16

Ludwig Bemelmans
Billy Collins
Tom Feelings
Tina Fey
Joy Hakim
Polly Horvath
Tim LaHaye and
    Jerry B. Jenkins
Donna Jo Napoli
Christopher Paolini
Lori Aurelia William

Business Leaders

VOLUME 1
Warren Buffett
Peter Capolino
Michael Dell
Earl Graves
Michele Hoskins
Judy McGrath
Arturo R. Moreno
Pleasant T. Rowland
Martha Stewart
Oprah Winfrey

Performing Artists

VOLUME 1
Jackie Chan
Dixie Chicks
Kirsten Dunst
Suzanne Farrell
Bernie Mac
Shakira
Isaac Stern
Julie Taymor
Usher
Christina Vidal

VOLUME 2
Ashanti
Tyra Banks
Peter Jackson
Norah Jones
Quincy Jones
Avril Lavigne
George López
Marcel Marceau
Eddie Murphy
Julia Stiles

VOLUME 3
Michelle Branch
Cameron Diaz
Missy Elliott
Evelyn Glennie
Benji Madden
Joel Madden
Mike Myers
Fred Rogers

Twyla Tharp
Tom Welling
Yuen Wo-Ping

Scientists & Inventors

VOLUME 1
John Bardeen
Sylvia Earle
Dian Fossey
Jane Goodall
Bernadine Healy
Jack Horner
Mathilde Krim
Edwin Land
Louise & Mary Leakey
Rita Levi-Montalcini
J. Robert Oppenheimer
Albert Sabin
Carl Sagan
James D. Watson

VOLUME 2
Jane Brody
Seymour Cray
Paul Erdös
Walter Gilbert
Stephen Jay Gould
Shirley Ann Jackson
Raymond Kurzweil
Shannon Lucid
Margaret Mead
Garrett Morgan
Bill Nye
Eloy Rodriguez
An Wang

VOLUME 3
Luis W. Alvarez
Hans A. Bethe
Gro Harlem Brundtland
Mary S. Calderone
Ioana Dumitriu
Temple Grandin
John Langston
   Gwaltney
Bernard Harris
Jerome Lemelson
Susan Love
Ruth Patrick
Oliver Sacks
Richie Stachowski

VOLUME 4
David Attenborough
Robert Ballard
Ben Carson
Eileen Collins
Biruté Galdikas
Lonnie Johnson
Meg Lowman
Forrest Mars Sr.
Akio Morita
Janese Swanson

VOLUME 5
Steve Case
Douglas Engelbart
Shawn Fanning
Sarah Flannery
Bill Gates
Laura Groppe
Grace Murray Hopper
Steven Jobs
Rand and Robyn Miller
Shigeru Miyamoto
Steve Wozniak

VOLUME 6
Hazel Barton
Alexa Canady
Arthur Caplan
Francis Collins
Gertrude Elion
Henry Heimlich
David Ho
Kenneth Kamler
Lucy Spelman
Lydia Villa-Komaroff

VOLUME 7
Tim Berners-Lee
France Córdova
Anthony S. Fauci
Sue Hendrickson
Steve Irwin
John Forbes Nash, Jr.
Jerri Nielsen
Ryan Patterson
Nina Vasan
Gloria WilderBrathwaite

VOLUME 8
Deborah Blum
Richard Carmona
Helene Gayle
Dave Kapell
Adriana C. Ocampo

John Romero
Jamie Rubin
Jill Tarter
Earl Warrick
Edward O. Wilson

VOLUME 9
Robert Barron
Regina Benjamin
Jim Cantore
Marion Donovan
Michael Fay
Laura L. Kiessling
Alvin Poussaint
Sandra Steingraber
Edward Teller
Peggy Whitson

Sports

VOLUME 1
Hank Aaron
Kareem Abdul-Jabbar
Hassiba Boulmerka
Susan Butcher
Beth Daniel
Chris Evert
Ken Griffey, Jr.
Florence Griffith Joyner
Grant Hill
Greg LeMond
Pelé
Uta Pippig
Cal Ripken, Jr.
Arantxa Sanchez
   Vicario
Deion Sanders
Tiger Woods

VOLUME 2
Muhammad Ali
Donovan Bailey
Gail Devers
John Elway
Brett Favre
Mia Hamm
Anfernee "Penny"
   Hardaway
Martina Hingis
Gordie Howe
Jack Nicklaus
Richard Petty
Dot Richardson
Sheryl Swoopes
Steve Yzerman

VOLUME 3

Joe Dumars
Jim Harbaugh
Dominik Hasek
Michelle Kwan
Rebecca Lobo
Greg Maddux
Fatuma Roba
Jackie Robinson
John Stockton
Picabo Street
Pat Summitt
Amy Van Dyken

VOLUME 4

Wilt Chamberlain
Brandi Chastain
Derek Jeter
Karch Kiraly
Alex Lowe
Randy Moss
Se Ri Pak
Dawn Riley
Karen Smyers
Kurt Warner
Serena Williams

VOLUME 5

Vince Carter
Lindsay Davenport
Lisa Fernandez
Fu Mingxia
Jaromir Jagr
Marion Jones
Pedro Martinez
Warren Sapp
Jenny Thompson
Karrie Webb

VOLUME 6

Jennifer Capriati
Stacy Dragila
Kevin Garnett
Eddie George
Alex Rodriguez
Joe Sakic
Annika Sorenstam
Jackie Stiles
Tiger Woods
Aliy Zirkle

VOLUME 7

Tom Brady
Tara Dakides
Alison Dunlap

Sergio Garcia
Allen Iverson
Shirley Muldowney
Ty Murray
Patrick Roy
Tasha Schwiker

VOLUME 8

Simon Ammann
Shannon Bahrke
Kelly Clark
Vonetta Flowers
Cammi Granato
Chris Klug
Jonny Moseley
Apolo Ohno
Sylke Otto
Ryne Sanborn
Jim Shea, Jr.

VOLUME 9

Tori Allen
Layne Beachley
Sue Bird
Fabiola da Silva
Randy Johnson
Jason Kidd
Tony Stewart
Michael Vick
Ted Williams
Jay Yelas

VOLUME 10

Ryan Boyle
Natalie Coughlin
Allyson Felix
Dallas Friday
Jean-Sébastien Giguère
Phil Jackson
Keyshawn Johnson
Tiffeny Milbrett
Alfonso Soriano
Diana Taurasi

VOLUME 11

Laila Ali
Josh Beckett
Cheryl Ford
Tony Gonzalez
Ellen MacArthur
Tracy McGrady
Steve McNair
Ryan Newman
Tanya Streeter
Natasha Watley

VOLUME 12

Freddy Adu
Tina Basich
Sasha Cohen
Dale Earnhardt, Jr.
LeBron James
Carly Patterson
Albert Pujols
Michael Strahan
Teresa Weatherspoon

Order Annual
of *Biography 1*
and Save 20% C
Regular Pri

Now, you can save time and money by purchasing *Biography Today* in Annual Sets! Save 20% off the regular price and get every single biography we publish in a year. Billed upon publication of the first volume, subsequent volumes are shipped throughout the year upon publication. Keep your *Biography Today* library current and complete with Annual Sets!

Place a standing order for annual sets and receive an additional 10% off!

Regular price $278
2005 Annual Set $222
You Save $56

Biography Today 2005 Annual Set

8 volumes. 0-7808-0782-0. Annual set, $222. Includes:

2004 subscription (3 softcover issues);
2004 Hardbound Annual; Authors, Vols. 17 and 18;
Scientists & Inventors, Vol. 11; Sports, Vol. 13

Regular price $374
2004 Annual Set $299
You Save $75

Biography Today 2004 Annual Set

9 volumes. 0-7808-0731-6. Annual set, $299. Includes:

2004 Hardbound Annual; Authors, Vols. 15 and 16;
Business Leaders, Vol. 1; Performing Artists, Vol. 3;
Scientists & Inventors, Vols. 9 and 10;
Sports, Vols. 11 and 12

Regular price $335
2003 Annual Set $268
You Save $67

Biography Today 2003 Annual Set

8 volumes. 0-7808-0730-8. Annual set, $268. Includes:

2003 Hardbound Annual; Authors, Vols. 13 and 14;
Performing Artists, Vols. 1 and 2;
Scientists & Inventors, Vol. 8; Sports, Vols. 9 and 10

Regular price $297
2002 Annual Set $237
You Save $60

Biography Today 2002 Annual Set

7 volumes. 0-7808-0729-4. Annual set, $237. Includes:

2002 Hardbound Annual; Authors, Vols. 11 and 12;
Scientists & Inventors, Vols. 6 and 7;
Sports, Vols. 7 and 8